David Foster was born in the Blue Mountains in 1944 and has lived for the past twenty years in the Southern Highlands. He was trained as a scientist to post-doctoral level, and his interests include music, martial art and gardening. He was awarded a Keating Fellowship in 1991.

David Foster has six children, two stepchildren and ten grandchildren. His wife, Gerda, is a former jazz vocalist who now works as a counsellor in a men's prison.

By the same author

North South West
The Pure Land
Plumbum
Moonlite
Dog Rock
The Adventures of Christian Rosy Cross
The Pale Blue Crochet Coathanger Cover
Testostero
Hitting the Wall
Mates of Mars
The Ballad of Erinungarah

THE GLADE WITHIN THE GROVE

DAVID FOSTER

V

A Vintage Book
published by
Random House Australia Pty Ltd
20 Alfred Street, Milson's Point, NSW 2061
http://www.randomhouse.com.au

Sydney New York Toronto
London Auckland Johannesburg
and agencies throughout the world

First published in 1996

This Vintage edition first published in 1997

National Library of Australia
Cataloguing–in–Publication Data

Foster, David, 1944–.
The glade within the grove.

ISBN 0 09 183214 4.

I. Title.

A823.3

Cover design by Yolande Gray
Typeset by Midland Typesetters, Maryborough
Printed by Griffin Press Pty Ltd, Adelaide

10 9 8 7 6 5

For Kit Guyatt and Rory Shannon

Acknowledgements

The narrator's botany is designed to obscure, rather than reveal, the whereabouts of the Erinungarah. His indebtedness to the scholarship of Toynbee, Frazer, Gibbon and many others (see Bibliography) is appreciable.

The financial support of the Australian Government, in the form of a Keating Fellowship, is appreciated, so too a brief residency at the University of New South Wales. Many thanks to Roger Milliss, Nicholas Jose and E. Annie Proulx for suggesting amendments.

Non datur ad musas currere lata via
Propertius

Preamble

You find some funny stuff in old mailbags. False teeth, British Empire medals. Always worth a look though, you never know when you might happen on a valuable stamp, a five-shilling bridge. As it happens, my vocation lent itself to rummaging through old mailbags. You might even say it was part of the job.

Each mailbag, once it has been emptied of mail, is supposed to be inverted before reutilisation, but many a young, long-haired postman finds he has better things to do, apparently. How else to account for those piles of surplus, all-but-uninverted mailbags, often to be found in the corners of rural bike sheds, the careful inversion of which can provide a mature relief postman—who may not wish to spend all his off-duty hours in the pub—with a carefree half-hour.

Towards the end of my working life with Australia Post, concerning which the less said the better, I found myself on a two-week stint at a small town in Far Eastern Gippsland—New South Wales, actually, but Far Eastern Gippsland to my mind, far Far Eastern Gippsland—Obliqua Creek. Border country. The place functioned as the local postcode, which meant that all mail dispatched from the various hamlets hereabouts was dumped in the bike shed, under lock and key, before being picked up by road lorry to be taken to the nearest mail centre. I had the lock and key and I don't think I ever saw such a heap of old mailbags as what I found in that bike shed. It was a treasure trove of old mailbags. There were old-fashioned blue ones, new-fangled yellow ones, everything in between. Most, of course, were those grubby, off-white linen jobs, manufactured in prison workshops, and big enough for burials at sea, that loom large in your nightmares when you wake in a sweat, as so often I do these days. Something to do with my current chemotherapy.

I had a light mail one morning. It happens. Too early to head off to the pub, as I never like to be first in the door, so I moseyed round to the bike shed, started inverting a few of those old bags. The heart was pumping, but the heart was always pumping when I inverted uninverted mailbags, uninvited. I was addicted to my job.

June 1990. It's funny how mail can change your life. I changed a few lives in my time as a postman, judging by the tears, the lacerations and, yes, the kisses I have seen mail sustain. A piece of mail has now given me a purpose, and a thrill, and a fright. It has given me a hint as to what may lurk in the darkness that lies around me, and before me. It has imparted meaning to my life. I now know why I migrated to Australia, and why I became a postman, and I'm glad of that. I'd have hated to have died never knowing. I don't recall if I was ill back then, June 1990, as I never had a memory, except for mail and faces. Put me in a strange town, though, I'd have that town down, every last letterbox, inside a week. Not every postman can do that. It's a gift.

So you've got your arm down your mailbag, up to the shoulder, you're fossicking round like a mutton-birder plucking a squab from a mutton-bird hole, hoping to Christ you don't feel the fangs of a funnelweb spider or tiger snake. You're humming a bit of Mahler, taking in the view of the town, through the open door of the bike shed. Your free hand could be rolling a smoke, ashing the one you're on. And then you feel it. There's something there. A strike, from a Nefarious Cult.

Householder? Could be. Bit bulky for junk mail though. Item of mail that should have been delivered? That puts you in a quandary. What do you do with it? Deliver it? Destroy it? That puts someone else in a quandary. Either way, it could spell trouble. Though I have delivered a cheque in pounds shillings and pence, twenty-five years late, and not a word was said.

Trawl it up, like a creature from the deeps, like an orange

roughy from the deep sea slopes. Sit it on the concrete step. Check it out.

Oversized. Standard large envelope, bursting at the seams, like an orange roughy's eyes. Should have been taxed. No stamp, maybe the stamp fell off. No datestamp. Rummage about a bit, try to find the stamp. Invert the bag, no stamp. Never had a stamp.

Can't make out the addressee. No return address. Handwriting pale and ghostly. Out with the reading glasses now, all sense of time disappearing.

'To Whom it may Concern.'

Well, you would, wouldn't you. You would throw a thing like that aside, if you had heavy mail to break up. You'd toss it in a bag, and it wouldn't plague your conscience overmuch, if you never saw it again.

Well, maybe I should open it, I thought to myself. Just to be on the safe side.

Poetry. What a disappointment, something from the bloody prison farm. Woe is me, to the refrain of the righteous, rubbing together the fourth fingertip and thumb, as the world's smallest violin orchestra. If you can't do the time, don't commit the crime.

I glance, of course, at the first few lines, in the manner of a busy editor. With the reading glasses.

Hmm. Interesting. Read on. Something mesmeric about this. Keep an open mind. Tuck it in the trousers, take it back to the digs. Study it at leisure, on the concave bed of my room at the Terminus Hotel. Edit it a bit, but only where it needs it. Weird piece of work. Back then, 1990, I'm not sure I understood the implications. But I have thought about little else since. And Mysteries never yield themselves entirely to the Intellect. They are not meant to. The word 'Mystery' means, in Greek, 'That which is not to be discussed.' But it didn't stop the Pope, so it won't stop me.

I thought I found an argument that proved I was the Pope. I looked again and saw it was a bar of mottled soap. Lewis Carroll.

Dark themes. Emasculation. Goddesses. A Greenbrown Man who appears to be enmantled with living ferns and mosses. The story of a mortal we shall call Attis, enamoured of a goddess of the glade, name of Brigid, and the superficially tragic consequences of their love. All apparently set, in an unselfconscious manner, by a scarcely tutored mind, locally.

Intimations of Courtly Love, and its Sacred Antithesis.

I vaguely recognise a Greek myth, unaccountably overlooked by the Romantics. Is this my chance to redeem myself? I sidles up to the postmaster, on my last day on relief in the place. Casual like.

'Recognise this handwritin, Boss?' I says, obtruding the crumpled envelope before him.

But he's processing a passport application for a woman who has changed her name five times. He can be of no assistance.

'Yes, the woman who appeared upon the waters of the weir when Finn MacCool looked in was seen here too'—that's a line from the poem. What we find in this poem is a White Dreaming, cognate with the Aboriginal landscape, but defiantly pastoral, the way the hippies were. And the Irish came hereabouts, in some number, which may account for the context. I did track down the man who wrote that poem, the best piece of postal detective work ever I undertook.

For I have found myself an independent informant. And Kimbo affirms that a goddess by name Brigid appeared to them in that Valley, during a period when they were effectively cut off from this world, or could have been, had they more sagaciously quiesced in their Dispensation, mid-79 to May '86, or thereabouts. They won't speak of Her now. Their lips are sealed and so are mine. You don't want to risk blaspheming the gods, when you're on your last legs. Brigid, perhaps an apparition— the blue meanie, a psilocybin mushroom, grew abundantly at one time in that Valley, though it is now extinct—Brigid persuaded the men to emasculate themselves, although there were three would have no part of this New Dispensation. All communes, of course, break down, and this one, despite evident advantages, broke down in the usual manner, as soon as isolation ended, and the younger generation gained access to TV, with a gradual attrition of vision and resolve manifesting in a lust for cash, with concomitant leakage of the able-bodied from the Valley, up the Yellow Track. To the point where the commune became unviable. The final blow was the abduction of the children, for their own welfare, by the State, in '89. No, you didn't read about it in the papers; Rupert adjudged it in the children's best interests the matter be kept from the people.

There was a complication: during the Period of Autarky, a few communards metamorphosed. Disappeared, to reappear as trees. Well, you can understand the reaction of the Welfare, and it made no sense to me, till I recalled that the word 'Brigid' is etymologically related, in Gaelic, to the word 'Phrygian'. Could it be, I asked myself, that what occurred in that Valley is a manifestation, abortive, and at two removes, of the Anatolian Cult of the Great Mother? We know it spread as far afield as Heligoland. And we must surmise that certain Irish tribes came to Ireland from Anatolia. The Galatians were Celts.

We may surmise, I should have said; and specifically, the province of Phrygia. You will recall that Phrygia grew substantially, over the years of Greek and Roman occupation.

What follows is a gloss, a supplement to the Ballad of Erinungarah. A view from the Mind, to be read in conjunction with the view from the poet's Heart, to effect a stereopsis. The Gospel according to the scholiast. As to the poem, well, I sent it to a literary agency, but they haven't as yet gotten back. I can't waste any more time.

I'm not an experienced writer, of other than short, sharp warnings detailing sequestrations pursuant to non-containment of cattledogs and contingencies pertaining to the chronic non-provision of a letterbox, but I did take a Course in Creative Writing once, and passed, which gives me confidence. Should that confidence prove misguided, may I crave indulgence, all the more as my health is failing, fast as the health of the Postmodern PostChristian PostWestern Civilisation around me.

Oh why did I bother, why do I trouble myself with this bizarre and unsubstantiable tale? Because my researches indicate the poem has an historical foundation, and because everything has gone terribly wrong for this civilisation. In the view of F.R. Leavis, our prosperity cannot be regarded as a matter for happy contemplation. Cults spring from fertile ground. I can scarcely bring myself to visit the blessed church up the hill, and you do want a bit of spiritual comfort when you're dying, and you've no family. If what they claim happened in that Valley did happen, or even if it *didn't*—there, I've said it—I am forced to conclude that Valley became, for seven years, a Land of the Ever Young. And if Brigid's talk of a 'broken pledge' that the poet reiterates is taken seriously, it suggests, does it not, that the Christian Church ran off the rails very early on, like me. I suppose Gibbon would call me a 'Phrygian', in reference to that early, proscribed sect of the Church. But all this overpopulation today, all this degradation of farmland and forest, all these unrealistic demands being made on men, this Greenhouse effect, this salination, these Christian Brothers molesting boys, all these women deacons who want to be ordained, these priests demanding to be married, this body piercing and sexual sadism that goes on, this waxing of shoulders—there is a reason for it. It tends towards something. It tends towards solution. There is a solution to it. I found that solution, I believe, in a piece of dead mail at the bottom of an uninverted mailbag, in the bike shed of a post office, since become an agency, at Obliqua Creek, a small town on the arse end of this world.

To Whom it may Concern. Christ was a Eunuch.

We have built us a dome
On our beautiful plantation
And we all have one home
And one family relation
Song of the Oneida, New York, Community, 1848

Quis tamen adfirmat nil actum in montibus aut in speluncis?
(Who says they got up to nothing out in the sticks?)
Juvenal

All these people, looked at from above, present mostly a dreary or
laughable comedy; and yet they are as impressively simple as those
Galileans who were once called blessed.
Carl Jung

Keep going to your wars, you fools, as of yore
I'm the civilisation you're fighting for
Hugh MacDiarmid

Workers of the world, disperse
Fred Richardson, 1970

Contents

Act 5

The Principal Characters

As they were in 1968, with their status in 1995, if known, in brackets.

Mother and Father of the Revolution
Phryx Pfingstl. Late sixties. Plump, broken-nosed, becharcoaled eunuch, emasculated by the Sacred Pump. Consort of Gwendolyn the Witch (murdered by Mehmed).
Gwendolyn Bletherstone Mayall. Late sixties. The Witch of the Ballad, whose vision, inspired by the Sacred Stone, portends the Epiphany (murdered by Mehmed).

Sundry Loners
Michael Ginnsy. Mid-twenties. Red waist-length hair, tall emaciated frame. Guitarist. Top hat, dark glasses. Long arms. Custodian of the Sacred Pump. Always off his face. Became a eunuch (afflicted with the Alzheimer's).
Barbara Byng. Early twenties. Slight, fair, freckle-faced, big ears, braces on her teeth. Student organiser. Mother-to-be of Dawn, by Derek Frodsham (currently senator and minister).
Derek Frodsham. Mid-twenties. Small, dark, acned, prematurely balding working-class scientist from the north of England. Nail-biter. Trotskyist. Father-to-be of Dawn, by Barbara Byng. Became a eunuch (last seen working as a mail sorter, Sydney West Mail Exchange).

Mehmed Contramundum. Early thirties. Big, tough, tattooed Chechen. Deep ecologist and mercenary soldier. Defender of the Grove. Introduced the Phrygian cap to the Valley. Appears in the *Ballad* as the Greenbrown Man, after years of anchoritic mortification in the Valley. Killer of Gwen and Phryx. Emasculator of Smitty. Adoptive father of Attis (suspected of Metamorphosis).

Balthazar Beauregard. Mid-twenties. Brown-haired, muscular soft-drug dealer/landscape gardener-cum-jeweller. Long-time communard. Purveyor of penis ring to Mehmed. Devotee of Indian guru. Father-to-be of Mist, by Paula Zoshka; Galaxy and Nebula, by Sister Annunciata. Became a eunuch (missing, thought deceased).

Sister Annunciata. Late twenties. Nun, who dropped out of the Patriarchal Church in search of the Real Jesus. She it was, according to Kimbo, who first saw the goddess Brigid. Mother-to-be of Galaxy and Nebula (twins) by Balthazar Beauregard (cleaner, Leura).

Johnny Dakota. Late thirties. Part-Indian Canadian vocalist. Guest at the Latin Quarter nightclub in Sydney. Used Michael Ginnsy on one of his albums (appeared recently at the Three Weeds Hotel, Rozelle, according to the *Herald Metro*).

Maximilian Worboise. Mid-twenties. Overweight anti-nuclear demonstrator, who left the Valley in May '86 (overweight anti-nuclear demonstrator still. Active in Greenpeace. Crewman, Rainbow Warrior. Wears his greasy grey hair in a ponytail).

Grainger. Mid-twenties. Like Maximilian, left the Valley on, or about, the Day of the Passion. The Silent One. Made a pledge to remain silent till the Vietnam War was over, but when the Vietnam War was over, resolved to remain silent (senior policy adviser, Anti-Discrimination Board).

Fiona. Mid or possibly late twenties. Diabetic. Fat, hospitable girl, well liked by Sister Annunciata (lived in the Cave, and apparently died there).

Smitty. Late twenties. Ganger on the Forestry. Champion axeman. Husband of Breda, Kimberley Moon's ex-wife. She had the marriage annulled. Foreman on the coupe when Mehmed made a last kill. Emasculated and sexually assaulted by Mehmed (committed suicide).

Wozza. Mid-seventies in 1968. Very part-Aboriginal retired fossicker. Lived, for decades, at Wozza's Camp on Fossicker's Flat,
but more recently, Ruffit Lodge, Wozzawunwun. Blind. Knows
more about the commune than prepared to divulge, in case his
comments may find their way to the National Library Oral
History Unit, which he holds in fear (still roughing it at Ruffit
Lodge).

Monica's Clan

Monica Ecks. Late twenties. Green-eyed, blonde-haired Southern belle and sometime *Playboy* centrefold. Mother of Alexander
(by her first husband, who does not appear in this Saga), Cindy
Ecks, by her second husband Calvin Ecks (who does), and
mother-to-be of Harley and Norton, by Darryl MacAnaspie.
Grandmother of Passionflower (now remarried, domiciled in
Florence. That's Florence, Italy, not Florence, Alabama).

Calvin Ecks. Late twenties. Green-eyed, blond-haired bioscientist, from the US Midwest. Husband of Monica Ecks. Inventor
of the Green Munga, a nutritious but unpalatable paste made
from the leaves of the gum. Father of Cindy, by Monica Ecks,
and father-to-be of Plum Pine, by Nisi Papadimitriou. Grandfather of Passionflower. Never became a eunuch (unemployed,
Wooddenbong, 2476).

Eugene Ecks. Early twenties. Calvin's younger brother, traumatised by service in Vietnam, as a conscript. Shot through on R
and R, from Sydney. Dome enthusiast and votary of R. Buckminster Fuller. Heroin addict, never became a eunuch (unemployed, Byron Bay. On the Done program).

Cindy Ecks. Preschooler in '68. Beautiful, charming daughter of
Monica and Calvin Ecks. Fell in love with Timothy. Abandoned
by Timothy. Thus responsible, indirectly, for the writing of the
Ballad by Timothy. Mother of Passionflower, by Timothy
(unemployed, Wooddenbong, no postcode).

Nisi's Clan

Nisi Papadimitriou. Late twenties. Overweight scrubber from the
Western Division of NSW, but possessed of a certain sexual

allure. Anti-war activist. Horse enthusiast. Mother of the poet 'Orion' (Timothy Papadimitriou), mother of Aloysius O'Looby, mother-to-be of Phascogale, by Olaf Abernathy, Plum Pine, by Calvin Ecks, and Turpentine, by Kimberley Moon. Common-law wife of Olaf Abernathy, a full ten years her junior (grazier, Camooweal).

Olaf Abernathy. Twenty. Gawky, bespectacled loser. Granny glasses. Good handyman, though. Vietnam conscript. Deserter. Common-law husband of Nisi Papadimitriou, stepfather of Timothy Papadimitriou (Orion the poet) and Aloysius O'Looby. Father-to-be of Phascogale, by Nisi Papadimitriou. Became a eunuch (last seen, working as storeman and packer, Cairns region. Tranny now, calls himself 'Olive').

Timothy Papadimitriou. Preschooler. Orion the Poet, wrote *The Ballad of Erinungarah*. Father-to-be of Passionflower, by Cindy Ecks. Having been sent to the local high school here, eloped to Sydney with that Johnson piece from Bunoo Bunoo. Computer whiz. Degree in electrical engineering. Became a eunuch (now resident Bloomfield Asylum, Orange).

Aloysius O'Looby. Nine years old in '68. Troubled, disturbed, anti-social type. Loved West Indian music (couldn't track him down, but pursuing various lines of inquiry).

Diane's Clan

Diane Zoshka. Mid-teens. High school dropout anarchist. The driving force behind the commune. Common-law wife of Attis and mother of his children, Dusk and Sun. Defender of the Family. Converted to a goddess, according to the *Ballad*, by grace of the goddess Brigid. Deadly enemy of Brigid. Lit the fire that burnt the Dome (metamorphosed, with her children, to a waratah, peculiar to the Valley: *Telopea doliveresiana*, the crying wife).

Paula Zoshka. Mid-twenties. Barmaid and heiress. Elder, and more classically beautiful, of the two lovely Zoshka sisters. Always falling pregnant to men. Always regretting it. Mother-to-be of Mountain Gum, by Brian Chegwodden, and Mist, by Balthazar Beauregard. Made the Phrygian caps (unemployed, Double Bay).

Brian Chegwodden. Late twenties. Frustrated writer. Dark, good-looking, lopsided journo, whose mother married a quid. Went to a good school. Fond of the drink and the women, but aren't we all? Hopeless with his hands, but had a green thumb. Common-law husband-to-be of Paula Zoshka, father-to-be of Mountain Gum, by Paula Zoshka. Became a eunuch (currently editor, various computer trade journals, Hong Kong).

The MacAnaspie Clan

Horrie MacAnaspie. Mid-sixties. Earth mover, sawyer and cattle-man. World War Two veteran. Son of Charlie, father of Norman, Barney, Darryl and Fergus. Adoptive father of Attis. Hates goats and doesn't like his neighbours much (deceased).

Iris MacAnaspie. Mid-sixties. Wife of Horrie. Mother of five boys. Comes from the granite country. Forever cooking cakes. Forever washing dishes. Ambitious for Attis to become a lawyer (afflicted with Alzheimer's and stone deaf).

Charlie MacAnaspie. Early nineties. Patriarch of Wonderview and owner of the Valley. Gallipoli vet. Wears only the under-wear. Self-centred curmudgeon (deceased).

Barney MacAnaspie. Early thirties. Eldest of the MacAnaspie boys. Enlisted to fight in Vietnam (currently earthmoving con-tractor, cattleman, and supervisor, lumber yard, Obliqua Creek, resident Wonderview. Captain, Obliqua Creek bushfire brigade. Father of four daughters. Shows no interest in the Valley.).

Darryl MacAnaspie. Late twenties. Jinker driver, motorcyclist. Rastus the Rodeo Clown. Father-to-be of Harley and Norton, by Monica Ecks. Never became a eunuch (still living in the Valley with his sons. Remarried. Still logging the Valley).

Fergus MacAnaspie. Late twenties. Jinker driver. His father's favourite. Fights on a daily basis with Darryl. Became a eunuch, first abbot of the monastery (committed suicide, June '87).

Norman MacAnaspie. Early twenties. Developmentally disabled (still about and still a burden to his family).

Attis MacAnaspie. Mid-teens. Uncommonly good-looking but lacks personality, at least in the following work. Honey hunter and bushman extraordinary. Good at school. Found, at the softwood mill, as a newborn child, by Fergus MacAnaspie. Common-law husband of Diane Zoshka, father-to-be of Sun and Dusk, by Diane Zoshka. Adopted son of both Horrie MacAnaspie and the Greenbrown Man. The Chosen One of Brigid. The Exemplar (metamorphosed to a mallee, upon self-emasculation. DNA testing indicates a hybrid, of several local species).

Kimberley Moon. Kimbo. Me little mate. Me little cob. Late twenties. Friend of Darryl and Fergus. Hypersensitive horseman and bush balladeer. Rodeo star. Represented the nation in the Open Saddleride. Close-set eyes, gammy leg. Threw his saddle off Sunrise Lookdown. Annulled husband of Breda Smith. Father-to-be of Turpentine, by Nisi Papadimitriou. Became a eunuch, but receives hormone treatment (runs the Wozzawunwun store. Sold Phrygian caps there.).

Your Narrator

D'Arcy D'Oliveres. Mid-sixties in 1995. Justice of the Peace, certified Creative Writer. Anglo-Celtic ex-postal worker and sometime migratory beekeeper. Senior Deputy Captain, Obliqua Creek bushfire brigade, Senior Vice-president, Obliqua Creek Bowling Club. Amateur of Anatolia. Founded and edited *The Ballad of Erinungarah*. A Voice of Late Twentieth Century Scepticism (deceased).

Prologue

Beyond the mallee heaths, over the sandstone seacliffs, skirting the smokestacks of the Leisure Coast. Inland, we descry the high plain of the Monaro. We can make out windbreaks of Monterey Cypress, boisterous white cockatoos mounting silo raids.

Leaving the vehicle parked in the desolate Delegate cemetery, let us strike out for the beckoning Tasman, to the tune of Barber's *Adagio for Strings*. Soon, in some old growth forest, where the soil is rich and deep, we see before us the tallest flowering plants on Spaceship Earth: messmate, mountain gum, manna gum, monkey gum and, most beautiful eucalypt of all 700 subspecies, shining gum. But the basalt soon gives out, the sub-basalt, we're into the rough stuff. Between the seacoast and ourselves is a fastness, a wilderness of watersheds. Were there a bob in clearing this country, rest assured it would have been. Where can a man buy a packet of smokes, a tank of gas? Thank God, here's a general store and, behind this lofty plateau to the east, signs of habitation in the next valley along. Let's time our visit to postdate the reopening of the Gap Road, May '86. The *coup de grâce*. We can drive a logging truck in now, but we won't; we shall walk down, like gentlemen. And ladies, given the venue.

Lilly pilly and prickly tree fern, native daphne—one of a myriad—muttonwood and mock olive. The rainforest through which we descend evokes a pristine Peloponnese; it is not entirely to be marvelled at, we feel so much at ease. Our fore-fathers loathed the bush of Sydney, admiring the rainforests of Wollongong. Unhappily, the rainforests proved easier to clear, as their species, with a few topical exceptions—bolwarra, bastard rosewood, native laurel—won't sucker, after being burned. Of a sudden, a midsummer night's dream of cerris oak and sweet bay. We hear the Embden geese genuflecting on the creek flat, adding their voices to those of the purling creek and discreet bellbirds. A water monitor basks on a rock, invigilating the late light. The approaches to the narrow creek—whether caved-in black banks or sandy reaches—are poached, as we see, by cloven hooves, and overrun with blackberries and broadleaf brambles. The steep, farside riverbank, pasture at one time, is infested with madeira winter cherry and fireweed groundsel. You can barely make out the Ronaldson Tippett three-horse-power petrol/kero engine hooked up to the double action piston pump on the nearside bank. The proximal acres of lush creek flat, matted in places with pennyroyal, and showing traces, here and there of lucerne and wall fumitory, have been recently replanted with tree seedlings, shining gum, guarded with wire to protect them against the depredations of feral goats, who can ringbark a tree to a height of twenty feet, by a gentle and judicious backpedalling. Looking up and around, we see that every cranny of this Valley harbours the remains of former dwellings, indifferent in style. Some, reminiscent of the houses flung up by the first Ionian colonists, could be demolished by a strong man in a single day. You wouldn't need a ladder to paint them. Others, still intact, have smoke curling from their chimneys, and V8 vehicles parked beside their middens, and the odd jinker. Many a ruined bush plot remains, to delight the lyre bird, and jonquils, wombat-spurned, mark the site of a once magnificent garden of exotics. All dwellings, but one, have floors of beaten earth, sealed with beeswax and linseed oil, and all but one are built of mudbrick and grey, well-weathered river red gum; which might surprise a botanist unfamiliar with the hole made by a dogspike, as no river red gum grows within a hundred miles of this Valley. The one conventional dwelling, next to what was once the Southern Hemisphere's biggest three-frequency, five-eighth geodesic dome—evocative, insofar as the ruin consists of one of the seven red cedar pillars that formerly supported the floor of that seventh wonder of the ancient world, the Temple of Diana at Ephesus, which survives, in modern Turkey, as a solitary column with a stork's nest on top—this one conventional dwelling, grown over with wombat berry and lawyer vine, commands from a commodious verandah the best view in the Valley, for it sits, fair in the middle of the Flat, with only a huge, majestic, stock-rubbed blackwood, dripping with felt fern, standing between it and the creek, which is lined, below the Falls, with northern sassafras and shining gum, an unusual combination, but here with kanooka, manna gum and ironwood, and washing over the grey and white stones of an Aboriginal Zen garden. And if we could rewind the clock, so that Koala Kottage with two K's were still the only house in the entire Valley, and much of the Flat a vineyard, we might observe an elderly couple, sitting on the verandah in the last light of a late October afternoon. Each afternoon they sit here, listening to the derivative lyrebird, as, somewhere up on a west-facing cliff, he makes in perfect reproduction now the resonant hoon-call of a pied currawong, now the self-effacing backing vocals of an eastern rosella, now the 'eee-chong, jooey-jooey-jooey' of the rufous whistler, now the descending warble of the satin bowerbird, roo-hopping bane of the market garden. And during a break in this recitative, the old man, Phryx Pfingstl, addresses the old woman, Gwen Bletherstone Mayall, in a BBC accent.

'You predicted a coloured Kombi would come into the Valley, Gwen, but now the Etheric Peace has been disturbed, so that the road to the Outside World is entirely blocked, and the crop eaten by scrubbers.'

Plump Phryx has the habit of daubing his eyelids and eyebrows with charcoal. His face is smooth, if disfigured by a badly broken nose, and his voice high-pitched. The plummy baritone *de rigueur* with the BBC accent is not there. Long gone.

'We have still time to plant new crops,' replies the old woman, 'as to those other matters, I see both confusion and polarisation in the cities, Phryx, and I detect much self-righteous anger, and self-piteous indignation. But, at the same time, I see the Soul Magic of the Seventh Ray, manifesting in its highest aspect, through a stimulation of the awareness, of the Healing Power, of Group Consciousness.'

'But these are surely non-integrated beings,' protests the old man. 'They are, at best, impure Brothers of the Shadow.'

'Nonetheless,' retorts the old woman, 'a Village of Custodial Light will manifest, if each Group member can accept the Power within, without feeling an obligation to express it, on every occasion. But before this Transformation can occur, these purely intellectual and physical beings must be purged, and purged again.'

Gwendolyn has extraordinary physical beauty for a woman of her advanced age. Blessed with good hair and good facial bones, a trim figure, she retains her looks. From a distance, that is to say, from a clifftop. Through a telescopic rifle sight.

'There will be trysts and assignations, Gwen.'

'There will be many Points of Procedure raised in this Valley, Phryx. There will be day-long, daily trysts and assignations.'

'And will the Chosen Ones be gathered at these trysts and assignations?'

'We have prayed to the Stone, and purified the Spirits.'

'Oh Gwen, I am so very tired. I'm fairly worn out, maintaining this old farmhouse, which must be maintained. It's high time, I'm sure, some younger man took over.'

Phryx Pfingstl: late sixties. Plump, broken-nosed, becharcoaled eunuch, emasculated by the Sacred Pump. Consort of Gwendolyn the Witch.

Gwendolyn Bletherstone Mayall: late sixties. The Witch of the *Ballad*, whose vision, inspired by the Sacred Stone, portends the Epiphany.

Both murdered by Mehmed. Thought to be buried beneath the Dome.

It is winter here in Obliqua Creek, but the weather is so changeable you have to be close by to get the most out of a fine day. If, however, you are far off in a city, sitting in front of a television one evening, watching the news, and the weather man displays a high-pressure system, very stable, over the southeast corner of the island continent, get yourself into a vehicle, and by driving all night you might arrive on the steppe before the blue sky turns its more customary grey, and the sleet, and the rain, and often as not a gale, blows up. 'Tis then our menfolk leave to plant out frozen pine seedlings in the snow. How we love these fine June days! Not before winter's end do we list our homes for sale. The shadows made by the small white cumulus clouds over our denuded landscape barely move, while the leaves on our few remaining eucalypts positively glitter. The only flower about in the bush is the variable bossiaea. And if we sit in front of a north-facing window, behind a cherry laurel hedge, we may find ourself stripping the milk-white torso to the bra, or singlet, as the case may be. On such a day, a man or woman will wake, six-thirty in the morning Eastern Standard Time, thinking, oh no, it's clouded over! But the sky becomes a pure blue above that thick white fog in some of the moister gullies, and the haze is due entirely to smoke. You can savour that smoke, if you're not yourself a smoker, and if you are, you're like me, a damn fool, because I'm still smoking. Yes, I've been reduced, at times, to smoking the hair off my own legs, with a little coir matting, wrapped in paper from the Book of Common Prayer, but the Whitehall Study of '68, which remains the only controlled trial ever undertaken on the effects of giving up, demonstrated no statistically significant change in mortality from lung cancer. Ah huh, ah huh, pardon me.

In the still days the smoke from the wood fires in our town hangs low over the town, the wood being generally speaking damp, and recently plucked from the mulch, rather than cut, a year or two before, from a freestanding dead snow gum. Accordingly, in the late afternoon, when a lounge room fire is being prepared, it doesn't draw well, and the boy in a grey pullover and blue shirt is forever being instructed to open the side door of the black stove in order to give the fire a boost, either by blowing upon it, or by puffing at it with a set of broken bellows, or more generally, and less intermittently, by blasting it with a sister's purloined hair dryer, if there be an appropriate power point. And the serried embers will then glow, and the damp wood smoke visibly for a time, but only whilst that door is open; for when the door is again closed, and whatever the aperture setting on the flue, the wood, however redeployed, will smoulder, so that no red glow can be observed through the japanned mica or glass, not that the boy would notice; he has his gaze firmly fixed upon *Monkey* or *Teenage Mutant Ninja Turtles* or their equivalents—I sold my tele in '88, so I'm *démodé*—and truth to tell, he can't see the need for a fire on such a night, as he'll be in bed before the dew starts dampening the soot on the iron roofs. He's not permitted to watch the mid-week movie or Panasonic Cup Rugby League match, and rightly so, but it is not, you may be relieved to learn, of my own dull life in this humble abode, in this bleak Boeotian landscape, that I wish to speak, nor of how, rolling over before utterly discomfiting my lumpsum, I retired early from the Australian Postal Service, both to play bowls—for, unlike Diocletian, I have grown my share of cabbages—and to effect a *risorgimento* of my long-lapsed scholarly inclinations for the task at hand, for unlike Descartes, I cannot pride myself on having forgotten all my Greek. It is nothing less than a *Saga* which I must here recount, taking the word in its modern meaning of an epic-like narrative, that is, not the story of a group of Icelandic heroes, prior to the momentous *Althing* of June AD 1000, when Thorgeir, Priest of Lightwater and Old Speaker of the Law, lay all the long day (rather like the Scythian discoverers of hemp), on the rocky Hill of Laws, with a cloak over his head, before he rose and, according to the *Njals Saga*, spake as follows: 'Now all men shall be Christian here in this land, and leave off all idol worship, and not expose children to perish, nor eat horseflesh. It shall be outlawry if these things are proved openly against any man; but if these things be done by stealth, then it shall be blameless.'

The *Sagas*, mind, were written some 200 years subsequently, by scholars of impeccably Christian upbringing, for scholars and Christians, it appears, are suited to compile, though may not feature in, *Sagas*, which gives me heart, as the heroes of my own *Saga* are neither Christian nor scholarly, while I have been both, after my fashion. And though it could be claimed that the *Saga* of which I must speak has not concluded, in that hewers of wood and drawers of water live still in that far, remote Valley of Erinungarah, then I must retort that Icelanders live in Iceland today, as Poms do in the Old Dart, which proves only that the body outlives the spirit.

No, my fear is that this *Saga* not be committed to the word processor and thus lost, for it is suspected that those who were 'of', as it were, the Valley, are some of the most amotivational Anglo-Celtic people to be found outside the New South Wales North Coast or the Tennessee Appalachians; while those not of the Valley who knew something of it have either failed to grasp the significance of what went on there, or else lack a capacity to put it into legible handwriting, let alone historical perspective. It thus falls to me to do the job, and perhaps as well, for I, too, have come across the sea (if not recently, and if not unto Ionia), and am bound to use the language and tone of voice appropriate to the *Saga*, for to paraphrase Nietzsche, there is, in all talk, a grain of contempt.

I regret I cannot make of this *Saga* an *echte* Epic in the mode of the Homeric Odyssey; Aristotle, student of Homer, claims we prefer in our reading what is impossible but plausible, over what is possible but incredible. During the winter of 1794 the Dutch fleet, frozen in the ice, was captured by the French cavalry; but who would not rather read of a bow that only one man could draw, or of a mob of truly wild brumbies, yarded by one diminutive lad? I will give you the *Saga*. Another gives us the *Ballad*. You may be the judge.

I certainly hope we will not sully the manly, ironic tone of the *Saga* with the low, scurrilous, scabrous tone of the satire, but if we do (*et quando uberior vitiorum copia?*—and when were there worse bastards about?) it will be of comfort that the first Phrygian response to the Hittite

Great Mother (Kubaba) was a comic object, that the Passion of Christ was prefigured in the farce of Aristophanes—though whether he wrote as Aeschylus did, and as I do, drunk, we have no evidence—that Apuleius, tongue half in cheek, finished what Homer had begun, and that Juvenal, according to no less an authority than Hume, was the last great Latin writer of genius. And this astringent bachelor, unmentioned by any other writer in his lifetime, forgotten the moment he was dead, and not subsequently looked at for 200 years—at one stage, cheetah-like, he was down to a few breeding pair—wrote, you may recall (for Memory, says Aeschylus, is the Mother of the Muses) not in the days of Nero or Domitian, as one might suppose from a reading of the satires, but a little later, in the halcyon days of the Roman Empire, according to Gibbon, when it was under the rule of Nerva, and of Trajan, and of Hadrian, when, stretching to its furthest marches from Berenice to Eboricum, it knew both peace and comparative prosperity without, and utter hopelessness within, which is pretty much my own state of mind these days, and that of my neighbours, as far as I can suss them out. We all bask in the yellow submarine of world-historian Toynbee's Indian summer. What boots it that I fear a moribund god while they, bless them, acknowledge none? 'Of all customs,' says Plutarch, 'first and greatest is belief in gods ... you might find communities without walls, letters, kings, houses or money, with no knowledge of theatres or gymnasia; but a community without holy rite, without a god, that uses not prayer, nor oath, nor divination, nor sacrifice, no man ever saw, or ever will see.' Oh dear. We must, however, concede, that of all sedentary barbarians, the white Australian is perhaps the only one for whom a nocturnal cemetery holds no terrors, as yet.

Where then to begin? Begin at the beginning is what she advised, when we took the Creative Writing Course, but it all goes back forever, doesn't it. Anyone with half a brain could see it. We are the product of ancestral genes as well as of social conditioning, now let us pray.

Hermes, thou most loquacious of gods, hear our prayer! Was it not you who said to Charon, in the imagination of Lucian, 'Some there are whose eyes are open to discern good and evil. They stand aloof from the rest of mankind, and scoff at all that goes on. Nothing is as they would have it.' Lend us the wit to understand, the pension and the passion to pursue, the skill to evoke, the patience to persist, and may they appreciate, once for all, that although we ride an ex-Postal motorbike, and wear this old postman's uniform, we are not necessarily prepared to convey their Postmodern correspondence to the Post Office.

To begin.

Incipe, Calliope. Licet et considere (Let's go, Muses. Don't bother standing up).

The West Coast of Southern Chile, which shares with the southwest coast of the South Island of New Zealand, and the southwest coast of Tasmania, the most miserable climate on this planet and, perhaps in consequence, the last remaining wilderness of cool temperate rainforest—chiefly, species of the southern beech *Nothofagus*, of which tanglefoot is one and 'myrtle' another—is drenched by the roaring forties, which bring buckets of very cold, semi-solid rain annually. And yet it seldom snows. To the north of Chile, in contrast, the Atacama Desert is the driest place on earth, there being parts where no rain has ever been recorded; an interesting, in fact absolute, contrast in rainfall patterns.

Never more than 250 miles wide, Chile is 2661 miles long, though no sensible man would choose to live beyond 200 miles of Santiago, the centrally situated capital city. Around Santiago, the rainfall pattern found elsewhere only in the Andes, on the high plateau of the cordilleras, extends towards the Pacific Ocean, until, as we move south, no rain at all very rapidly becomes too much rain for our comfort. In this fertile central region of Chile, the rain gauges record ten to eighty inches annually, a precipitation to the liking of that portion of the evergreen sclerophyllous biome, which here faces, across 8000 miles of Pacific Ocean, its more illustrious Australian counterpart. To the north, presumably, it peters out; to the south, where the annual rainfall is closer to eighty inches than ten, where fogs and mists abound, and where rivers and lakes have not yet become glaciated masses of solid ice, the evergreen sclerophyllous biome has wet ears and wet feet, a circumstance which, towards the Pacific Coast from where this writer pens these lines, would surely evoke the mountain grey gum, the messmate stringybark and the brown barrel, the last known to our local timbermen as cuttail. But in Chile, we are marching, with the old Imperial Incas, who acted, like the Romans before them, as margraves to their civilisation, up against the huge Gondwanan rainforests, at first subtropical rather than temperate, and rooted in deep, fertile soils, produced by the region's innumerable volcanoes. And to those who define Civilisation as any place conducive to the cultivation of the spud, or potato, this is sacred ground, for the evidence suggests that *Solanum tuberosum*, a nightshade, originated in these uplands of southern Chile—although, like the related tomato and capsicum, it does appear to have been first domesticated further north, on the verge of its natural range, domestication being favoured on the verge of a species' natural range, for it is here desperate measures are required—where the evergreen sclerophyllous biome, and the Andean Civilisation, marched over against the rainforests, and the savages from Tierra del Fuego, who were subsisting off sea urchins and Magellan's currants, and doing no harm to the environment, at the time of a seasick Charles Darwin's visit in the 1830s, by which date half the inhabitants of Scotland, and all the Irish, were living nine months of the year on a pabulum of potatoes.

The 40-year-old Empire of the Incas was overthrown by Pizarro in 1530. Forty-seven years later Sir Francis Drake discovered the potato. Fifty-five years later, Sir Walter Raleigh reburied it in Ireland on his Cork estate, where it proved an immediate success, being tolerant of the moist climate, the long summer days, and the mean annual temperatures, though hankering, winter-long, to the depths of the beady little eyes on its tubers, for the glimpse of an evergreen, sclerophyllous shrub. It was the potato blight caused the famine of 1845 and led to the Great Emigration of Celts to northern Tasmania, northern California, to Gippsland, Canada, the State of Idaho—to anywhere, in short, where conditions were found to comport with the propagation of the ancestral aliment.

Act 1 Scene 1

1. *Ginnsy meets Barbara.*

People are forever staring at Michael Ginnsy because of his red, waist-length hair and his tall, emaciated frame. There is something about him doesn't compute, the drug-induced indifference to others sitting strangely with the deferential hunch. Though forever stuffing himself with food, Ginnsy never puts on weight. Only hair. From the habit tall, shy adolescents acquire of stooping to be polite, the shoulders are rounded; the Hibernian locks fall down the pigeon chest. There, they interfere with his picking hand and make it hard for him to find his wallet. But life is not meant to be easy, though hair was not meant to be greasy.

'Yes?'

'One small bucket, make that a large bucket. One large bucket of chips and a white coffee.'

'Sugar?'

'Four.'

He sits down, with his coffee and chips, and picks up the student paper, *Honi Soit*. It is 1968, a time when Australian men with long hair were stoned in the streets, so to speak. Where possible, Ginnsy selects a vacant table for himself. With his dark, reflective glasses and dark, unreflective intelligence, he lives life in a see-through mirror, from the inside of an ambulance. He can see other people, but they can't see him, can't see his eyes, which are fearful, and distracted. So much of what Ginnsy sees and hears is phantasmal.

Avoid white powders.

It's lunchtime and the cafeteria is crowded. The only vacant seats at the tables are littered with dirty dishes, but that doesn't deter Ginnsy. He sits down, not even troubling himself to clear away. With the remnants of someone's meal before him— plastic sandwich wrappings, milkshake containers, the remains of a cream bun—he spreads over all of it the student paper, and flicks through the paper, slurping his coffee. Two overthin lips move as he reads.

Girls opposite, one Chinese, are staring at him now. He looks up, grins affectedly, gives them the finger, tosses a chip high in the air, makes a grab for it with his green and yellow teeth, his seven-potater maw, misses. He turns back to his paper, but his mind, as he tucks into the chips, and they are good—fat, wrinkle-cut French fries*, cooked to perfection with plenty of salt and vinegar—is brooding over an incident that occurred some time in the recent past—and even in the witness box, as a witness to the murder of his own brain, he could be no more specific—when, on his way out to buy some strings, and checking out the record racks in one of the city's biggest stores, he could find not one copy . . .

'Hello? Mind if I join you?'

Not one single copy. Barbara Byng, a fair, slight, freckle-faced girl with big ears and braces on her teeth, has followed Ginnsy all the way from the Free Concert on the Front Lawn, which is still raging without his Hot Club of France rhythm guitar, a musical joke that fell flat as a nightcarter's hat.

Ginnsy moves his neck turtle-wise, methodically munching and chomping chips. He belches in the girl's face, inadvertently.

'There's something I'd like to discuss with you,' says the girl, undisconcerted. 'That's if I'm not disturbing you, Michael.'

He listens carefully. They always want something. Reaching down, he unzips his fly, or as far as the non-pubic hairs caught in the zip permit, then pulls from a fob a wallet stuffed with big notes, slamming it on the table. He then turns back to his paper, which is bloody boring. Normally, at this juncture, they have the decency to get up and leave, but no; she initiates an allocution concerning the Vietnam situation, concluding with the need for celebrities like him—that's a good one—to do their bit, to lend a hand.

'Oh, you want me to speak, is that it? OK, I'll make a speech right now. Achtung!'

He scrambles onto the table, scattering the paper plates with his hand-tooled boots. His fly is still undone.

'Pcheow! We gotta stop all this shit bout fightin in

---

* Were these available then? I have the feeling they were. Defrosting my freezer on moving house, I discovered a cache of frozen foods I estimate dates to the late sixties. I'm sure I saw a packet of Birdseye crinkle cut fries.

4

Vietnam,' he bellows, shy by nature, but feral under the influence of angel dust cut with bleach. 'Let's hear it for Ho Chi Minh, Ho ho ho ho, ha ha ha, a bottle o'rum, and a number, for 'r'on.'

He scrambles back down. He was a student himself here a few years back, and no one took any notice of him then, though he was a far better guitarist then than he is now, far better. Failed Economics One twice.

Thrusting a fist into the chip bucket, to garner the last few broken chips, he does up his fly with his free hand. The chick is wearing an Indian smock, you can see her bra, sort of, and her eyes are red, she's biting her lip, he's upset her.

She reminds him a bit of his sister Colleen; another foundation member of the Itty Bitty Titty Committee.

'Hey' he says, 'I've embarrassed you.' The tone of his voice is warm now, and seductive. But could the focus of the eyes be determined, Barbara would note he was staring over her shoulder. In some alarm.

She denies embarrassment. The whole table is watching. The whole cafeteria is listening.

'Hey, I can't think at this time o' day. I dunno what I'm sayin 'n doin. I should be in bed.'

He winks, to no effect perforce. The apparition.

'I'm sorry, I shouldn't have approached you.'

'Naa, it's nothin. What's your name?'

'I already told you my name. It doesn't matter.'

He watches as she walks out. Episode closed. She looks like his sister Colleen, except his sister Colleen would not be reading, as she walked, Joske's *The Law and Procedure of Meetings*, but might indeed have a playful bruise on her upper arm.

Lunchtime is almost over. The first lecture of the afternoon will have commenced. Ginnsy saunters to the counter. The warm sun is peering through the windows.

'Yes?'

'What's your name?'

'Hurry up. What do you want please.'

'I want two Swiss potato cakes. I'll pay a hundred dollars. I want them now, I crave them. Do you have a grater?'

'I'm busy.'

'Here's the money. Pcheow! Count it. Fifty now, fifty later. You're beautiful.'

'Please don't waste my time.'

'No one need know. I'm not a student. I'm a wealthy ex-student. Now then, where's that grater? Here's how we go about it. We'll take some butter and oil in the pan, and in the meanwhile, parboil the potatoes.'

'I'm going to call the supervisor.'

'Why? Grate the potatoes, add salt, pepper, some grated cheese. What kind of cheese you got here? Brown and toss. Mm baby, those country cakes. Look, I don't have time to go to the shops right now. Just sell me the potatoes.'

'Really!'

'You are so conventional. Must the whacks take *all* my money? Can't I give some to you? Don't you believe in service? I mean, you look like a working-class woman. Are you offended I'm not trying to root you?'

'OK buster, what is going on here?'

'He's trying to buy some potatoes. I tell him the chips are already prefrozen but he doesn't listen.'

Michael Ginnsy: mid-twenties. Red waist-length hair, tall emaciated frame. Guitarist. Dark glasses. Always off his face. Became a eunuch.

Barbara Byng: early twenties. Slight, fair, freckle-faced, big ears, braces on her teeth. Student organiser. Became a senator.

2. *Barbara chairs a meeting. Frodsham and Mehmed attend.*

'Surely we need a police permit?'

Barbara Byng addresses herself exclusively to men, if there are men present. She is open, however, to misinterpretation in other respects, and this is duly acknowledged, in the form of an appreciative snort, by the impavid Derek Frodsham, who never looks anyone in the eye. Frodsham—a small, dark, acned man, prematurely balding—has either misread or, as a relative neo-phyte, failed to read Byng's eagerness to please, which forbids irony and expresses itself, towards men, through exaggerated facial mannerisms, instinct with courtesy and submission, that are sure to please ideologues of every age and all denominations. Combined with undoubted but well-concealed intelligence, her bureaucratic efficiency, it has made a sexually alluring apparat-chick from unpromising raw materials: flat chested, freckled, round shouldered, short sighted, Barbara Byng never wants for boyfriends, to the contrary. Her winsome 'personality'—her readiness to listen, her apparent interest in what men say, the habit she has of leaning forward in her chair, combined with an inveterate sexual availability—nullifies the protruding ears, the braces, and an appalling dress sense. Sex is not all tits and bums, but till he meets a raver of the intellectual type, a man could be forgiven for thinking otherwise.

And who is this Frodsham, so insensitive to feminine wiles? He is a member of the International Committee for the Recon-struction of the Fourth International and a brilliant student of physics.

The anti-war movement, quiet, since the visit to Sydney eighteen months before of US President Johnson, is quiet no longer. This particular meeting, convened in a wainscoted with-drawing room of the University of Sydney, can claim no his-torical precedence, though it is not inferior, in terms of the passions aroused—and passions, it could be argued, if more usually insisted upon, are what count—to similar meetings taking place, with a similar lack of buckram, in the US. Here, as there, draft dodgers, dole bludgers, dope dealers, dropouts and deserters, mingle with radical nuns, Maoists, Stalinists, anarchists, Trotskyists and Quakers. And then there are the students.

Poor sequacious colony, destined never to be first cab off the rank. Yet what nation-state ever existed with greater potential for autarky than Australia?

'You have sold us all short!'

Those present who in all conscience find they must oppose violence are ranged against *sicarii*, fanatics who have no objec-tion to the execution of tyrants. And really, these two have no

7

business in being in the same room, let alone on the same committee (Students for a Draft Dodging Society) organising the same march. The concord arising from the fact they both disapprove of what is happening in Vietnam—and Australia, as a staunch US ally, has conscript ground forces there—is the concord a vegetarian strikes up with a gourmet near Harry's *Café de Wheels*, the Woolloomooloo pie and pea concession; heartwarming, but only insofar as it is evanescent, and not meant to be pursued, like the glance a young engaged woman on a train will give a married man on the platform, but only after the carriage doors have been safely closed, and the guard's whistle blown.

Brotherly, and oft times Sexual, Love, in a modern city is a touch, a word, a glance. Those with *savoir vivre* keep their bodily fluids to themselves. They know how to walk away, and are content to do so.

'This is the man, I might add, who didn't have the guts ...'

'I beg your pardon!'

'Didn't have the bloody *guts*! Didn't have the common courtesy ...'

They smile, they dream, they use their intelligence. They return to an empty apartment. They admire, from a window, harbour views. They dread embrace, no longer wish to be harangued by people with arseholes.

They pick up the weekend magazine, with its soft porn, its social concern.

'Siddown, ya wanker. It's people like you ...'

'On a point of order, Madam Speaker!'

Within five years, there will be unisex toilets downstairs in the Men's Union. Unisex toilets with urinals. A show of hands indeed.

And order comes, profound as an *ange passe*. The meeting is silenced by a total stranger, unknown to any person present, yet unlikely, it is thought, to be an undercover policeman. A stocky person, he boasts a curious cap, a sleeveless flak jacket, safety boots and blue jeans. Born in Siberia, a Chechen from the Caucausus, he wears, affixed to his jacket, no North Vietnamese flag, no Red Chinese flag, no Black Power badge. He has sleepers in both nipples, centurion-style, but you don't know this unless you know him well. A knife wound disfigures his left cheekbone. He has an AK 47 bullet scar on his right bicep. His arms are heavily tattooed with grinning skulls and cartoon road-runners. Frowning, a cartoon figure in his own right, he looks about the room, as though seeking a tart, or a V twin.

'Take my seat' whispers one of the academics, and with a dignified nod of assent the offer is accepted. Mehmed Contramundum sits bolt upright, spilling from his seat, hands stiff on his knees. A deep ecologist and mercenary soldier, Mehmed is destined to have great impact on the campus anti-war movement, chiefly in raising the level of debate; from the moment he entered this room this evening, not another four letter word was heard to be uttered.

Barbara Byng: early twenties. Slight, fair, freckle-faced, big ears, braces on her teeth. Student organiser. Future senator.
Derek Frodsham: mid-twenties. Small, dark, acned, prematurely balding, working-class scientist from the north of England. Nail-biter. Trotskyist. Father-to-be of Dawn by Barbara Byng. Future mail sorter. Became a eunuch.
Mehmed Contramundum: early thirties. Big, tough, tattooed Chechen, deep ecologist and mercenary soldier. Defender of the Grove. Appears in the *Ballad* as the Greenbrown Man, after years of anchoritic mortification in the Valley. Adoptive father of Attis. Suspected of Metamorphosis.

3. *Monica takes up with Balthazar. Calvin visits the Shoalhaven Gorge.*

During the first years of her second marriage, Monica Ecks travelled. Her husband, a Yankee from the Midwest, Calvin, studied for a time in Oxford, then later moved to Europe, completing his education at a Max Planck Institute. The couple arrived in Australia a few years before Derek Frodsham arrived from London, and, like Frodsham, flew in from Singapore: after scrutinising his bank book, and finding it empty as a Jim Beam bottle at a sixteenth birthday party—Monica wouldn't work, but had a taste for Paris—Calvin concluded he could no longer afford to travel via the US. This was a mistake, as not long after the arrival of these two good-looking Americans—so alike they were often mistaken for twins—in Canberra, where Calvin took up a five-year appointment as research fellow in the John Curtin School for Medical Research, Monica's father died, having written a strange letter to his daughter expressing the intention of visiting her in her new home, a duplex in the Canberra suburb of Campbell. How this affected a woman who had paternal difficulties and never wrote her father, we can but guess, but we know she commenced an extra-marital liaison shortly after, the first of her second marriage, and her first ever with an Australian, because, after moving on to Sydney, and tenure, with a family that now comprised her long-suffering but dearly beloved second husband, her four-year-old daughter Cindy and a nine-year-old son Alexander by her first marriage, Monica's Australian paramour, distressed perhaps by the thought of endless reverse charge telephone conversations from public telephones, crashed his racing pushbike into an Embassy fence (but not seriously) as a subconscious means of drawing attention to his plight and the police, inappropriately, were informed. Monica had a potent effect on men, for though schooled in California she was raised in Alabama, and her voice retained a sexy Confederate twang till the end of her days in the Valley, where she is still remembered by the sons that she abandoned there.

Today she remains, no doubt, a beautiful woman, but she is married to a Frenchman now and lives in Florence. In her mid-twenties she must have been a stunner, all bustle and magnolia. South of the Mason-Dixon line, coquetry, I venture, has a style all its own, and you cannot expect to flaunt a Southern girl with party-going impunity, especially if she's a Decatur belle with big white teeth, and big brown hips, and big brown and white D-cup boobs, and you're the kind of nerd who regards all conversation not concerned with jazz, or wilderness, or immunoassay, as a waste of your time. A foreigner, moreover, enjoys exotic status among Australian womanisers, and to possess her might well prove something to someone. Had Monica, spare the day, been mine, I should have stayed home, I think, or converted to Islam. She had a Gene Tierney overbite, with a gap between her two front teeth, the better for whistling Dixie.

We will take up the story of Monica Ecks and her many men* about the time Balthazar Beauregard began building a birdbath for Monica's next-door homosexual neighbours. This would have been a few months after Olaf Abernathy moved in with Nisi Papadimitriou and Nisi's two children, Timothy Papadimitriou and Aloysius O'Looby. And if you're having trouble keeping up with these surnames, spare a thought for the contemporary postman, whose only respite from the pressures of the job is a substance that pickles the perspicuity, though it's amazing what you recall when you're actually out on the beat. People think nothing of approaching to inquire if you had any mail for the mother-in-law the day before yesterday, and the wonder is you can usually tell them, through a process of visualisation. I maintain envisaging any sort of array tones and stimulates the grey cells, and I once memorised the name of every Roman Emperor, from Augustus to Maurice, by ascribing the name of an emperor to each letterbox of my beat.

I have now in my notes to circumstantiate an act of fornication, that occurred one morning between Monica Ecks and Balthazar Beauregard while Calvin Ecks was walking in the bush, on a rare day off, but I'd be more comfortable in the bush with Calvin, though I should not be at my ease. I'm no Manichaean, but we won't be getting between the sheets with Balthazar and Monica. We knows what goes on, and I never thought it made for compelling reading. Show me the video *Debbie Does Dallas*, an *Outlaw Biker* with a blonde on a bike, and I'll behave like most men, with interest. Read me an account of what someone did with someone else—next he shoved it up her nostril, then he put it under her armpit—I remain unmoved. I'm no Harlequin Mills and Boon subscriber, but The Lord has given us a finite anatomy, which no amount of fetishistic desiderata (not to say contraceptive

---

* *Nam ut se ament efflictim non modo incolae, verum etiam indi vel Aethiopes utrique vel ipsi Anticthones.* For she allures, not just her own kind, but Indians, black fellas, even Antipodeans. Apuleius.

impedimenta) can mask. In the end, we have three or four lubricable apertures, a dozen insertable appurtenances, and as that portion of the hindbrain, or limbic system, which responds to the sexual stimulus is both illiterate—as witness the fact it never learns—and irrational—as witness the fact it never wants to—I will not defer to it in this *Saga*, which will, however, describe in some amplitude what happens when the venereal appetite is sated. It is time, in short, for Cupid to be set loose a season, with a whistle in his teeth.

'I'm going bush' says Calvin to Monica, 'I'll take the tent, for I may stay overnight. I want some shots of that white-faced heron, the grey bird that flies over late in the evenings when we're camping out, later than the wood duck, in the last light. Know the bird I mean? A grey waterfowl with a harsh cry. Craark, cra-ark. Know the bird I mean?'

Monica's at the sink, watching Balthazar Beauregard through the kitchen window over the paling fence, and the last question she's asking herself is whether this boy has both oars in the water.

'Know the bird I mean, woman? I'll probably go down to the Shoalhaven, there's plenty there, I'll take the car. All right with you?'

'Take it, for God's sake!'

'Do you need money?'

Calvin is a bird lover. He chucks his packs and cameras into the car, and drives off at 4 a.m. next day with a sense of annoyance. He is fed up with life in the Antipodes*, tired of having to force himself to go bush, his only outdoor recreation. 'In our own wild nature,' writes Nietzsche, 'we find the best recreation from our un-nature, from our spirituality.' So even in her adultery, there is a nexus between this Postmodern man and his wife.

As he drives though the sparse city traffic, he thinks of the bush awaiting him today, the bush of the Shoalhaven Gorge to the south of Sydney, without a *soupçon* of the anticipation that

---

* The eighth century Irish scholar, Virgil, Bishop of Salzburg, was unfrocked by Pope Zacharias for professing a belief in the Antipodes.

the woods of Britain and the United States and Bavaria traditionally afford. Here, the trees are the same always. You can never tell what season of the year it is.

'Mark ye the leaves, for men are like thereto.' Homer. But the evergreen sclerophyllous biome is not in concert with Homer. This green is not a true green. There is no annual season in which these leaves change colour and fall. There is no spring explosion of bud, no aureole of venous spring verdure, no panoply of leaf in high summer. There is not even a period in winter when these trees are bereft of leaves. They do not shriek the solstices.

So? No. It is not a question of asking if this matters, but of gauging the extent to which it *does* matter, *has* mattered, by the disconcertion the bush produces in us. All Europe, before the Hellenic Civilisation, and disregarding the Mediterranean moiety, the pine, olive and evergreen oak which spread northward under the influence of man, was covered with huge, deciduous forests of oak, elm and chestnut. An oak forest, of what I should imagine was deciduous Valonia oak, stood at the foot of Mt Cithaeron, in northwest Attica, as late as the second century. Some Germans questioned by Caesar once travelled two months through the Hercynian Forest, which stretched eastward from the Rhine. Non-bog Ireland, in St Pat's time, was a forest of sessile oak, containing not a single town or city. But by the end of the fourteenth century these forests had been cleared, from the coast of the Atlantic through to the Urals, and what survived the charcoal makers in Britain and Ireland could not survive the shipbuilders. By the eighteenth century, Ireland was importing staves for barrels.

Now all the main branches of the Aryan stock in Europe had as their chief divinity that god of Thunder and the Oak, known to the Romans as Jupiter. Men, according to Roman lore, are *rupto robore nati*, born of a broken oak (Juvenal). Why Thunder and the Oak? Because the oak, in virtue of its conductivity, is struck by lightning with more frequency than any other forest tree of Europe, according to the anthropologist Frazer.

Suppose a Caucasian venture into a deciduous wood one

autumn, the man being in a bad mood; the forest will commiserate with him, reinforcing his mood. If, to the contrary, he's in a good mood, there will be a dialogue between the forest and himself. So whatever the season of year it may be, always there will be an exchange, and I don't think we realised, till ignored by the evergreen sclerophyllous biome, how important this dialectic had become to us. The cult of Christ, in contemporary Australia, commands about the same degree of fervour as the cult of Vespasian did in Antioch, or the cult of Domitian in Ephesus. This I ascribe less to the fact that we started as convicts and Irishmen than that all the festivals of the Christian Church (and though Jesus may have preached in the country, Paul built Christianity in, and for, cities: don't forget pagan means bumpkin) are celebrated six months out of kilter here, which renders them diabolically inappropriate, an inversion of the natural order being characteristic of satanism, as you'd know if you'd ever celebrated the winter solstice at the summer solstice*, or sat down to murder a hot cross bun on some gloomy day in autumn.

I know people who actually have the habit of sending off cards to slight acquaintances, in the last pre-Xmas mail.

Eucalypts don't lose their leaves *en bloc* and we may disregard the sole remaining Australian deciduous native of note (disregarding the cedars), tanglefoot, a bastard beech, as the Tasmanian southwest, where tanglefoot occurs, is now believed to be of Antarctic provenance. Sixty million years ago, we were connected, through Antarctica, to South America. Platypus teeth have been found in Patagonia.

I didn't think platypus had teeth.

---

* The Festival of Christmas was taken, in the fourth century, from the worship of the Danubian sun god *Sol Invictus*, Invincible Sun. Temperate man has a natural proclivity to celebrate the rebirth of the year in midwinter. At that time, though at its lowest, the life force may be expected to increase. Contrarily, in midsummer, a declination sets in. This is no occasion for celebration. Midsummer's Day, St John's Day, was, in pagan Europe, a day to be dreaded. This was the day the water spirits of German rivers demanded drownings, the Celtic Beltane, on which Druids immolated human victims, a day of brooding, of divination.

Pine trees, of course, don't lose their leaves, and our adoration of the Christmas tree is a rite that, like Easter, we have taken from the worship of Cybele, the Hellenised *Magna Mater* of the Anatolian Hittite civilisation. We can no longer attend a midnight mass, but we still put up the pine tree.

I shall state it plainly, insofar as a Mystery can be: the Christianity of Western Christendom was 'Oriental' and *all* higher religions of the 'Orient' (Anatolia and Canaan) derive from what is commonly described as tree and crop worship, as though the two were compatible; all derive from the worship of Tammuz and Ishtar, in their various guises.

Now the annual rebirth of an apparently dead tree is a cardinal metaphor to our Northern Faith, and Spengler the historian regards this Northern Faith, which he terms 'Faustian', as a distinct religion, not to be confused with the Christianity of the Martyrs and the Anchorites—and, dare one say it, the Celtic Christian Church of Ireland, before the Synod of Whitby. I agree (nowdays the Pope avails himself of surgery, while the Bishop of Canberra, up on a sex charge, threatened heart attack and got off) and I maintain that without this metaphor Catholic Christianity is sorely tested, even fatally impaired. The 'Faustian Faith', incidentally, which contains a strong admixture of Jupiter worship, came into its own around the end of the first millennium AD, through an ebullition, principally, of the Mithraic (Church Militant) component of The Christ—Who, as the victorious Brat among the many conceived through the fornications of Jove, Yahwe and Ahuramazda, with Ma, Mut and Astarte in the realm of the Great Pander Seleucus, took His Siblings (Mithras, Attis, the Hellenised Baal Jupiter Dolichenus) unto Himself, as a matter of *Weltpolitik*.

While now, at the end of the second millennium AD, it is the turn of Attis.

I don't know where I'd be, without my deciduous liquidambar in my backyard. Small wonder Calvin feels his heart sink to his atheistic walking boots, at the thought of another day in this evergreen sclerophyllous biome, because the trees here show no interest in him, and scorn his (northern European) spiritual essence. And the eucalypt has yet, outside the Erinungarah Valley, to supplant the pine as a symbol of the eternal.

I am told Attis MacAnaspie, born from a pine in the pine plantation, metamorphosed hereabouts to a eucalyptus tree. I have here his left hand sitting on my desk as a paperweight. He lost the tip of his index finger.

Kimberley Moon, that bandy little eunuch who runs the store in Wozzawunwun, he had that stashed away. Cost me half me super. Must have seen me comin.

See, if Attis became a eucalypt, and if the climate here is warming, and if the eucalypt is expanding, then there is no future for farming.

Back in the house in Paddo, all is quiet. Whatever daemon was demanding to be heard has spoken, and been suitably thwarted, and rests exhausted.

'You're so cute,' says Monica, after a time. 'I gotta buy you a present, come on. You need a pair o' shoes.'

'Settle down,' grins barefoot Balthazar, but Monica is off the bed, wiggling into her patchwork harem pants. 'Get up,' she says, 'I got things to do. Gotta collect my daughter at the pre-school. Shift your pretty butt.'

It's a big ask. Monica hasn't given him the chance to regret what he's done, which would have taken only a few more minutes, and lasted, moreover, only a few minutes more. The sight of that big shapely bum wiggling into those harem pants and the smell of it—something like a rabid musk-ox, in a drought, chewing on a fresh salmon—has done the trick, and he wants her back in bed. 'Look,' he says.

'Come on,' says Monica, who's seen a few of these, 'we gotta walk. My old man took the car.'

There's no hint of feminine solicitude, and Balthazar feels its absence keenly. He wants to talk, but she won't listen to him. On the way to the shops—and she doesn't seem to care if people see them together, at one point stopping to chat with neighbours—he tries to tell her about himself, but she waves him away as though she's heard it all before.

'Oh you're into all that,' she says. 'I thought all that went out with the Ark. I took you for an art student. How old are you anyway?'

Rivers and waterways, thank God for them. Cut through the evergreen sclerophyllous biome till you find the rivers and watercourses, and they will speak to you, and console you and threaten you, as always they have done, at all times, and in all places, for they are the same the world over. They are the sea and we are aquatic apes. Even the vegetation that, spate-twisted, grows by the waters is more involving, the bent casuarinas which look like pines, the watergums which look like oleanders. Halfway down the steep Assay Buttress, heading for the Great Horseshoe Bend, Calvin can feel himself relaxing, but not completely. He sees the big river now on both sides, and no one else is out here today, no vehicles in the carpark of sorts, no one else on the trail.

Calvin, a lanky, well-built man with the blond hair and olive skin of a surfer, has been an outdoorsman long enough to know you don't perve on the Wilderness. You don't idle in the Wilderness. When you enter Wilderness, it must be with respect, with a purpose in mind. You may fish or canoe, pan for gold, climb, trek or paraglide, but you must set yourself a goal out here, because Wilderness will not yield to a man's direct gaze. She's like a hill gorilla, you can't stare at her. She's shy. And besides, young men should be active. They must take risks in the Wilderness, small but constant, to focus the mind. Only when the mind is focused on survival, can the mind relax. The Wilderness appears in retrospect, in dreams, through peripheral vision.

The grey gums roll down from the trig opposite like folds in a big velvet dressing gown. The old stockmen used to drive cattle down this precipitous bridle trail, to water them by the river yards, having first advised newchums to sew up their waistcoat pockets, because if your horse relieved himself on the way down his dung fell in your waistcoat pockets—and the trail is littered with animal dung now, square wombat pellets affixed to cairns of greywacke to mark out wombat territory and, unsurprisingly, pebbles of sheep dung. There are wild sheep in this gorge, unmustered remnants from the old days when they ran free, treble fleecers even then, thick with burrs, trailing dags, feral sheep. Calvin has seen them downstream, by Badgery's Crossing. There is always there a small mob of wild sheep, scrambling round on the steep pink folded slates, among the blackboys.

The scale of the landscape is practically Pictish, and down below, far below, the river tumbles over a chevron on the map, sending up a white glint. One of these days Calvin will buy a rubber ducky and haul it down this Ordovician buttress and float right through to the Pacific. For this is one of the few rivers anywhere that flows through a Great Divide. For a time Calvin took his family with him camping, but they didn't enjoy it, and neither did he. There was nothing to do at night, no television, and Calvin was forever screaming at the kids to shut up: he doesn't like the sanctity of Wilderness disturbed. He doesn't like to speak aloud in the Wilderness—Monica would accuse him of sulking—but his inner voice is still jabbering away strongly, now, at this very moment. Insufficient time, two days, to silence the inner voice. He might walk out tonight. He is heading for a campsite on Nerrimunga Creek, upstream of Little Horseshoe Bend, but the river is up, so who knows? It might be a good idea to spend tomorrow maybe taking the kids to a movie.

That smell. There it is again.

Half an hour later, by the river, Calvin locates the source of the offensive odour. It is a mixture of putrescine, cadaverine, stercobilin, turpentine and Monica. Wild goats, a small mob of a dozen or so wild goats, with one black kid, are grazing on and among the sheoaks. The billy goats are imposing beasts. One even thinks twice about backing off, when Calvin approaches.

Thinking about it later, he appreciates they could have killed him. This thought occurs to him that night, at home, in bed, where he can smile. In the wild, the goats' horns are longer, and straighter, more your Scottish than your Irish feral billy, and their bodies more massive, though they spend their days here on stony slopes, not in pens and paddocks. Calvin spends the entire day tracking the goats. If he loses them, he can find them again, from the stench of the males. He has never tracked game with his nose before. It's a novelty, to have his anosmia dispelled by these reeking billies. High above him on the buttress, among the thick-leaved yellow bloodwoods, they send down a constant shower of scree, sometimes quite hefty. He gets good exercise, nice footage of the goats, and as he succeeds in forgetting himself in the chase, his purpose for the day is achieved. The Wilderness will *never* let you down in this regard, but you cannot foresee that once you have left Her. From time to time the white-faced heron meanders up the river, but as Calvin explains later that night, the bird was just a pretext.

He returns home late. The day has exhilarated him. He found something *unexpected*. He would like to share the experience.

'You feel like pancakes?' he inquires of Monica. 'Let's have supper out and listen to some jazz. That's if you're not too tired.'

'Fine' she agrees, hunting for her handbag, 'Think the kids'll be OK? It's only Australian jazz, you know.'

'Sure they will.'

And they are. No harm comes to the kids.

Monica Ecks: late twenties. Green-eyed, blonde-haired Southern belle and sometime *Playboy* centrefold. Mother of Alexander (by her first husband, who does not appear here), Cindy by her second husband Calvin Ecks, and mother-to-be of Harley and Norton by Darryl MacAnaspie. Grandmother of Passionflower, the daughter of the poet.

Calvin Ecks: late twenties. Green-eyed, blond-haired American bioscientist, from the US Midwest. Husband of Monica, father of Cindy by Monica, and father-to-be of Plum Pine, by Nisi Papadimitriou. Grandfather of Passionflower. Never became a eunuch.

Balthazar Beauregard: mid-twenties. Brown-haired, muscular, soft-drug dealer/landscape gardener-cum-jeweller. Long-time communard. Devotee of Indian guru. Father-to-be of Mist by Paula Zoshka, and Galaxy and Nebula by Sister Annunciata. Became a eunuch. Believed dead.

4. *Balthazar Beauregard.*

'Hello, me old mate, you look a bit cold, Christ, you're shiverin like a dog shittin razor blades. Here, have a peach. Scrounged these this morning. Too good to throw away, ay. Old uncle of mine used to grow peaches, he was a bit of a bird. Had the old thunderbox out the back, you know, goannas crossin the road? But delicious fruit mate, just as ripe as you'd like it, ooo, really made the old mouth slobber.'

It's one of those beer-gutted, flat-arsed type of men whose jeans are always falling off their bums, so that you can always see the beginnings of the crack of an arse above the back of their belt. Railways workers, usually. This one lobbed in last night with the drinkers. He's trying to console a strung-out young junkie, whose *modus vivendi* is this rats' nest of a squat, this stately mansion fallen on hard times, and sold to developers. Pending demolition, it shelters men who lack the nous to find work in a country boasting full employment.

The name of the house is Fiddlewood: now to me that's any tree of the genus *Citharexylum*, family *Verbenacaea*. Family-wise, I don't recall seeing a fiddlewood in Pyrmont, and lantana, which was introduced here from South America, is a well-known noxious weed. You should see the way it's taken over Nimbin, Minnamurra and Apple Tree Flat, on the Shoalhaven, but it is a popular suburban hedgerow, and I am fond of its little red and yellow or purple flowers, and the scent of the leaves.

All we have wild is the native clerodendron, an understory shrub of the wet sclerophyll. Grows in the Valley. Besides, what's in a house name? There's a house called 'LLYDALE' down the road from me, which I imagined belonging to a homesick Welshman. I found the other day it's 'LILLYDALE' with the first 2 letters fallen off. Well, I think it's rented out, it must be, I saw a horse on the verandah yesterday, but I must cease these digressions, and teach myself discrimination, or we'll not get to the interesting part of the *Saga*. I've been given six months to live, by an expert, and that was two years ago.

Lung cancer. Inoperable. Whom The Lord loveth he chasteneth, and scourgeth every son whom he receiveth.

I'll level with you. I don't know much about people. I don't

20

know much about the late 1960s, I often think I'm stuck in the fifteenth century. And I don't know much about city life, I've mostly been a countryman. Moreover, the sixties activists I've interviewed—and the anarchists drifted to the countryside, while the socialists remained in the cities—don't remember the sixties themselves, so we have a problem with verisimilitude. Fortunately, a change came over these same folk when they moved out to the country, so much so that twenty-seven years down the track, they are hard to distinguish from their yokel neighbours, and here I expect to be on surer ground. So be patient and bear with us, as a PM once said to a lady journalist—we sharpen the knives as we confer the purple, we're a Roman sort of people, we Australians—while I continue to introduce our *dramatis personae*, or such as I have tracked down.

Now a commune similar to that in Erinungarah was once described to me as a 'Hamlet Development'. How apt. In the beginning, our little phalanstery was in fact known as The Moody Valley Candle Company Co-op, which failed, incidentally, to thrive; there's not much demand for the beeswax candle as I, of all men, could have told them—something eerie in the way they drip wax, suits them to the set of the Phantom of the Opera. But one of the Hamlets who developed the co-op was the man we are now about to meet, the multimedia artist Balthazar Beauregard.

Frontis nulla fides. Never judge the contents of a letter by the envelope. Picture a vain, lonely man with epicene appearance and a studied innocence. I wish I could describe him as nasty, brutish and short, but that sounds more like me. The lustrous brown locks, like those of a Regency rake, fall in ringlets to the shoulder, but the abdomen is muscular, and the torso, if hairless, unmistakeably masculine. The hips are those of a negro dancer. Balthazar is given to the wearing of fine jewellery, which here retains a magic, as distinct from purely aesthetic function—rings, armbands, earrings and the like—designed by himself and fashioned by himself from sterling silver and bronze, filigreed of late with flourishes from the cursive Persian script of Urdu. He is a painter, a sculptor, a dancer, but also, of necessity, a landscape gardener, and the many stupas and prayerwheels that have sprung up round the inner suburbs in recent months bear, each of them, his

21

imprint. When it comes to embellishing the Sydney Federation style of bungalow with Tantric Mahayana fishponds, here's your man. I never heard a good word spoken of him, but everyone I spoke to had 'slept' with him. I suspect that, like the composer Purcell, he sang both bass and countertenor.

Dressed in a sarong, he is greeting the sun as we in turn greet him on this warm morning, stretching, like a bored cat, the ligaments and tendons of his lithesome limbs in the manner prescribed by Hatha Yoga,* breathing, as he performs with sweet breath those rudimentary asanas, eyes half-shut in meditation, oblivious to the peak-hour traffic outside, which is as nothing compared to the traffic of India. When he has money enough saved, Balthazar will return to his guru, and living in a squat is only for him a convenient means of saving on rent,

Sell out, says the Devil. Sell out and buy a waterfrontage, in which to kick back and relax.

I have in my possession a diary of Balthazar Beauregard's, and what an exquisite piece of octavo craftsmanship. With its fine calligraphy, its wealth of hand-painted illustrations, it puts me in mind of a Kufic Koran from the Topkapi Treasury. Even has that same, defiant air of amateurism transcended. And to think he fashioned it himself from recycled copies of *The Sydney Morning Herald*, worthless chips of opal gangue, and a melted-down length of copper wire, on permanent loan from Sassafras County Council.

You know, when I think of these young Balthazars, I'm reminded of those rampant box trailers you see, rearing up on their roo legs at you in car yards. Freshly painted, newly registered, tyres blacked, nary a speck of rust on the springs, they

---

* You'd have to go back to the Silk Routes, I should say, to discover a comparable religious promiscuity. In 1253 Friar William of Rubruk encountered in the court of Manghu Khan a kind of Adyar Bookshop of Orthodox Christian Alans, Tibetan Lamaic Buddhists, Muslim Turks, Monophysite Armenians, Nestorian Mongols, Manichaean Uighurs, not to mention Chinese Taoists and Korean Confucians.

In the last days of the fifth century AD, the neoplatonist philosopher Proclus apparently observed the holy days of every religion on earth.

Welcome to the festival of Mind, Body and Spirit.

look as ready for a freezer or compressor, as any big haul of firewood, yet twenty-seven years later they're rusted out, you're lucky if one dozy blinker bulb winks, the mudguards have been bashed that often into gateposts they're barely hanging on, and there they sit, despondent on the lawns, the gooseneck drooping in the clover. Everything—well, practically everything—gets harder as you grow older. Twenty-seven years ago, it was that wet here you needed gumboots to hang out the wash. Today, if you took a chip at the ground with a mattock it'd jump up and hit you in the bloody eye. Dry as a nun's tit.

Bloody El Ninos. I have a confession, in verse 84 of the *Ballad*, I have edited out the drought, and made it this one, the drought of '95, which is the worst I can recall.

Now I don't suppose these youthful Beauregards or Byngs or Abernathys were different to my generation. We wanted what they wanted, but they were able to get what they wanted, I dare say, whereas we were not. Intellectual austerity, combined with a simultaneous sexual depravity, has been the hallmark of other civilisations in decline; notably, the Hittite, the Hellenic, and the Mayic. Here, it has to do with the weakness, I believe, of the parents in question, who, placed in an untenable situation by the state of Western Civilisation as they found it, spent their lives gambling. It is certainly true our Postmodern, PostChristian Western Civilisation attained a precocious degree of development in the Antipodes, both technologically—as witness the fact that New Zealand, a nation of fewer than three million inhabitants, invented both the paper clip *and* the automatic stamp vending machine—and materially, for Melbourne and Sydney spawned the first high-leisure Western societies, and even now Australia has the highest standard of living in the world, if on the tick, and fuck the figures.

Sorry. I should have said 'stuff the statistics' had I been able to do so.

Now where's my box of paper clips? I want to give my front plate a scratch.

Balthazar Beauregard: mid-twenties. Brown-haired, muscular soft-drug dealer/landscape gardener-cum-womanising jeweller. Devotee of Indian guru. Father-to-be of Mist, by Paula Zoshka, Galaxy and Nebula by Sister Annunciata. Became a eunuch. Disappeared on a visit to India, in the late eighties. Assumed dead.

5. An Australian Mystery.

Speaking of gambling, to the Byzantine Greeks Constantinople was simply 'the City' as Athens once had been. As to why Constantinople got 'the works'—to quote from the lyric of a popular song which was among the first Olaf Abernathy ever learned—it appears (*vide Peregrinus Wiccamicus*) that the Ottoman Turkish 'Istanbul' is a garbled version of the Megarian Doric Greek phrase 'to the City' (pronounced 'Stambolin') which some non-Greek speaking invader apparently mistook for the name of the city itself.

The Dardanian soldier-emperor Constantine founded Constantinople on the site of Byzantium, a colonial, Megarian Greek city-state, as a consequence of a vision in which he saw a cross athwart the sun, on the eve of the battle of the Milvian Bridge, AD 312. Although, with Hadrianic *laissez-faire*, Constantine continued to mint coin featuring the Mithraic *Sol Invictus*, Invincible Sun, for another twelve years (and his son subsequently conferred, in defiance of ecclesiastical policy, the birthday of the Danubian sun god on the putative Galilean), he also determined that from its foundation the City would be a Christian city, though fewer than one in ten Roman citizens were Christians at the time. But showing great prescience and prudence he made to this policy one important exception; he shrewdly provided the people of the City with a Temple to Tyche, Roman Goddess of Chance, and this temple survived not just the definitive triumph of Christianity, which Toynbee dates to the reign of the bigot Theodosius (*imperabat* 379–395), but also the final collapse of the Hellenic Civilisation, in the latter part of the sixth century. I am indebted to Toynbee for this observation.

What is more, the worship of Tyche is practised to this very day, which happens to be a public service pay day, in a colony of a civilisation affiliated to the Hellenic, at a time when the Christian churches in this colony, though extant, are all but unheated, and I have had the good fortune, if you like, to observe the initiation of a postulant into the Penetralia of this Temple, not once, but many times; an Australian Mystery, then.

The postulant, wearing his best clothes—no thongs or shorts permitted—is conducted, usually by an aged initiate, to a queue in the temple foyer. Here, dazzled by the banks of reflecting surfaces, plate glass dividers and wall mirrors that signify the transitory and illusory nature of the material universe, he may, while checking his shoulders for dandruff, grow conscious that in taking this physical body for his real self, he is forfeiting the opportunity of unfolding his indivisible and immortal soul.

Next, he has to sign his name in the Visitor's Book, left-hand column. In doing so, he expresses a desire to join the ranks of the Immortals, right-hand column, while attesting that having reached the age of sexual consent and being legally entitled to be served fermented liquors, he is fully prepared to undergo the hazardous ordeals that await him.

Sexual intermingling is strictly forbidden in the Chamber of the Lower Mysteries. On entering this chamber—a dark cavern symbolising the bondage of material existence—the postulant is dazed and confused by a battery of strange and fearsome-looking poker machines. As his eyes grow accustomed to the smoky, chthonian light, he sees that each of these machines has entranced some poor tormented soul, whose hideous groans, intermingled with high-pitched beeping, and less frequently a metallic clatter, dominate the precinct.

Taking the candidate now firmly by the elbow and leading him over the blood-red carpet, which signifies the chasm of carnal appetite dividing the world of the Living from the Dead, the hierophant conducts him down a narrow corridor, flanked by the asymmetric shoulders of the damned. In their dread that this intruder may wish to seize one of their pokies, the damned, glancing about them like papal sbirri, are heard loudly deploring the ancestry that gave them one head, and not three. Another arm would have come in handy, too.

At the far end of this corridor, surrounded by corkscrews, stands a male figure in a black bowtie, representing Hades, consort of Tyche. Should any machine be found malfunctional, he, and he alone, can declare it out of order. He holds in his hand a brimming goblet of *Lethe*, the amber fluid that renders all who drink it insensible to their lot.

Having downed one glass and ordered another, the postulant, now seized with an irresistible desire to squander his week's wages, strolls over to Persephone the cashier and hits her with a blue swimmer. Abducted from the local savings bank by Hades and forced to become his acolyte, she sits, forlorn and bored shitless, in a tiny cubicle, dispensing coin in translucent plastic cylinders.

With full solemnity, the psychopompus leads his young charge to a vacant pokie. He explains, how contrary to vulgar opinion, this machine is not the child of *Chance* but owes its origin to *Certainty* who, in despair of persuading Jove, the god of the living, of its efficacy, conveyed it instead in a fit of pique to Hades the god of the dead. Thus it is the secrets of the Rites of Sabazius, Dodonean Oracle *et cetera*, find their way into present-day hands .

The fundamental unity behind the apparent diversity of the material world is shown in the fact that, while these machines look different, there's nothing to choose between Inca King and Humdinger, when it comes to a payout. The candidate is made to gaze on a typical Aristocrat four-reeler; Snowball, say, or Wild Goose. He first observes the flashing lights that play about the payout console: exoterically, a textbook instance of classic Skinnerian conditioning, esoterically, these represent the continuous flux of material phenomena that so dull the brain it never thinks of asking the most obvious questions of itself; as, for example, how many kings, queens, jacks, eights and sevens do we actually *have* on these reels?

He next observes that while he has no way of knowing whether this machine is rigged, he must obey in using it a whole host of ethical precepts. A player, for instance, may not play more than one machine at a time.

This is an exhortation to marital fidelity and mindful concentration, pure and simple. It may look easy, but unless the missus is sweet, and a player free to concentrate with his *whole being* on that window, who's to say he won't wipe out a winning combination, even a jackpot? To this end, he must treat as distraction all extraneous input. At first, this takes the form of shutting out the din from the games room and the other machines. At a more advanced level, the importuning of the bladder can be overcome; and who could forget the tale of that great master, Jack Flynn of the Como Bowling Club, who steadfastly kept playing his machine, while the clubhouse burnt down round his ears and over them?

It is in fact our own human body confronted in a clockwork mirror we see here, and if we're to pull that jackpot, if we're to walk out the doors of Life bearing more than we brought in through them, nothing less than our complete dedication to the goal is going to be sufficient.

Ever tempted to take a short cut in the form of harmful drug or occult practice? Anyone caught using foreign objects to manipulate the reels will be asked to leave the premises.

You the kind goes on a bender every time you don't get your own way? Abuse of machines by rough handling absolutely forbidden.

Got the idea you can get all you want out of books and do nothing yourself? Only coin of legal tender to be used in playing the machines.

Let us now turn to the reels themselves and the playing card symbols thereon. The four suits represent the *Grail hallows*. What ought to be the lowest and most worthless card, the ace, turns out to be the highest. The king is *Time*, omnipotent ruler. In Him all things reach completion and all losses will be recouped. Just keep pulling that handle.

The Queen is *Wisdom*, Time's live-in lady; jackpots of 250 bucks and over to be paid to a visitor by cheque. If you didn't sign the Visitor's Book in your real name, you did yourself out of a jackpot.

The stupid-looking Jack is actually the *Fool* of the old Tarot pack, by no means foolish. There is a great arcanum in this card; it is understood fully only by those who have ruined their lives, quote unquote, through gambling.

Note the 8 is worth more than the 10 and the 7 worth more than the 9.

Eight was sacred to the Eleusinian Mysteries and takes its form from the Hermetic caduceus. Its key word is 'convenience'.

Seven was sacred to the Cabbalistic Mysteries, and its key word is 'judgement'.

Nine falls short of the perfect decad by one; its key word is 'limitation'.

Ten, normally perfect, is in the special context of this chamber, *manqué*. Its key word is 'half-heartedness', for it is sacred to those who'll play a Rambling Rose when they could be playing a Super Quadreel: those who'll play the ten-cent machines when they could be playing the twenties. Those who feel, if they walk out having lost half what they might have, they're in front. Negative thinkers.

As to the Chamber of the Upper Mysteries? New tenders are being called for.

6. *Olaf Abernathy visits the Blue Mountains. Encounters Nisi.*

It is, let us remind ourselves, the year the Eden chip mill opened, the year the Australian Conservation Foundation called for an extension of the South West National Park in Tasmania. Sixty-eight, the beginning of the end. The year of the Tet Offensive, the Prague Spring. The year Apollo Eight gave us the first views of our planet from the moon, the year the San Fran leathermen gave us a brand new sexual perversion, the fist fuck.

Olaf Abernathy, an odd job man of nineteen, with no education in the classics or the Bible, a member, in short, of the first utterly illiterate generation in Western history, hesitates on the way to his front door, and again, as he walks back to the bedroom for his granny glasses, which he has misplaced. He opens the front door, which is jammed, and the intense sun, risen already above the crown of the nearest London plane tree owing to the lateness of the hour, strikes him in the face, and makes him squint. He has a freckled face. The white-painted wall of the terrace house opposite, coped in one corner, with a stand of dark bamboo, further reflects and radiates the subtropical summer heat. A woman restraining a large black and tan dog on a choker chain strolls by. Abernathy glances at them both, without a thought of liberating either. It is Sydney, Balmain, mid-week, mid-morning, January, the middle of a mail strike and a heatwave, too late, really, to initiate a journey of substance. Abernathy had hoped to rise early so as to capitalise on the charm of the dawn, and avoid the worst of the traffic, but he knows himself too well to set an alarm.

His hesitancy, habitual, is ascribable here to the fear that he will regret this undertaking within an hour of setting off. Clearly, there was a time he could look forward to such a journey with pleasure. Equally clearly, there came a time when such a journey had become a chore, to be anticipated with no more pleasure than a visit to the supermarket. If he looks forward to this journey—and he is not sure that he does—it is despite the fact that more recent experience has endued him with a caution, which, translated into physical movement, makes his gait slow and hesitant, seemingly relaxed while in fact the converse. He drives as though an oncoming vehicle had just flashed its lights at him, and he can't decide if this was accidental. In conversation, likewise, his tone—neutral, diffident—bespeaks, to a casual acquaintance, a dispassionate control that more truly reflects an emotional stalemate, an equipoise set up between the expectations from a now distant past with those from a more recent past. Olaf Abernathy was born in Mt Gambier, South Australia, where his stepfather was a schoolmaster, and his family subsequently moved to the central west of New South Wales. He is not in the habit of reviewing this childhood, which, at the time, and on the whole, was painful to him, but he has a recurrent dream which centres on a large building, very possibly a high school, situated near a railway line, in a town that is reached by a long descent down a vast slope, on a smooth inclined road. Regardless of the action the landscape in this dream seems never to vary, and because Olaf cannot recognise the landscape, though he appreciates it must have significance, the recollection of this dream provides him, when he wakes, with bemusement, that is both a stimulus and a relaxation to him, and a source as well of cautious optimism; for Olaf intensely admires in himself this capacity for innocent reverie, especially when it costs him no effort. The dream recurred last night, and has put him in a good mood this morning: it indicates there is something about himself he does not understand; he, who understands himself so well, in most respects. There is hope, in other words, if not much hope perhaps.

The car is his biggest problem at present. No GTS Monaro, she is, to the contrary, one of those nondescript, off-white three-speed lawnmowers I associate with women wearing cheesecloth kaftans. When she has been sitting in the sun so long the kerbside slicks have damned a nest, the smell is that of a school playground, under a spreading Moreton Bay fig. And supposing she fires, clouding the street with a blue-black gust of smoke—the way the old Landrovers used to, the ones with the cast-iron blocks—then Olaf can relax, which he does by lighting up a Chesterfield king, and hitting the windscreen wipers. Beyond the segments the wipers have scratched is a region dark as his own subconscious. If she won't, it'll be a matter of roll-starting and kangaroo-jumping her. There are jumper leads in the boot, but they're useless where a vehicle is boxed in. And since the handbrake is non-functional, roll-starting can be a task, too. The street is on a slope—Olaf won't live in a street that's not on a slope—where gathering together a team to lend a pound could take time, if not because there'd be a shortage of volunteers. It's just that this is a quiet street. Olaf won't live on a noisy one.

It is now almost ten-thirty, and Olaf drives past the Riverview Hotel, turns right at Darling Street, and crosses the Iron Cove bridge. An hour later he has cleared the traffic of Parramatta, and is heading towards Richmond, on the Nepean River. After a pause for a much-needed Coke and some fuel at the BP Supermix, he is climbing the glacis of the Blue Mountains via Bell's Line of Road, a tortuous route on which overtaking slow vehicles can be dangerous, and Olaf is holding up the traffic. He may sustain a puncture, blow a head gasket in this heat, and where will he be then? It's a courageous, temerarious act, bringing this old vehicle up here, which had he thought more about, he might well have reconsidered. If he thinks hard about any project he's intent on, these days, he rarely proceeds. Figuratively, Olaf has left the River Flats and entered upon Rocky Slopes, where bramble and bracken fern abound. There is sustenance here, but it must be searched out, and since, like a good farmer, Olaf expects all change to be for the worse, he doesn't emigrate, will not educate himself, and refuses to marry, although he is often in love, loathes Sydney, and deplores the tardy-apishness of Colonial culture.

Just to let the queue pass, he is constrained eventually to pull over, and would have done so sooner had he seen sooner a place where he could park in safety. At length, he espies a small dirt track, like a safety ramp, off to his left. He determines to stop and go for a short walk, for he loves the notion of loving the bush, and despises himself that he cannot seem to do so. He is on the northern side of the majestic Grose Valley, traversing one of the wildest temperate plateaux of the Great Divide. He has, of course, been here before, but only as a child, and usually in darkness. Because of the rugged nature of this terrain, the dearth of habitation, a tow to the nearest garage would cost him more than his own vehicle is worth. In contrast, his stepfather drove a most reliable vehicle.

Why, Olaf? When it is your customary palladium to travel via the Great Western Highway, a well-travelled track through a myriad little mountain towns, strung out like droplets of mist on a March morning web. The fact is that driving in his customary daze, he was through Kurrajong before he knew what he was doing. As though of a sudden, he is winding down the window at the hairpin where the bellbirds tintinnabulate.

Later in life, making an effort to comprehend this momentous day—for it constitutes a Turning Point—he is forced to conclude it began with a careless error (as so many concatenations of moment have, including the Big Bang, if there was one): an error which his subconscious autopilot failed to countermand.

Now staring at the Blue Mountains is not like staring at the sea. The sea is a continuum in time and space, and we know the sea. And whether we are viewing the Aegean, the North Sea, or the Tasman Sea, and whether it be the dark Southern Ocean, or the blue Pacific Ocean we are contemplating, the sea is a lifeline to us, and a highway, and a familiar face, for any sea is every sea. So that staring at the sea, from an island or a headland, or a seagoing craft, or a beachside condominium, is a comfort to us (algal blooms notwithstanding) and a solace in our exile, and we prefer to live by the sea, and we love seafood. A real estate agent from Sutherland Shire in Sydney—with whom I had some dealings once, over and through a private box—confided to me that a couple in that shire pursue in their domestic history an immemorial progression. At the time of their engagement they rent, or purchase, a one-bedroom home unit lacking water views; at the birth of their first child they upgrade to a house lacking water views, or a two-bedroom unit containing them; the children being old enough for the wife to resume work, they move to a house possessed of water views; and if fortune smiles upon them, they end their days in a house rejoicing in a genuine waterfrontage from which in their dotage they may be reconsigned, only to a waterfront unit or seaside nursing facility. There is just one aim in all this; to get as close to the water and as far from their fellow Colonials as possible, and the values of the property market reflect, I am assured, this intelligent desire. At no time in the process, incidentally, is it necessary to leave Sutherland Shire, and no modern resident ever does, unless Lycra-clad on the seat of a chrome-moly cycle, for it is effectively the birthplace of our nation, where Captain James Cook set foot on what is now a sacred site, commemorating the third, and most recent, takeover on this continent. First, eucalypts, second Java man, thirty-four million and one hundred thousand years ago, respectively. I came out in '53.

Do you know the second verse of our National Anthem? It's not often sung round here.

> When gallant Cook from Albion sailed
> To trace wide oceans o'er
> True British courage bore him on
> Till he landed on our sho'er.
> Then here he raised old England's flag
> The standard of the brave
> For all her faults, we love her yet
> Britannia, rule the waves!
> For all her faults, we love her yet
> Britannia, rule the waves.

An Englishman, incidentally, will not use the word 'British' unless there's a Scotsman standing by, which round here, there usually is.

Cook (that devotee of the comma splice): 'The woods do not produce any great variety of trees, there are only 2 or 3 sorts that can be called timber; the largest is the Gum Tree, which growes all over the Countrey, the wood of this tree is too hard and ponderous for most common uses.'

No, there is no nostrum like the sea for the troubled in spirit (if not the sick to their stomachs) and Sutherland Shire is the quintessential Sydney in this respect, as in most others. Just to know the sea is there is not sufficient, though: one must smell her, one must betimes hear her, one must catch a glimpse of her; and then vacuuming, ironing, shaving, cleaning the pool can all become rituals of worship. The irrepudiable comfort of the Sea, that Great Blue Nubby, the Bosom of the Ancestress, that ever-changing, never-changing, Spirit Goddess, the Shakti of Big Syd.

John White, surgeon-general to the First Settlement: 'The timber of this country is very unfit for the purpose of building. Nor do I know of any purpose for which it will serve, except for firewood; and for that it is excellent; but in other respects it is the worst wood that any country or climate ever produced.'

Whereas the Blue Mountains are the sea's antithesis. They are not blue, if by blue we mean the colour of a postman's shirt, or of a middle-aged male satin bowerbird, or of the sky reflected in the summer sea, but it is more the case that the natural green of the chlorophyll molecules in the gum leaves is pushed, when seen from a distance, towards the blue end of the visual spectrum, by the droplets of eucalypt oil that emanate from those same leaves, so that the blue is no more than a suggestion, or hint, of blue, as in the leaves of the 'blue-leafed' stringybark, *Eucalyptus agglomerata*, or the boles of the 'Blue Mountain blue gum' *Eucalyptus deanei*. Nonetheless, the effect is striking, reminiscent of the blue hills of Turkey (where it is due to the terpenes from the pines), and further differentiates a view that differs from any comparable English view to the extent a 'gum tree' differs from a myrtle. Moreover, after five

33

millennia of civilisation, disregarding Catal Huyuk, only patches today remain of the dry, evergreen forests of the Mediterranean, while those of California and Chile, and South Africa's Cape Province, are mostly scrub. This, in fact, is the finest specimen extant of the evergreen sclerophyllous biome, a circumstance of significance to our *Saga*. Indeed, Olaf cannot stand at the pipe and wire of any of the many lookouts that horizontally festoon the more habitated ridge to the south, and scrutinise the wilderness of sclerophyll forest stretching before him to the horizon, broken only by the faces of sandstone and shale too sheer for vegetation, and *passim* by the richer green of a rainforest along a watercourse, without reflecting on his own sadness because of his indifference at the spectacle, so contrary to what he might feel faced with the Swiss Alps, or even the Malvern Hills. This is a landscape in which species have names only taxonomists know, names that mean nothing to anyone unschooled in Latin and Attic Greek, languages that seem an inordinately long way from home in the Antipodes, if not climatically. Why was no convict poet assigned to give the bush flowers of Sydney common names? If you want to go beyond simple wedge pea, you bruise your lip on *Gompholobium*. Even the glorious, golden yellow guinea flower, *Hibbertia* species, has no adequate sobriquet. You wouldn't get a guinea for one today.

There is precious little bush tucker, not much game either, and most of that nocturnal, or crepuscular, except for the spiders and snakes. Passing Aborigines would scarcely have paused, except to light fires. Not much worthwhile, accessible timber, too frosty. The sandy ridges are worthless as farmland, the blacksoil valleys locked up in National Park. The orchards are negatively geared. The once-mighty rivers that carved out the gullies have been reduced, over the aeons, to polluted streams. The peaks, very ancient, gently uplifted, scarcely tilted, have been weathered and flattened, more a debrided plateau than a mountain range as such. Nature is here aloof, rather than awe-inspiring, and while a tourist might well return to his coach completely satisfied, for those whose toilet-tissue-strewn heritage this happens to be—and Olaf is one of them—the landscape is an enigma still. He misses the crimson rosellas, but the prickly, drab, vertical bush of these sandstone counterscarps, so hard to come to terms with, so utterly unaccommodating to man, seems to Olaf to lack a *Leitmotiv*. He never dreams of it. He never longs for it. It has moods of which he is vaguely aware, but they make no reference to him. It has never been claimed on his behalf, and it seems he cannot claim it for himself. Indeed, quite recently, the canard was being upheld, by the more fatuous of local literati, that D.H. Lawrence's confession of utter and total ignorance and alienation says all there is to be said on the time-worn subject of the Australian bush. If the sea, to a suburbanite, is reassuringly familiar, the Blue Mountains are correspondingly alien, and the well-adjusted Sydney child should aim to spend as much holiday time at Echo Point as on Manly Pier. Not before Manly Beach is uplifted and petrified—rather like one of its own ageing showgirls—can the two be reconciled, except through the agency of *mist*, which, as the sea's Cimmerian benison to its hinterland, confers on these Blue Mountains a sense of familiarity that gladdens and relaxes the hearts of those who dwell here.

But we don't get much mist any more, because of the bloody El Nino.

The sound of the traffic still loud in his ears, Olaf Abernathy walks up the little track, which, 200 yards from the road, takes a sharp turn out of sight. No botanist, he has no idea what kind of trees these are, but they seem quite large and some have what appear to be serrated leaves. Around the corner the track descends sharply. Olaf's mood is improving. He is walking through a patch of warm temperate rainforest, and the saw-leafed species are coachwood, sassafras and blackwattle.

When the ancient supercontinent Gondwana broke up, in the process articulating itself into Africa, Australia, Antarctica, and the rest, certain of its flora are believed to have withstood and survived the evolution of more modern plants, and are still to be found, contracted into pockets, all over the Australian Great Divide,* where they are known collectively as 'rainforest'. It could well be the subtropical rainforest—palms, figs—migrated

---

* and elsewhere: New Caledonia, South America, Lord Howe Island, New Zealand, New Guinea.

from Malaysia; but then, it could well be the concept of Evolution is wrong. Certainly, I've had the god-botherers knocking on my door to tell me so.

If you have driven (during summer) from Minehead in Somerset via the back road to Tiverton in Devon, you will know approximately what kind of forest this warm, temperate rainforest is, for it is very like an English West Country forest in summer. The leaves of these here smallish trees are green and shiny, and their trunks, like those of pear trees, mottled and narrow. Rainforests require a fireproof niche, continual water and a shale or basalt soil, so they don't usually grow to this altitude in the Blue Mountains. Without realising it, Olaf has stumbled on the highest patch of rainforest hereabouts, but the road attests he was not the first to do so, a road that, as he sees, is suitable only for motorcycles and four-wheel drive vehicles, and possibly, he thinks now, a firetrail. A small creek tumbles down the sandy gutters, eroding them away. The whistling wings of a pileate bird are heard and, where a small and recent landslide has cleared a partial view below the precipitous track, Olaf stops, amazed by the best mountain view he has ever seen, that is, a view that recalls to him a view he has seen before, at an early age, and forgotten, if indeed it was he who saw that view and not some ancestor of his. Tall eucalypts, maybe blue gums, cover the lower slopes of the hill and a forest of tree fern grows under them,* but what has caught Olaf's eye is that glade of green, surrounded by bush, on the floor of a valley in the far distance. It can only be a farm.

He pauses, unselfconsciously admiring the view, for two minutes. If you asked him, later, what he most admired in the view, he would not be able to say. If you asked him what was wrong with the view, he would not be able to tell you, and yet there persists in him a deeply felt spiritual objection to the evergreen forest, it being evergreen. Now he walks on there is a vigour and purpose in his stride that was not there previously. Does he imagine that, if he walks sufficiently hard and fast, the

---

* A poignant sight to be seen in County Kerry are the Australian soft tree ferns, *Dicksonia antarctica*, standing tall in abandoned gardens on Valentia Island, Dingle Bay.

road will lead him to the glade? Scarcely. But he has forgotten himself a moment, in the temporary, subconscious illusion of a bourne. He pulls a marihuana reefer from his pocket, ignites the tip and inhales. Imagine his delight when, shortly thereafter, rounding a bend, he comes upon a house, set back off the road, and, what is more difficult—something like finding a self-addressed envelope in the mail perhaps—imagine further his surprise, when he sees affixed to a nearby lilly pilly a cardboard sign, made by writing on the back of a beer carton with a black Texta pen, bearing an arrow directing him to the house, and depending from this sign, on string, a dozen brightly coloured, all but totally deflated, party balloons.

A birthday party is being held in the house, for Timothy Papadimitriou. Olaf wanders in, is made to feel welcome, and falls in love with Nisi Papadimitriou, Timothy's mother.

Olaf Abernathy: Twenty years old. Granny glasses. Gawky loser. Good handyman, though, whose talents were not to be fully utilised outside the Valley. Common-law husband-to-be of Nisi Papadimitriou. Became a eunuch.

7. *Brian Chegwodden visits the Southern Highlands. Loses his temper, because of Paula.*

The warmth, the charm, the beauty, the devotion of his mother envelops Brian Chegwodden, a lopsided man whose right shoulder is six inches lower than his left—he blames this on a heavy schoolcase, till orthopaedic consultations put him straight, while his head, as if in compensation, inclines habitually the other way—and secure in his mother's never-wavering love he is free, as usual, to shrug testily. She has just asked him, how things are. Beyond her, through the colonial frame windows of her mansion, he sees a grove of golden elm, with leaves the colour of lime, that reminds him, for some reason, of schooldays, and in the grove an antique fountain, or perhaps a reproduction, suitably distressed, the style and virtue of which, were he possessed of the *savoir vivre* that the money spent on his education ought by rights to have guaranteed, might well prompt some facile comment here and thus inject into the duologue that tone of specificity, of sophistication, which the setting, the expensive prints on the walls, the antique furnishings, his mother's clothing, all deserve, yet so conspicuously lack.

'Our little girl is looking well?'

She could not frame the most trifling remark without an invitation to be contradicted.

'Come home from kindie cryin th'other day, 'cordin te the missus.'

'Goodness? Whatever for?'

No matter her bridge partner would formulate such a response with eyebrows arched; Brian's mother moves forward on the *chaise longue*, eyes imbued with genuine concern.

'Those red lips o' hers. Boys were teasin her 'bout 'em. Ya got lipstick on, ya gunna get married. Sump'n to that effect.'

'Poor little thing!'

From the kitchen is heard a peal of false laughter. Prompted by some remark from Prim, Brian's wife. At my expense, no doubt, thinks Brian.

'The garden is looking well. Would you care to walk round it with me?'

You are happiest in the company of your brat, is what Nigel, his stepfather says, and it may be true. But then again, he is a fine young man, of whom any (deaf) mother might be proud. Brian's mother takes Brian by the arm, pointing out this and that aspect of the garden. The *mise-en-scène*, the grounds of this highland mansion, has become the woman's bailiwick. By virtue of her husband's position they have to entertain a great deal. He is even speaking of renting out his city apartments, or one of them.

'Did I tell you Nigel is thinking of renting Elizabeth Bay? Are those friends of yours still interested, do you think?'

'Doubt they could afford the rent, Mum.'

'Well, of course we shouldn't rent it if we knew someone who could look after it for us. Tenants are such a worry.'

'I know 'eaps o' people could look after it for ya.'

'I think you know what I mean. Look! Isn't this a superb daphne? They *are so* difficult to strike.'

His thoughts drift, as she launches into a disquisition on grafting. She employs a gardener, a local man, for the big jobs, but guards the small ones jealously, kneeling to weed on an English racing green pneumatic semicircle that must have cost a motza. Her gardening gloves are kidskin.

Brian has found a new woman, and being alone to dream about this woman is his principal need at this point, hence the testiness. Time and again he rehearses in his mind the drama of coupling with the new woman, in the naive and disingenuous assumption that, far from assembling a sexual spell, he is indulging a harmless fantasy. Paula, a stacked brunette with grey eyes, works as a barmaid in a bar he frequents, and because of this, he cannot easily tell if she regards him as someone special.

'Do you envy my life here with Nigel, Brian?'

'No. I'm glad it's you and not me. What would the neighbours think?'

'Oh I am a silly billy, I never manage to say what I mean. But sometimes I think it's hardly fair on you.'

'Eh?'

'Well, Nigel could very well afford to help you more than he does, I think.'

'I don't want his bloody help!'

'Oh dear, I've upset you.'

'Look I know ya mean well Mum, and you've had a hard time in the past, and we're all glad things have worked out. But frankly, isn't this a bit obscene? I mean, how big a garden does a woman need?'

'I don't understand you. If you mean to imply Nigel has too much property, I perfectly agree. That's what I mean when I say we could well afford to help you establish yourself more.'

'You've done enough. I'm doin all right.'

'But it must be so tiresome for Prim when you work such long hours, Brian. And you'll soon have another mouth to feed.'

'It's part o' the job.'

'I know it is. I really don't think he'd mind. Shall I approach him for you?'

'No Mum! I don't want any more help from Nigel.'

'You don't like Nigel, do you.'

'If you're happy, I'm happy you're happy.'

'Is it because of him you don't visit?'

'Whattaya mean we don't visit? We're visitin now!'

'I just wish I could see more of Felicity.'

'Yeah, and we wish we had a babysitter. Come on, it was you moved out to the country.'

'It's not really the country. We're only two hours' drive from Sydney.'

'It's the country. This garden needs sheep. Why don't you visit us? You've even got poor bloody Nigel commutin.'

'This garden needs constant attention, Brian. Besides, he doesn't mind. He takes the Jag and only works three days a week now.'

Brian hurls his tumbler of vermouth at the wishing well. Later, when more mature, he'll better understand that though the siren call is unremitting—parents' voices, children's voices, wives' voices, colleagues' voices—in the absence of inspired voices, and because of the Babel of internal voices that characterise disintegration, the most eloquent voices one can hear are the silent voices, the dumb epiphanies, when, after a first or second glass, but always before a third, one contemplates a paving stone, or a tree, or a lichen on a tile, or a patch of moss on a letterbox, and the brevity and pointlessness of life on earth confront one momentarily. T'is but a tent.

'Sorry, Mum. I'm under a lot o' stress.'

More than you realise, old son. You cannot ponder the important questions, because your parents never sought to pose them, but they will exert their pressure on your psyche nonetheless, till, some day in middle age, they will burst into your conscious purview through the perforating ulcer of a long-suppressed grief. And then your mother will confide to her friends that you have suffered a (mild) nervous breakdown, but are feeling much better.

'Shall we return and join the others?'

That will be the question.

Brian Chegwodden: late twenties. Frustrated writer, dark, good-looking, mean-spirited journalist, whose mother married a quid. Went to a fine private school. Fond of the drink and the women. Hopeless with his hands, but not a bad gardener. Built the Bacchus fountain in the Valley. Common-law husband-to-be of Paula Zoshka, father-to-be of Mountain Gum by Paula Zoshka. Became a eunuch.

8. *Monica meets Nisi, through preschool. Calvin encounters Frodsham in the Physics Department of Sydney University.*

To the amusement of both Monica Ecks and Nisi Papadimitriou, Cindy and Tim, their preschoolers, prefer each other's company. No sooner has Cindy caught sight of Tim than she makes straight for him, beaming. Even then.

'Uh oh, he's after all the gals,' laughs Monica. 'Is this Tim? Cindy's always talkin 'bout Tim and hopin he might come round to play some afternoon. Maybe we can arrange that.'

Nisi, who though dumpy and overweight, wears a white vinyl miniskirt that barely covers her bottom, feels tongue-tied in front of the American blonde, whose accent, waist-length unsplit hair, green eyes and high yaller skin are so impressive.

'That'd be wonderful,' agrees Nisi. 'The problem is, we don't live here any more.'

'Oh? Where *do* you live? Cindy, *Cindy*, don't hit your little friend! It's funny, she's so possessive when she's here. At home she would never do a thing like that.'

'It must be a strain on all of them. I'm wondering whether to send Tim to school next year.'

'How's that, honey?'

'Well, you know, it is taking something away. I think it forces them to conform.'

'Yeah, right. So where do you live?'

'We live in the Blue Mountains.'

'Wow, that must be real nice.'

'Well it's not so nice in many ways. It's very cold in winter, and wet, and there can be bushfires. I had Tim booked in at the preschool here from when we used to live in Paddington, so I thought we should take advantage of it.'

'Only Fridays? Boy, he must be quite a lady's man. He certainly made a big impression on Cindy.'

'Isn't she beautiful? I wish I had a daughter like her.'

'Say, would you like to have coffee with me? I'm only right over the street. My name's Monica, by the way, or "Mon" as you Australians say it. I never can get used to that.'

'I'm Nisi. Berenice. Why, that'd be nice, Mon, thanks. I'd love a coffee. I find the train trip so tiring.'

'Oh, you took the train down?'

'Part of the way. I have a car but it's not a very good one.'

Monica's walls are covered with primitive art. No posters of Che or Jimi or the Viet Cong woman in the cone hat.

'So is Tim your only child, Nisi? Would you care for a cookie, dear?'

As Monica reaches above the sink for the cookie tin, she comes face to face with Balthazar Beauregard, who is trespassing, staring over the next-door fence with a pleading, uncomprehending expression. Monica smiles at him, flutters her fingers, snaps shut the venetian blind.

'Oh that guy is really gettin to me. I made the mistake of ballin him a while back Nisi, and now he won't leave me alone. So what you do in town Friday? Shop?'

Nisi, swallowing hard, sips her coffee then speaks, without looking up.

'I'm involved in the Vietnam Protest Movement, Monica. I belong to the Vietnam Action Committee. We have a small office in Goulburn Street behind Bob Gould's bookshop. Do you know it?'

'Goulburn Street, Goulburn Street ... No, I don't think I do.'

'We hold rallies Friday afternoons but unfortunately, because of my timetable, I can't be there. So I usually spend Friday in the office, mailing out protest information.'

'Wow, it's really heated up since Tet, hasn't it? My husband

42

has a younger brother in Nam at the moment. Just a grunt. He's comin out here for his R&R. Coffee OK honey?'

'Lovely! This is the best coffee I ever tasted, outside a coffee shop. And do you have other children, Mon?'

'I have a son nine.'

'Goodness! So do I.'

'We both started too young. We *must* get together some time. I don't seem to talk with many other women. Maybe I'm wrong, Nisi, but I have the impression Australian women don't like Americans.'

Nisi is pondering the appropriate *démarche* when a strange sound makes her glance up. Her new friend's eyes are filling with tears, but it's worse than that, far worse, she can tell, and before Nisi knows quite what she is doing, and responding purely through instinct, she has struggled, with a sigh of effort, to her feet, and is holding Monica, who is now free to howl.

'There, there,' says Nisi. 'It's true some of us blame Americans for what is happening in Vietnam, but people are people.'

'My God, I'm so sorry. I'm so embarrassed. My daddy died recently Nisi, and I haven't ... I mean, I can't seem ... MmBrraa!'

'Hey, come on now.'

'MmmPprrra!'

'Come on, it's OK.'

'Nnnggha!'

'That's better.'

'Hrrra. You're so kind. Can *you* be my friend? Even sluts need friends. I invited so many of the other mothers but none of them would ever come. Mmpffaa.'

'We *are* a bit scared of Americans. And you're so beautiful. They probably feel threatened by you, Monica.'

'Oh Nisi, I'm in a *mess*, honey. I need to talk to a woman *real bad*.'

'Go on then. Talk.'

'But you have to go to work.'

'No I don't. I'm only a volunteer. I don't have to do anything. I can stay here all morning. Would you like me to freshen up this cup of coffee for you?'

'Oh Nisi honey, you're an angel.'

Nisi Papadimitriou: late twenties. Anti-war activist. Horse enthusiast. Mother of the poet 'Orion' (Timothy Papadimitriou), mother of Aloysius O'Looby. Common-law wife of Olaf Abernathy.

Monica Ecks: late twenties. Glamorous blonde American nymphomaniac. Mother of Cindy, mother of Alex. Recurrently estranged wife of Calvin Ecks.

That afternoon, a knock is heard at the door of the cell in the Physics Building to which Derek Frodsham, acned theoretician, has been consigned.

'Just a moment, would you?'

Calvin Ecks, in the corridor, swears, sighs, shakes his head, settles down for a short wait. He's in no state to work today anyway. Through a door off the corridor, he watches a group of first-year Physics students, sitting on antique wooden stools at antique wooden benches, determining the charge on an electron through a replay of Millikan's oil drop experiment. Back home, coeds still kiss Millikan's statue's nose, for luck.

Frodsham is absorbed. Fridays p.m. he sets aside for what he calls 'Applied Physics' and since he works most nights till 10 p.m. and all day Sunday, he can spare the time. Later, donning a boilersuit with the pockets sewn up, he will lock the door and head off towards Bob Gould's bookshop, but in the meantime, he is drafting his infrequent 'Letter from Abroad' to the editor of *New Left Review*.

'Under Aarons,' writes Frodsham (and this is just a draft), 'the Communist Party of Australia is more sympathetic to the concept of Self-management, and less inclined to spring to the defence of the fiendish crimes of the Mao-Stalin parasitic oligarchy. They have dared, for instance, to criticise the arrest of Ginsburg and Galenskov. It can only be a matter of time before Sydney has its own Institute for Workers' Control.'

Someone at the door. But let him wait, as Lenin awaits burial.

'Regrettably, fresh upon their expulsion from the Australian Labor Party, the Balmain Trotskyist group has been expelled from the Fourth International in Paris, by the revisionist Mandel-Frank gang, and voted, at a meeting held in the old

Annandale Town Hall, to affiliate itself—in principle—with Pablo's revolutionary Marxist Tendency. The view has been expressed that Australia will be the first advanced capitalist country to undergo Revolution. Certainly, one feels the rising pulse of worker discontent. Widespread police corruption, conscription into the criminal activities of the American adventurists ...'

'Hey, listen you in there, I don't have all day. Are you the guy with the vacancy?'

Smiling at the man's audacity, and reflecting the CIA would be better served by recruiting locals as operatives, Frodsham conceals his typescript under a stack of S-matrices, takes from a drawer a badge which says 'Smash US Imperialism' and pinning it to his tie, opens the door.

'I'm sorry to have kept you waiting.'

'No problem. You the guy with the room to let? How much?'

'There'd be no formal charge.'

'I beg pardon?'

'It's a communal house. You pay what you can afford. And it *is* rather primitive. I doubt it's quite what you're looking for.'

'I just need someplace cheap and handy to Royal Prince Alfred Hospital. I need a place to sleep, mostly.'

'You could always sleep on a park bench. I've slept on park benches.'

'I slept in a bus shelter last night. Didn't get much sleep.'

'You realise, you suppose, you're wasting your time? We only use the place to sleep and cook in.'

'I'm not sure I understand you.'

'I'm not sure I understand myself! I presume you work at the university?'

'I'm over in the Department of Medicine. Are you going to give me the address, or what?'

'First, I have to put your application for admission before the house committee. That could take some time.'

'Oh, that's no good. You see, I'm in a bit of a hole. I have no bed, no money, and I don't get paid till next month.'

'Couldn't a colleague put you up?'

'I'm not that close to anyone in Sydney. I have a tent. Is there somewhere in your backyard I could erect a tent?'

Frodsham is biting his nails. Calvin, for his part, is weary, and this whole drama has been most unwelcome to him. He's clutching at straws.

'How do you know about the room?'

'I saw it in the student paper.'

'But it wasn't advertised in the student paper.'

'Oh well, it was advertised in some paper that was open on a chair in the Med School cafeteria. I just assumed it was the student paper.'

'It was, in fact, the paper called *Socialist Perspective*. Do you realise what this means?'

'No, can't say I do. I'm very tired.'

'It means the residents of the house oppose, on principle, the Vietnam War.'

'That's fine by me. I got a brother drafted there at the moment. He's hating every minute of it.'

Frodsham bites his nails more deeply.

'Are your parents, perchance, recent emigrants from Europe?'

'Nope. We're Americans from way back. Look, I have no political views, if that's what's bothering you. I take no interest in politics. I'm just a scientist. If you must know, I have a domestic problem.'

'Could I ring your wife to confirm that?'

'Why don't you just take my word for it?'

Frodsham, a man who derived his own political views from first principles, smiles. He takes no one's word for anything.

And what true Doctor of Philosophy, in particular, what kind of American Scientist, boasts a lack of interest in Politics? Was not the *Aufklarung*, the Enlightenment, the product of Scientific Thought? Were not Diderot, Descartes, Bacon, Newton, Leibniz, Kepler, scientists in their way? Is not the American Constitution—though drafted by a man who kept 200 slaves and slept with the prettiest—the product of Philosophy? It was because scientists withdrew so early from the *Aufklarung*, that Polity ground to a halt, in the West, in this Liberal Democracy which, properly construed, is no more than a staging post on the path from Feudalism to Socialism. Scientific self-interest lends spurious weight to the disgusting premises of Locke and

46

Adam Smith, but now, fresh from victory over regressive Stalinist elements in the East, now is the time for Science—which remains independent of Culture—to reclaim its abnegated Sceptre, and long live the Philosopher-King! Let us, for God sake, have someone at the helm, of algorithmic complexity *and* thermodynamic depth.

Calvin Ecks: late twenties. Struggling American bioscientist, unable to concentrate on his research because of his wife's persistent misbehaviour. Devoted father of Cindy, reluctant stepfather to Alex.
Derek Frodsham: mid-twenties. Intellectual. Bites his nails. Trotskyite. No time for Americans. Would-be lover of Barbara Byng, last seen sorting mail. Became a eunuch.

9. *A Balmain Wake for Martin Luther King.*

Ain't No More Cane is a chain gang song. Now what in God's name could have prompted Michael Ginnsy to have brought this tape along tonight? Is he mad? Even given there were white men in chain gangs. Was it no more than a desire to impart his enthusiasm for the music? Or can it be he perceives, with Aristotle, the primary importance of musical education. Either way, it is music not vitiated by a cynical, urban *Weltanschauung*. It is pure Mississippi mud.

Ain't No More Cane is, we should say, a song from *ante-bellum* Arkansas and we're listening to it, rapt. It is of course The Band, The Hawks, recorded in the basement of Big Pink, their house at West Saugerties, New York, sometime between June and October of the previous year, with a single mike on someone's home recorder, and their Southern twang is unmistakeable on this, an Australasian premiere.

Ain't No More Cane is a *work* song. 'Rock music' writes the urbane Allan Bloom, whose views I find, on the whole, congenial, 'has one appeal only, a barbaric appeal, to sexual desire.

Young people know that rock has the beat of sexual intercourse.' Spoken like a true Chicago Jew. With respect, this is the comment of a man who never swung a hammer at a dogspike. There is more to rock than the pelvic thrust, Allan. Mars swaggers off to battle to its beat and Hermes keeps its rhythm on His datestamp. Rock is the rhythm of our hearts, the rhythm of jogging, the Four Seasons. *Solvitur saltando*, dancing is the answer. We are wired for rock as we are for language, and that's the problem.

'*Listen!*' orders Ginnsy, and the people listen though the sound is very faint. They listen, because these people are open to experience, and though the evening is supposedly a wake for Martin Luther King, the black April victim of Southern white oppression, no one has a problem in sitting back to listen to white Southern boys making music, because it's great music, and Aussie, like Dixie, was beaten to begin. By no person present is Ginnsy's gesture, in providing this music on this night, misconstrued, for ain't no such thing as taste, now the alchemical solvent has begun work. Taste is in reformulation, answers are being sought, instincts are being heeded and acted on: Bliss was it in that dawn to be alive, But to be young was very heaven. Sure beat the nineteen fifties.

We are on the corner of Cameron Street, Balmain, where the 441 bus turns left, in a two-storey building that was once a corner store, with a residence above it, for the storekeeper's family. The verandah, in such a state as to provoke uncertainty in passers-by glancing up, is cantilevered out over the footpath, and contained only by some ornate wrought iron, of the kind that made its way to the colony as ships' ballast in Victorian days. The cornice is an entablature, with finely tuck-pointed brick piers, in lieu of caryatids. Over the verandah, the bull-nosed sheets of rusting, corrugated iron grow more restless with each passing breeze and piss into a guttering that could be removed in minutes by a five-year-old boy, using his bare hands. At street level, the entrance is secantial to the kerb, and both the antique sandstone steps below the French doors are worn as the kerb itself; the same, weary beslippered feet that trod the kerb often as not went on into the shop, but by '68 the shop is become a residence, and the shop windows are hung with heavy curtains, and in the cracks between the curtains can be seen at night sometimes the glow of candlelight.

A symposium has been scheduled by Barbara Byng, one of the shophouse residents, to protest against the assassination of the Rev Dr Martin Luther King Jnr, shot dead in Memphis, where he'd planned on leading a dustmen's strike. It is hoped to explore means by which white Australians can express solidarity with adulterous clerics and black American dustmen.* Keynote speakers are bound to include Barbara, who has a particular interest in Blues music and civil rights, Nisi Papadimitriou, who has just finished reading *Soul on Ice* by Eldridge Cleaver, and Nisi's new friend Monica, who was raised in Alabama, and has seen plenty of negroes.

There has been a disappointing roll-up, according to Barbara, who must have been hoping they would spill onto the footpath. Certainly, the shop is full, and the music from the shop hi fi can be heard blocks away, at the police station. The music contains a strong West African element (excessive *portamento* in the vocals, the search for the ever-so-slightly flattened third, which here misses by a country mile), but the blues harmonica has the poignancy of oboe, and the rhythm guitar is a Gaelic strum. It's your Jewish one-man band, the boy from Duluth, Minnesota, 'where'—to quote from the jacket notes of *Planet Waves*, '74— 'Baudelaire lived, and Goya cashed in his chips, where Joshua brought the house down!'

Too soon for *Hurricane*, *They Killed Him*, *George Jackson*— songs written with the Black Civil Rights Movement in mind— but well in time for *Oxford Town*, inspired by James Meredith, and *Blowin' in the Wind* is an anthem of the sixties, and it is on the disc being spun now, over and again, *The Freewheelin Bob Dylan*.

These are the battle hymns of the Revolution. Cain't you hear that slave boy holler in his hut? Cain't you hear dat choo

---

* And sucks to the local blackfella. Charlie Perkins' freedom ride excepted, Paul Coe's outburst after the '70 Moratorium provides the first inkling here that charity begins at home. In the words of Emerson. 'Never varnish your hard, uncharitable ambition with this incredible tenderness for black folk a thousand miles off. Thy love afar is spite at home.'

choo train, comin roun de bend? I don't know that Bob ever actually worked on Maggie's Farm, but his mentor, Woody Guthrie, certainly did.

Now, as underscored by Allan Bloom, the ancient Greeks understood the importance of music to Civilisation, and they used music as a means of subduing the barbarous elements in the human soul, in much the same way Balthazar Beauregard, the yogin, uses breath to gain mastery over his autonomic nervous system. Plato's *Republic* ('the spirit of law must be imparted to them in music') and Aristotle's *Politics* discuss musical education at length. 'We Arcadians,' boasts Polybius of Megalopolis, 'are trained from our childhood to sing, and when we feast, we provide the music ourselves: we don't hire musicians.' It is recorded of Arcadian Cynaetha that the city, lapsed into barbarism through a neglect of the Arcadian institution of compulsory universal education in community singing.

Contrarily, the Semites and 'subterraneans' used stringed instruments, cymbals and drums, to induce a kind of wild, ecstatic trance, as also induced by the holotropic breathing techniques of Leonard Orr, featured in Rebirthing, and reEarthing. The musical stairs which lead from Passion to Reason can lead back down again more easily, if, at the top of those stairs, one finds an elevator shaft, or a door with no handle.

> *Facilis decensus Averno*
> *Noctes atque dies patet janua Ditis*
> *Sed revocare gradum, superasque evadere ad auras*
> *Hoc opus, hic labor est.*
> *(Easy enough to slide downhill*
> *The doors of hell are open night and day*
> *But working your way back up top again*
> *That's a wee bit of a different story.)*
> —*Virgil*

'Member the old Led Zeppelin classic *Stairway to Heaven?* You would, if you'd ever played pool at the Belmore Hotel. More of a greasy pole, covered in hog fat, ay. If you don't know

Stairway and *The House of the Rising Sun*, you are thought to be no guitarist in Obliqua Creek.

For generations, after the breakdown of the Hellenic Civilisation through the Atheno-Peloponnesian War, the oldies went round deploring the vulgarisation of music, and the pernicious effect on their Hellenic ethos of the corruption of this seminal art.

Sure enough, turning the pages, we find, in the late nineteenth century AD, the syphilitic lunatic Nietzsche, who could describe a postman as 'the mediator of impolite incursions', calling on the Rev Little Richard to pump up the jam. 'How little is required for pleasure,' says Nietzsche, who had the ear of a coal scuttle. 'The sound of a bagpipe. Without music, life would be an error.'

'Ear 'ear. I believe no sensitive soul could attend these songs of Bob Dylan (aka Robert Zimmerman), without being filled with *indignation* and the hankering for a porch with rural Jews, er, views.* Sure, and it's the down-home music of a fifth-generation emigrant from Ulster, infused with a negro slave's despair and the gimcrack credo of Weimar Berlin. It is anyway Bob's harmonica, and Bob's voice, and Bob's guitar, that provide the soundtrack to our Erinungarah *Saga*, that whining, querulous, half-ironic voice, that foreign voice, accompanied by an off-key mouthharp. Bob cain't sing and cain't play his horns; who could be more democratic than Bob?

On the other hand, he *is* a great songwriter. *Poeta nascitur, non fit.* Poets are born, not made. There is nothing democratic in the gift of melodic invention. As the Greeks knew, it is the rarest and most precious of all the gifts the gods bestow. Orpheus captured the hearts of barbarians through the music of his lyre, and Orphism was a religion invented by the Greeks, not inherited by them.

Bob has The Gift. It is rare as true mathematical flair and unrelated to technical proficiency. It expresses itself, most perfectly, in tunes a mere Post Man could whistle, and does. God has smiled on Bob Dylan, notwithstanding the big hooked beak

---

* Leon Trotsky (aka Lev Bronstein) was a rural Jew.

which, incidentally, is Hittite, not Jewish. You see it in Turks and Armenians too.

Barbara Byng: future senator. Anxious to commemorate the death of Martin King. How would her electorate respond to the revelation she has had a child taken into care?

Michael Ginnsy: emaciated muso, off his face at all times. Long arms, can't swim freestyle at the shallow end of a pool. But apparently present in Big Pink, when The Band was putting down The Music.

Act 2 Scene 1

10. *Wonderview. The MacAnaspies. Attis sends a letter, but not to Diane. Horrie receives setback.*

I doubt it has changed. I doubt one need use one's imagination to see Wonderview as it would have been then, twenty-seven years ago now, because they don't change much, do they, these places, and not because they don't get their windfalls, because they don't see a need for change. Their inexpugnable strength is in fortitude and consistency. And any inhabitant not content with things as they are knows where to go.

Each day at Wonderview begins with a dispute as to the correct pronunciation of the owners' surname. 'Mc Mc Mc Mc Mc Mc Mc Mc*Gark*' is the emphatic view of one party, while 'Mc Mc Mc Mc Mc Mc Mc Mc*Gerk*' has its equally clamorous advocate. I would say neither is within a bull's roar of the correct pronunciation, which, so far as a man can gauge it from the very tattered and yellowed piece of paper affixed to the wall of Obliqua Creek Post Office agency, would have to be 'MacAnaspie'.

MacAnaspie, H.J. and I.C. Wonderview Hereford Stud.

October 1990, first time I went to Wonderview, which is a very isolated neck of our local woods, it was misty and wet, as so rarely it is any more. The ochre sand on the recently graded gravel access track was flinging up under the mudguards of my rice-burner, and when I got home, I had quite a job, I found, to clean my little grub. In among the sandy loams, and the tanbark from the cattleyards, was a kind of whitish clay, which a professional potter might pinch and sniff and roll between his fingers. But I could think only of Darryl MacAnaspie—better known to you, perhaps, as Rastus the Rodeo Clown—boring down the track on his motorcycle, the Bonneville Triumph. It must have been close on midnight when Darryl hit that dirt, because he drank, I am told, every night till closing time at the Terminus Hotel, not that he was a big drinker; no, he was a man who enjoyed a bit of intelligent conversation. I can reconstruct his ride home, just looking at the map. The fog patches would have begun here, in this hollow, on the outskirts of town, but the only trees here are poplars, lining the beds of the creeks as they do on the Anatolian steppe. The real bush begins here.

By the time Darryl hit the dirt, his wonderview would have consisted of a headlight beam, diffracted to a nimbus, three feet in front of his face.

By Jove, he would have thrown the leg shivering every time. He would have stood, with his hands and kidneys to the fuel stove, a good few minutes before retiring, either pondering some of the conversation he'd enjoyed earlier on in the evening, or humming to himself the latest hit by the Everly Brothers, Don and Phil, with the droplets of moisture from his hair, and his damp woollen shirt (for he never wore leathers) hissing as they hit the hob. There'd have been damp clothes hanging everywhere, back in '68, off racks, off the saucepan hooks, off the cup hooks, off the backs of chairs, and some of these would have been the hand-me-down blue school shirts and grey shorts of Attis MacAnaspie, the youngest MacAnaspie, who had a five-mile barefoot walk to the school bus in shorts, winter and summer. Strange, ay, to think that down in the Valley even now are folk, who, if you presented them with a scrap of clothing authentically worn by Attis MacAnaspie, would finger it with thought, or with awe, if not reverence.

That's his left hand, lying there.

This is the house in which he was raised, young Attis MacAnaspie, and these the unlikely folk who raised him, though they never claimed him as one of their own. He was a foundling, as the whole district knew, abandoned by his mother—probably some local schoolgirl—on the damp sawdust at the softwood mill, naked as a Spartan or a Viking, but still alive and kicking when they found him, so that Fergus MacAnaspie, who was working at the mill then as apprentice electrical fitter, a cow of a job, and who was forever bringing home kittens and magpies with broken wings, and orphaned wombats, brought him home, for it was autumn—you can't be eight months pregnant and your mother not know it in midsummer—and his birth, through some oversight, was never registered. There was blood on the sawdust, and his afterbirth was found near some treated windsplits.

You would need to know precisely where you were, coming down the track to Wonderview by night. There are no guide-posts and heavy equipment is parked everywhere. Many a

B-Model Mack, the six-ton tipper for the ditchwitch, the old Studebaker six-wheel drive—that's the beast with the accelerator pedal between the clutch and the brake—the beavertail floats for the backhoes and the bobcats: the Macks are Superliners now, Barney's recently upgraded, but apart from this, nothing much would have changed, I shouldn't think. Barney keeps the show afloat. Jinkers, the upraised arms of their bolsters supplicating for old-growth sawlogs.

The day I went out, there was a low-loader with a D8 dozer on it, both covered in mud, slung across the track, being guarded by a gaggle of semi-domestic geese. Not the sort of place you'd expect to find a selection of champagne corks within a cricket pitch arc of the back door, though there were a couple, and they date back to the late sixties, the era to which we are alluding here as well, in fact they date back to the same day. What looked like a Staffie, with a studded collar, was dozing on the dozer the day I went out, and while they can be very agreeable animals, I didn't make a closer inspection, but I recognised the D8, as anyone would who's seen a dam being dug round here.

That big six-wheeler Atkinson tipper that scoots round full of firewood, that's Barney's, but mostly, as of yore, our Darryl works with the Forestry, jinking high in the hills, and his jinker, well you never see it unless you're so unlucky as to be coming the other way down some slippery forestry road, because he leaves home at 4 a.m. to get to the coupes by first light, and he's on the coast roads till after dark. It's a bloody long way from the Valley to the woodchip mill.

On occasion, the MacAnaspies would load up cattle at bush yards, constructed down forgotten firetrails.

They're a strange family. A bit offbeat, always were. For instance, the proper Australian name for a property by a swamp is Springvale, or Hillview, if it has the view of a hill, but Wonderview, though it sits right on the edge of the plateau, and ought, in theory, to command a wondrous view of the Erinungarah Valley, has a view only of regrowth mountain gum, with the odd narrow-leafed peppermint and a few straggly Monterey pines and some disused deer fencing, of which more anon, so that in the fog, and disregarding what sound like steam trains at the pinecones, and which are, in fact, small family groups of our yellow-tailed black cockatoo, with whingeing young, you might imagine yourself in California, up north, somewhere near Eureka, in which case your eucalypts would be introduced, and your radiata pines autochthonous.

So is our *Saga* a pan-Pacific *Saga* then, a story which might as easily have taken place on the Other Side? How dearly I wish it were. But I cannot see how I can translocate this *Saga*. There is, haunting the lives of my protagonists, despair that does not accord with a Californian milieu. If we're a long way from the chip mill here, we're a bloody sight further from Silicon Valley. No, I think I'll have to tell it as it was, and set it where it did, in fact, happen. Sorry.

Breathe deep now. Flashback. Early '68. Iris MacAnaspie has no daughters, so Attis becomes the youngest of her five sons. H.J. MacAnaspie's father, C.K., lives with the family too, and H.J. and C.K., former sawyers both, have fourteen whole fingers and thumbs between them. Barmen complain they never know whether Horrie wants four beers or two. Charlie, though a dreadful hypochondriac who visits the doctor for a check-up every week, and twice in the week before Anzac Day, forever exerts the power of the weak and defenceless over his long-suffering grandsons, who don't like to punch him back, but have to retroflex to avoid it. Old Charlie is notorious for never wearing clothes. The coppers tell me that whenever they pull the old curmudgeon over—and he's still driving a B-Model Mack well into his eighties—all he would ever be wearing was a Jacky Howe singlet* and a pair of jocks. Down at the mill they wear singlets, but they wear workpants too, and if it's particularly cold they'll don a shirt or a cardigan. Not Charlie: I have seen photos of Norman's twenty-first birthday party, which was held in the Country Women's Hall here, and all Charlie wore to that august occasion was a singlet and a pair of jocks. The man had a phobia, but you can understand his daughter-in-law not wanting to display him

---

* Jacky Howe shore 300 sheep in a single day with a pair of hand clippers, at Alice Downs Station in 1892. Of course, Australians being what they are, no one went up to shake him by the hand.

any further afield than the doctor's surgery, where he always went to the head of the queue, no matter how many were waiting.

Now the property adjoining Wonderview, which had been deserted for decades, suddenly sprouted 'Keep Out' signs and warnings that Trespassers would be Prosecuted. As the Mac-Anaspies considered it part of their run, and had been cutting sawlogs off this land, and depasturing starvers on it in spring, they at once dispatched Barney, the eldest, to Council, to see what was going on, because they didn't believe in telephones: if you wanted them for a job of work you left a message at the mill. That evening, while Mrs MacAnaspie served dinner to the clan, Barney conveys to the rest of them the information he has garnered.

'Total Goat Control,' he tells them. 'That's the name of the geezer.'

'Total Goat Control,' puts in Charlie from the fuel stove, from where he is being asked to shift himself every thirty seconds. 'There is no such plurry thing as total goat control.'

'You fool!' says H.J. to Barney. 'I asked you to find out the names of the new owners of our adjoining property and you can't even do that for a man.'

Barney frowns, the way he does when under assault, and picks the marrow from his T-bone. 'Do it yourself,' he advises.

'I will,' avers H.J. and next morning H.J. confronts the Town Clerk, an old cricketing colleague, in person. 'Has he paid the outstanding rates then, Mick, this Comptroller of Goats, because I reckon there'd be a few bob owin. I thought all this was Crown Land. By Crikey, it's windy today. Sort of day the bails are forever blowin off the stumps.'

'No, no, this block here, see? Right up one side of your access track. Isn't it all fenced?'

'I wouldn't call it fenced. Few star pickets. Nothin that'd keep a goat in. Look, we don't want goats devastatin our land. We must have a name and address on him. No caravan about.'

'This is his address. Erinungarah Road. Of course, he only just bought the place.'

'Who sold it to him?'

'Council took possession for non-payment of rates years back now. It's been up for auction every year since. Didn't I see you at one of those auctions?'

'I doubt it. Now listen, Mick, we don't want goats in our shire.'

'There's no law against goats. You'll just have to get on with your new neighbours, Horrie. You've been spoilt, mate. Everyone else has neighbours.'

At first, nothing. Then a letter from Total Goat Control in the mail. 'Would you be interested,' it says, 'in undertaking, strictly cash for me, a big fencing job?'

'I think we should do it' says Fergus. 'If we put the fence up ourselves, we have only ourselves to blame if the goats get out.'

'Well, that just shows how much you don't know about goats.' H.J., though previously unacquainted with them, now regards himself as an expert. 'He had a right to come out and see me, this man, and introduce himself to me, and if the truth were known, he should have asked my permission to move in, which I would not have granted. And I don't know what sort of control a man expects to exert over goats who can't even put up his own blunny fences! Sounds a bit of a blatherskite. Probly some city fella, one o' these hands on hippers.'

Well, a fence, in due course, went up, courtesy of a team of fencers from some foreign shire, and substantial fencing it was, and then the goats arrived while everyone was out one day. Mohair goats, thousands of them. The first in the district. Among the first in the State.

'They're very attractive animals, Dad. Did you see them?'

'Just let me get this bubbly down. Yes Iris, I seen 'em. Haven't set eyes on their Comptroller yet, though.'

'Well, we have better things to think about now, haven't we, Charlie?'

'Don't think this matter is settled, Iris. It's not settled by a long chalk.'

'Why, what do you mean?'

'Well I haven't decided yet. I may very well pull those fences down and let the goats out yet. I haven't decided.'

'Oh Dad! You worry me, when you talk like that.'

'You're not wasting my plurry money on fines.'

'I can't sleep properly any more, Charlie. I can't relax now in my own home.'

'You never had neighbours before, did you, Horrie?'

'You know I didn't. And I don't want them now either, I'm too old for it.'

'The Lord says we must love our neighbours.'

'The Lord was a drifter, Iris. That's as good as Solomon telling us not to commit adultery. And I took the boy in, didn't I? Raised him as one of my own? My conscience is clear.'

'Just don't do anything stupid, Horrie. I couldn't stand the shame.'

Only Attis and his mother were home when the police car drove up a few months later. Iris, as usual, was fussing over the sink while Attis did his homework at the table. At school, he would always depict his mother standing over a sink.

'My God, he has gone and done it' was all she could say, because the police, though they often had lawful reason, never came to Wonderview. They were apprehensive, as most locals are, of the MacAnaspie reputation for being ogres, which is documented. You will find, that according to statistics released by the Department of Primary Industry, the MacAnaspies slaughtered, in the year of 1965 alone, 149 head of cattle for their own personal consumption. A hecatomb. My God, they would have needed the six-ton tipper, just to remove the bones and offal.

'Is it Darryl?' inquires Mrs MacAnaspie of the young, green, uniformed constable, who has brought out the pursuit car, a Cooper S, not a vehicle suited to the mud.

Actually, they're pretty laid back around here. Only time I ever heard a siren was when they were delivering Santa Claus to the preschool Christmas Party. I bought my house in Obliqua Creek, it would have been August '91.

'Horrie,' replies the copper, white as chalk. 'I have here a summons for a parking fine it seems was never paid.'

'Oh you're not going to fine him for *that*,' she says. 'He was only doing an old soldier a favour. You know old Mr Mac-Anaspie? Well, he decided to change doctors recently, because he's cranky with Dr Phoukas, because Dr Phoukas says his ulcer is because he won the lottery and not because of the Great War.

Horrie was only parked outside the surgery with the low-loader to pick up his father's files.'

Charlie MacAnaspie: early nineties. Patriarch of Wonderview. Gallipoli vet, wears only the underwear. Self-centred curmudgeon.

Horrie MacAnaspie: mid-sixties. Earth mover, sawyer and cattleman. Son of Charlie, father of Barney, Norman, Darryl and Fergus. Adoptive father of Attis. Hates goats and doesn't like his neighbours.

Iris MacAnaspie: mid-sixties. Wife of Horrie. Mother of five boys. Countrywoman, forever cooking cakes. Now suffering from the after-effects of a diet of toast and tea. Points east when she speaks of Wonderview, though it's south of the nursing home.

Darryl MacAnaspie: late twenties. Jinker driver, motorcyclist. Rastus the Rodeo Clown. Fights, on a daily basis, with Fergus. Father-to-be of Harley and Norton, by Monica Ecks. Never became a eunuch. Reopened the Gap Road, May '86. Owns the Valley, logs the Valley. Doesn't welcome intruders. Hates postmen in particular.

Fergus MacAnaspie: late twenties. Jinker driver. His father's favourite. Fights on a daily basis with Darryl. Became a eunuch. First abbot of the monastery.

Barney MacAnaspie: early thirties. Eldest of the MacAnaspie boys. Enlisted to fight in Vietnam. Present-day owner of Wonderview.

Norman MacAnaspie: early twenties. Developmentally disabled.

Attis MacAnaspie: mid-teens. Uncommonly good-looking, but lacks personality, in my depiction. But there is a reason for this. (Fear. Awe.) Honey hunter and bushman extraordinary. Good at schoolwork too. Found, at the softwood mill, as a newborn child, by Fergus MacAnaspie. Common-law husband of Diane Zoshka, father-to-be of Sun and Dusk, by Diane Zoshka, adopted son of both Horrie MacAnaspie and The Greenbrown Man (Mehmed Contramundum). The Chosen One of Brigid. The Exemplar. First communard to emasculate himself.

We have returned to the era when a postie rode a pushbike with Major Taylor handlebars. They were great days.

As an adolescent, Attis is prone to decorate his envelopes the way girls do, not that he receives, or sends, a great deal of personal mail; an identity exists between seeing what other people consider normal and your own expectations. If, like myself, you've lived on a street where it's normal for the postie to switch off the engine at every second drop, then your attitude towards the art of correspondence will soar above that of the private boxholder, whose habit it may be to grope his box, 4.30 a.m. once a month, tossing, with contempt, any advertising matter straight back down the chute, and the remainder—peeping out at him through windows—into the throbbing cab of a throbbing rig, where it may remain under the hamburger wrappers and next to the safety repair kit (Minties, for leaking fuel tanks; Wrigley's gum, for radiator repairs; cans of beer, to be shaken and used as extinguishers, in the event of fire) up to a month. Some folk, in other words, don't know what they're missing, and the wonder is Attis ever came to realise mail can be used for Higher Purposes, because his entire adoptive family had no inkling of the notion; to be fair, when Darryl went away, in '88, he did scratch home some pretty poor stuff, actually, from Box 32, Cessnock.

That's the prison. Lot of keen poets in prison.

'Are you goin ta town today, Mum? Could you post this for us please?'

'As if I haven't enough to do. What's this you've drawn on the back of this envelope, Attis?'

'Can't you recognise her?'

'Well, she's a possum of some kind.'

'She's a yellow bellied glider, Mum, look. See? There's her flap.'

'And why have you covered the envelope edges in little blue stripes, son?'

'So's to look like a proper airmail envelope.'

'Well I never. Off to New Caledonia, too. See the drawin he's done here, Dad? Good, isn't it.'

'I hope you're payin for the stamp. All the way to New Caledonia indeed. Who do you write to there?'

'His new French penfriend, in Noumea. She's a girl.'

'Well, just make sure he pays for the stamp himself. Now we know what he's up to, when he's s'posed to be doin his homework. Writin to women all over the world. Look at the smile on his dial.'

'You know he spent his money on Norman's birthday present. I think it's wonderful he writes letters.'

'I was workin at his age, for less than he gets in pocket money. Never learnt to write letters, though I can still read'em, don't you worry. How'd you meet up with this French bird, Att? Haven't been hangin round the docks when you're s'posed to have been at school, I hope?'

Only by the broad wink Horrie, deadpan, may deign to flash an interlocutor, can the same gauge his dissimulation. On this occasion, he doesn't wink. His intercourse is largely raillery; he will introduce himself at a menswear store with some such remark as, 'What are you doin there, you lazy, good-for nothin bastard, goan to serve us here or aren't ya?' The true Aussie wit, that so often expires, during Happy Hour at the Black Stump, in fisticuffs.

'He's blushin, look at him. God strike us, how old's the boy?'

'Leave him alone. Come on, Attis, hurry now, or you'll be late.'

'What, he's been missin the school bus?'

'Only the once.'

'That we know of.'

'Done your teeth, son?'

'Yes.'

'Don't you go missin that school bus. Come on, off with you now, quick sticks.'

'What's wrong with you today? Forever snappin 'n snarlin.'

'Get yourself another boyfriend, if I don't suit. Find yourself a Caledonian penfriend. Ask Fergie when he comes home, he'll tell ya. He was there, saw the whole shemozzle.'

'What, you won nothin again?'

'Didn't score a single card. I'm on the point of doin somethin, too. Got talkin to Didier Lovaduk in the pub, sayin as how I didn't see how that red cockerel pair could have missed, or that little silkie, and you know what he said? Overheard that goat

Isbester sayin to Mr Justice Safehouse, I recognise all Mac-Anaspie's birds, and I won't give them a card.'

'What?'

'Won't give them a blunny card! That's what he said. Dunno why a man bothers liftin a finger. I'll be glad when I'm out of this world. Come on, give me another cup of java and hasten my departure. Has that boy gone off to school yet? *Attis!*'

'Don't take it out on him, please. He's gone. There he goes. See?'

'He's a blunny dreamer, look at him. Can't see him bein of use to an employer. Lives in a world of his own.'

'You're forgettin he's good at school, he's just sixteen, and he keeps you in honey.'

'Probly wind up a beekeeper. Now there's a dead-end job.'

'You couldn't find someone to take him on, just for the school hols? He could learn bookkeeping. Are you going to work today?'

'No.'

'Why not?'

'Because I have to work on the plant, don't I? And frankly, if I never worked again, I've done my fair share, Iris. Most men are retired by the time they reach my age. What we need in this household is a diesel mechanic.'

'Don't start talkin like that. That boy's not going to be a diesel mechanic. It's all because of those blessed chooks. Speakin of which, you could kill one for me, if you're goin to hang round all day.'

'You can have those red cockerels. I'm gettin rid o' them.'

Attis leaves home at 6 a.m. to get to his high school by nine. A school bus delays, but only if he's waiting, where the Erinungarah Road leaves the coast road, just up from where that 'Form One Lane' sign had a 'p' and a 't' added to the front and back of the third word, and if he's left home late, or dawdled on the way, he takes a short cut through the woods, that none of his brothers would have deemed one, because it would have taken them longer. A fair sort of swamp hereabouts, a lot of prickly beard heath and dagger hakea, but Attis gets down on all fours, and follows a wombat pad through the melaleucas. Even in depth of winter, there's light enough at six to see where you're going, if you know where you're going, and the great advantage of being off the track at this hour, you get to meet the natives.

'At piccaninny dawn in the Erinungarah Range, before the colour sinks into the Gap, singing commences, and many voices apprehend the day ahead. By midday, it can get very hot, and this hour, the hour of dawn, forgotten.

'Colour infuses the plateau now, and all the creatures that lie down still in the heat of the day move freely about. Not before dusk, when colour fades, will they be seen and heard again.'

That's from the ballad by Timothy Papadimitriou, the poem I found in the mailbag. 'Orion', to accord him his *nom de plume*, and the Aussie balladeer must have a *nom de plume*. He was given his *nom de plume* by a nun, the first woman to see Brigid. Would she have been eating the mushrooms? I can't see a nun eating mushrooms.

Pausing under a small drumsticks plant, which part-way up contains the abandoned nest of a white-cheeked honeyeater, made, as so often they are, of cowhair, Attis, not yet three miles from home, and running late, and sweating, and with fresh scratches bleeding, pulls from his pocket the pale blue letters he has thus far received from his penfriend, and rereads them and rereads them. They're probably written in what I always call postcard Creole ('My brother visits in this year high school,' etc), but we can't be sure, as we don't open mail, unless it's addressed to Santa Claus or the Easter Bunny. That's me. The letters crinkle like a blue synthetic flag when you fold them after a hot, windy day, because the boy can't leave them concealed in his pocket, or under his pillow, ten minutes. The adrenalin of anticipation, the endorphin of serenity, with which the boy's mind and body alternatively tingle and repose, galvanise the pages. These emotions are novel to the lad, untainted, as yet, by carnality, and thus completely holy and delightful. Most amazing, he can't understand how his new French penfriend got hold of his moniker.

'So it is with the voices of our hearts. Silent at night and in the noonday sun, loudest at dusk and in the piccaninny dawn.'

Eros.

Horrie MacAnaspie: mid-sixties. Disappointed fowl fancier, disenchanted with modern life. A kind, loving person, to some.

Iris MacAnaspie: mid-sixties. Long-suffering *materfamilias*. Keen to see one of the boys do well, i.e. move to the city and prosper. Had only she eaten her own delectable preserves, she would have her wits about her still. But they went to charity, sold off card tables outside the post office agency here.

Attis MacAnaspie: mid-teens. Growing up in the same country, in much the same style, as Wilfred Burchett. But Christ wouldn't join the Maccabees and Attis was never an activist. He married one, though, in Diane Zoshka.

11. *Fergus finds his father in the tractor shed. Darryl arrives, fights with Fergus. Kimberley Moon attempts to cadge an inner tube. Phryx and Gwen. A brumby muster planned.*

Another day, another dollar, April '68. Around about the time that Barney went to fight in Vietnam. Fergus fangs into the yard and leaps from the seat of the great ten-wheeler before it is fully stationary. Dust hangs in a cloud. Pausing on the way to light a cigarette, he strides past some demolition scantling towards the bush-pole tractor shed and workshop, in which his elderly father has taken dispirited refuge. So many lengths of pipe and conduit nestle under the iron roof, you'd have to stare pretty hard and long to make out the sapling battens.

'You're home early.'

'Barely got up the coupe this mornin, Dad. After that rain, be no chance.'

'I'll have a word with the man. You're losing too much time on that road, Fergus.'

The walls of the old tractor shed are roofing iron, nailed to turpentine posts, joined with double lengths of fencing wire, tied with a Cobb & Co hitch. Huge, wide, dust-gathering championship sashes, imperial green, purple and blue, adorn the walls. A dozen or so yellow or red ones have been consigned to a cardboard box. We learn that Horrie's weaners (like Juvenal's satires) do better on the hook. A pre-war runabout, covered in rust patches and dust, alternatively mud, sits up on red stringy-bark blocks, tray covered with thick blond plywood, seams rising. Over this tray, Horrie, without so much as looking from his work, could let rove the mutilated right hand to come upon a bottle of meths, or a bossing mallet, or a bakelite switch, or a long-throw bucket hoist, or give a touch-up to a kero tin half containing vaseline, jointing cement and female connectors; or scratch himself with a farrier's pritchel, or stroke a black welder's helmet, or spar with a fretsaw blade or two, or a suction syphon; or pore over a purloined milkcrate, packed with measures, claw hammers and brushes, bristling with wood glue; or prod the fruitbox, stuffed with welding gloves and welding electrodes, while, with the mutilated left hand, actuating the actuator or spreading a pelt on the fleshing beam to take to it with a skiving knife.

'What y'up to then?'

Fugly, I can't look at a man's digital amputations. Hate the way the skin folds in on the stumps.

'Fiddlin with this blunny thing. Why won't this go on, Fergie?'

'Left-hand thread?'

'I'll be damned.'

Between the Fordson and the Dodge is an ancient rotary hoe, which serves now as a shelf for scraps of spent sarking. Behind the tractor, to which is hitched an old homemade coachwood trailer, is the piston from a steam lawnmower, a mechanical reaper that looks like the one spoken of by Pliny as in use in first-century Gaul, a stack of bee boxes riddled with wax moth, grease-encrusted Esso oil drums, and a workbench, covered in drawers from old treadle sewing machines, neatly inscribed 'autoelectrical', 'used plugs', 'door handles', 'deck spikes', 'gate latches'. A bench grinder and a multi-speed drill contest the oil-soaked earth floor with jack hammers, truck hoists, boxes of taps and dies and socket sets, but the *pièce de résistance*, with its distinctive cooling tank, its Napoleonic hat silencer and water jacket atop crankcase and fueltank base, between two big twenty-two-inch flywheels, on its little undercarriage, with its hardwood shafts fitted with runners for the dray harness, two of its four cast-iron wheels skewwhiff and buried in the dirt, is the MacAnaspie seven-horsepower Sunshine portable two stroke petrol engine, which, by means of a belt like a Mobius strip, used to drive the chaffcutter in the days before tariffs were used to destroy this country's leadership in world rural technology, when graders ran on chaff and lucerne grew on the Flat, and men wore waistcoats and white shirts and short-brimmed hats to do manual labour. The oilcan and funnel, the spare diaphragm discs for the carbie, and all the British imperial spanners are long gone from the toolbox cum driver's seat; of the four oil drip-feed lubricators, three appear to be missing; the chain that drives the magneto is hanging off the crankshaft in thin air, while the magneto itself has disappeared: but the bolts look sound, and there's not much rust on the cast iron, and no borers in the wood. Even the hoses on the thermosyphon, to and from the cylinder jacket, from and to the reservoir, are unperished. And if you removed the inspection door, at the front of the crankcase, which would be no trouble, you'd see that the phosphor bronze big-end bearing—in which wear may be taken up by the simple, and patent, expedient of tightening and slackening the nuts that secure the bearing flanges to the crankcase flanges, as distinct from the more usual rigmarole, best undertaken by a qualified fitter—well, it looks good as new, and the joints seem airtight.

'What ya doin down here, Dad? Drop somethin, you'll never find it.'

'I'll find it, same way as you'd find yer arse. It's a question o' knowin what you're lookin for.'

Fergus cracks up, choking on smoke. Twenty-nine years old, he's a bit of a Dad's boy. Come home from Sydney once with the word 'Dad' tattooed to his arm. Drunk at the time, had no recollection. Woke up with the sheet stuck to his arm and wondered why.

I provided myself with a tatt the very day I retired, July '91. From Dutchy, down there by Liverpool Station, the Comanchero hangout. Just an Australia Post symbol, and under that, in a scroll, the quintessential tattoo. I am tough, and I have proved it.

'Christ, you got some stuff down here.'

69

'Yes, and I know where everything is. I'm usin the Central Station Outward Parcel System. See if you can't find me a washer for this nut, son, save me gettin off me haunches. Walkin round like blunny Groucho Marx I was, this mornin, after a session on the ram pump valve spring. Throw me the WD 40, too, I think I've a touch of arthritis. You'll find the jar of washers above the stock saddle trees, behind the cycle gears, between the toasters, and after the fan belts.'

'Christ, look at all this trace leather harness, all this workin horse tack. *Years* since I been down this place.'

Hanging off hooks, below a dusty graduate diploma from the University of Adversity, are hames, collars, ridgepads, bridles, nosebags, all well maintained till recently.

'Think you'll be needin this tack again, Dad?'

'Well, I hope not, but the way the world's shapin, I shouldn't be surprised. Your mother is always goin on at me cause I throw nothin away, but you don't see me wastin petrol, runnin to town when I need some little thing. I find I need a rasp, or a crystal set component, or the runnin board for a '27 Chevy, I've got one handy. How's your bum for grubs? We'll be runnin a drive shortly, bring in those twenty head of cattle we're down. He's not keepin those, and bein as he is, the kind o' man who'd steal your eyes, spit in the holes and swear to Christ you'd been born blind, he'll be plannin a muster, to impound them for himself. They'll get the cramps, if we don't shift'em soon. Either that, or find their way to the Valley and upset the tenants.'

'Eat the bracken too, ay Dad. Uh oh, look what the bloody wind's blown in.'

A second jinker rig, same as the first, pulls into the yard and swings round. The jinker is up itself, so too the driver.

'Down here, little brother!'

Roy Orbison the second in dark glasses, suave image vitiated by the bark off his knuckles and the permanent half-moons of sump oil under his nails, strolls down.

'You takin an early mark too, are ya, Darryl?'

'Gotta nip in the bike shop, pick up some filters 'n sprockets. Thought I might do some shoppin.'

'Couldn't your mother have done it for ya? She went to town today. Shoulda called you Hurricane Lamp, you're not very bright. Pon my soul, it's runnin in and out of town's keepin you poor, Darryl, can't you see it? Each night you spend in that boozer is two days off your lifespan, to boot. *I* was a boy, a trip to town from here was an expedition. And you don't sit in a wagon, wearin a pair of dark glasses, when you're drivin bullocks. Ask Charlie. You walk beside'm or half o'them don't pull.'

'Yeah, well them days is over, Pops, and good riddance.'

'Don't talk to yer father like that, y'ignorant cunt! Man who can't fart and chew gum at the same time, show some respect.'

'Who told you to stick your bib in, Gus? Keep a civil tongue in yer 'ead or I'll rattle your daags till your nose bleeds!'

'Now then boys ... '

'He ain't gonna speak to me like that, Dad.'

'Try me on, dickhead! That's if you want more o'what ya got last time.'

'Yeah?'

'Listen boys ... '

'Same time same place?'

'What's wrong with here and now?'

'Boys, take off your shirts, if you don't mind, and swill off, fore you come back in the house. I'll have a brew waitin.'

Horrie MacAnaspie: mid-sixties. Father to the fighting brothers and a great hoarder of tools.

Fergus MacAnaspie: late twenties. Jinker driver and not a bad horseman. Fights, on a daily basis with Darryl, since Darryl accused him of cheating once, in a marble swallowing contest.

Darryl MacAnaspie: late twenties. Jinker driver and Roy Orbison lookalike. Goes to town, every night, on his Bonneville Triumph to drink at the Terminus.

May '68.

'Kimberley Moon is here to see us, Dad.'

'What does he want? If he's after a tool, he can't have it.'

The Moons are notoriously hard on their tools. Worse than plumbers.

'Got a sick calf. Wants to know if we've any big inner tube we don't want.'

'Oh very well, ask him in. Hello, Kimberley me boy, how are ya? Sit yourself down and have a cup of tea with us.'

Kimberley, a wiry, dark little fellow with five nephews older than himself, of simian appearance but sensitive, nods a curt greeting to Iris MacAnaspie—'Silky Purple Flag' as he calls her—bids Attis move up the books and sits, to stare defiantly at Horrie, a convivial Australian mode of greeting, and always preceded, in a public bar, by the slamming down of all one's small change.

'They tell me you've been away, boy.'

Kimberley inclines his head in acquiescence, and emits a non-committal grunt.

'What, you've been workin up north again, have ya? Musterin? What did you do in the Wet? Hole up?'

Another inclination of the head, no grunt. Kimberley's eyes, deep and close-set, under thick brows, are of frightening intensity. They are wounded eyes, and they never move from the eyes of an interlocutor.

'I'll never forget the time he turned up at the Bombala Show with his horse on the tabletop, member that, Mum? No sides, or nothin. Metal tray. Horse was shod too, all saddled ready to go. Give the dressage toffs a turn.'

'Taught him balance.'

'Course it did. People underestimate horses. If dogs can ride on the tanks of bikes, why can't horses do as *they* likes? Still writin poetry, Kimbo?'

It's Attis Kimberley fixes with a smile of infinite compassion, though his gaze goes through the side of the house to fix on the Valley, as he nods, in the negative.

'They don't want my poetry.'

'Of course they don't. But it must be very hard.'

Old Charlie, coughing and barking, emerges from the hallway to spit on the fire. He's reached that age where a man can't sleep five hours on the trot, for fear his joints freeze. Largely for his benefit, the MacAnaspie stove is lit first thing every morning, and burns all day every day, till Darryl, three sheets to the wind, gives it the last riddle round midnight. Charlie's mottled skin, under his white singlet, is loose as the skin on a jugged hare, and the palms of his hands, as he rubs them over the hotplate, cracked as the mud in a drought-stricken dam.

'You got the rent down the Valley yet?' he inquires, ignoring the visitor.

'Not this month. Doesn't buy much.'

'They're a month in arrears.'

'What, you think something may have happened to them, is that what you're trying to say?'

'When I seen the doctor this mornin, he asked had I seen Frick's missus, cause Frick's missus was due for a check-up last week, and never come in. Now she always comes to town once a month, to deposit the rent.'

'I see. Didn't realise she hadn't been comin to town.'

'Who's this we're talkin about, boss?'

'Phryx Pfingstl and Gwen Bletherstone Mayall, Kimberley. They live in the Valley, in the old farmhouse.'

'You're the boy always got the wet patch on his trousers pocket, aren't ya. Suffer from catarrh, don't ya. Like your uncles.'

'Often got a wet patch on me crotch too, mate, from ridin horses in the rain. Makes me look like I pissed meself.'

'First up, it fills your boots, then down the back o' your neck, and finally your crotch. You said it. Kimberley's been musterin, Dad.'

'When did he ever do a high country muster? Wouldn't call him a stockman. What, out west?'

'Up the Gulf, mate. Normanton.'

'Huh. Heard you'd been out west, doin it hard. Been gettin it dry out there, too. Mind you, this'd be close on the worst drought we ever had round here. Everytime someone goes to war, we get a drought.'

'Dry all over, Mr MacAnaspie.'

'Drier than this in 14–15, when I went off to war. Very dry again 1919–20. I member it rained here June 25 and by August the creeks was in flood.'

'Would you like another cup of tea, Kimberley?'

'Had a run of good seasons up to '29. Not too bad all through the thirties, very dry again by the mid-40s. That was when

Horrie and his brothers went to war, and only Horrie come back. Forty-four, I member all the narrow-leafed peppermints dyin, and that big cryptomeria outside the Council Chambers, that was the year that died too. By rights, they should remove it. No second cut down on the Numeralla flats '44, but the highest rainfall ever we had here was in 1950. Two hundred and fifty seven inches and the sheep died o' liver fluke.'

'I'd been meanin to visit the Valley, as I feel sure the cattle will be there in the drought. Attis says he saw a coloured Kombi head down there, too, with some barber starver in it. Never seen it come back out.'

'When are we gonna get them cattle?'

'Very soon, Dad, though I've struck some resistance with your grandsons. We're bound to use horses, as we want the lot, and we don't want that fool of a neighbour wise to the fact we're cuttin through his fences.'

'I'll come.'

'Good on yer, Kimberley. I was hopin you might say that. You're the best young horseman in the district, since Barney went to Vietnam. And I want Attis to come too, get his head outta those books. I don't think he's been on a horse, since he won the juvenile campdraft at the Omeo Rodeo.'

'What horses we usin, boss?'

'Oh, there's some out there, somewhere. You doin anything Mondey? I thought we might break in the horses Tuesdey and catch'em Mondey. That'll be a long day. Wednesdey we'll set off. Norman, isn't it your bath night tonight? Don't you think it's high time you got the tub out, son?'

Kimberley Moon: late twenties. A Moon—the Moons, with the MacAnaspies, being the pioneers of that rough country between Obliqua Creek and the coast. Champion horseman, and quite a throwback, as he takes his bush ballad writing seriously. Concedes it was him got young Orion interested in the ballad form. Paranoid, umbrageous cove. Father-to-be of Turpentine, by Nisi Papadimitriou. Became a eunuch, but repented him of it, and receives hormone treatment from the hospital now. Runs the Wozzawunwun store. Sold me my

Phrygian cap, and the Holy Hand, which he nicked from the monastery.

12. *Description of a Land of the Ever Young.*

Northeast of Erinungarah Gap is the southernmost horn of that tiny Tertiary volcanic basalt cap, of which the old Potato Ground is the sole surviving MacAnaspie remnant. Between the Second World War and the Vietnam War, they bought potatoes at the shop. The remainder, including the scrap of plateau rainforest you see from the Valley floor, is in the hands of the Bunoo Bunoo (pronounced Bunabunoo) Pastoral Company, registered office Fivedock. That Johnson girl, Timothy Papadimitriou's wife, came from there. A parcel of land that might feed the Snowy Mountains if converted to a terraced garden is thus assured of growing nothing but grass and fattening scenic Angus vealers. The odd huge ribbon gum survives, to provide shade.

The rest of the Valley wall is dominated by a tough, infertile Permian sandstone, owned, pretty much, by the National Parks and the Forestry, which yields to a blue Permian shale, just above the talus, and a narrow coalmeasure. The plateau, from which the Valley is excoriated, is 2000 feet above sea level, and the hard floor of the Valley, though dropping away, half to a third of that height. The main road through to the coast used to negotiate this Valley, but then they built the new road, and then they built the dam. In the early Silurian Epoch, when this area was underwater, the Valley and its surrounds would have been part of the abysmal mud plain, which lay off the shallow continental shelf, which at that time extended to round Murrumbateman, while the Australian continent was still conjoined with the Antarctic. The combined coast extended no further east than Wantabadgery. A mid-Devonian interlude of instability, known as the Tabberabberan Orogeny, produced hereabouts, on the margins of the plutons, the odd patch of auriferous ore, but bypassed Erinungarah, as we can assume since we know of no local gold rush, and there wouldn't be a gully, or a creekbed, on the whole East Coast of this country, that was not assiduously scrutinised for gold by some poor rebarbative bastard wearing bowyangs. Thrice, during the Permian, the sea reinvaded what had now become an upraised river valley, and some huge Permian river delta deposited clay from a hinterland. Today, that clay is shale, but not yet slate; the sand, a tough sandstone, not yet quartzite; the organic debris from the putative intervening peat swamps coal, but not yet oil. There were trees, but they had no flowers then, and the reptiles had no feathers or fur.

Here where I live, so to speak, we're in the granite of a Carboniferous intrusion. The right arm of Wozzawunwun Creek is siltstone and there is mudstone below the dam, but the floor of the Erinungarah Gorge, which has of course been flooded by the dam, is an early Devonian conglomerate, and limestone from some ancient coral reef can be found above the white cedar behind Fool's Dope Flat. Near where Mehmed built his lair.

Geologically, the Valley is a curio twenty-five miles long, but almost ten of those twenty-five miles flooded, another ten sheer cliff, warmer than it has any right to be and full of biological upstarts, to mention only the plants. On the map, you will find the lower-case p's that delimit a National Park skirting the scarp. The Park's advisory committee would dearly love to see the Valley gazetted in the Park. Unfortunately, it is freehold land, owned by the MacAnaspies, and they won't sell.

Mehmed: Fled and hid in the Valley after murdering a local woodcutter. Reappears in the *Ballad* as the Greenbrown Man. One of the Valley deities, the others being Attis, Diane and Diane's children. Dusk and Sun disappeared the day their mother did, to reappear as waratahs.

ACT 1 Scene 2

13. Timothy Papadimitriou and Aloysius O'Looby. Olaf and Nisi arrive at the Wake early.

May '68. The Wake for Martin Luther King. The trainee teacher who answers the door knows nothing of any scheduled meeting, though it has been widely advertised, courtesy of Barbara's long-suffering Gestetner. The air smells of coal dust and soap.

'You sure you got the right address?'

'This is Barbara's place, isn't it? We know we're a little early.'

An hour and a half early for the Wake for Martin Luther King. Olaf Abernathy dissociates himself from the sordid fiasco. He does it through a pained expression, and by turning his back on his lady.

Olaf is wearing the clothes he would wear to a Lucky Grills/ Lucky Starr doubleheader at the Blacktown Workers' Club: cream and blue Paisley body shirt, Presley purple pants, with flared bell bottoms, punctate oxblood shoes over platform heels: *Swingin Shepherd Blues*, please Maestro. Because none of these items has a pocket (to prevent the bulky male wallet ruining the visual line) he is, in accordance with the revolutionary precepts of certain menswear designers, with limp wrists, obliged to carry his money and tickets in a hand-tooled handbag, slung athwart his torso. His concomitant effeminacy of appearance is comically offset by muttonchop whiskers. The car blew up the day before yesterday.

Nisi, many years Olaf's senior, has combined a short and unflattering A-line miniskirt, with false eyelashes, scads of make-up, but no protein wave. Her vinyl boots were not made for walking. Neither feels the need for sweaters in what is, to them, the mild Sydney climate, compounding an appearance of seedy poverty. They look a somewhat poverty-stricken, seedy, bourgeois couple. They even look as though they intend to move in; either carries a cheap green quilted cotton army disposal type sleeping bag, as do the boys, and Nisi, along with the Gossamer hairspray, and some foodstuffs wrapped in white butcher's paper, holds a packet of Maggi chicken noodle soup (eleven cents at Moran and Cato), a bottle of blackcurrant and apple juice, some Kraft cheddar in the blue pack, and a

Sunbeam electric Frymaster. The Frymaster has just been purchased from a pawnshop by Central Station, but a sixth sense cautions the man on the door against letting these people in.

'Is Barbara home?'

The man in the doorway doesn't know and doesn't like to leave the door to find out. The door cannot easily be secured. His feeling is, he may return to find the Frymaster frying up a storm.

Now another man who lives in the house is at the door, trying to get in. A solicitor, but not in a suit, he can't get past Aloysius, who has taken an instant disliking to him. Whichever way the good-natured young fellow moves, Aloysius blocks his path.

'Could you please take him for a walk?' begs Nisi. Her gaze expresses, to Olaf, four months of intimacy and the promise of more. She appreciates that Aloysius is difficult, and Olaf is not the boy's father.

'Come, Aloysius.' Olaf grabs the little bastard who, turning, throws an inconsequent punch. The solicitor fends it with his briefcase.

Two steps ahead of Aloysius, for whom he feels a guilt-stricken loathing, Olaf Abernathy heads off towards his former residence. From the day of Timothy's birthday party, advertised by balloons—into which, from that sinuous mountain track, Olaf wandered uninvited—Olaf's attention has been totally focused on Timothy's mother, Nisi Papadimitriou. Olaf is obsessed with the woman, owing to a basic misapprehension. He feels, for the second time in his life, an unequivocal, if aleatory, commitment. The first occurred when, like all mankind, he was born to the parents to whom he was born. He is not a Pom. He is not a female, nor a short dark man, nor a tall blond one. We may legitimately suspect, that had it been up to Olaf, to decide what race, what sex, what height to be, he'd still be pondering the problem. But somehow, we all contrived the resolution, described in the *Bardo Thodol*,* of the reborn spirit, heading for the womb, having failed to attain the Great Straight Upward Path at the moment of death. And few,

---

* Tibetan Book of the Dead

80

at this juncture, have the wit to declare, 'Ah! I ought to take birth as a Universal Emperor, or as a Brahmin like a great sal-tree, or as the son of an adept, in siddhic powers, or as a rural Post Man.' In Varanisi. It is a comfort, that The Blowing Out of the Flame of All Selfish Longing, which is Nirvana, may be accomplished from the *Bardo*, or from this life, or from Heaven, or from Hell: ask Balthazar Beauregard. But when it comes to deciding which womb, of the multitude available, were the more choiceworthy, then consciousness—which survives forty-nine days after death, according to Lamaic teachings, and there's a rub—employs no other criteria, than sexual attraction combined with jealousy, and is not this *Sidpa Bardo*, this last, and lowest, residue of the after-death state, which follows the *Chikhai Bardo*, the Clear Light, also glimpsed from the realm of clinical death—followed by the intermediate *Chonyid Bardo* of Karmic Illusion, the realm of alchemy—is not this *Sidpa Bardo* precisely that region of the Nietzschean *id*, identified by Freud as the irrational source of our anxiety, art and higher religion? And are not the delights of the kind described by Freud as 'poly-morphous and infantile' precisely those promised our Genera-tion of Sixty Eight, after their mandatory Revolution? I am indebted to Allan Bloom for this observation.

Choice, to Olaf Abernathy, appears infinite. He could live anywhere, work at any occupation (assuming he chooses to work), shack up with anyone he fancies—well no, not quite, not yet; it certainly helps he has found a woman who lives in a remote fastness here—wear what he wants, live how he likes. The effect of this overwhelming freedom is, paradoxically, a paralysis of the will.

Taste, according to Bloom, as the faculty of discernment, is an attribute of aristocracy; it relies, in its development, on a sense of tradition not seen to be arbitrary, but lapidary. *Ipse dixit*. In democracy, nothing is necessary and we are tormented by parallel lives. The power of doctrinaire abstraction, in democracies, first remarked on by Toqueville and confirmed by Saul Bellow, expresses the fact that, when the father is a welder, the son a lawyer, the grandson a chef, they have no choice but to temporise over their Xmas bonbons.

'The banishment of rusticity among a people,' says Hume, 'is seldom attended with any remarkable perfection in particular persons.' To the contrary, Ulpian says there were village schoolmasters as far afield as Egypt, by the third century AD. But this spread of primary education throughout the Roman Empire was accompanied, not merely by the extinction of a selfish intellectual tradition stretching back to Miletus, but, as Toynbee points out, by the overthrow of the *Pax Augusta*. A little learning is a dangerous thing.

By the time Olaf returns with Aloysius (now clutching the latest *MAD* magazine) Barbara Byng has been found, and she and Nisi are sprawled on the seagrass matting, in the velveteen beanbags, making a dent in a flagon of the dreaded Orlando Coolabah claret.

'Hello, Olaf,' says Barbara. 'Have you found a new short motor for your car?

Olaf Abernathy: Gawky, lost soul in granny glasses. Over-whelmed by democratic choice. Besotted with Nisi Papadimitriou. Comforted by her ample bosom. Reluctant stepfather to poet Orion, and most reluctant stepfather to the troubled Aloysius O'Looby. Good handyman, though: used to work as a builder's labourer.

Nisi Papadimitriou: late twenties. Plump networker, anti-war activist. Social worker's nightmare. Wound up with five kids by five different men, and lost them all. Poor Orion.

Timothy Papadimitriou: four years old at this stage, the second son of Nisi. A bright boy, who seems to blame himself for what happened in that Valley. As Orion, he wrote the *Ballad*, before he emasculated himself. There's a fair bit of Bob in the *Ballad*, and a touch of Kimberley Moon. Tim threw the *Ballad* in the outgoing mail, at the postbox, Obliqua Creek, and had he not done so, who's to say this story would be going on record? He dumped Cindy Ecks, when he got to high school, and ran off with that Johnson piece, from Bunoo Bunoo. Computer whiz. They put him in a mental home, where I can't see him, now my travelling days are over.

Aloysius O'Looby: nine years old in '68, eldest son of Nisi. A real handful. Hated Valley life, but loved West Indian music. A mate

82

of Alexander, centrefold Monica's son, but I can't track Aloysius, and have drawn a blank with Alex. So much for Freedom of Information. Alexander was/is one of those people no one notices. *Barbara Byng*: future senator, and ineffectual Minister for Housing. Forever being rolled in the Senate.

14. *Barbara's powers of observation.*

Now Barbara has never even met Olaf, though she knows his name and has guessed what's on his mind. We can attribute this to a phenomenal memory, the urge to put people at their ease, but some suspect there is more involved. It is certain, that putting the right name to a face, while pressing the flesh, is a vital political skill, and Barbara is blessed with preternatural facility. People are an obsession with her. She keeps huge scrapbooks and takes clippings from the daily papers, and the local papers too. Of particular interest are team games, orchestras, class reunions, conferences, funerals, wedding receptions. By the time she was captain of a big, prestigious girls' school, she knew the name of every girl in the whole school, and the name of every girl who had gone to the school in her time there, and the names of all the school prefects and captains going back to the First World War, and the names of all staff members, still living, whether teaching or no, and already she'd begun using these names as a basis for working into the wider community. She soon knew the names of the parents, and siblings, of every girl in the senior school, and the names of their boyfriends, past and present, and their penfriends, and their girlfriends outside the school, and their brothers' girlfriends, and the friends of their brothers' girlfriends, and the husbands, and children, of the married staff. At school concerts, she was able to address every person present by their proper name, and knew their interests sufficiently well to be able to exchange a few chosen words, whether concerning their recent hospitalisation, or their niece's performance at the previous concert, or their son-in-law's prospects in the forthcoming yacht race, or the likelihood of the relevant Council approving their neighbours' subdivision. All these topics she selected with uncanny, if apparently unconscious, tact. She never boobed. She never bailed you up concerning the divorced, or the deceased, or the disabled. I've no doubt she would have made a fine postman, but she had more ambition than I did.

Having commenced with her own family and friends, and working her confident way outwards, she is, at twenty-one, on speaking terms with a varsity nursery to the demographic hump, and speaking of humps, I never would. Only the more far-flung engineers and veterinarians are proving intractable. It is said she knows every resident of Darlington and Chippendale by sight, if not by name, all the shopkeepers of Newtown, by name *and* sight, all the publicans of Glebe, together with their usefuls and regulars, every member of the Anti-War Movement, in its various manifestations, and most of the residents of Balmain, Rozelle, Leichhardt, Lilyfield and Annandale, Eastwood, Epping, Denistone, West Ryde, Ermington, Cheltenham and Thornleigh. During the university vacation, she works as a bus conductress. I have heard she has been known, when drunk, to make tentative stabs at total strangers. 'Hello Claude,' she might say, 'is your little doggie feeling better?' Now I can pick a Rayleen, or a Prudence, or a Lisa, and so can any man, but I'm a damn fool when it comes to the fine distinctions among the Waynes, Shanes, Dwaynes and Jasons. As for walking up to a stranger, in the manner of an old acquaintance . . .

I suspect Barbara wants to know the name, and a few of the interests, of every Australian citizen. It's a shame she ended up in the Senate. I'm not even sure she wants to be PM, though it's hard to see how we'd keep her out. It is more the genuine interest in people, motivates Barbara Byng. She likes people. She wants to help people, if she possibly can, all people, everywhere. All people, without distinction. North Vietnamese people. Afro-American people.

Not certain he can face the prospect, straight, of encountering unfamiliar people, Olaf has mildly confused himself, with a surreptitious mull-up, at the oval. It is true, however, that pot, in '68, is pretty much the property of Surfdom and Show Biz.

Barbara Byng: should she get up as PM, this book becomes an unauthorised biography.

15. *Cindy Ecks. Calvin and Monica reawaken friendship.*

It's 2 a.m., after the wake and Monica Ecks has returned to the Paddington terrace. Young Alexander is tucked up in bed, sleeping soundly, but four-year-old Cindy is too excited to sleep, couldn't sleep at the party, hasn't slept all night. Can't get to sleep.

'Mommy!' she yells, for the umpteenth time.

Monica lifts her dishevelled head from the pillow. She is tired, drunk, and wants to dream of home.

'Now listen Cindy, you're gonna have to go to *sleep* now! I'm gonna be angry with you, presently. It's 2 a.m. and you haven't been to sleep all night, child. You got preschool tomorrow.'

'Will Tim be there?'

'I don't know. You wanna go pee pee? Wanna glass of water?'

'Daddy's here, Mommy.'

'Hello, Monica.'

'What the hell you doin here, Calvin? Whatta you want this hour o'night? Why you in the child's room?'

'Wanted to see my daughter.'

'She gotta go to sleep now, God knows.'

'Thought you would have changed the locks, Monica.'

'Cain't we go someplace else and talk, Calvin?'

'You always change the locks.'

'That's if we must talk. Now Cindy, if you don't hush up an go to sleep ...'

'I wanta kiss Daddy.'

'Nighty night, Cindy.'

'Daddy, do you know Tim has a real horse and he's gonna take me on rides?'

'That's great, Honey. You go to sleep now. Nighty night.'

'Daddy, will you be here at breakfast?'

'Don't know. That depends on Mommy.'

'Jesus, you are a shit. Let's go to the living room.'

'Ain't you gonna slip into something less comfortable, Monica?'

'Dunno why I'm the one actin deferential.'

'You wouldn't know deferential from a gearbox, Calvin.'

'He was there tonight.'

'Wouldn't know. Didn't notice.'

'Too busy eyein off some other man.'

'Listen Calvin, if you came here to sulk and pout . . .'

'Don't you sass mouth me, you bitch. I am sleepin in a goddam tent, three metres from a railroad track, cause of you. Not gonna keep doin it.'

'This is not the right time, Cap'n. Really don't feel I can argue right now, too tired 'n drunk.'

'Monica, why do you do it?'

'Don't know. No one knows why they do it, cept for you.'

'Yes, I know why I do it. I do it to express my love fr a particular woman.'

'You're too good for me, Calvin. We both know that.'

'Don't say I'm too good for you. But I do have to *understand* you, Monica.'

'I don't understand myself. And why does it have to be now?'

'Just want to help y'out.'

'This is when the drug squad call.'

'I won't sleep another night in that pup tent. I'm a senior research fellow, you forget that. A rat ran over my face last night.'

'I'm prepared to fly back to the States tomorrow. I think we should quit, Calvin, I'm not meant for marriage. Hey, may's well just kill myself. Oh wow.'

'I want to help you, Monica. If only we could *understand* your behaviour.'

'I cain't keep askin you to go through hell cause o' me, honey.'

'Does bein married mean a thing to you?'

'Well it does. You're a fine man, Calvin, an a good provider an a good father, an you deserve better. I'm tryin to help you, fuckwit, by gettin out of your life.'

'I don't want you out of my life. Don't you care what I want?'

'You're a fool. And I never heard you talk so much. You drop a tab of that strawberry fields? Saw it goin round.'

'Just a tiny piece o' blotting paper had no effect.'

'Jesus Calvin, what am Ah doin to you.'

'Ah know what Ah'd *like* you to be doing to me, Monica.'

'No no, it's a fake compassion, man. Wears off, believe me.'

'Monica, I still love you.'

'Calvin, please. No!'

'Don't tell me you don't love me a bit.'

'You're one of only three men I ever loved.'

'Then why do you go messin with these Hootchy Kootchy boys?'

'Don't you feel attracted t'other women?'

'We all yielded t'every impulse that we feel, whole world'd be like those freaks out in Balmain. Maybe, just this once, you could talk to me about it.'

'No, because you'll only throw it all back at me later. Men always do.'

'"Men always do." I hate it when you treat me like I was just another man.'

'You are just another man, Baby, and I'm just another woman. You can do better than me, Calvin. You owe it to your mother and yourself. As you say, you're a senior fellow. That's not shit, an I'm just a slut.'

'I won't ask if his cock was bigger 'n mine.'

'Good. Calvin, I am truly sorry. I wish, as always, I hadn't done it. I do not understand why I told you, but I suspect I may do it again, and I cannot put you through this again, honey. You're too fine a man.'

'Hey, don't you want Cindy to have her *real* Mommy bring her up?'

'You know I do. What do you mean?'

'Together, we can lick this thang.'

'You got a one track mind, and you're trippin, Calvin. I don't believe you ever tripped before. I cain't live through another six months o' your jealousy.'

'Yes, but, ar, how many crimes must a husbaind forgive?'

'Why don't you go beat him up? That's your problem. You're cowardly.'

'I'm not your first husband or your everlovin Daddy. I was raised a Christian. I won't do things that way, cause it don't solve nothin.'

'Solve this thing, understand that thing. Oh boy. We're in math class here. I need a drink.'

'Want a smoke instead?'

'Do what?'

'I got some grass.'

'Jesus, Calvin, you're turnin into a drug fiend.'

'When in Rome. Sides, my brother's comin out, an Ah got to get in shape. Ah'd like to think Ah could entertain him here, in m'own home. He's been through Hell.'

'I'll leave. I don' want to humiliate you.'

'I'd like you to stay. And if it happens you find my brother attractive, well *go* for it. You have my word on that.'

'Look Sicko, I'll only smoke this if you promise we can talk bout something else, OK? Deal?'

'I'm goin fuck you later, Baby. You know I am.'

'Guess you have that right. But later, OK? It's a real trip, see you trippin.'

'I did enjoy your spiel tonight, Monica, to change the subject briefly. Your paean to Family an the ole South. I fess I miss yer Daddy.'

'Liar. Yeah, cause they don't understand spades. I get tired o' bein sandbagged, Calvin.'

'Course you do. We all do. They don't understand things have changed since the days of the early Civil Rights Movement. Hell, I was involved in the Freedom Rides.'

'That's how we met.'

'That's how we met. Today, it's a matter o' Black Pride, Brother. Panthers don't want no truck with whites, Uncle Toms, or anyone else. You know they drew up that ten-point program in the North Oakland Poverty Centre? That is government funded.'

'They just want equal rights, Calvin. Same as you.'

'No, Monica. They got equal rights *de jure* since the Civil Rights Act o' '57, and *de facto* since the Freedom Rides o' '61.

Trouble is, equal rights don't guarantee equal performance. All men are equal is a democratic prejudice.'

'It's the basis for our American constitution, Calvin.'

'Hoss shit! Constitution guarantees freedom to reason. No mention of unreason.'

'Now you promised you wouldn't talk about that.'

'Show us your titties, then.'

'Mommy!'

'Oh Christ, that child is still awake.'

'He a nice guy, this Balthazar Beauregard?'

'He is utterly self-centred, honey. A complete prick. Did he sell you that grass?'

'Hell no, found it on the floor, next to the stovepipe hat. I suspect that stovepipe hat has a false flue.'

'False flue, hope it's not catching. Now don't you go way now, Calvin.'

'Look at that wall. My God, it's moving.'

Monica Ecks: has it all. Social position, looks, poise, education. Orgasms with total strangers.

Calvin Ecks: her male counterpart. Often taken for her twin. A cultured, beautiful, well-formed man, but unlike Monica, riddled with doubt. Aware, as a heterosexual male and scientist, he is the Blight of Spaceship Earth. Spasmodically impotent, hated by the *Zeitgeist*. But never became a eunuch.

I'd like to see him make some money, yes I really would. I wrote him, poste restante Mullumbimby, proposing a literary collaboration between us, *When You're Ageing and Your Partner Isn't*, by Dr Calvin Ecks, PhD. Me to edit.

16. *Ginnsy's bootleg tape played at the Wake for Martin Luther King.*

Ginnsy it was, Michael Ginnsy wore the stovepipe hat to the wake for Martin Luther King. Michael Ginnsy, the beanpole guitar player with the foetid breath. The topper was the hat he wore when he wasn't wearing his Red Baron special.

At some stage during the evening, Barbara knows she must act autocratically. 'Silence is the Offense,' says the badge on her breast, but she orders the hi fi switched off, without so much as calling for a vote. *Bringing It All Back Home* is the album that announced Bob's conversion to electric rock, with the sound that got him howled off of the stage at the '65 Newport Folk Festival. Half the mourners are on their feet, bopping to his *Subterranean Homesick Blues*, it's turning into a party. Pot is going every which way, and pot, in those days, had a kick. It is a fact, if a crying shame, our Cool One Million cannot seem to get down unless they are totally out of it. Their higher faculties stand in the way of free movement of the hips. When Martin Heidegger proclaimed our need to 'loosen up', to be 'authentic', he was speaking, unbeknown to him, the language of Howlin Wolf.

Nisi Papadimitriou, who discountenances pot, is on her feet, opposite the bombed-out Olaf Abernathy, who is playing air guitar with the spasticity of Joe Cocker at Woodstock. Something petite, there is, and curiously demure, in her twee little shrugs and twitches, though it would be inappropriate to judge her by these clumsy locomotions, which are neither art nor courtship, but the search for that unrestrained bodily movement, to the Heartbeat of the Laughing God (120 beats per minute) which was perhaps the first casualty of civilisations of the second generation. It survived, as the Rites of Dionysus, exclusively dance, in the Greek Bacchanalia, which the Romans, in the year 186 BC, saw fit to ban from their capital. Well, fair enough. They already had the Berecyntian Mysteries. The Pessinuntine Stone of the Great Mother, a black meteorite, was conveyed from Anatolia by five quinqueremes and installed in the Temple of Victory on the Palatine Hill by *vir optimus Romae*, the best man in all Rome, P. Cornelius Scipio Nasica, during the Punic Wars. There was, though, a problem, worshipping Cybele, in that She prefers eunuchs, and in particular, Her eunuch priests, known to the Romans as *Galli*.

Hic turpis Cybeles: Hail, the filth of Cybele. Juvenal. But he was thinking more of the Sleaze Ball and the Gay and Lesbian

Mardi Gras. The eunuch priests of the Syrian goddess get short shrift from Apuleius, too. Actually, Gay Lib began in the West, nine months after Women's Lib, June '69, when police raided the Greenwich Village gay bar, The Stonewall, and the patrons fought back, Well, one of the fuzz actually touched a drag queen's face, you don't never do that. By '81, a former colleague of Martin Luther King was instructing the New York Gay Men's Health Crisis in techniques of civil disobedience. By '91, the paedophile North American Man Boy Love Association could state (in applying for UN recognition): 'Differences in age do not preclude mutual, loving interactions any more than differences in race or class.'

Welcome to Secular Democracy.

'All right,' says Barbara Byng, 'I think we'd agree it's time we made a start, so may I hereby call this meeting to order?'

'My God,' whispers Olaf Abernathy to Nisi Papadimitriou, 'isn't that Michael Ginnsy?' The object of his awe is wreathed in native laurel, having recently completed a stint with Taj Mahal.

'We might ask Monica Ecks to speak first, and this, I feel, would be appropriate, because Monica, whom I haven't yet had the pleasure of meeting, is American.'

But it's Ginnsy, an Australian, takes the floor, albeit in a stovepipe hat, with stars 'n stripes.

Donning now my own clairvoyant's hat, which also features a few stars and stripes, I go so far as to prognosticate that, when the Moon is in the Seventh Phase, and Jupiter aligned with Mars, many here tonight will smile, in later years, at the recollection of a man wearing jeans with a top hat, long after they have forgotten every rural picnic race meeting they ever saw a picture of.

Have you wondered why witches, heretics, dunces and astrologers wear the Ku Klux Klansman's hood? This tall, pointed cone, so instinct with opprobrium, strictly speaking, a hood, first appears on the heads of warriors in the frieze of the Hittite sanctum at Yazyly Qaya, above the Hittite capital of Hattusas, near the present-day Turkish town of Bogazkoy. It was worn by Ottoman palace waiters and the Mevlevi dervishes of Anatolia down to 1925, when the order was dissolved by fiat of the

Westernising Hero of Gallipoli, 'Attaboy. Clearly, the Mevlevis, who whirled and danced to the strains of handdrums and the Phrygian flute were heirs to the Corybantes (Greek for 'high hats'), which was the cognomen given the notoriously boisterous priests of the Roman/Lydian/Phrygian Mother Goddess, by unbelievers, dancing to the beat of a different cymbal. The evidence, adduced by Toynbee, suggests a common Anatolian impetus for the Bacchi, the Corybantes and the Jewish prophets. And the vatic impulse again burst forth, around the time of which we speak, 'sixty-eight.

Stiffened, the hood becomes your red plastic witch's hat, lobbed out by your modern Council pepper-and-salt gang; relaxed, your Phrygian cap, as worn by Dopey, Santa and Wee Willy Winkie, your cocky's comb; relaxed further, the medieval *liripipium* on your supermarket can of Dante* olive oil; eventually, collapsed completely, the hood on your academic gown, and there wouldn't be many pointy-headed intellectchools not entitled to wear one.

Ecstatic prophecy? Yes, we'll give it a try. Why should the vatic 'world thinkers' of Findhorn, the fatidic 'hope freaks' of the Big Sur have all the fun? Pass us that bong. Flick us that roach. Hand us that tab of trippy eccy.

St Peter's was built atop the Temple to Cybele, on the Vatican Hill. The Rites of Cybele were practised in Rome for at least 400 years, having been incorporated into the established religion of Rome by the Emperor Claudius. Records of the celebration of the rite of the Taurobolium break off in AD 241, but the priests of Attis, dancing and singing, beating handdrums and clashing cymbals—sound familiar?—were still to be seen in the streets of Carthage, in the time, and much to the displeasure of, Augustine.

The Etruscans were Hittite colonials. The worship of Mary, where it is not the worship of Isis, is the worship of Cybele, the Etruscan *haruspex*, the Grand Inquisitor; both wear the conical cap. The Etruscan *bulla* to avert the evil eye, as worn by Romans—origin of the crucifix?

---

* Dante was a Tuscan, i.e. Etruscan, or Colonial Hittite.

The witch's hat, as worn by Yoko Ono, the Madonna on *Rage* and the greengrocer's wall, Bobby Dylan's big hooked beak, the *liripipium* in the portrait of the poet on the Dante olive oil can in the chrome checkout gurney, the hat on the Disney figurine; the academic gown in the Kodak ad at the chemist's shop, the plastic Christmas tree all lit up with plastic lights in the same shop—remnants of Hittite culture. But the Corybantes were down in the Valley, and though they wore Phrygian caps, the only stiff, tall hat they possessed would, I guess, be the one we are now admiring, Ginnsy's Uncle Sam topper, which acquired a gunshot wound. It became common property. The kids thought it good for a laugh. Ginnsy has doffed it, and puts it on a chair, whence the four-year-olds, Tim and Cindy, effect its removal. Eleven years on, Cindy might wear it the night she conceives her daughter, Passion-flower. Guilt, over dumping Cindy, who adored him from the moment she set eyes on him, unhinged Tim. But every man who made himself a eunuch down there had a bad conscience over women, don't we all? T'is the constant betrayal of women defines a man, in our monogamous culture, for male and female desires intersect, not precisely but imprecisely. Monogamy, in a man, is sacrificial, never, I suspect, congenial. And who can demand a sacrifice, that is not prepared to make one? That is why we dramatists are never out of a job. In their struggle for equality, women overlook that male fidelity in marriage is unnatural—just as unnatural, in fact, as a woman subordinating her will to a male will. The men of the Erinungarah joined their women in a rebellion against Nature, for tragically, men, though incapable of it, do aspire towards monogamy. That is made very clear in the *Ballad*, where in order to psych himself up for the Deed, the candidate repines the shabbiness of sex, and sees himself as having betrayed the woman within, through the woman without. As Kimbo points out, one spunk was adequate to serve all the women in that Valley, and Darryl and Eugene, indifferent to the loss of their immortality, took up the challenge. Which freed the remainder of the men for the Higher Calling of the Goddess Brigid.

Now for my prophecies. The carbonaceous chondrite of the

Kaaba and the Kalighat, also worshipped as the Diapete (*She of the Rock*),* will become the most sacred hallow of our third millennium AD. Symphony of pre-solar starstuff, Mother of the Gods, where the party started.

And, on a more prosaic note, the Aussie eucalypt, following in the footsteps of the Aussie crow, will colonise a warming earth.

Michael Ginnsy: deranged musician. Top hat, dark glasses. Became a eunuch.

Barbara Byng: student organiser. Slight, fair, braces on her teeth. Future senator.

Nisi Papadimitriou: dumpy, fat, not much of a dancer. Hates to see Olaf on pot.

Olaf Abernathy: Nisi's boyfriend. Also plays guitar, but cover versions only.

Timothy Papadimitriou: Orion the poet, son of Nisi. Cheeky little chap, full of beans. I wish I'd taken more notice of children, that I might bring Tim to life a bit here. But I didn't, so I can't.

Cindy Ecks: a delightful child, the daughter of Monica and Calvin. The kind of child makes you weep, to think her parents can't get on. She and Tim were encouraged to marry when they were just fourteen, and their daughter, Passionflower, was two years old in '79, and two years old, in '86, according to my calculations.

---

* A 16kg meteorite which fell to earth in Phetchabun Province of the Kingdom of Thailand in June '93 became, prior to its confiscation by the local governor, an instant object of veneration to the Buddhist villagers. The dimensions of the black Cybele are lost; it may be buried under the Vatican. The stone which Saturn vomited up, which is kept in the Kaaba at Mecca, would be about two feet in diameter, judging by the size of its original gold casing, which is on display in the reliquary of the Calif, at Stamboul. Indeed, the practice of stone worship is very ancient. The numen of the sun god Elagabolus, and of the ancient Roman god of Boundaries, Terminus, were stones.

I recall that I first read the *Ballad* at the Terminus Hotel, while suffering a terminal illness.

17. *Brian visits Paula's cocktail bar. Diane Zoshka.*

Nineteen sixty-eight, although you could scarcely guess the month from the weather. Always so mild in the city of Sydney, though not as warm then as it is now.

'Hi. You're early.'

'Wanted to beat the rush.'

'What will you have?'

'The usual. So what did you think of the wake for Martin Luther King?'

Brian, wearing a gaberdine safari suit, drove to Balmain in his Sunbeam Alpine.

'I only went because of Diane.'

'I didn't realise she was so young.'

'She's fifteen. It's a nice age. Adult clothes, but slides down slippery dips. You can't believe how fired up she gets.'

'I saw it. Her eyes were shining. She was talking to herself. I watched her.'

'I know. She's a fanatic. And so persuasive. She makes me feel I don't care as much as I should about everything. In the world.'

'I know what you mean.'

'How could you? You think she looks like me?'

'Well, no. You're obviously sisters, Paula, but no, I wouldn't say so. She's not a younger version of you. She's not as pretty as you are.'

'I think she's very pretty. She has fire!'

'I didn't say she wasn't pretty. It's just you're exceptional, in my view.'

'Uh oh. Here comes that man again. I better look busy.'

'Hey ...'

'No really, Brian, I must go. I'm under a slight cloud here.'

'What do you mean?'

'Tell you some other time.'

'No! Tell me now, Paula! I'll have another drink.'

'Brian, I'm not an Asian bar girl. You shouldn't be drinking, just so's to talk to me.'

'It's not just so's to talk to you. I was drinking here before you started working here. Alternatively, see me outside. Then I wouldn't have to drink.'

'No,' she says, but she says it with a pout, like a naughty little girl, and thus gives Hope. And the giving of Hope was regarded by the medieval Courts of Love as the first Gift of Love.

'Why not?'

'Because you're married. Look, we've been into this before.'

'You were saying? About being under a cloud?'

He's good-looking and wealthy. Marriage is no defence against Love. We are never safe.

'Oh. Well, there's my sister again, for you. She persuaded me a brassiere is a sign of female enslavement, and we shouldn't wear them.'

'You're joking!'

'So I came in one day without a bra, like the girl in *Au Bout de Souffle* and the manager got upset. The union wouldn't back me up.'

'When was this?'

'While you were in London.'

'You mean you actually worked here all day, in this public place, half-dressed? I can't believe it.'

'It was only for an hour or two. I got sent home. Look, I really must . . .'

'No, I'll have another drink. Drambuie. In a balloon.'

'It's your funeral.'

'Why? Why would you come to work without a bra, Paula? Was it busy that day?'

'No, it was quiet. Maybe not as quiet as this.'

'I see. So men saw you. Oh my God. What blouse were you wearing?'

'Same as this, I think.'

'You can see through it!'

'Not really. You think so? You know, you're reacting just like the manager? Why does it upset you?'

'You don't know, do you. My God. How could you do this to me, Paula?'

'*You?* Oh really. I wonder how you'd feel if you had to wear these clothes all day, Brian. Shoes like these—just look at them—that throw out your back, and tight, uncomfortable

96

undergarments. I wonder how you would feel about it, Brian. By the end of the week.'

'You're being disingenuous, Paula. You know that isn't the point.'

'Oh, but I think it is the point. I think Diane is right. You know, she doesn't wear a bra *or* a girdle?'

'She doesn't need one. Skinny as a rake.'

'I won't argue with you.'

'Mustn't argue with the customers. You didn't stick to your guns, though, Paula. You backed off.'

'So? I'm a coward. I'm a girl.'

'You can get a better job than this. Dunno why you keep doin this job.'

'Yeah, well you got a pretty cushy job I must say. You can start drinking ten in the morning.'

'Brian, you're going to be so very drunk and I don't have time to talk with you now.'

'Wait! Don't assume you know what drink I want. Always ask me first, please Paulie.'

'Very well, Brian. What drink would you like now?'

'Schooner of advocaat, please. Paulie?'

'Yes Brian?'

'I have so much to say to you, and you just treat me with such contempt, don't you.'

'I don't mean to treat you with contempt. You're one of our most valued customers.'

'Now that is just what I mean. That was not very nice.'

> All the men you have ever loved
> Are incarnate in me
> They speak with voices I cannot hear
> They smile with eyes I do not see
> And when we kiss, they kiss as well
> They lie beside us in the night
> And listen as you list their faults
> And caution me against your spite.

If ever I am filled with pride
That I am here and they are not
They tell me that they felt the same
And that they understand my lot
Better than I understand theirs
For at the close of day
One sees a pattern in the game
One may not see at start of play. *

'Heineken beer, please Paula. Can't you see what you're doing to me?'

'I'd say you were doing it to yourself. Seriously, can you afford to sit here drinking all day?'

'Can't afford not to.'

'What do you mean?'

'Have to sort things out. Today. Don't want you to think of me 'sa drunk.'

'This will be your last drink.'

'What would it take for you t'see me? Have cuppa coffee with me? Hm?'

'I don't go out with married men. It's simple as that.'

'Bet Diane would.'

'You're probably right. She probably would. Why don't you ask her?'

'You're not being ver' nice.'

'I think it's you not being very nice. I happen to know you have a pregnant wife at home, because you told me, and while I understand you're feeling, how shall we put it? Lonely?'

'Bitch. Just another drunk, ay.'

Later that night, the phone rings down a sparsely furnished corridor. Paula, dripping water, runs up the hall.

'Hello?'

---

* That's a bit of the *Ballad* I had to edit out. Fits in well here, though.

'Paula.'

'Who is this?'

'Brian the bibulous. Look, I know I'm out of line ringin you at home, but er . . . thought you might like to know I've left my wife.'

'Come again?'

'Left my missus cause of you. See, I can't say I love you in a bar, can I.'

'Oh fuck. You hardly know me, Brian.'

'We hardly know anyone. Love is not knowing someone, not for me. More the opposite. With me, it happens in a moment of time. Not that I should generalise, cause it's only happened once, maybe twice. See, minute I saw those ber-bepper . . . look, I really don't feel comfortable talking this way on a phone. Will you see me now please?'

'I don't know. You must be so very drunk.'

'Oh God. Oh Jesus.'

'Brian, this is a dreadful thing you're doing.'

'It's done. I already done it. I did it so that you would see me, Paulie, nothin more. It really hurts those other barflies, who don't love you, have seen your tits. That, I suppose, was the crunch. Look, I understand it may well be different for you, and you probably need more time.'

Diane, who is walking by on her way to the bathroom, senses something is up, scrunches up her salient nose. 'Who is it?' she inquires.

Paula's hand goes over the mouthpiece. 'Some guy from work. Claims he's rapt. Left his wife for me.'

Diane's eyebrows rise and eyes widen. Black eyebrows, freckled face, big nose. But strangely lovely.

Paula's eyebrows follow suit. Be impressed, plead Paula's eyebrows.

Paula Zoshka: mid-twenties. Barmaid and heiress. Elder, and more classically lovely, of the two Zoshka sisters. Mother-to-be of Mountain Gum, by Brian Chegwodden, and Mist, by Balthazar Beauregard. Lost them both to the Welfare. With women like Paula and Monica, as lovely as they were promiscuous, you can see the attractions of life in the Valley for local jinker drivers.

Diane Zoshka: mid-teens. High school dropout anarchist. The driving force behind the Moody Valley Candle Company. Common-law wife of Attis and mother of his children, Dusk and Sun. Defender of the Family. Made into a goddess, by grace of the goddess Brigid. Deadly enemy of Brigid. Lit the fire that burnt the Dome down.

Brian Chegwodden: late twenties. Frustrated writer. Handsome, skewwhiff journo—imperfection (poor posture) made him more attractive, and heightened his vulnerability. His mother married a quid. Obvious to Paula, if not to me, from his accent, as well bred. He got into the gardening, in the Valley, and established that grove of exotics, most of which survive. Father-to-be of Mountain Gum, by Paula Zoshka. Became a eunuch.

18. *Frodsham disagrees with Diane. Sister Annunciata.*

August 1968. Barbara Byng, who in Balmain is making ready to chair this evening's meeting, was never a member of the Communist Party. Had she been, she would have been expelled, for not toeing the party line on Hungary. She cannot, therefore, be described as a fellow traveller, though Derek Frodsham, who fancies her, thinks of her as such. Her braces have just been removed, and indeed, she deplores violence and opposes censorship of every kind. More importantly, she understands, as Derek Frodsham never will, the intrinsically unAustralian nature of Communism, which has more to do with its idealism than the nature of those ideals. If one may generalise and one *must* generalise, though I don't like to: you always libel someone: Australians are naive pragmatists, who distrust ideologues, so that Barbara, with her instinctive political acumen, dare not become, or seem, too 'political', for fear of offending her potential constituency. As an earlier demagogue (Cleon) observed, dullness and sense are a more useful combination in politics than cleverness and licence. Barbara does not consequently acknowledge, even in soliloquy, her political ambitions. At the same time, it suits the men to have a woman playing the role of amateur conciliator. As in the parliament, where everyone addresses the Speaker while looking at someone else, Barbara is an indispensable figurehead, who threatens no man, and is taken by no man seriously. Not a single member of the various, and populous, committees of which she is chair remotely suspects her of biding her time.

Jeff Grono, a ginger-haired mugwump, with a flushed, rubicund face, arrives at the meeting place early. He is in the front rank of every May Day march.

'Hello Sister,' says Jeff politely, for though happy to quote Lenin, book and verse, on the scourge of superstition ('Religion is one of the forms of spiritual oppression—*thump*—which everywhere weighs down heavily upon the masses of the people—*thump*—over-burdened by their perpetual work for others, by want and isolation'), nothing in his manner of greeting this nun will betray his unregenerate heart. But take him to the Vatican, and introduce him there to the World's Richest Bachelor, and watch him spit chips.

Sister Annunciata is in mufti, as always. Were she a priest, there'd be nothing but a tiny, stark cross on the lapel of her sports jacket to show it, with the arms drooping in despair, to form the Death of Man motif on the CND emblem. She'd swear and drink and punt.

'Is Archie coming?' she inquires.

It was about this time nuns began breaking loose from convents to shack up with ex-seminarians.

'Archie?'

'Archie, yes. Is he coming tonight do you know?'

'I have no contact with him, Sister, outside of these meetings.'

'I thought someone told me you lived together, Mr Grono. I am sorry.'

'Did you want to go in?'

'I think we're a bit early.'

'I saw Barbara going in.'

'All right. You know, it's a terrible thing they arrested you, Mr Grono.'

'And why is that, Sister?'

'Because you're a married, family man.'

'I am not.'

'I do beg your pardon. I thought someone told me you were a married, family man.'

'I see where the Pope's rejected birth control. I wonder does he realise the world's population is increasing at the rate of fifty million people a year?'

'Hey! Diane! Over here!'

Much later, after brooking many absurdities, Diane Zoshka's tirade among them, Derek Frodsham rises to his feet.

'I should like,' he says 'the indulgence of the chair, to speak against the motion just moved.

'Now no one who has just listened to this eloquent young woman can doubt the strength of her conviction. She is an anarchist, and proud of it, and wants the world to see she is serious. But, as a greater man than Dr Comfort, namely Lenin, pointed out, God has ordained the young should be stupid. For to die for your cause is, I suggest, less glorious than attaining your end, Diane, and if I may say so here without causing offence, a somewhat Australian sort of activity. The only way you're going to die tonight, love, is if you do the job yourself. Of course, there are precedents for this, but I ask you to reflect that when Miss Malpas, of Halstead, a CND member, killed herself when the Great Powers resumed atomic testing, she received next to no publicity compared with the Suffragette Emily Davison. This was back in '62.

'Let me attest, Madame Chair, I saw this young lady break the police line, July 4, outside the US Consulate, and could not doubt her courage, but did not observe members of the public, inflamed by her spirit and example, rushing to join her in the paddy wagon on that occasion. The course she proposes is more likely to result in bystanders making a citizen's arrest, than joining her with brickbats. The fact is, Diane, that by breaking the law in so childish a manner, you accept the limitations imposed on you by the bourgeoisie. They would be only too delighted, my dear, to see you immolate yourself, and your confidence, in being joined in the shambles, by others of like mind, is fantastic. Anyway, are these citizens, because they have been brainwashed into believing they are cowards, to be denied their democratic rights? Must they be slaughtered on the killing fields of Asia, because they have been bamboozled into supposing they don't want their heads broken with truncheons?'

'Chinovnik.'

'Shut up.'

'Thermidorian. Petty Bourgeois Restorationist.'

'Shut your stupid face, you goose. And shame on you, Diane, for your spiritual pride. You're a doctrinaire elitist and adventurist. You must never go outside your people's experience! By isolating yourself, as you have tonight, you have shown the folly of your criminal conceit. The litmus test of an activist, Diane, as you may some day learn, is to find an issue, like Vietnam, important to the masses of the people, and to rally the people around you, not behind you. To quote Trotsky, at the trial which earnt him a life sentence in Siberia, though he promptly escaped, "Gentlemen the judges, a popular insurrection cannot be staged, it can only be foreseen." The democrat seeks the will of the people. She does not seek to prescribe to the people, like a common businessman.'

'Or a pope.'

'Or a pope.'

Venceremos, Tovarishch.

Barbara Byng: future senator. Chairs any committee.

Derek Frodsham: Trotskyite. Marched against the bomb at Aldermaston with all those old Left Book Club subscribers.

Diane Zoshka: wild-eyed anarchist, who never lost her faith.

Sister Annunciata: late twenties. Tough-minded, mundane nun, on the verge of spitting the dummy with the Church. She it was, according to Kimbo, first saw Brigid, at the site of the Sacred Stone. Mother-to-be of Galaxy and Nebula, twins, by Balthazar Beauregard. They were identical twins, and I think they were separated by the Welfare. Now if a man could track them down ...

19. *Nisi argues with Olaf, concerning Aloysius O'Looby.*

Winter '68. There can be no more miserable winter than that endured by Australians in the high country. That is because there is no Festive Season, to look forward to, in the midst of it all. It just goes on and on.

Yet, by breaking our Northern cake of custom; by denying us the possibility of Aryan worship in these Antipodes; by forcing us to contemplate the birth of 'Our Lord' (Adonis) from his 'House of Bread' (Bethlehem) in midsummer, the foolish fathers of our First Fleet did us, I believe, an inadvertent favour. They rushed us into the Nietzschean abyss, ahead of the rest. They pulled Our Saviour from His Heaven, where an emperor set him up—and frankly, we feel no great need to appease the sun out here—burying him back in the cornfield, His rightful and traditional home. The Rites of Adonis, in Athens at least, were celebrated midsummer. Two thousand years of error rectified, with numinous results.

Nisi Papadimitriou gets back into bed with Olaf Abernathy, who dreamed his dream again last night, and sighs, a sematic sigh. 'Jack's crib-biting now,' she complains.

'I don't know why we don't sell that horse,' says Olaf, jumping in a bit too quick. 'He can't be happy out there in the shade. I don't think it's fair on him.'

'I don't ask you to give up smoking.'

'I'm not thinking of you, love. I'm thinking of the horse. I mean, in summer, when grass is growing . . .'

'He needs more room. Aloysius! Would you light the stove, please.'

'Hasn't he lit that bloody fire yet? Aloysius! Come ere at once.'

'Don't talk to my boy like that. Who do you think you are? All you've done, since you've been in this house, is make everyone else miserable.'

'All right, I'll leave. I'll go this morning. You pack my things after breakfast.'

'You're so self-deceiving. Why must you constantly threaten to leave? Can't I express a point of view, without you acting like a child?'

104

'It's obvious last night meant nothing to you. Oh. Aloysius.'

'Didn't you just say . . .'

'Get out. Go on. Light the fire! That's your job! How many more bloody times?'

'Don't speak to him like that, Olaf.'

'You're too soft on the boy, Nisi. That's why he won't do as he's asked.'

'He's just a normal little lad. You're going to have to make a bigger effort with them both.'

'Please don't sulk. He'll be all right. Boy needs his father to be firm.'

'How could you say last night meant nothing to me? You're so cruel, and so tyrannical, and I don't think you really care about the horse.'

'We've never been together *alone*, for Christ sake! Oh God, what's the matter now?'

'There's no dry paper or sticks.'

'Didn't I ask you to bring some in last night, son? Use straw.'

'I don't think it's going to work out, Olaf.'

'But it is working out, love. It's working out fine.'

'But it's so awful, isn't it. There's so much about you I can't stand and you must feel the same.'

'No. Now when you say The Shrdlu is biting his crib, what exactly do you mean?'

'Don't change the subject. And don't touch me there please, I'm not in the mood. Oh God, it's raining. I haven't washed your uniform for tonight.'

'Then you'd better get up and wash it at once. Hey, come ere.'

'No.'

'Come ere, y'bitch.'

'No.'

Nisi Papadimitriou: overweight femme fatale, holed up in the Blue Mountains. Horse enthusiast.

Olaf Abernathy: Geek. Not a bad handyman, but left the building sites, to work in a Shadows tribute band, for the Blacktown area.

Aloysius O'Looby: Nisi's elder boy. If he's in the City of the Plain, he'll be driving one of those speaker boxes on wheels, those vehicles that go 'cheopadippa chippadippa chippadippa chip' when they're pulled up at the traffic lights with the ragtop down.

20. *Diane's arrest. Brian instrumental in gaining her release. Johnny Dakota.*

July the second 1968, fifty students, among them Paula Zoshka's sister Diane, are arrested at an anti-war demonstration in central Sydney. Two days later, Thursday the fourth, another forty-five protesters, including Diane Zoshka again, are arrested outside the US Consulate.

It has been a winter of discontent. Bobby Kennedy, in favour of arms for 'Israel' (should be Judah), shot dead by a Palestinian. Tony Hancock, British comic, suicides in a Sydney hotel room.

Exhausted, Brian Chegwodden, who has been covering the Siege of the Glenfield Gunman, is lying on a chenille bedspread in his Campbelltown motel room, watching *Thunderbirds* on TV, when the phone rings.

'Chegwodden.'

'Oh. Is that you, Brian?'

'Paula! What a pleasant surprise!'

'They gave me this number to contact you, at work. I hope you don't mind me ringing. Brian, I have a problem. I was hoping you might be able to help. It concerns my sister.'

'Diane? Why, what's she done?'

'Oh, just got herself arrested for the second time this week.'

'Good God.'

'Anti-Vietnam protesting. You may know about it. When she was arrested Tuesday, at the War Memorial, she was released on bail.'

'Just a moment. Did you bail her out?'

'No. There was someone there from the demonstration bailed them all out, Tuesday.'

'Right.'

'Brian, I thought she was at school.'

'Naturally.'

'They're going to expel her, but that's the least of my worries.'

'They can't do it, Paula.'

'Yes they can. It appears she hasn't been attending school for weeks. She goes off in the morning in her school uniform, so I assumed she was going to school. I don't know where she goes.'

'How could you? And now she's living with you.'

'When Dad kicked her out, she had no place else.'

'I see. So naturally, you're concerned about her being expelled from school.'

'She *is* my sister. Her photo was in Tuesday's paper, punching a cop, in her school uniform. Did you see it? Of course, she denies she was punching him. She claims he had grabbed her by the arm, and that she was pulling her arm free, and that when a person suddenly releases your arm like that, it often looks in the photo as though the person concerned was punching the other person? Press photographers do it all the time, she says, is that right? Did you see the photo?'

'Ar no, I've been busy. So naturally, you are concerned about what to say to the headmistress.'

'Not at all. That's the least of my worries. She can go to hell, to Tech with her. She was arrested again today, Brian, and they're holding her at the station. They won't let her go.'

'But they can't do that!'

'You sure?'

'Well, they can delay things, Paula, and often will, if they're feeling particularly bloody-minded, but sooner or later, they'll have to let her go. Twenty-four hours maximum. It's a question of civil liberties. Has bail been mentioned?'

'I had a phone call from the sergeant who claims he made the arrest, and he wants me to go in there. Brian, you don't know what she's like.'

'Would you like me to come to the station with you?'

'Oh Brian, would you mind? You see, you're experienced, and there's no one else I can turn to, and I am feeling so *angry* with that girl, because of all the grief she has caused me, I can't handle it.'

'OK. Sit tight. I'll be there in a couple of hours.'

The arresting sergeant is friendly towards them both, initially.

'Would you like a cup of coffee?' he inquires.

'Thank you. Brian?'

'Yes please.'

'Help yourself. It's over there.'

'Paula. You're having a cup of coffee with me.'

'Where's my sister?'

'All in good time. Now you say you're the sister. Where's the parents?'

'She's been living with me.'

'I think I understand. Diane Zoshka ... she was here Tuesday. You'd have laughed to have seen it, Paula. Everyone milling around, trying to work out who's arrested who.'

'Yes, we know all about that, Sergeant. If you don't mind, it *is* getting late. Can we see Diane please?'

'Are you the boyfriend?'

'Have you any right to be holding her? What exactly is she charged with?'

'Did I say she was charged?'

'No, but we presumed ...'

'Did you. When I spoke to the young lady on the phone, did I say to you, Paula, your sister had been charged?'

'No.'

'What did I say?'

'You just asked would I come in.'

'That's right. I asked would you come in. Now I don't understand why this young man ...'

'I am a friend of the family.'

'Glad to hear it, Mr Chegwodden. That's cleared that up for me. Paula, you realise your sister was charged, only two days back, with several serious offences? Casting my eye over the charge sheet I see "resisting arrest", I see "assaulting a police officer in the execution of his duties", "offensive behaviour" ...'

108

'Come now, Sergeant. Give the girl a break. She has been released on bail, and a charge does not constitute a conviction.'

'You sound like a lawyer, son. What *is* your occupation?'

'Journalist.'

'I see. Oh well, if that's the way you want to play ... '

'He can go outside, if you like. It's me you're supposed to be talking to. Why are you holding my sister? Why is she not free to go?'

'She was taken into protective custody. I understand she's not yet sixteen.'

'Why did you take her into protective custody, Sergeant?'

'To stop her getting her nose pulled, son. Twice now, she broke our line, ducking between someone's legs, and I never heard such language from a private schoolgirl. I will not be called an effing pee by a fifteen-year-old private schoolgirl. You realise I could bring a charge of offensive behaviour over it?'

'Look, why are we trying to upset this young woman, Sergeant? It has nothing to do with her.'

'I'm afraid it does. If she is the child's guardian, and she admits she has no control over the child's behaviour, then her sister is an uncontrollable child. She could be made a ward of the state, sent to a girls' home.'

'Oh please, there's no need for that, *please*. Can I take her home now?'

'Take her home and keep her home.'

'You bloody bitch! You little bastard, I could kill you. I could wring your neck, Diane. I mean it.'

'Look.'

'What?'

'Chewing gum in my hair. Look, Brian, it won't come out. What they do, they chew gum, and as they throw you in the trawler, they grind the gum in your hair? So you can't get it out again? Fucking pigs.'

'Shut up, Diane.'

'Don't get her anything alcoholic, please Brian. She'll have a Coke.'

'*Paula!* Look who just walked in.'

'Oh my God. It is too.'

Brian is mortified to see his two companions staring at some man, who must be standing by the door. He watches, appalled, at the zombie-like expressions the two dupes dutifully assume. He can pick them for sisters now. It is clear they are staring at a 'star', some total stranger who'll be able to assume with them the intimacy of an old friend. No man could wish for more salutary sexual standing with a local woman than a foreign star, unless a foreign superstar, and we have the media to thank for this. Casting a fretful glance round the room, the 'star'—who proves to be a plump man with the oriental eyes of a native Indian—spots Brian, and makes straight towards him.

'Brian! How ya doin, man? It's Brian, isn't it? You interviewed me for the rag, the other day. Johnny Dakota, the singer?'

'Of course, Johnny. Won't you sit down? Johnny, you've heard of the Andrews Sisters. I'd like you to meet the Zoshka sisters. This is Paula, and this is Diane.'

'Hi gals.'

'So what is new with Johnny Dakota? What brings Johnny to this part of town?'

'Oh work, you know, Brian. Endless work.'

'Concert appearances all done?'

'Hell no, man, that goes on forever. Hey, what are we drinkin, gals? Can I buy youse both a drink?'

'No thanks.'

'I'll have a large Scotch.'

'You will not!'

'Come on, let her have one. Don't be a party poopa.'

'She is just fifteen, Johnny.'

'I'm jailbait, Johnny. Better watch out for me. So what do you think about Vietnam?'

'I dunno. I'm Canadian.'

'But are you happy with the situation in Vietnam?'

'I think we opened a whole can o' worms.'

'Paula and I will get the drinks, Johnny. You talk to Diane about Vietnam. She was arrested at today's demo. We've been over the road, bailing her out.'

'Fourth of July. I get it. By the way, Brian, I don't drink. Hey, before you go, didn't happen to see a man with red hair down to his waist?'

'Don't think so.'

'I'm fillin in for Ricky at the Latin Quarter. My new guitarist was supposed to be startin tonight, but he never showed. The guys kinda think he's around, so we're spreadin out to look for him.'

'Maybe Diane could accompany you, Johnny,'

'What are you saying, Brian? What kind of irresponsible comment was that?'

'Sorry Paula. I'm very tired. It was meant as a joke.'

'It wasn't funny. '

'Hey Johnny. I really dug your version of "Let's Have a One Night Stand".'

'Thank you, Diane. You realise they banned that track in the UK? Banned in the country that gave free abortion and junk to registered addicts. What a world.'

'You should be complaining. They murdered Che Guevara.'

'Hey, I really love this kid. Gotta go, but keep an eye out for the guy with the titian ponytail, won'tcha. If you do see him, remind him of his commitments. Fuckin musos! Pardon my French. Used him on the last album. Found him in the Ozarks, livin in one o' those Finnish Futuro plastic pods. I would have to say he looks like a freshly smoked mummy, from in front. Head like a Dayak longhouse. Don't take care of himself, you know? Been in trouble, too. Lost his green card.'

'You remember him, Paula. He was at the wake for Martin Luther King. I didn't realise he was famous.'

'He's not.'

Paula Zoshka: heiress and barmaid, but lacks confidence. Promiscuous, low self-esteem. Molested as a child? Just a thought.
Brian Chegwodden: journalist. Paula's boyfriend, despite being married. The kind of man (to quote Agatha Christie) women like but men have no time for.
Diane Zoshka: Paula's younger sister. Lacks diplomacy. Hates

the US military. The type we admire, in theory, but desert, shrugging our shoulders, in practice.

Johnny Dakota: late thirties. Part-Indian Canadian. Had a hit with that Crash Craddock cover, what was the name of it again? Appeared at the Three Weeds Hotel, Rozelle, in the nineties. Needs a new agent.

21. *Brian at a country house. Paula makes a phone call. Brian visits Johnny Dakota, where Ginnsy speaks of a glade within a grove.*

August '68, Burradoo. You wouldn't believe me, if I was to tell you the number of postmen work out of Bowral. The nobs must have their morning mail to read as they eat their breakfast, see.

'I let you down, Brian. You needed a father.'

'Look I can't stay here, if you're going to keep goin on like this, Mum. You make me feel I can't be honest.'

'Well at least we've always been honest with each other, son. And I was only being honest when I told you I thought you were too young to marry. But you wouldn't wait and wouldn't be told.'

'Yeah well, I wanted to be married.'

'You still believe in marriage?'

'It's natural, if you love someone, you want to be married to them. Anything less is a compromise. You married again.'

'But not for love. I can say that, because I never pretended otherwise, with Nigel. I did say, I thought I could love him in time. He never asked again.'

'I don't think time comes into it. And I don't think anyone really knows what they mean by that word "love", do you?'

'Women know what they mean. Brian, I want you to promise, that no matter how you feel about Prim at the moment, you won't say anything to upset her further. I spoke to her last night.'

'What. She rang?'

'I rang her. She is my daughter-in-law and I feel responsible for her. She'll always be welcome in my house.'

'Great. I'm glad. I think that's a very civilised attitude.'

'Phone call for Mr Brian.'

'Thanks Lorraine. I'll take it in the lounge room. Is it a lady?'

'Didn't sound like one.'

'Aha. A tart.'

'Brian, you're going to have to speak with Prim, sooner or later. I won't have this nonsense going on indefinitely. How you can allow such a silly disagreement to get so out of hand, at a time like this, is beyond me. It's only because I feel you're not entirely to blame I can have you here at all.'

'Hello?'

'Hi Brian. This is Johnny Dakota. Remember me?'

'Of course, Johnny. What can I do for you?'

'I just saw yesterday's paper. You did a job on me, man.'

'Oh yeah. Who gave you this number to ring?'

'I'm sorry. I take it your privacy is not to be invaded. Tell you what, I been around, but I was never white-anted like this. I'm thinkin o' seein a lawyer.'

'You do that, Johnny. I think you'll find you're wasting your precious time and money. Course, you have plenty of both. Talent, too.'

'I oughta come down there an ...'

'Don't make threats at me, Buster. I'll take you for every cent.'

'Why, you fuckin ...'

'Bye, Johnny.'

'Who was that?'

'Oh just some arsehole I interviewed for the rag. Wouldn't it rock ya?'

'Brian, I really can't stand any more of this foul language. It's so tiresome. There was a time a man would never use language like that, in front of a barmaid. I'm not used to it. And people are always saying you're so negative, in all that you write.'

'Yeah? What people are these?'

'Friends of mine, who are very widely read.'

Purple leaf prunus and box elder colour up well and drop their leaves early, so these are the species Brian's mother planted, behind her daffodil beds. For true autumn colour she has gone for the maple, claret ash and Persian witch hazel. A particular feature of Fall in the highlands are the flocks of berry-seeking gang gang cockatoos, to appease which the old hawthorn hedges of Withycombe have been left intact. Rowan and firethorn in topiary form, reminiscent of the brushes of a carwash, have been planted along the drive and by the tennis courts. But autumn, now, is gone, and the spring bulbs have finished flowering, though it's not yet spring. The daffodils, as so often they do here, flowered with the jonquils in autumn, but, providentially, the prunus was afflicted with shot-hole fungus, so they got what you might call 'scattered' sunlight.

Earlier in the week, a truck disgorged a load of supposedly sandstone bushrock, and Brian Chegwodden will now distribute this, under his mother's close supervision. In fact, it is mostly conglomerate.

'Well, shall we make a start? I hope you don't mind me giving Jock the week off, Brian. I thought, so long as you were here ...'

'No worries, Mum. Glad to be of help. I need the exercise. You must be real happy, the way yer garden's lookin.'

'It rarely does itself justice. It looks rather ordinary today, for instance, so dry. But sometimes, when the light is right, when there's been a lot of rain, and the sun, as it sets, comes out from under the clouds, and bathes the whole garden in that soft light, that light that lends such depth to things, well, you should see the colours then. *So* fetching. All the flowers come into their own. It's the main reason I never leave Withycombe. I couldn't bear it, do you see, if the light were to come when I wasn't here. One can never predict when the light will admit of being right, and even though it's never right more than two or three times each year, and though it never lasts more than ten or fifteen minutes a time, if I can be in my garden then, well, that's all I really ask from life. Am I being selfish? I do so hope you will see it, and share that experience with me some day, that *light*. Then you will understand. The way everything becomes more real, more deep, when the light is right. It's quite astonishing.'

'I see. And this is what you live for, is it, Mum?'

'That, and my family, of course. I can't express myself as eloquently as you, but it's more than just the colour in the flowers.'

'I reckon. Where do ya want this bludger?'

Brian, a pen pusher, strains his back, and next morning, has difficulty straightening up. So instead of labouring in the garden, he takes his mother for a spin in the Cresta.

'Look at them starlins. *Millions* o' the bludgers. What Pommy clown brought those into the country?'

'Perhaps they were here to begin with, Brian. I learned the other day that self-heal is a native. Brian, please turn off the radio. Having to listen to that rubbish is quite spoiling the drive.'

'The world's goin mad, Mum. I don't think I can hack the job for much longer. Ya cop the lot.'

'Whatever can you mean, Brian?'

'Well, you're always upsettin people, aren't ya. See, anything you write that's honest, or a true account of things as they are, it upsets someone. I envy musicians, know why? Cause they're not held accountable. They can jump up, in a furious rage, and play their music straight out of hell, and no one holds them accountable, cause they don't have to use *words*. They're lucky. They can't cause offence.'

'Oh, I wouldn't say that. I think we get the message. I do, anyway. Brian, stop at the shops, please. I want some ice cream, for when the babe arrives, and some champagne. Will you buy the champagne?'

'Yep.'

'I know that once you see this babe, everything will be just fine.'

'There was a phone call while you were out, sir.'

The help's come in to remove the plate of coloured cocktail onions on toothpicks.

'Please don't call me "sir", Lorraine. This is the Land of the Free. Did they leave a number?'

115

'It might be the orspital, Brian.'

Oh my God, it's *her* number. Close the door quick, it was Paula.

Dial. Thump.

'Brian?'

'Paula, I didn't expect to hear from you. Paula, is it still OK between us? I have to know.'

'We'll see. That's not why I rang.'

'Oh don't tell me Diane is in strife again.'

'Well, I am worried about her. What else is new? Where are you staying?'

'I'm staying with me mum, out in the country. God, she makes me tired. Why do they make you so *tired*? Who gave you the phone number?'

'Never mind. Brian, what do you know about communes?'

'Communes? Look, I can't talk over the phone about communes. You're going to have to meet me, I'm afraid.'

'Diane is thinking of joining one.'

'That'd be right. She can't stay a teenage rebel forever, so has to find some totally unacceptable way of growing up.'

'Is it safe, do you think, for a young girl?'

'Not over the phone, mate, please. Can't I come to your flat?'

'I guess so. Brian, I'm scared, it's like watching a good friend convert.'

'You do miss me a bit?'

'I guess so. Brian, you can't stay here.'

'Course not. I wouldn't suggest it. Not while Diane was there, anyway. She is still there, I take it?'

'For the moment. Brian, that was a cruel piece you wrote about Johnny Dakota. Poor Johnny! Why did you dud him like that? It was savage.'

'I dunno. Stress, It's my job. I got upset and he got in the way. It's all true anyway. Who knows? Think I should ring to apologise?'

'Yes, I do. I'll see you later, but only if you promise to ring Johnny first.'

'Hey, I was joking!'

This is ridiculous. Brian *ne regret rien*. Dakota knew the risk he took when he spoke to an Aussie journo. They do it to big-note themselves.

'Oh hi. Look, I'm trying to contact Johnny Dakota. Is he there?'

'Palooka! Phone! Who shall I say is ringing?'

'Doesn't matter.'

'I think he's in the loo.'

'Look, it doesn't matter. It's not important. I may call by, later. Tell him that. Will he be in this afternoon?'

'If he doesn't go out in the meanwhile.'

'I may call by, on the offchance.'

The band is gagging, having consumed a cocktail of imported Listerine with orange juice.

'Who was that?'

'Wouldn't leave a name. Said he might call by later.'

'Oh no. You shoulda put him off. How ya feelin, man? Cool?'

'Yeah feelin good, feelin fine. No bad breath.'

'Ginnsy?'

'No sweat. To me, this is just another trip. I've had millions.'

'No, this is not just another trip. Even hipsters lose their grip, with this stuff. This is a crazy, rhythm trip. They make it in Newark, 'n I got the scrip. Get Down Dust, it's called, and you'll flip.'

'Fark! You guys feel that just then? What was *that* about, my frien'?'

'Anyone not on the nod would recognise the Iron Rod. And now, my boys, so help me God, we'll synchronise this whole pad to that Iron Rod. Gerry, you take the kitchen hotplate, the one that crackles when you turn it on, mate. Ginnsy, you take the leaking laundry tap, the one that goes "plip drip", old chap. Remember, we have all day, and all night, to get down, and that's a promise. James Brown, even Les Brown, with his Band of Renown, 'll have nothin on us.'

'What will you be doing while we play the spouts?'

'I will get the vacuum cleaner outs.'

Brian picks up a pizza, family size, and they eat the pizza, and the strings of the mozzarella, as it drools from their mouths, makes them cack themselves. Paula, after a short absence, takes his breath away, and confirms his good judgement.

Or maybe it was the bottle of Mateus Rosé took his breath away. It always took *my* breath away. Acme of sophistication, the squat, distinctive tipple, and *de rigueur* when you flinched at the price of one of those chianti bottles, the which, empty in their wickerwork baskets, adorned the living rooms of young ladies' flats.

'So you're living with your mother now, Brian?'

Paula has chosen velvet bell bottoms, bare feet, white organza blouse; Diane, a torn pair of faded men's jeans, many sizes too small, and a man's herringbone blazer, many sizes too large.

'Just a temporary thing, Diane. Just till things sort themselves out.'

'Oh, things sort themselves out? How convenient. I thought human beings had a role to play.'

'Please, Diane. When someone buys you a feed, have the good grace to wolf it down without comment. There's a good little girl. Nice pizza, ay. They make the best pizza in Sydney.'

'Oh wow Paula, how could you pass this guy up? He's a mine of consumer information. Who cares if he's also a rat who just walked out on a pregnant wife?'

'Leave us alone for a while now, Diane. Didn't you have a meeting to attend?'

'With pleasure, my dears, but first I must wolf down my pizza. Wolf wolf! Paula tell you I'm thinking of joining a commune, Brian?'

'Yeah, but she didn't say where.'

'I don't know myself yet.'

'That's right. You *don't* know yourself yet, Diane, and I think you should wait until you are older, say twenty-one, before you make these important decisions. So many people have joined communes to find it's a one-way road to nowhere.'

'How was that again? A one-way road to nowhere! Are you fe real, Brian?'

'How will we solve the world's problems, from a rural backwater, Diane?'

'Who says we're leaving the city?'

'I thought the whole purpose of communes was to get back to basics. You know, mud? Cowshit?'

'We have to begin with ourselves, Brian. We start by making our own pizzas.'

'Oh, spare me. This, after you've just eaten more than half of the one I purchased!'

'I *am* a growing girl. Course, I wouldn't expect you to understand that. You just walked out on your own daughter. Prick.'

'I know more about gardening than you, kid. I spent all last week shifting bushrock, and as for my own daughter, for your information . . .'

'Sorry, must run. Most impressed. Thanks for the pizza. Paula, can you lend me five dollars please? I'm off to my meeting. Be good kiddies. I'll be back around ten.'

'Is that a promise? Here, take this. Keep the change, and buy some make-up.'

How many guys have pulled on these? He wishes he didn't have to ask.

And she can't remember. Doesn't care. Just shrugs, when he insists.

He decides to amuse, with a short story. She's lying on top, pressing her full, red mouth against his, when he'll let her, but he'd rather push her shoulders back, and ease her up, so her big plump boobs, one of which has a hair next to the nipple, hang down over his mouth. Phrygian Tantalus, in the Orphic myth, for divulging the Secrets of the gods, was tortured by having a cluster of luscious fruit hang just out of reach. Well, even when he got his mouth around the fruit, he found it still out of reach, and he found the bitter-sweet juice he could work from it making him more thirsty, rather than less so.

Paula has stripped to the waist, but there'll be nothing below the belt, not tonight. This was an age in which girls said no, and guys took no for an answer.

'Mmbleer. Did I tell you I called round to see Johnny Dakota as requested? Mmph.'

119

'No. Oh, what are you doing now? Don't do that. I'm getting a cramp.'

'Let me rub it for you. It was a most amazing scene. I must have interrupted something, but what? Mmpfuph.'

'Come on, that's enough now. Let's get dressed. I'm cold.'

'OK. Yeah, they had all the kitchenware out, and they were going round tapping things, and stroking things, and all the while listening intently, and all the taps in the place were dripping, and all the appliances were switched on. It was Bedlam. They'd been drinking mouthwash. I could smell it on them. That guy with the long red hair was there, right into it. Wearing a Biggles hat. You know, the one that got busted? Ginnsy?'

'Did you apologise?'

'Yeah. Johnny was quite friendly, actually. Hey.'

'Hmm?'

'I love you.'

'You just love these. Now you've had a taste, I don't expect to see you again. Do me up, please.'

'Oh, you're so unfair. Yeah, they all wanted to talk at once. My God, they wouldn't shut up! When he heard I was a journo, the guy with the long red hair started raving on about this secret Valley he found, somewhere down on the far South Coast or East Gippsland, and how he'd been isolated down there, and cut off from the world, and all the weird things that had happened to him, and how beautiful it was, and oh, the wonderful people that live there, and of course, he made me think of Diane. An enthusiast. He lost his dog down there. The van got trapped. He's absolutely desperate to get back.'

'What's stopping him?'

'Can't find the place. Doesn't remember where it was.'

Brian Chegwodden: had, I am told, a blissed-out look, like someone who's just run the City to Surf. Which may account for Paula's infatuation with him. Shows his social class, in his proclivity for petting.

Paula Zoshka: gorgeous, amenable, but something wrong somewhere, her nipples don't get hard when they're sucked. Of course, that may have only been when Kimberley Moon was sucking them. Kimbo had slept with Paula. Everyone slept with everyone down there, excepting Attis and Diane. The same thing happened in all these communes, according to what I've heard. What of Soul was left, we wonder, when the kissing had to stop? (Browning)

Diane Zoshka: possessed of the warrior spirit makes for the best anti-war demonstrator.

Johnny Dakota: introduced Get Down Dust to Australia. Under its influence, the user speaks compulsively in four-bar patterns, the same rhythm Orion uses to write the *Ballad of Erinungarah*. This rhythm is not arbitrary: it is the rhythm of the beating of the heart, the most fundamental of all rhythms. Hymns to Cybele, in ancient Greece, were written in Galliambic metre. This is the metre the Roman poet Catullus employs, two thousand years back, in the last extant hymn to Cybele written before Orion's. I think it fair to call Orion's *Ballad* a hymn to Cybele.

Super alta vectus Attis celeri rate maria
Phrygium ut nemus citato cupide pede tetigit (et cetera)

Seven stresses with a breath for the eighth. Stupid bloody academics, have no rhythm, can't see the eighth beat. They mistake the Galliambic metre for a seven-beat bar, but it's eight, of course. Classical blues beat, classical reel beat. The original rock, samba, reggae beat.

All Roman writers, not just Juvenal, disparage the Great Mother. The priest of Attis, according to Catullus, above quoted, is to be pitied. Orion has not just written the only hymn to Cybele in two thousand years; his is the first positive portrayal of emasculation in all literature. Because the sacred originals have not survived.

Makes you think, ay, gives you pause. We live in terrible times.

Act 3

22. *The plight of civilised peoples. Communes. Mehmed orders a ring from Balthazar.*

'In consequence of the successive violent deluges that have occurred over the past 9000 years,' writes Plato in the *Critias*, 'there has been a constant movement of soil away from the high altitudes; and, owing to the shelving relief of the coast, this soil, instead of laying down alluvium, as it does elsewhere, has been perpetually deposited in the deep sea round the periphery of the country or, in other words, lost; so that Attica has undergone the process observable on small islands, and what remains of her substance is like the skeleton of a body emaciated by disease, as compared with her original relief. All the rich, soft soil has moulted away, leaving a country of skin and bones. At the period, however, with which we are dealing, when Attica was still intact, what are now her mountains were lofty, soil-clad hills; her so-called shingle plains of the present day were full of rich soil; and the mountains were heavily afforested, a fact of which there are still visible traces. There are mountains in Attica which can now keep nothing but bees, but which were clothed, not so long ago, with fine trees producing timber suitable for roofing the largest buildings; the roofs hewn from this timber are still in existence. The annual supply of rainfall was not lost, as it is at present, through being allowed to flow over the denuded surface into the sea, but was received by the country, in all its abundance, into her bosom, where she stored it in her impervious potter's earth and so was able to discharge the drainage of the heights into the hollows in the form of springs and rivers with an abundant volume and a wide territorial distribution. The shrines that survive to the present day on the sites of extinct water supplies, are evidence for the correctness of my present hypothesis.'

In fact, it was Themistocles tore down the forests of Athens, to build his fleet. The Roman Imperial Public Baths destroyed what remained.

Plato was a virgin-born divine man, according to his countrymen.

This reduction, by the fourth century BC, of the Attic peninsula to yet another olive grove (the same thing happened to

125

Palestine, following Joshua's injunction to the Jews)—and bear in mind the Messiah is literally the 'Christ', the Anointed One, the man with the olive oil on his head—this reduction stimulates Solon's economic revolution; the replacement of subsistence farming by cash crop farming, the development of money, of a merchant marine, of potteries in which to build the pots in which to export the olive oil; and also accounts for the building of the Parthenon from stone, in the absence of a supply of Lebanese cedar. Further north, the victor in the Pythian Games at the Delphic amphictyony, originally a shrine to Cybele, can no longer be awarded a wreath of oak, and must make do with a laurel wreath.

Hear this: let me float this one past you, as we say. I propose that Civilisation, as we know it, is a ruse to evade the consequence of sylvan degradation. The view of Civilisation as an enormity, in response to abandonment by God, is the theme of Moses' *Genesis*, Plato's *Politicus* and Virgil's *Fourth Eclogue*. It appears, in the West, most forcibly, in the anti-Enlightenment thought of Rousseau, yet I do not know that any of these thinkers specifically identifies deforestation as the prime evil. If it is, it is unsurprising to find our growing reverence for trees and forests, accompanying the general Postmodern reversion to a barbarism of West African origins, itself the condign consequence of the late modern Western slave trade. It's not that the cutting down of trees threatens Civilisation; more that Civilisation can't begin till the trees are gone.

In little more than 200 years, we Europeans and (lately) Japanese have clearfelled about eighty per cent of the tree cover in the land of the stump-jump plough; yet in slowing down, to the extent we have, and whatever the merits of this (in)decision, I claim we have disavailed ourselves of the comfort of our tutelary deities. In theory, forests are renewable; in practice, they have never been renewed. As we cannot forever persist in our present irresolution, and while still we import the bulk of our olive oil— there's no export market for the Green Munga, as Calvin found to his dismay—we must thus revert to an aboriginal barbarism (which even the Aborigines don't want), or invent a new form of Western Civilisation, or more likely, accept that our own Civilisation, if not *all* Civilisation, is doomed, take up the

Challenge of New Ground, as they did in the Vale of Erinungarah, and devise, or disinter, a religion to act as a chrysalis for some as yet unborn affiliate.

Communes: the postmaster at Nimbin claims ninety per cent of the local population of 4000-odd souls was on the dole, or the single mother's benefit, or some other form of social security, by '84. Back in '68, when the population would have been closer to 400, I estimate that no more than fifty per cent of the population would have been on welfare.

Now the Northern Rivers area of NSW was the first in this country to be colonised by the young folk whom Zablocki ('81) has so eloquently categorised as 'classless, white, urban, liberally, but not professionally educated, and insulated both from any real danger of slipping into poverty, and from any real opportunity of becoming absorbed into a demanding, and worthwhile, career'. Nothing a degree in sociology, or a motorcycle rider's licence, couldn't have put right.

Shares in the Tuntable Falls Commune, $200 a throw, were not made available to the general public till '73, and it's fair to say this commune, near Nimbin, with its 300-odd members, remains the best known, as well as one of the biggest, and oldest, about. But what is *not* so widely appreciated is that, according to the postmistress at Tabulam, there was an even larger community in the Happy Valley, on the Upper Duck Creek at Old Bonalbo, as long ago as '68, i.e. contemporaneous with Oz, in Pennsylvania, and California's Paper Farm, but it lasted only two months; and the citizens of *this* community (the Happy Valley Candle Company Co-op, as they styled themselves)—which was, of course, a commune in name only, as the Hamlet Development Act, that formula for introspection, was not promulgated till the '70s—would have brought their beeswax candles, their flooded gum honey, all inherited or purchased, into The Channon, and there, during their brief spell in the sun, they would have set up on card tables, outside the old dairy, on a Saturday morning, their produce (radishes), their coloured stones, their woven rattanwear hats, and people from far afield would have come along to buy.

Some time after the Balmain Wake for Martin Luther King, Balthazar Beauregard returned to the North Coast of New South Wales. He has set up his jewellery stall at The Channon, and Mehmed Contramundum is looking for a ring, so it's inevitable the two should fall into conversation. They are vaguely familiar to each other, having met at Barbara Byng's wake for the Reverend Doctor King, on one of their frequent, though independent, visits to what the poem calls 'The City of the Plain' in reference to Sodom. They had a Bible in the Valley.

Balthazar has cured himself of his longing for Monica Ecks, as he thinks, by flight and expeditious cohabitation with someone drab. His stall assistant Rainbow, though a pleasant enough girl, is no head-turner. No scarlet lips here, nor tight jeans with high heels, nor cashmere sweater, to flaunt the small of her back: no make-up of any kind, and a tatty floral cotton smock, and buffalo hide besandalled toes, with dirty toenails. But significantly, no perverse and manipulative revelling in her impact on men, because there is none: Mehmed doesn't give her a second glance.

Mehmed Contramundum is wearing his heavy round hat, or telpek, made of goat fur, with a faded rawhide jacket and a pair of Kazakh trousers, under ugg boots. He has recently partaken of a bowl of yoghurt, and globules of yoghurt, and not necessarily the yoghurt of which he has recently partaken, adhere to his beard and moustaches. These are the whiskers of a man who will never kiss a woman or consult a mirror, and the matutinal bowl of cold water, in which he undertakes ablution, and, later in the day, rinses the dishes and spoons from the day before, is both too ineffectually applied to his face and insufficiently warm to dissolve the residue of a diet based on dairy fats and pumpkin soups. Planning a raid, he will often look up from a map, as though in thought, and it is then that his tongue makes its degustatory sorties, as far as it can reach. Mehmed has just returned from a binge. A binge drinker of the old school, he disappears during a binge and afterwards reproaches himself. During a binge he drinks vodka by the crate and eats only mutton plov.

He seizes an armband, and weighs it with a discriminating forefinger. Next, he picks up a silver bracelet, and holds it to his nose. Finally, he scoops a selection of roach clips, and, hiding these behind his back, raises his gaze to Balthazar's, who hopes there will be no trouble.

'May we help you?' inquires Balthazar.

Mehmed thinks. As he does, he looks at the scene beyond the *souk* and gives thanks. Mehmed looks the kind of man might seize two roach clips, and apply them to his own nipples, or yours. He was never a people-oriented person, more a number cruncher, but every tree remains a miracle to him. Paradise (Old Persian, *pairidaeza*, a garden) is here and now for Mehmed, and like the primitive Muslim Arab, he fights the good fight, under a plain green banner.

'You make all these?' he inquires.

Balthazar has seen him only the once and he's not a man you would forget, although you'd try. Tattooed, like an Assyrian *gallus*. His manner, his bearing, his scars, contrive a mockery of the *Zeitgeist*, as understood here. Can't he appreciate he's not welcome?

'Some I import from India.'

'Hand baggage of friends?'

'Some are imported from India, yes.'

Mehmed glances left and right, like a man about to take a piss by the road. 'Ask the girl to go away,' he says. 'I want to speak with you, man to man.'

'Why?'

'Ulcers to your soul, just do as I ask. Here, girl. Buy three slices of carrot cake, with this.'

'Go, Rainbow. It's all right.'

'You've been laughing, selling, buying. Count your cash, and you'll be crying, but I give you the chance to make real money. You got penis rings?'

'Penis rings. They wouldn't fall off?'

'Not if inserted properly.'

'Inserted.'

'Yes, you put them in. Of course they fall off, if you put them on. You don't make them?'

'Not as yet.'

'Yet you say you know India?'

'Go there often. Rainbow and I are planning a trip.'

'You never saw an ampallang?'

Mehmed presses the four fingers of his left hand together, with his left thumb. He could hold a hundred letters in this hand and still ride a motorcycle. Then he lays his right middle finger over the top of the simulated glans.

'It's a piece of threaded rod. It goes through the head, here, and normally, you keep it capped with ivory studs. Then, when you want to go with a woman, you replace the studs with small balls. Sometimes, not so small.'

'If that's what you're after, why not try the hardware store in Casino?'

'I mentioned it, because you mentioned India, ulcers to Her soul.'

'I never saw an Indian penis. They turn their back, or squat, when they piss.'

'I've seen a cardboard box full. Many wore ampallangs.'

'Oh really, look I . . .'

'Have the goodness to hear me out. I am not in the business of pleasuring women, but there are times when a man, for practical considerations, needs to restrain his movement. As you may be aware, the Prince Albert wore a penis ring, on ceremonial occasions.'

'No, I didn't know that.'

'The Prince Albert is a nose ring, but it goes through the tip of the urethra, not the septum. You make bull rings?'

'Not as yet.'

'Get your act together. In the middle of a beef and dairy district you must make bull rings. Look, I tell you what, I buy you a bull ring, from the vet, and you make me a copy, in gold. Size should be about right.'

'Listen Pal, have you thought this through? I mean, if you've got two holes in your cock, what happens when you piss?'

'And what happens, on a movement detector, as you dash naked, tree to tree? Don't hang noodles on my ears. You are so obsessed with women you think a penis gourd is for modesty?'

'Carrot cake,'

'Thank you, Rainbow. What is this thing called, Love?'

'Those are Rainbow's runes. They are not for sale.'

Balthazar Beauregard: good jeweller. I had an ear pierced at the same time as I got my tatt, and I'm wearing one of Balthazar's sleepers. Well, if you're not prepared to keep up with the times, how can you hope to understand them?

Mehmed Contramundum: the Greenbrown Man. Kimbo, who's been the main source of my information—I have tried to talk with Darryl MacAnaspie, but he just threatens me with a shotgun: Harley and Norton, his boys, interest me, and Darryl must take me for a pederast—Kimbo wasn't clear as to what kind of tree Mehmed metamorphosed to, but suggested casuarina.

I should never have shown Kimbo that poem. Too late. And what of Mehmed's 'last stand'? That may refer to what he did with Smitty, or what Attis did to him, I don't know. I do know they were shit-scared of him down there in the Valley, except Diane. He was shit-scared of her.

23. *Obergurgl Lodge. The Phrygian Cap. Kimberley Moon in Wozzawunwun. Calvin and Monica visit Nisi and Olaf.*

Talking about those stalls at The Channon has put me in mind of how I stumbled on the Phrygian cap. As I mentioned, I'd been working for years as a relief postman, which is a great strain—if you don't know a married woman's maiden name, you can't do a proper job—but only in New South Wales and Victoria. The final straw was being asked to attend the Stay Upright Course, if I wanted to keep my job. Stay upright, I said, you've got to be joking! But as it turned out, he wasn't, and he was only some clown, acting up. Singlets, we called him, he was never off your back.

I did speak to the Union rep, but he did nothin. Mirrors, we called him. He was always going to look into it.

I'd had the *Ballad* for a year or so, I was puzzling over it. Orion changed the names of the characters, which is a wise course, but didn't help me. I was still delivering mail, so my time for detective work at Obliqua Creek was limited. I couldn't

131

get back there often enough, and my inquiries had drawn a blank. To be frank, I was starting to think the poem was the product of a warped imagination.

I am forced to conclude that poem was posted no more than a week before I found it, although its vague chronology suggests it was conceived and written over a period of years. The Valley was cut off from the outside world, by rockfall, in mid-79. Orion speaks of an 'Indian Summer', which means, in my book, April or May, but there is a slight chronological inconsistency further on when he speaks of his first trip back as having occurred on 'Queen's Birthday Weekend'. Cindy, that same day, speaks of the communards as having been drunk at a Solstice Party. Now both these events occur in June, though he has the order confused, but I think we can safely infer the goddess Brigid appeared sometime that month. The Gap Road was reopened by Darryl and his team in May '86. Timothy Papadimitriou, diagnosed schizophrenic, was committed to the Bloomfield Lunatic Asylum, in Orange, in autumn 1990.

I can't see him there. They won't let me in.

Winter '91 I was holidaying at Obergurgl Lodge, the Postal Institute cottage in Thredbo, very popular, and booked out years in advance. On the fateful morning, it was clear and bright, so I took the Crackenback chairlift to the top. Do you know that night I couldn't sleep? I became delirious. Mistook my sheet for a sheet of stamps.

Yes, something I had seen on the slopes had left me with a sense of unease. I hadn't a clue what it might have been, so cleared my mind, best I could, and went into angel gear over a tall, frothy glass or four. As with some address you can't recall, it's no good torturing yourself: you must, however, readdress the problem, for fear it evanesce.

On my second last day in Thredbo, by which time I'd recovered from my fever, I was coming back down the chairlift when it stopped to allow for the loading aboard of a skier with a broken leg. I was put in mind of the time I rode the Cha Cha at the Cow Flat Show, for a bet. The attendant, thinking he was doing me a favour, left me up there for half an hour. On this occasion, I was left, suspended, hanging over the creek, and as I sat there shivering—for I found my Australia Post wet-weather gear unsuited to the conditions, and could only wish I had socks on under my gumboots, as both eventually fell off—I saw her again, and knew the instant I saw her a second time, that girl had occasioned my unease.

It wasn't so much her as the hat she wore. I'm too old for love. A piece of smart snow-wear it might have seemed to you; Santa wears the Phrygian cap, as do Grumpy and Wee Willie Winkie. And being, as it was, midwinter, the Phrygian cap looked *à propos*. For here was no *libertinus* wearing a *pileus*, the Roman freedman in his Phrygian cap of red felt, which became the *bonnet rouge* of the French Revolutionary. Our cap in question was no nightcap, for it had no white pompom, and it wasn't felt but velvet, and it wasn't red but sky-blue, and star-spangled, like the roof of the Hampton Court Chapel. It was those stars must have set me off. They glowed in the snow, as I recall. I also recall Attis was given just such a cap, by his consort Cybele.

The original Attis.

Was this, perhaps, one of those caps I knew so well from my *Ballad*? I asked the girl had she made the cap herself, when later I caught up with her. No, she replied, got it from the shop at Wozzawunwun. Know the place?

Only by the postcode, I confessed, playing Mister Beasley to her Blondie.

I rode out next day, and I found Wozzawunwun at the end of a long, winding dirt track, full of potholes, and it looked to me a place that had died in the arse, and not for the first time. An abandoned railhead, on a derelict branch line, with an abandoned sawmill, consoling a dead Ford Blitz truck, blackberries spewing through the windows, and the main street, unsealed, lined with dusty grey Bhutan cypress. I was excited; I knew mail written here would fall into the catchment for Obliqua Creek, which is not far off as the crow flies. Dead showground. Ruined tennis courts. Couple of fibro dwellings, and each of them with a jagged, triangular hole by the front door, and they were smeared with mud and moss and sump oil. The church, of corrugated iron, was painted red, like the one at Golspie. A tethered goat of a town, a plastic rose of a town, in a Vegemite bottle. Its sole redeeming feature was the view, to the east, of

133

the Erinungarah Plateau, rising sheer from Wozzawunwun Creek. From a couple of miles further on, they tell me, you're looking down the throat of the gorge, towards the lights of some coastal town. I wouldn't know. *Non scire fas est omnia.* You can't expect a man to know everything. Even a Post man.

Yet behind the bowser on the footpath stood an Avalon cafe, with its faded, rainbow awning; this royal blue-coloured general store-cum-caff, for sale, as they always are, that dealt in second-hand books and Devonshire teas, handcrafts, sliced bread, Aquarian remainders and reminders, Pepsi, you name it. Today, it'd be full of videos. The store was closed, but the craftware consisting of stuffed canetoads sitting on dunnies, I turned to leave. As I did, I heard someone with a bad knee scrambling down a flight of stairs.

'You wantin somethin?' he shouted after me, desperation in his high-pitched voice.

'No, it's quite all right,' I replied. 'I was just having a quick look round.' I'd made up my mind, by this stage, to return to my ancestral seat. You can only take so much.

But he followed me as I walked back to the bike, and he must have been studying me intently, because as I reached for my yellow helmet he clamped his good foot on my centre stand.

Kimberley Moon, the erstwhile stirrup king. He drove that centre stand into the ground an inch.

'Come on, son,' I says, 'get your foot off that. I'm not to be underestimated. I've taken out a good few bluetongue lizards, in me day.'

'You're a man who reads' he pronounced, having noted my Coke bottle bifocal lenses, 'you wouldn't care to see some slightly foxed second-hand books?'

'Rather see a star-spangled skiing cap,' I told him. 'Wouldn't have one glows in the dark?'

'Oh there may be one left,' he says. 'Don't get them any more. Girl who made them has left the district.'

Paula. She's back in Double Bay now, spends a lot of time in coffee shops, chatting up dagoes.

Well, there was one left, the green one I wear as I pen these divagatory lines, and I think it was Kimbo's, actually, but he sold it me. Must have seen me comin. Cost me half me super.

We keep in touch. I had a phone call from him the other day.

'Something just come in has made me think of you,' he says, with all the conviction of that 'Good, no bills' people give you, when you've got no mail for them. Unfortunately, I already own two copies of the *Srimad Bhagavatam*, by His Divine Grace A.C. Bhaktivedanta Swami Prabhupada.

Kimberley Moon: bought the store at Wozzawunwun, and now can't unload it. Rides from there to the hospital, cross-country, once a week, for hormone treatment. Gets a bit of trade from the snowfields. Been a great help to me, in composing this *Saga*. It was all over, of course, by the time we met. You could date the end of the *Saga* to the reopening of the Gap Road by Darryl and his team, May '86. I will escort you that far. The Welfare, three years later, put the nail in the coffin by taking the kids, because the kids were given to sneaking into town, to thieve and perve on television sets. They would walk down the main street, I am told, smashing the windows for sport. They were naive. And here's a funny thing: those kids—Turpentine excepted—were all born, according to Kimberley Moon, in the early seventies, in consequence of that explosion of Eros that follows the founding of any commune. Which means that Mountain Gum was pushing twenty, by the time they were taken into care. Of course, they didn't know how old they were, no one else did either, as their births had never been registered and memories in the Valley were unsound, to put it mildly. So it fell to the social workers who processed their cases to estimate their ages. And here is a real Mystery; here is the Mystery of Mysteries: even conceding the notorious ineptitude of public servants, it seems unlikely the Welfare could have been out by more than a year, as there are physiological indicators of ageing, which we won't go into here: yet every one of those Valley children was estimated to be not more than twelve years of age, by 1989.

Olaf Abernathy moved in with Nisi Papadimitriou in February '68. By midwinter, Nisi feels it is time they enjoyed some social life together. In consequence of their age difference, they have nothing in common, friends included, so Nisi has invited Monica and Calvin Ecks to visit her and Olaf, in the Blue Mountains shack they share with Nisi's boys, Timothy Papadimitriou and Aloysius O'Looby. This, then, is mid-68, about the time Diane is being arrested, in Sydney, for upsetting the Ally.

'I was brought up,' reminisces Nisi, 'in a country town out West, and my horses were always getting out of the paddocks that I kept them in. I had them on those little vacant blocks every country town has, those small abandoned paddocks with their tatty, makeshift fences. First horse I ever owned was called Prince. He was an old stockhorse of twenty-three.'

'Wow! That sure is old.'

'He was white with age, Mon, and he had a Roman nose and big, dawky ears. And he used to snort when he cantered. Ha! Ha! No matter how much wire I fed into a fence, or how tight I thought I'd strained it, he would get out. Once, I caught him down on his knees, wiggling under the lowest strand.'

'Cindy, don't hurt your knees doing that.'

'I'm a horse, Mommy. Watch me run. Neigh-gh-gh!'

'Cindy, Ah do not like your behaviour. You will receive no attention from me. Oh, it's so nice, bein out here in the country. Let's move out in the country, Calvin.'

'It's not always like this, Monica. We usually don't have time to sit back.'

'Shit on you!'

'You guys think Olaf'll be OK? Maybe I should go look for him.'

'Oh no, he'll be all right. Go for a walk if you want to, but he should be back by now, Calvin. I thought he'd be back by this. He has to work tonight. I told him you were coming.'

'He won't miss us, Nisi, cause we'll be stayin late. I'll soon be in no condition to drive. Intend to get shickered.'

Olaf remains, concealed, awaiting the words that will confirm his unimportance. When Monica and Nisi move to the kitchen to make soup for lunch, he focuses on Calvin. Calvin belch. How relaxed the man seem. Speak with the aplomb of a Paul Ehrlich.

Wish I could be like that, thinks Olaf. Wish I could be famous, or Californian, or both.

'Hello.'

'Oh hi man! We were getting worried about you. You must be Olaf. I'm Calvin, Monica's husband.'

Calvin extends a muscular hand with the grip of a wire strainer. Olaf proffers a dead fish. The heart has gone from Olaf.

'Brought you some beers.'

'Ta.'

'Nice place you got here.'

'It's not ours. We only rent.'

'Nisi says you built the stables.'

'Yeah. Why is the horse out?'

'Kids musta let him out. They won't admit to it. Guess he'll go back in, when he's hungry.'

'Hope not.'

'Oh?'

'I hate the fuckin horse.'

'Yeah, I don't like horses. I think they're an obsession. I couldn't believe it when Nisi was telling Monica what it eats.'

'Zat your daughter?'

'Yeah, that's Cindy. She's always talking about your Tim.'

'He's not mine. Don't encourage her to ride the horse.'

'I won't. Don't worry.'

'There are hidden costs.'

'I bet. Have a swig, kid.'

'Ta.'

'Beers in the fridge.'

'Later. Agistment, fencing, drenching, shoeing. Food. Stables.'

'Right. Sorry to hear you got called up, man.'

'Heavyweight rug for winter. Lightweight rug for summer. Hood, bridle. Saddle, halter.'

'Sounds like it never ends.'

'Lead, brushes. Shampoo, whip. Riding lessons. Lunging rein. Jodhpurs, boots. Riding coat. Gloves. Float hire.'

'Not to mention the cost of the horse in the first place.'

'That's the least of your worries. People give them away.'

'By the way man, don't leave me alone with your girl, when I'm stewed. I can't be trusted.'

Nisi Papadimitriou: horse enthusiast. If only their fathers had carried them on their shoulders more often, when they were young girls.
Olaf Abernathy: granny glasses now revealed as affectation. Passed his military medical.
Calvin Ecks: father-to-be of Plum Pine, by Nisi Papadimitriou.

Act 2 Scene 2

24. *The brumby muster. Kimberley throws his saddle off Sunrise Lookdown.*

The road into the Erinungarah Valley was blocked by rockfall in '68, some time after the Balmain Wake for Martin Luther King. This occurred while Michael Ginnsy, off his face, was visiting the Valley. Phryx and Gwen, those two old timers who lived there on the Flat—now don't confuse the two rockfalls, will you: there was a rockfall blocked the road ('68) and a rockfall blocked the track ('79)—they were still alive, at this point, but prevented from paying their rent. Ginnsy, obliged to leave his van in the Valley, returned to Sydney, promptly forgetting both where he had been and where he had left his van. We know he appeared with Johnny Dakota at the Latin Quarter nightclub in August. It was during the interim period, between April and August, when his van was in the Valley but Michael, the man himself, was not, that the MacAnaspie clan decided to run a brumby muster, as they needed their horses to muster the cattle on what was to be the last great drive.

Our party of potential horsebreakers pauses, before leaving the precinct of Wonderview, to check someone has brought along the container with the corned beef sandwiches. They don't intend to be sleeping out. Two big wings, of binding twine and newsprint, are in place to guide the horses into the house yards, and it's early. Kookaburras are just starting to sing, if you call that singing. Bats are scooting about. The grass is wet, the sand sticks to riding boots, though no one's riding. Darryl and Fergus wear their riding boots in the cabs of their logging trucks. Kimberley's tough little bay mountain gelding, brought over on the tabletop, is tethered to the race. According to Horrie, so well trained are these MacAnaspie horses, and such the length of their memories, a clap or two, and a shout of 'hello' will see them fairly racing towards these yards, once the fence is down.

The paddock on which the horses are stored is coterminous, from their viewpoint, with the run on which the cattle are depastured, in that no fence, or natural border, delimits one from the other. Urn-fruited peppermint and silvertop ash emerge, on both, every ten or twenty feet, from a ground cover of gorse bitter pea, spiny sunbush, native holly and prickly moses. White, at certain times of year, with platysace, beard heaths and mountain flannel and rice flowers, the terrain presents a navigational challenge to the walker, an all-but-impenetrable thicket to the conventional cattledog, a sanctuary to the rare, endangered brush-tailed phascogale, and a motorcycle motocross course and tyre dump to Darryl MacAnaspie. Gullies of turpentine and burrawang that deride, in desiccated parody, the shining gum and soft tree fern stands on the wet sclerophyll lower down, fall sharply away, left and right, through outcrops of native fucshia, and weeping baeckia.

'We feed'em, you know. Darryl here throws 'em a biscuit of hay, every so often. Isn't that so, Darryl?'

Darryl makes no reply. Fergus grins at Attis, and Horrie picks up on the grin at once.

'You do feed 'em, don't you, Darryl?'

'Naah, not exactly. Too good for 'em.'

'What do you mean? You're the one comes in here with his motorcycle club! Hasn't it always been understood it was your job feedin the horses?'

'Baarney's bin doin it.'

'Barney! Barney's been away for months. You mean to tell me the horses haven't been fed in months? You dweeb. You frootlupe. You lazy, good for nothin, bone idle bastard, man ought to take to ya with a draftin cane.'

'Try it.'

'What do we do now then, boss?'

'Yeah, don' matter. Useless animals eat all that hay, could be put on some daangerous corner.'

'Dunno, Kimberley. Dunno. Maybe just walk out in the bush a bit, see if we can pick up a spoor. Never bein fed, they could be anywhere over the entire run by now. You blunny fool!'

'Might be quicker drop over my place, boss, pick up some orses there.'

'Use bikes.'

'Yes, you would say that. You'll be fetchin those horses on that bike of yours, Darryl, *get* on yer bike! Your horses'd be no good for what we have in mind, Kimberley. Thank you very much for your kind offer, but you don't know this run. Those twenty head will be nickin with the scrubbers. Always plenty of scrubbers out here, ay Dad.'

'Been here since the thirties.'

'Since the thirties. Fancy that. See what I mean, Kimberley? Been here since the 1830s. Know the place. It was us, remember, put beeves on this country, we was here before you Moons, and it's our opinion only horses bred on this run can muster off it. Too rugged for any horse but an Erinungarahan Ugandan whaler. Old uncle of ours brought back some whalers from the Royal Ugandan Mounted Rifles, Oo, blunny magnificent hunters over rough country, what. This was after the Sudan War. Boysa bin usin motorcycles, but I don't care what you say, there's places a horse will go a motorcycle won't.'

'Only up some other orse's clacker. Get with it, y'old fool.'

'Oh you think so, do ya. In the time you've been motorcycle musterin, Darryl, you're bringin in fewer and fewer head. They're awake up to yer. And you must be on a horse, to catch a stallion. I'm speakin of catch, not chase. Motorcycle stockman can't even catch one o' them little Japanese riceburners. I hate to think how many wild scrubbers we've out here now, but one thing's certain, we're bringin 'em in this week, scrubbers, the works, which is why we're not usin motorcycles. They're not scared of the noise you make, what are you gonna do? Dismount and hit'em over the head? See, your options is limited. You're already usin both hands and feet. Nother coupla pair of feet comes in handy, as you may learn, or you may not, cause this'll be the last muster off this run. Yes, like it or not, we can no longer think of this MacAnaspie run as ours. Truth is, that aside from this house paddock, and that barely feeds a dozen head and it's not worth clearin, least I'm not doin it—the run is in the hands of the neighbour's goats, what's not owned by the National Parks and Wildlife. So we have to wash our hands of the run, and get on with our lives.'

'Still own the Valley though, don't yez?'

'Yes, but we don't own the run, and stock move freely between the two, once they get the cramps.'

'Mountain goats, mate. Wait till ya see'm.'

'Want to buy it off yez, don't they?'

'Yes, and we'll sell too, when the price is right. Won't we, Dad?'

'Dunno. They'll need to change their tune fore I'll do business with rangers. Forever complainin bout the dogs! I says to them, I says, how we s'posed to muster our cattle without dogs?'

'What dogs are these, Mr MacAnaspie?'

'Oh, they live out on the run. You'll be seein 'em.'

'You know Kimberley, you're the first non-MacAnaspie to be taken on a MacAnaspie muster. You're gonna learn all our trade secrets. We're the only men left can run cattle on this country.'

'Too late to do me any good though, ay boss.'

'That's the only reason we're takin ya.'

It is soon apparent what was intended as a few days' work might take weeks. The manly and honourable mustering contract settles over these men, as does the non-drought-breaking rain. Fogs descend. Rock walls glisten in mists. The imprecations of a customer with a half-excavated dam, threats from the chip mill, even pleas from the high school that Attis should be studying—the dogs bark, but the postmen move on.

And the more rain, the more problematical the muster. Midwinter, morning tea time, 9 a.m., dripping wet in their Drizabone capes, weeping from smoke, the party of six mills round the struggling campfire, sipping a restorative cuppa. The billy depends from an inverted jam tin, on a tripod of sticks, by a length of fencing wire. My God, but it's cold. Breath from the horses, and steam off the two motorcycle exhaust systems, mingles with the fog, of which these men take no more note than a postman of a NO JUNK MAIL directive. Gibbon, alluding to the cavalry of the Roman Emperor Licinius, says, 'As the cavalry was drawn from Phrygia, we may conceive a more favourable opinion of the beauty of the horses, than of the courage and dexterity of their riders.' Here, the converse is true.

'Did you remember to throw an ants nest to the chooks and a wallaby to the pigs, Darryl? It amuses me my rooster knows he's the father of all my hens, yet none of the hens has the slightest notion of who she might be the mother of. Did you bring the ENOS, Fergie, for the damper, and after the damper?'

'Yes Dad.'

'Don't think we'da bin better off with a packhorse, boys? Not too late to go back and get one.'

Both motorcycles, huge, homemade beasts, of one-litre capacity, with dimpled long-distance tanks and heavy duty forks and knobby tyres, are carrying a brace of bulging panniers, from each of which projects a rattlesack and a bushsaw. The horses carry only blanket rolls. Whether Kimberley's horses can cope with running horses here is moot, so Horrie's plan is to run the horses with the bikes, while the men on horseback erect yards, then, when the horses are half-broken, to use the freshly half-broken horses to muster the cattle. Fully broken horses can't, or won't.

Reconnaissance of the house paddock having failed to disclose a beast, the party has moved onto the run proper, that wild plateau close to thirty miles long, and a few miles to barely a tenth of a mile in width. Something of a panhandle, the pan being owned by the neighbour for the most part, and the Forestry, and bordered to the east by the 2000-feet-deep Erinungarah Gorge and to the west by the Left Arm of Wozzawunwun Creek, not so deep but just as sheer, the run pokes fingers up to a mile long out many a narrow neck, and down many a rolling poddy spur. Once past the Ford on the Falls, it's National Park, but rangers never come out here. There's a fire-trail of sorts, leading off the Erinungarah Road above the Gap, but it's washed away, and overgrown, with big-leaf geebung and hairpin banksia and sweet-smelling tea tree hiding bloodwood stumps that took out the sump on the last fire tanker ventured over it. The local bushfire brigade wants it graded, pronto, but the Parks and Wildlife won't be coming here for fear of disturbing the habitat of the brush-tailed phascogale, which hereabouts appears to have ventured from the sanctuary of the rainforest. Anyway, they don't want firetrails in Wilderness. Encourages hoons.

'Look' says Charlie, 'the mist's liftin. You can see into the Valley.'

Indeed, the mist has momentarily lifted, and Kimberley can see, not so much the Valley, which is still immured in fog, but the campfire, three feet from the Gorge, and that his horse has

145

been tethered, by a broadly grinning Darryl, to a stunted white stringy that clings to a ledge.

'Smartarse.' Kimberley, spurs jangling, bandy as a coot, strides off to Sunrise Lookdown.

'Think it's his saddle he's worried about, boys. Wouldn't give y'a zac for that horse.'

'Yes, it's a beautiful saddle, Kimberley. I've been admiring it all morning. What, is it hand-tooled, is it?'

'Got it in Texas, boss. Picked it up while I was over there rodeoin.'

'And what would it be worth?'

'Dunno. Paid two grand then.'

'Ever thought of enterin the bareback, boy? I know you always wins the saddleride, but don't you think a man who needs a saddle on a bronc …'

'Shut up, Dad, for Chrissake. What the hell would you know?'

'No, no, let him have his say. What do you mean, Mr MacAnaspie?'

'Nothin.'

'Perfectly clear to me. He's sayin a man needs a saddle on a orse is, well, you know, bit of a siss. Ain't that right, Faardy?'

Years later, when parting the white panicles of a possumwood on the talus some kids in Phrygian caps—caught in a Spell, never to age, never to die—discover this beautiful artifact, nesting low in a possumwood tree, Kimberley, black eyes blazing, removes again the saddle from his pony and draws it back, at first, away from the cliff, but higher now. And then it is in the air, sailing out over the gorge, further, higher, tumbling down past the two-tone grey of the white box on the Valley's west-facing wall, and the party drink again the rest of their tea and rum in enamelled silence, and move off into the mist, which comes down again, on Kimberley, riding bareback.

Charlie MacAnaspie: too old, in his nineties, to take part in any muster. I'm beat to see how he got his leg in the air and over the horse. See, I have a step-through Honda, so I don't have that problem.

Horrie MacAnaspie: grew up, not so much in a saddle, as walking beside a team. Not a great horseman, too much meat on his arse, according to Kimbo.

Kimberley Moon: a superb horseman, who rides bareback now, though he says a saddle wouldn't discomfort him now, the way it used to. Good he can laugh at himself! The toughness of these mountain men—Darryl, Fergus, Kimberley—was an indispensable factor in the Cult of the Erinungarah. They needed guts to do what they did, they had no anaesthetics down there. Where did the guts come from? City wimps? As if.

Fergus MacAnaspie: Like his brother Barney and Kimbo, a real horseman. But, except to pick up at the Rodeo, he never rode, after he moved to the Valley.

Darryl MacAnaspie: A very bitter man, ever since he got out of boob. No longer drinks in the pub, and when he does come to town now, he gets his hair cut, and he's always wearing his suit, for a court appearance. Acquitted, as he always is, on a charge of overloading jinkers or dangerous driving, he leaves town in a burst of fury that sets off the magistrate's car alarm.

Speaking of which, I have to chat with Harley and Norton, but Darryl has promised me that he will shoot me, if I do. I take a threat from him seriously. He wasn't charged, but Darryl it was destroyed the Greenpeace Camp near Eden.

25. *Brumby muster continued. Kimberley has a fateful fall.*

Water being temporarily abundant, a trap yard is out of the question, so while Fergus and Darryl gun off on the bikes to do more reconnoitring—which involves fanging from ridge to ridge, standing on the footpegs, from time to time—the rest of the party set about building yards on a piece of sedgeland bordered by swamp gum, *Eucalyptus ovata*, where the headwaters of a creek emerge from a poorly drained heath. It's a traditional MacAnaspie yard site, one of twenty or more over the run. Horses, being driven towards the heath, head for the sedge every time, as the shrubby heathland here is higher than a

147

horse's head for the most part. A man walking on a compass setting soon finds himself looking for wombat pads.

'What about buildin two yards?'

'Two yards?'

'Yeah, get 'em into a second yard, makes it easier to drop a rail. Don't like droppin a rail with a stallion chargin down.'

'Oh, we won't be yardin stallions, Kimbo. They've gotta be run down. Put 'em fresh in a yard like this, they'll kill 'emselves, belt 'emselves to death. Seen it as a kid. Wild buggers. This is for the faster mares. By the time they get to the wing, any forward mares shoulda dropped off. Dad'll run in and get the rail down, won't you, Dad, after the stallion has decamped. He needs ten seconds on the best mare, so we build a big yard, and it needs to be high. They so much as get a foot over, they'll somersault out and break their blunny necks.'

'An we're gonna be ridin these roosters.'

'All we gotta do is jump on and hang on. Dogs do most o' the work. See they got no mouths but they won't buck. Any horse ever so much as looked like buckin, we shot it there and then. Kept the dogs happy. They will try, of course, to dislodge you, on any overhanging branch or ledge, but I dare say, horseman that you are, you'll be able to handle that. Take this bushsaw, Att, and go fell some swampies for the posts. Sure a rail be all right, Dad? Wouldn't like us to run y'up a gate? Wouldn't take four of us more'n a day.'

Attis has no scruples sawing down swamp gum, as it will coppice back. To kill one, you would need to ringbark, poison or uproot it. They like fire, and droughts, unless accompanied by a plague of cup moth larvae, don't faze them, which is why many an old codger, like Charlie, thinks dieback the best thing since sliced bread.

Horses are seen, and some yards with two huge wings of binding twine duly erected. Then on a morning when the mist is raining under the larger trees, and as soon as they have emptied their bowels and kicked a few leaves over the toilet paper, it's down to business. The skill involved in riding bikes hard over this country surpasses horsemanship. You can't give a motorcycle its head, as they long for death and will go straight to ground. But the fighting brothers, who've been fighting daily since the one accused the other of cheating in a marble swallowing contest, can stand their bikes stock still and put a front wheel in the air most any time. Each rider will wear out his pair of riding boots. The noise these bikes emit, off the canyon walls of this fastness!

A harem is found, head-down on a green of node-sedge and streaked leak orchid, by a shelf of glittering sandstone. The mist lifts; pellucid droplets will have formed, quivering, in the hollows of peltate leaves. The cauliflowers by the chookpen will be sparkling. The creatures of this plateau, native and feral both, are inured to the internal combustion engine, and it's not till the wary stallion catches sight of the motorcycles as they shower down on him that he acts. He moves his mob off at a full gallop, and as they have a furlong lead no way are the bikes going to catch them up through the woods, but they must be pressed: otherwise, the mares will go under, over or through a makeshift prison.

At the outset, the stallion is in the rear, nipping laggards on the rump. Soon, however, one gutty mare drops off, peeling away with her foal. Darryl and Fergus, on seeing this, whoop an unselfconscious hunting cry. Fergus throws a doughnut, for he knows the stallion will feel compelled to move into the lead, which he does. By the time the wings of the yard are in view, the duds, with foals, have dropped off, leaving only the three fastest mares, accompanying the stallion, and by Christ, he's hiking.

Horrie curses when he sees the speed at which the brumbies wheel into the yards. Dogs shoulda run 'em round a bit more, speaking of which, where *are* the blunny dogs? Attis, hidden behind a tree, rushes out to drop the rail, but he's slow, and a mare escapes with the stallion, leaving two horses only. The yards resound.

Horrie smartly gallops down to sit on the stallion's arse. The mare wasn't meant to be part of the equation, but no muster ever goes according to plan. Horrie wants the mare, but though he carries a rope he daren't throw it. Kimberley's second pony is a nice steed, going like the clappers, but Horrie is half-holding him back. Age, injury and disillusion take the ticker out of a man.

Dismounted, Kimberley, hidden behind a narrowleaf stringy, hears the three horses approach. He stubs out his fag and mounts as he sees the stallion, followed by the lead mare and Horrie, who's lost his hat. Kimberley springs out, and the stallion, seeing the ambuscade, veers off at an obtuse angle. Horrie is shouting something Kimberley can't hear, something about the mare. For close on two miles Kimberley presses her, half-aware of Horrie, though neither looks back. Single file, the brumbies cut through a densely timbered gully, then up the other side. Here, the plateau opens out. Knackered, the mare has dropped back to a canter, when she comes upon a tree down in front of her; four feet of turpentine bole, covered in the parasitic devil's twine. The stallion clears it without missing a beat, but the mare, not so lucky, clips a branch and goes down, belly up. Seconds later, Kimberley joins her, on his right folded forearm, as his own mount misjudges the long jump. He is on his feet, grinning, within seconds, but might have been better off to have rolled through the mat-rush.

'You OK, boy?' Horrie throws his rope at the neck of the stunned mare and frowns, as he picks up a front foot.

'No worries. Better get on with it, ay, see ya back at the yards, hey? Gi's yer stockwhip.'

Three hours later Kimberley Moon is back in the yards with the stallion, on hackamore, in tow, and being persuaded of the pecking order by being half-choked to death, and continually pushed off-balance, and thrashed over the head with the whip butt. Quite a feat of horsemanship, this, without a saddle. The fighting brothers, back from building a wing for the cattleyard, cheer ironically. Always ironic, the cheer here.

Released into the yard, the stallion is greeted by his mares, whom he shapes up to kick in the slats.

'You're goin home, Kimbo, and you can take Norman with you.' Fiat from the stockboss, while the billy boils. Norman turned up, uninvited. He's greatly given to prowling through the bush, head thrown back, staring at the stars.

'Whattaya mean, boss? I'm not goin nowhere.'

'You are goin home. You are goin home tonight. I saw what happened to you. You went down, flat strap, on that arm, and ya never even rolled. Gi's a look at your right shoulder. There! What I tell ya? Sittin up like a roo at sunrise. I'd say you musta gone close to dislocatin that shoulder. At the least, you've a subluxation o' the AC joint.'

'Feels all right. Just a bit o' bark off, I reckon.'

'Course it feels all right. Dare say it feels better 'n all right. Think I don't know that feeling? Think I don't know that sensation of jubilation, when you jump up after some fall off a horse, or bike, that mighta killed ya, but you're still not dead, and yer don't even hurt? Half the reason we ride the blunny things. Oh sure, you felt good at the time, and you're feelin pretty good now, and you'd feel even better, this evenin, after a few beers, had you access to'em. But you know, and I know, it's gonna be a wee bit of a different story in the mornin. You've torn most every ligament in that shoulder, son. You won't be ridin no horse in that condition. You'll be groanin when you get out o' your roll, and you won't mend for weeks if not months. Every step'll jar ya. Go home, while you can. It'd take an exceptional horseman, the kind we don't expect to see any more in this day 'n age, to ride in your condition.'

'I'm not goin till the job's done.'

'Very well, you take a rear wing. Fergus, you can take a front wing, I'll tail. Attis can lead. Dad can go home with Norman and the other horses and Darryl, who's so very keen to get back to work, or more likely, pub. I'm goin to bed. See yez in the mornin.'

'Who says I'm goin home?'

'You are goin home, cause I'm not havin you ridin bareback, Dad. And you have no choice, as you must know, if you're any kind of man.'

I'll fix you, thinks Charlie. I won't say now, what I saw by the Gap.

'Listen!'

Ubi cymbalum sonat vox, ubi tympana reboant. Where the cymbal sounds its voice, where the drums reverberate. Catullus. Above the crepuscular cry of currawong and lyrebird is heard a barbarous, man-made music, from somewhere down in the Valley. It is Phryx Pfingstl and Gwen Bletherstone Mayall, absorbed in their religious observances, with the dingoes and wild dogs, who should be at the muster, looking on, and joining in.

Norman MacAnaspie: I should have made more of Norman. I should have made more of Attis. But a couple of standard deviations from the mean, I lose confidence in my characterisations. Sorry.

Phryx and Gwen: ditto. I keep seeing Gwen and Phryx as old-fashioned occultists, of the kind that form spirit circles in manor houses back home. Order of the Golden Dawn, Madame Blavatsky, that kind of thing. Meetings over tarot cards in twin sets and cardigans. Those conversant with Findhorn will recognise the connection here. But this persistent image in my mind does not accord with the imagery of the poem, where Gwen is presented as a Celtic witch, and Phryx as a drunk. Pass.

26. *Fergus and Attis resolve to leave home.*

Now the bush treatment for a shoulder dislocation, or subluxation, accords with that arrived at independently, by modern physiotherapy.

Keep it moving, work it. Don't, on any account, let it freeze. The shoulder joint, as it heals, is prone to the formation of adhesive scars, and there is no better way of losing movement in the shoulder—as I have learned, to my cost—than by putting the entire arm in a sling, to nurse a fractured ulna. Last time I ever went to a locum.

It goes without saying no badly injured shoulder will be the same again. Inelastic scar tissue constitutes the mend, so the shoulder will always be weaker than it was, and more susceptible to subsequent injury. But if all goes well; if the damaged joint is worked hard in the beginning, close to full resumption of movement may be anticipated. You will look back and laugh at those weeks of excruciating pain you endured, when the injury was fresh, and though you could speak of it, you couldn't sleep on it, and aside from the grinding and crunching that you hear, or feel—it is hard to say which—whenever you reach forward to turn off the hot water tap in the bath, or stretch to prune the gravenstein, or attempt to paint a ceiling without using a ladder—which you can very nearly do, in most modern project homes—as I say, but for these minor inconveniences, you will be as good as you are going to get. But only, as I cannot stress sufficiently, if you are hard on yourself to begin, and mindful of keeping that painful joint in motion, in every original direction.

And I suppose the older you are, and the closer you feel yourself to your grave, the harder it will be, and the longer it will take, and the less incentive you will feel in doing it, which is why we must marvel at Charlie MacAnaspie, who receives a *Gallipoli Gazette*, for being as fully determined as Kimberley Moon, a man in his late twenties, to recover from a shoulder injury sustained in the course of the last, abortive muster—which saw not one single head of cattle yarded—in the course of each being thrown from a horse, which he was so foolhardy as to be riding bareback over rough ground. Which means that while Charlie is still groaning and shrieking, despite himself, and weeping like a boy with the pain, as he does his shoulder exercises—which he does for a full hour, every three hours, night and day—Kimberley has so far recovered as to be no longer obliged to wince when he stumbles, or gets a scare and jolts himself, though he still has that strange proprioception that tells him the joint is not yet 'right', that eerie, blunt, abysmal feeling you feel, where there shouldn't be a feeling. I suppose the word 'faith' has no more basic meaning than this—the trust a man must place in his body's recuperative mechanisms, over which he has more control, I suspect, than it pleases him to concede. And women don't have to get pregnant. As they proved in the Valley, towards the end. Anyway, Charlie's recuperation has been in progress some time, and Fergus, for one, has had a gutful. 'Give up!'

he shouts, woken from sleep by the groaning of his Fardy in the next room. Looking at his watch, he sees it's 3 a.m. Looking at the bunk opposite, he sees his younger brother awake.

'This can't go on' he tells Attis. 'We're spittin the dummy.'

And during the meal that evening, when the whole family is gathered, with even Barney's usual place being set for him, who is over in Vietnam, Fergus elaborates his viewpoint to Horrie, especially, and to Charlie, and to Iris.

'I *am* sayin he must learn to take into account the needs of others! Give us a break, Dad. You know as well as me, only reason's this family's done well is because we're prepared to work. Well, to work, you need sleep.'

'This is my home and I'm not leavin. I helped build this house. No plurry whingein kid's goin to drive me out o' me own home, at my age.'

'You're the one's doin the whingein. It's your bloody whingein that's the issue. Man can't get any sleep at night, and he's got to be on the road by four.'

'Wait a minute, wait a minute. Perhaps we can effect a compromise. I mean, the boy has a point, Dad. When you built this house, you built the internal walls too thin, and you should never have used woollybutt. We have no secrets from each other, in this house. See, you may not be aware of it yourself. He's probly not aware of it, Fergie. He's probly just rollin on his shoulder, in his sleep.'

'No, he's up and exercisin. I can hear him gettin about.'

'Is this true, Dad? Are you gettin up at all hours of the night to exercise that shoulder?'

'Give 'im a sleepin draaft.'

'Is he botherin' you too, Darryl?'

'Nup. Never 'ear a thing. Once me ead its that pillar, I'm dead. I'm gone.'

'You said you wasn't gonna drink any more, son.'

'You said you wasn't gonna send Xmas cards any more, Mum.'

'I dunno. What do you say, Dad? Would you be prepared to sleep in the shed a bit? Just till the shoulder's healed?'

'Shoulder never's gonna heal.'

154

'What!'

'Oh for God's sake, how old is the man now? Why does he need his shoulder for? Never does any heavy liftin.'

'Ho, that's all you know. Who do you suppose waters the chooks and ducks when you're at work?'

'Look, if you won't do it for me, have some thought for Attis. How can the boy study with this endless screechin 'n groanin goin on? How can he get his proper sleep?'

'Ow much sleep yez need, wimps?'

'We're not all like you, Darryl. You shoulda been a fisherman. Most people need five hours.'

'Yes, well I must have this shoulder mended, if I'm to move those old folk from the Valley.'

'Old folk, who you callin old folk? They're twenty years younger'n you, if they're a day.'

'And another thing. No one but me knows the way in and out o' there, now.'

'You could tell us. We'd listen.'

'It's my responsibility. Soon as I'm mended, I intend to go down and evict 'em. Won't pay rent.'

'*Can't* pay rent. Wonder is, they're not starvin down there.'

'Always on the piss, too.'

'You're a pig-headed old fool.'

'Don't speak to ya Fardy like that! Man'll have to teach you respect for yer elders, I kin see.'

'I'm pullin the plug. I can't drive a jinker all day over dangerous mountain roads ...'

'"Daangerous mountain roads," what are ya? Man's a wimp, Dad, let 'im go. I'm stayin.'

'Dunno. Don't like this, Charlie. Family's breakin up, cause of you. Boys are leavin home. What do you think, Mother? What's your views on this?'

'If Fergus takes Attis with him, he'd be doin Att a favour, at this stage. Then Att won't need to waste so much time on the school bus, during his final exams. I'll go in and do their washin for 'em, and cook, and clean the place, once a week.'

'I dunno. I reckon there's too much temptation in these towns. They tell me they're comin and goin from that Bowlin

Club, all hours of the night. You can't tell me two young men won't get in all sorts of mischief. What, yez'll rent a flat, will yers?'

'Yeah, rent a flat. Rent a house. Just for the time bein, like. Just till Fardy's mended.'

'No one here but me knows that Sit on Yer Arse Pass. Dad and me found that pass. That's where those cattle go up and down, I'll bet. Sit on Yer Arse Pass, only rowt into the Valley, now the road's gone. Still wanta get them cattle, don't we?'

'Yes, well I spoke to someone at Council about the road. And someone from the Parks and Wildlife spoke about the cattle to me.'

'What did Council say about it?'

'They'll be gettin round to it. Low priority. Now you're not stayin at Graceland, boys. Bunch of no hopers down there. Someone told me someone from those flats put out a whole heap o' *National Geographics*, last clean-up. Well I mean, what sort of low mentality would you need to do a thing like that?'

Charlie MacAnaspie: hard old codger. It is a fact that those with least to live for are the most determined that they shall never die.

Horrie MacAnaspie: seen here in conciliatory mode. When it came to a showdown with the neighbours, he would not brook conciliation. Inconsistent? No. Only the eunuch can love his neighbour as he loves himself. The man who does not love his own family better than he loves his neighbours' family had no business fathering his family in the first place.

Fergus MacAnaspie: his love for Attis, the fact he had found Attis at the mill, prompted him to follow in Attis' footsteps, in the Valley. According to Kimbo, Fergus was next, after Attis, to emasculate himself. God they had courage, though Kimbo tells it's not all that painful. It is, however, permanent, in the absence of microsurgical attention. Whether Fergus thought that he, too, would become a tree as a result, is unclear. What is clear is he established the monastery, which is just a mudhut with a nice bottle wall, and there the eunuchs would gather, to celebrate, whenever another resolved to join them. Kimberley's a bit coy about the ceremonial detail—or perhaps he has totally forgotten and I, for once, cannot prompt his memory—but he did say old Wozza turned up, in the middle of a ceremony, once. I shall have to check that out.

I wouldn't mind bettin bull's blood was involved. And I mean bull's blood, not that odious Bulgarian claret so popular in London, when last I was there.

27. Graceland. Fergus at the coupe. Smitty. Attis asked to pick up for the Rodeo.

Each country town has its Graceland. In the southern part of New South Wales they date from the mid-fifties, and are of fibro/iron construction, on a brick foundation. When a Graceland with an asbestos roof was demolished in Canberra in the '80s, to make room for an institution, what looked like spacemen removed it and it was taken to Queanbeyan, under police escort. I was looking on, stuffing a *Reader's Digest* into a letterbox—just about every household gets the *Reader's Digest* there. Despite these precautions, five passers-by have since come down with chest pain, and their case for compensation is being heard before Mr Justice Safehouse of the Supreme Court. I could have worn that horsehair hat meself, had I been a man of fewer scruples and less learning. I have the required sense of superiority.

If, or when, a Graceland is tarted up, always prior to sale—for they are constantly changing hands, and nothing is done, at the tenants' request—it is felt Mission Brown* is the go here for the windows and the iron roof, while the fibro cleans up so very nicely with a touch of sugar soap, the paint intended for the walls has been known to find its way onto the black market. No one knows who lives in these flats, not even the tenants.

---

* Commercial paint tint

When a relief postie leafs through his beatbook, more thoroughly perforce, on his second day in a new town, he never expects to find a name against a flat in the local Graceland. A future PM may have pencilled in the addressee on the last electricity account, but so manifest the palimpsest we pay it no heed. Mail, for any flat in Graceland, will be delivered as addressed, and you don't see it again. It won't reappear, to throw out your datestamp. No complaints, from anyone, either, if some little item goes missing. They're not ones to know, and they're not ones to complain, if they do. Like me, they have given up.

Dreary places, dank in winter. Always shaded by Monterey pine. Snowdroppers wouldn't bother. Only colour is the vehicle duco, and the glossy junk mail, lying by the boxes. No one cares for the garden, which is privet and camphor laurel, with here and there a stone gnome, like a young Rafflesia flower, or a mural on a fat bob tank or an Escort panel van, and I recall many a charming tatt, too, on the forearms of weedy men who, cursing, lay under HQ Holdens, being watched by big fat liminal de factos.

And always, some little distance off, and never, apparently, observed, until there was insufficient Mission Brown left in the tin to wet the brush, flat number one, or flat number ten, being a freestanding house.

Aluminium windows in the westerly weatherboards weathered back to the wood. Annexe of contrasting vertical boards, varnished cypress, nailholes black. Brick chimney, with two rusty flues, and a series of rear fibro extensions, all but the last, which is skillion roofed, constructed by a certain well-known chainsaw carpenter-cum-angle-grinder stonemason.

'This must be it,' says Fergus, surveying with evident satisfaction the modern, mass-produced numeral, which is black against a silver ground on the wooden door. 'Flat number one. Even a pile of firewood, or maybe those are the bargeboards. We shall have to get the agent onto this screen door. Flies will be gettin in, come summer. Hope you like the place, like the place, Attis? I wanted something to remind us of home, as I know it's important we slot straight in, with those exams comin up. Now then, where's the tack shed? This it, over here? No, this must be an old dairy. Whoever last used the churn didn't wash it.'

Attis is soon set up in the best place for study, the kitchen table, beside him an acervate congeries of the canonical mediocrities of English prose fiction; pedestrian Orwell, tin-eared Conrad, pea-brained Woolf; never any Conan Doyle.

Fergus can park the Mack in the adjacent vacant block, which for him is an attraction of the place. And concerning the neighbours, whose view he's destroyed on the rare occasions when he is home, it could be worse: he's not driving a pantech with an ad the length of the trailer. And if they're peeved at being woken before four, they don't let on. This is no Tidy Town. This is a Timber Town, as the shingle on its outskirts defiantly proclaims.

Obliqua Creek Timber Town, where Greens Cost Jobs.

But that's now. Let's go back to '68. For an hour after he leaves the bitumen, Fergus climbs an anfractuous corkscrew. He is still applying the headlights when he reaches the coupe, and he's never first rig in. The felling gang—nowdays, in the mid-nineties, two fallers, a D7 dozer driver and a skidder driver—are camped on the coupe. Fergus rocks off the jinker, dons hardhat, then strolls away for a smoke and a piss.

Late winter, '68. If Fergus could see the Valley, there'd be steam rising off the Valley as well, but you can't see the Valley from where he stands. What will become a 200-acre coupe has just opened for business. The fallers—inevitably young men— use no muscular strength. You can swing up a chainsaw, with a flick of the hip, and let it bite, so the two-stroke does the work. This deep basalt slope, covered in massive trees, would get very muddy in rain, and it's a good choice of coupe to be working in a drought, and perhaps unworkable at other times. The rig, *Simply the Best*, has been left at a lean-on which would cause a hobby farmer heartburn.

One after another, these old-growth mountain grey gums and messmate stringys will be felled, but not all: of a fresh and following folded rank, one will remain, every acre of so, and in theory, it's just a matter of resowing, with seed, from the air, to watch the coupe grow back. But it's cold hereabouts, with montane rainforest growing along the watercourses. Can you spare 200 years? It is thought to take that long before a tree attains the girth of these monsters, while the foresters find they

159

cannot get more than a third of these coupes to regenerate. One problem is the hot-burn policy in this *arrondissement** reduces botanical diversity, another, that on a slope like this, the topsoil tends to wash away. Come back in five years' time and you'll likely find a thicket of green wattle, on a clay pan.

More sinister, the climate itself changes when you clear the timber. Irish weather has steadily deteriorated over the past thousand years, and the treeline has actually dropped a thousand feet, since the coming of the Celt, with his iron axe.

Now all these men here chain-smoke, and they light up, every one, before dawn. The day-long roar of their engines is so fierce they'll never hear a gang gang, which'd be the least of their worries. The biggest trees, often one to a jinker, will be milled for handwood scantling, while the smaller stuff will be chipped and dispatched, direct as woodchip, to Japan. We like the idea of plantations, but we haven't got time to wait for them to grow.

Omnis enim populo mercedem pendere iussa est arbor. As a present for the mob, let's have all the poor bloody trees knocked over. Juvenal.

---

* It would appear that eucalypt prefers the hot to the cool burn, i.e., prefers a firestorm (incompatible with civilisation, buckles your tankstand) to a risk-reducing hazard reduction. A policy of systematic and regular hazard reduction burning reduces eucalypt population density and clears the underbrush. But we seldom do it, because we've short memories, and it's hard work and creates air pollution. So we have firestorms. Ash Wednesday, NSW, January '94. Good spring that year, top spring, '93. I recall the bees did so well off the clover I extracted before Christmas. But the week after Christmas, there were days of fierce, cold gales, snow on the Alps, and all the abundant new growth burnt off, and was left hanging off the trees, dead. Then a winter weather pattern set in; nor'westerly gales, bugger-all humidity, then days of century heat and more gales. The whole state went up, except where arsonists couldn't get to light their fires. You can't fight a firestorm. The fire crowns, walls of flame 200 feet high and miles wide. Spotting up to six miles downwind, air full of cinders and firebrands. Blast knocks trees flat before the fire hits. Helicopter pilots reported fireballs at 1200 feet in '94. I was there in me yellow overalls; senior deputy captain, Obliqua Creek. Barney, who's captain, can't recall the fire Orion speaks of; it sounds like a firestorm, from the description, but must have been unusually circumscribed. Certainly, the urn-fruited peppermints out there are black as pitch, but then they always are.

160

'Seed pickers workin?' inquires Fergus, making conversation with the man who will load him. 'Plenty o' seed on them messmates.'

'Ah, get a few snig tracks in, might see a few. Think I musta buried one, last coupe. One's gone missin, any road. Hey! Got a butt for ya here, boy. She's a ripper too. What about this?'

'Farck! Won't get the chains round it.'

'Darryl says keep that for me big brother. Oh yeah, he also says you're to give Kimberley Moon a bell. Somepin 'bout the Rodeo.'

'Goin in the woodchop this year, Smitty, at the Show?'

'Might enter the missus instead.'

'Pity. Six-cut front man, like you.'

'Pig's arse! Never seem to draw the right end o' the log. F'rever addin to me 'andicap.'

Sometime later that same evening.

'Sorry to interrupt, Attis, but how would you feel about pickin up with me, at the Rodeo? Talkin to Kimberley this afternoon, he don't think his shoulder'll be ready by October. If you was to do it, you'd be paid, o' course, and it's not hard work, mate. Horseman like you'd shit it in. I'll do the dismounts. Seen me 'n Kim work, haven't ya? Wait either side o' the chute, and when the gate opens, keep the bronc in our sights, and if the man makes the time, move in, one each side, and I'll lift the rider free while you release the kicker strap. Course, if he don't make the time, it's a matter o' keepin the horse away from his head. Common sense. Darryl a be workin. Reckon it'd please the old fella no end, see all the pickin up bein done by MacAnaspies. Darryl's got the hard job, clown picks up on the bull ride, and they're gettin the glove in the rope that tight, he's had to slice a few fingers. Real bummer for the kiddies, I reckon, watchin a clown cut a man's hand. Never get'im back in the Mackas* again. Know somethin? I'm missin

---

* An anachronism. The first Mackas restaurant in this country was the Yagoona Mackas, which opened, according to the wall plaque, February '72. It was the Kentucky Fried opened in '68.

the little bastard. Wouldn't like to give us a punch-up 'fore bed, I s'pose? No? That's all right. You're gonna be a lawyer instead. Tell you what, I'll go down the pub and bail the bastard up there. What's the time now?'

Nineteen sixty-eight, the Thursday before the last weekend of October (that is to say, the weekend after Paula's engagement party to the north), on the Erinungarah Plateau, which is upwind of the Tidbinbilla tracking station, except in the rare event of a nor'wester, at Wonderview, an isolated residence surrounded by dozers on beavertail loaders and housing four strong personalities, Fergus and Attis MacAnaspie return home for a square meal, at their mother's insistence.

'Hello, strangers! Come on in. Dad! Where is he now?'

'Darryl about, Mum?'

'No, he just went out. Gettin twitchy, you know how he gets, before Rodeo. How's Kimberley's shoulder, son?'

'Oh, ar, he's gonna be all right.'

'Shoulder mended? Norman, you go and find your father, please, and don't wake Fardy, while you're doin it. Tell him the boys are here. So how's life in town, boys?'

'Oh you know, Mum, keepin us busy. Goin to the Rodeo this year?'

'I always go to the Rodeo, Fergus. Why do you ask? I hope you haven't roped Attis into the pickin up, when I asked ya not to.'

'Yeah, well, I did ask Darryl ...'

'Oh don't tell me! Don't say it! I don't want to hear another word. He's in his final year, Fergus.'

'Someone has to do it, Mum. I asked bloody Darryl, but he said he'd only do it if we both rode bikes, Well, I mean, Hello. Speak o' the Devil. Tell your mother why you wouldn't do the pickin up with me, Shit-for-brains.'

'Fergus! Norman, did you hear what I just said to you?'

'Got more sense, ay. Won't catch me gettin on a bloody orse, not aafter what I seen one do to Faardy. Too daangerous.'

'Here's your father now. Boys! I don't want no fightin at this table.'

162

'Who parked their blunny rig fair in the middle of the driveway? Man can't get his tractor in. Darryl, did you throw a wallaby to the pigs? Pigs sound hungry.'

'Good Lord, look at you. You're all covered in dirt and grease. Go and wash your face and hands before you come in my kitchen.'

'I'll have a glass of beer first.'

'Well, you're in a nice mood to be greetin your boys.'

'Just spent half an hour takin the blessed gate off its hinges, didn't I. Locked meself in. Don't you dare laugh.'

'Bogged 'is tractor, laast week. Had to pull 'im out.'

'Ah! Thank you Fergie. Here's cheers.'

'Dad, you're not lockin the gates.'

'Too right I'm lockin the blunny gates, woman. Old man Moon got ripped off, t'other day. Lost twelve head, he estimates. Don't think he knows how many he's got.'

'What do you mean, "ripped off"? Use the Queen's English, in front of the boys.'

'Don't talk to me about that creature in the turquoise pillbox hat.'

'Oh you are in a mood.'

'Any man'd be in a mood, after seein what I seen today. Heifer o' mine just dropped a half-Angus calf. Now what bull's come all the way from Bunoo Bunoo to serve that heifer? How many fences must he have got through?'

'When was this then, Dad?'

'Oh when would you blunny think? Two hundred and eighty three days ago, wouldn't you say, give or take a week? And they musta come down and got 'im—cause, as you know, they can never get out, although they can always get in, unlike chicks, which can always get out, but never can get back—without lettin a man know. Gettin to the point, man can't run a stud operation here. See where next door's changed hands? Total Goat Control moved out, and Better Fritter Batter, o' Melbourne's, moved in. Better Fritter Batter just went and bought himself a truckful o' Friesian steers. Huh! Old man Batter'll be gettin the same for them in two years, as what he paid for 'em.'

'Oh that's enough now, Dad. The boys don't want to hear all this.'

'No, I dare say they don't. Att and Norm are the only ones ever showed the slightest interest in this farm. Is *this* all I'm gettin? Come on, I'm dyin to try it, not tryin to diet.'

'*I*'d like to look at yer cattle someday . . .'

'Would you indeed, Darryl. Well you've left your run too late. They're goin to the sale Mondey. Man can't do everything. I'm dispersin 'em.'

'Oh Dad! What are you gonna do with your time, when you retire?'

'Stand in front of this fuel stove and drive you mad. It's no good, Iris, me mind's made up. I already got 'em in the yard.'

'I was hopin you might come to the Rodeo, Dad. All the pickin up this year's bein done by your three sons.'

'Can't see Darryl pickin nothin up. London Fog, we shoulda called him, he never lifts. No, I don't think I'll have time, Fergus. I'm rippin up that red soil, if I can find the disc plough, and puttin in a crop o' spuds.'

'Didn't you make a barbecue out of the disc plough, Dad?'

'That was the disc harrow.'

Iris MacAnaspie: stuck in the nursing home here on the edge of town. Barney hasn't time to visit her, Norman can't get about—afflicted with the osteoarthritis—and Darryl only comes to town when he has to go to court. She is deaf as a post, poor old bugger, but she tries to lip-read. Doesn't get you far with Darryl.

28. *Resurrection of the Physical Body. A Millenarian Mystery.*

Uno itinere non potest perveniri ad tam grande secretum. One pathway is inadequate to penetrate the heart of so grand a secret. Symmachus, last apologist of pagan Rome, quoted by Toynbee. Symmachus kept a pet crocodile that died, because it wouldn't eat.

Funny the things that stay in your mind.

Almighty God, if there be one—so ran the Stoic prayer—I no longer anticipate Your Second Coming in a form I might recognise, I have to get it off me chest. I was drawn to the Gospel according to St Mark, though St Severinus is my main man. I recall still the thrill of reading, in Eugippius, how Severinus walked, unarmed, through the swords of the barbarians, and made the King of the Alemanni tremble in the face of his intrepidity. I used to invoke him, on the postal run.

Mark is an Heresiarch, wouldn't You agree? According to Mark, and his Gospel was the first Gospel to appear, the Incarnation of Christ occurred at the moment of Baptism, and the implications of Mark's adoptionist, as opposed to Luke's conceptionist, Christology—though, interestingly, both Mark and Luke trace Jesus' genealogy through Joseph—are that I, too, may be as Christ (*et ille Christus, et nos Christi*) and that if Christ were not born divine, farewell the cardboard nativity foldout. His Mother is of no more concern to me than the woman next door.

Where the worm dieth not, and the fire is not quenched.

I thus die a disaffected Anglo-Protestant, because I won't stick out my tongue for a woman's wafer. In the moribund Hellenism of the fourth century, women came to dominate the philosophical life. Think of an Hypatia, a Sosipatra.

'The invisible spirit which they had kindled,' says Gibbon, referring to the much maligned Cathars, 'still lived and breathed in the Western World. In the State, in the Church, and even in the cloister, a latent succession was preserved of the disciples of St Paul; who protested against the tyranny of Rome*, embraced the Bible as the rule of faith, and purified their creed from all the visions of the Gnostic theology. The struggles of Wycliff in England, of Huss in Bohemia, were premature and ineffectual; but the names of Zuinglius, Luther and Calvin are pronounced with gratitude, as the deliverers of nations.'

---

* As Toynbee points out, the Iconoclast, Islamic and, specifically, Protestant attacks on Mariolatry, were countered, in Rome, by the advent of the theses of Immaculate Conception and Assumption. Sheer fantasy . . .

Premature and ineffectual. Words that could be used to define Hell on Earth.

Nations, moreover, which in Gibbon's day were solely, and exclusively, the preserve of *men*.

'Men again,' I hear the dulcet voice of the gentle reader chime in. 'How paternalistic and patriarchal. Firstly, the arrogance. *He* can be as Christ, and Christ being a man, where does this leave wimin?' On the outer. Just as in the old world, wimin had no vote, civil rights being deemed to be purchased as the price of military service, what a joke. And secondly, the implications for this planet, and the species (though biology, as we now know, is not destiny) of striking out the consort of a gentile deity (Tammuz, for those with eyes to see: Apart from the well-known Greeks who became gods—Heracles, Dionysus, Ganymede, Asclepius—it is interesting, as Toynbee notes, that in the region of Galilee arose not one, but three religions, worshipping divine men. In the time of Christ, the cult of Simon Magus, responsible for the dreaded Irish tonsure, which survived down to the third century, arose in Samaria, while a thousand years later, the Shi'ite heretic Hakim became the locus of a dissident cult that survives among the Druses of Lebanon. Is it Campsie has the Maronites, Lakemba the Hezbollah? I'll never make a Sydney cabdriver; of striking out the consort of a gentile deity, the better to identify Him with His putative Hebrew Guardian, the Warlord Yahwe, the Galileans being gentiles, converted to Judaism, *by the sword*, during the rule of Alexander Jannaeus, a mere 100 BC.

And there be eunuchs, which have made themselves eunuchs, for the kingdom of heaven's sake. He that is able to receive it, let him receive it. Matthew. See also Isaiah.

And those that were unable to receive it have taught the word as a trope. *Phrygio quos tempus erat iam more supervacuam cultris abrumpere carnem.*

The time is long past when, Phrygian style, they ought to have lopped off the old boy. Juvenal.

St Mark begat Paul of Samosata, who begat Arius of Alexandria—whose followers included the Emperor Valens and the Vandals, Goths and Lombards who sacked the Roman Empire, and who didn't believe Christ was a god but thought of him more as a prophet; Augustine tells how Alaric, the Visigoth who sacked Rome in 410 AD, granted asylum to such of the populace as took refuge in the Christian churches—and Arius begat Nestorius, excommunicated at the Council of Ephesus for daring to suggest that though Mary was the Mother of Jesus, she could scarcely be the Mother of God—and Nestorius begat Luther, and Luther begat Descartes, who took up where the preSocratic Ionians left off. The way of the non-emasculated male is Power, War, Self-Knowledge, Dominion over Nature, while for you? Sweet Lady: the opportunity of having given birth to the better part of me. What more could you ask? Or can it be you're as weary of giving birth to the better part of me, as I am of attempting to catch the fickle eye of the worser part of you?

Alas, you have no Y chromosome, Love. So I can encompass you. But you can never encompass me. The male of our species is a specialised female, and the male of our species parasitises the female.

I have heard sex is a tactic that keeps us one step ahead of the infusorian.

Invocation of the Immaculate Virgin, Our Lady of Perpetual Succour, Mater Dolorosa, Mystic Rose, Queen of Heaven, all the rest of that, was something I never understood, and frankly, not something I admired. I cannot worship a goddess. Blind I may be, but I'm no Venetian. I am no Anatolian. I couldn't worship my own mother, which may be the key to it all. We only met, on three occasions, but then—no, I tell a lie, it was four—I couldn't worship my own father, and so I think I may have ended up worshipping my own potential, but my own potential for what, in view of my undoubted, and all-encompassing, underachievement?

Manliness? Lack of it? Hideous, to think, in these final days, or hours, the question looms again large, provoked by this sybaritic sodality of Postmodern bushwhacking misfits.

But a Faith, to survive, needs missions: a closed order of eunuchs, that stink of pennyroyal and eucalypt oil, will not achieve the desired end.

I have wasted much valuable time this past year, studying the works of Abelard and Origen. I did so, because they were both eunuchs and both Christian theologians. The only interesting concurrence I found is that both consider God could not do what He has not done, i.e., that He was not free. The *tertium quid*, then, is not tortured, as a real man is, by possibility, by the thought of what might have been.

Those four late votive reliefs of Cybele, now in the Selcuk museum. Each features a trinity. She is in the middle, flanked by a younger man in profile, to her right. To her left stands an older, full-bearded, patriarchal type.

Attis, Cybele, Zeus?

Christ, Mary, God the Father?

Let me float this one past you: Eunuch, Woman, Man. Then it all starts to make some sense.

Act 1 Scene 3

29. *Olaf writes to Nisi from Puckapunyal Army Camp. Brian encounters Eugene, worse for wear, in Woolloomooloo.*

Second Recruit
Training Battalion
Puckapunyal
October 26 1968

Dear Nisi,

Well, this is to be my home for the next 9 weeks, and though it's warmer here than the Blue Mountains, it is a pretty cheerless hole. 2 RTB are isolated from the rest of the camp, which includes the Armoured Corps, and a couple of infantry battalions. The barrack huts and admin buildings are painted grey, the parade ground and all the open spaces between the huts are grey stones, and the pathways are grey concrete slabs. When we got in on the buses, at 6 a.m., there were 2 guys doing laps of the parade ground, carrying rocks. They got here the day before us, and were being punished for having put their gaiters on back to front. One has since filled out a stat dec (statutory declaration), to claim he's a CO (conscientious objector).

I'm in C, or Charlie, Company (this is probably of no interest, but I can't think of anything else to say. Brainwashed.). Our company colour is blue. Alpha is red, Bravo yellow, Delta green. We have a blue flag on our parade ground, and blue lettering in our huts, which goes nicely with the grey. My platoon is mostly from Perth and Adelaide. There are 32 to a platoon, about 5 platoons in a company (I think). We live 16 to a hut, in alphabetical order. I'm in A-B hut. A's up one end, B's down the other. We each have a bed, a locker, and a writing table with a chair, all painted grey. I'm sitting on my grey chair, at my grey desk, as I write this note.

Our platoon commander is a second lieutenant, or one pipper, who's a Nasho himself, a 90-day wonder (as the Duntroon and Parksea graduates call them) from the Officer Training Unit (OTU) at Scheyville. After 4 weeks here, or Kapooka, where 1 RTB is based, officer candidates are transferred. They take themselves pretty seriously. All former school prefects, or cadet NCO's. Arseholes.

Next in command is the platoon sergeant, then the corporal RDI's, the regimental drill instructors. I spend most of my life at the mercy of these turkeys. They get up before us, and are belting on the sides of our huts, by 6 a.m. One is always threatening to insert his size 10 boot up my arse, to the sixth bootlace, and telling me how I stand out on parade like a dog's dick in a rice pudding. We have a company ser-major (CSM), who's also a complete arsehole, a major OC (Officer Commanding) and a few captains. Our battalion CO is a colonel, so we don't get to see much of him.

Soon as we arrived, we were each given a haircut, whether we needed it or not, and a series of injections, and were made to complete an IQ and a personality test. It is rumoured anyone intelligent, or of sound personality, is cashiered. Then we got kitted out. I am the proud possessor of 2 pairs boots, 1 pair shoes dress, 3 pairs socks, 1 pair sandshoes black, 2 sets jungle greens, 2 sets battledress woollen, 1 jumper (khaki), 3 sets underwear (khaki), 1 pair shorts drill, 2 shirts (khaki), 1 tie, 1 hat slouch, 1 beret, 1 belt webbing—khaki, but our first job was to blacken it with polish boot and spirits methylated—rifle, bayonet, cleaning gear, and so on. All this must be kept spit polished and brassoed daily.

If you like the idea of a beret (as I did), wait till you see mine. It's horrible. Large and floppy, and covers one ear completely. The cavalry wear small, black berets, which look quite smart actually, so a couple of guys in my platoon decided they would shrink theirs, to look like the cavalry. They were duly abused on parade, and had to buy new ones.

Each morning we are woken, 6 a.m., by a scratchy record of a bugle, and The Last Post is played at 10 p.m. We fall out for roll call, in our greatcoats and thongs—I don't think I mentioned those, did I?—and have to have a shower, shave, shit and shampoo by breakfast at 6.30. The food's not bad. Sundays, we get to sleep in till seven, and except for compulsory Church parade, which is a great yawn, have a free day, but there's nothing to do here, and nowhere to go.

Basic training so far has been mostly parade drill, with weapons, and PT. I find I'm rather unfit, and am doing it hard. Later, we get to do more interesting stuff, like map reading.

After 5 weeks we get 4 days off, and God, am I looking forward to it. A special train will take us to Melbourne, and I intend to fly straight to Sydney. I really should be at Kapooka, as you know. I'm hoping we could spend the time together, Nisi, can Mon look after the boys? I'll let you know exactly when this will be, a little later.

About halfway through our basic training, we have to nominate first and second choice for Corps training. Apart from the fact we'll all be eligible for cheap housing loans, the only bright piece of news I have had is I can apply for Infantry bandsman. Now the army bands are all Infantry, except for the Armoured Corps band, but if I could get into a Command band, of which there is one in each state capital, I wouldn't have to go to Vietnam. Mind you, if I only make a battalion band, then I may have to go to Vietnam as a stretcher bearer, and they have as big a chance of being shot as anyone. Of course, if I don't make a band, I've nominated Infantry (Vietnam). No one in his right mind would nominate Infantry, first choice. So maybe I should just nominate Ordnance, Medical, something like that, what do you think? It's a big gamble.

Yes, I know they don't have guitars in military bands, as yet, but I've heard they have been known to put keyboard players, and guitarists, straight onto clarinet, from scratch. It's amazing how fast you learn, when your life depends on it.

Did you see where the Melbourne postman was sentenced to 2 years jail for disobeying his call-up notice? He's not even a pacifist. He apparently told the judge he objected to Australia's role in Vietnam. Well I don't know that Pentridge Gaol could be worse than here, but I guess we're only here for 10 weeks, God willing.

Pray for me, Nisi, and give my love to the horse, and Aloysius and Tim. I do miss you all, and don't forget what I said about Calvin Ecks. He is not to be trusted.

Olaf Abernathy: Passes for a woman now, calls herself 'Olive'. Very likely now regrets she never fought in Vietnam. All those baby boomers now regret they never fought in Vietnam.

Patria, o mei creatrix! Patria, o mea genetrix!
Ego quam miser relinquens, dominos ut erifugae
Famuli solent ...
Homeland, My Creator! Homeland, my very life stuff!
I, miserable bastard, who pissed off like a runaway slave ...

Catullus

Australia is so dull, such a backwater, so derivative of foreign trends, the scribe with ambition gets out soon as he can, to ape those trends, the more assiduously; while we, to show our pride in the scribe and express our heartfelt gratitude, inscribe the scribe's name on a brass plaque, and even award him, or her, the highly esteemed Wombat Gong.

What manner of folk are we, *au fond*? In view of the national debt, we may safely say of ourselves (as the Cynic said to Lycinus) that local productions will not do for us, but the world must be our storehouse; that our native land and its seas are quite insufficient; that we purchase our pleasures from the ends of the earth, prefer the exotic to the homegrown, the costly to the cheap, and the rare to the common; in fact, that we would rather have troubles and complications than avoid them.

Patriotism? Last refuge of the scoundrel, old son. According to some bloated, carious, up-himself Fleet Street hack, whose asinine apothegm is held to outrank the Proper and Natural promptings of the gods of the Hearth. It was never easy, being a pioneer. Selling out? That was always easy.

And don't think we aren't snobs, because we're fools, and we're fools because, as Lucian says, those whose country is their true Mother love the land whereon they were born and bred, though it be narrow and rough and poor of soil.

The Royal George is the chief puking hole of the Bunch o' Cunts, that coterie of freethinking Sydney beatniks and their bourgeois claque, but Brian Chegwodden, not wanting to be tempted in the flesh, drinks nowdays at the Criterion, imbibing, with the beer, philosophies more liberal than libertarian. He is back with his wife, as Mum predicted, enjoying the new baby daughter heaps. In a way, he regrets what happened with Paula Zoshka, but he'd do it again. *Que sera, sera.*

This late October night, he decides to take a short stroll, as soon as the pub is shut, to sober up. The mood of the city is black as Brian's skivvy; Ron Clarke failed us in the 10,000 metres and Jackie Kennedy married Ari Onassis, why? Because she felt old age creeping on. Sockit t'me.

Fires have broken out in the Blue Mountains, and Brian Chegwodden has been covering these fires, if not with a wet blanket. Luckier scribes are in Mexico, checking out the Mescal. Ron Clarke may have let us down, but Ralph Doubell just scored an upset victory in the 800 metres. Only in sport, where there can be no question of who won, do Australians rate an ecumenical mention, and because we are such a forward-thinking folk, we take this hard, some of us.

For we *are* unique, and know it. Self-condemned as back-woodsmen, in fact, we are the Western World's avant-garde. Nietzsche's Last Man arrived in Europe and the US, scarcely before the Polish Pope. As Peter Coleman points out, he came to Australia with the First Fleet.

Doom of Tithonus. Yet can it be something is stirring here, for the first time in 200 years, give or take a midget sub? Some outside force prompting a response, some mobilisation of the social bone marrow, producing an alexin?

Wait a bit: this must be '68, it's a GI, stepping out from the doorway of Jimmy Carruthers' pub. He's in uniform, too. Drunk.

'Hey, buddy.' He waves at Brian. Is this a touch? Where are the girls?

'You lost, pal?'

'Yeah, but I could stay lost. Nice city you got here.'

'Thank you. What can we do for ya?'

'Oh I dunno. Whattaya got? Got any smoke?'

'Thought you were the guys with the weed.'

'Left my weed at home, man. Not talkin bout weed. You like to smoke?'

'Sometimes. Where are you staying? We should get you into a cab, I think. You look tired.'

'Yeah, I'm tired. What's your name, Buddy?'

'Brian. Brian Chegwodden.'

'Very *in*teresting. What do you do?'

'Nothin much. Write a bit for radio.'

'I'm a warrior. Hey—don't go, buddy. Talk to me, a whiles.'

'Sure. How long you been here?'

'Two days. I haven't been out of that bar in two days. Man, I never used to drink like that. What is happening to me?'

'You're tired, man. But you're out here for R&R, I take it, so it's OK. Relax.'

'Freedom from Fear, man. You don't know what that means. A cold beer, a soft bed, but Freedom from Fear is more important.'

'Absolutely. Would you care for a pie with peas? Hungry?'

'Smiling friendly faces. Sound of English in the streets. But more important than either one of these, Freedom from Fear. You don't know what it means.'

'No, you're right, I probably don't. See, I never fought in a war.'

'Don't do it! I got shot down, during Tet. Wasn't injured bad.'

'You were lucky. OK, let's walk a little ways. You like zoos? We have a great zoo here. Beautiful views of our harbour, from Taronga Park.'

'I couldn't handle it, man. See, *I* was in a cage, only recently. Got shot down over a North Vietnamese Army Regimental Base Camp. This was during Tet. They're tough mothers, man. Live off the land. All they carry is a shovel 'n a mattock head, couple of tin pots. Eat leaves. Shoes are inner tube. All I got to eat was salt water and pumpkin.'

'Good God.'

'Yeah, but I escaped. I did it. And now I'm here, to stay with my brother.'

'What? You got a brother in Sydney?'

'Oh yeah. I got a brother in Sydney. He works at the College of Knowledge.'

'Then there's no problem. We'll get you to your brother's house. Come on. What's the address?'

'Dunno. Forgot. Was in my wallet, but my wallet's gone. Think I musta been rolled. Doesn't matter.'

'I'd say it does! What about your money and papers?'

'Doesn't fuckin matter, man. What's money? Freedom from

Fear is the main thing. Let's walk round, and enjoy Freedom from Fear.'

'I won't notice it. Does that strike you as odd?'

'No. I remember that. We take all our freedoms for granted.'

'Hey, you're a mixed-up guy. I like you. What's your name?'

'Who gives a shit?'

'OK. But we could find your brother's house, if you could tell me your surname. Was he expecting you?'

'No. Wzzz my lighter?'

'You dropped it. Here.'

'Read what's written on it.'

'Ours not to Do and Die, ours but to Smoke and Stay High.'

'Man who knows has a Ronson Adonis. Yours, f'r gift. Gonna need a smoke soon, man.'

'I can rustle up some weed, I think.'

'Not talkin bout weed. What's this fuckin weed? Wanta know how I escaped?'

'Yeah, sure.'

'So do I. Don' remember. *Do* remember why. Nothin to smoke, in the cage.'

'Oh Christ, you mean heroin? Oh ho ...'

'Never chased the dragon man, don't knock it. Saved my life.'

'Bullshit, you're in deep shit now. You got a habit. Better watch what you're saying, too, I could write a story on this. How many like you, for Chrissake?'

'What do I care, man? I'm in the fuckin firin line. Why should I give a fuck about any fuckin thing?'

'Hey hey hey, settle down! We don't want the MPs round. Now listen, I think I know someone who may be able to put you onto some smack, though I can't guarantee it, and then we'll go round to your brother's place. How does that sound?'

'Very interesting. I'm not goin back to Nam. Give Peace a Chance. What do you say?'

'Yeah, fuck'em. That's what I say.'

Eugene Ecks: fathered no children, during his stay in the Valley, and like his older brother Calvin, never became a eunuch. You might wonder, as I do, how they knew who fathered whom

177

down there, but Kimbo asserts the women were never in doubt, so there you are. Secret Women's Business. Perhaps Eugene was sterile. According to Kimbo, the men became eunuchs during the Period of Autarky, when the Valley was cut off from the outside world, after the second rockfall. This was during the eighties. The Passion, according to the *Ballad*, occurred while Tim was at the high school here, which means it must have happened in 1980, or thereabouts. The Gap Road was reopened by Darryl and his team, May '86. During the Period of Autarky, which commenced mid-79, events described in the *Ballad* either occurred, or did not occur, but what is certain is that during that seven-year period, six male communards—Attis and Fergus MacAnaspie, Michael Ginnsy, Derek Frodsham, Olaf Abernathy and Kimberley Moon—emasculated themselves. Was a Spell broken when some man failed to perform his divine duty, and a year went by without the glade receiving its annual rent? Just a thought. Anyway, this contagious madness at first infuriated the women, who interpreted the men's abandonment of responsibility as dereliction. But how many men do you need? We're only a bloody nuisance. As implied in the poem, not all the men capitulated anyway; Grainger and Max apparently shot through, during the Passion Fire. Of those who remained, Calvin, a coward, began to argue for celibacy, while Darryl and Eugene exhausted themselves, in raids on each other's harem. But the women had dried crying wives in the huts, so there could be no pregnancies, and the children already born in the Valley were no longer ageing. The women and eunuchs were no longer ageing. Only surviving men were ageing. Now this may not have been generally perceived, by the men, but Tim would certainly have twigged. Passionflower still two years old, when her father sees her, seven years on! We know something blew his mind. He doesn't mention what.

Towards the ending of his *Ballad*, he implies emasculation of the young, but this, I'm sure, is poetic licence. There would have been prosecutions from the Welfare. No, the young voted with their feet. Spell broken, typical commune kids, they wanted no part of the Valley. Too restrictive down there. If Tim, first to turn his back on the New Dispensation, made restitution, the others—who were making themselves obnoxious in Obliqua Creek by this stage—were seized by the State in '89, and given surnames, and shoes, and a Postmodern education. Only Harley and Norton returned to the Valley, there to live the logger lifestyle, but they have replanted the Flat with eucalyptus, to give them their due. Shining gum.

30. *Nisi and children arrive to stay with Monica in Paddington. Monica argues with Brian. Balthazar's quandary. Frodsham's quandary.*

'Oh you got here, oh thank God. We been so concerned. Cindy's been up since 4 a.m. waiting for Tim to arrive. Hi Aloysius! Come on in, guys. Did you bring sleeping bags?'

'Mon, we can't stay.'

'Course you can, and yes you will. We owe that much to Olaf. It's OK with Calvin. He knows about forest fires. Never here anyway.'

'I still don't know.'

'You think about it, honey, while I make a pot of tea. Aloysius, if you like to go upstairs, you'll find Alex's room on the left. It's the one with the Jimi Hendrix poster. Don't play the hi fi too loud now. Cindy is over in preschool, Nisi, but the teachers know about the fires, and Tim is real welcome, I checked. Is your house threatened?'

'Well no, not at this stage, as the fire is down in the valley, but the whole Park is a tinderbox, Monica. You saw that.'

'Oh yeah, we saw it. Calvin was telling us how these eucalypt forests actually like fires. Spooky.'

'It's the horse I'm worried about. Smoke spooks him something dreadful. We only rent the house, and we own nothing of value. I took him back to the stables yesterday, but the smoke was actually thicker there, so then I found I couldn't pull the float back up the hill? Because the car was vapourising? And then it got suddenly cold and started to snow, and when I tried to get him out of the float, because I had jack-knifed it, trying to reverse, I couldn't get the tail down, because the bolts on these hire floats are so

179

rusted out, and he went berserk. Luckily, the bushfire brigade stopped, and some of the guys helped out, before he kicked the float to pieces. I think I'm going to have to buy my own float, and then I'll need a vehicle that can pull it.'

'And do you have the money for all this?'

'I guess you always find the money if you need it. There's always money for a funeral.'

'I guess so. How's Olaf?'

'I think he'll like being in the army, Mon. I really do.'

'Oh. Should we send little Tim over the road now?'

'Don't worry about him. He'll probably go back to sleep. He didn't get much sleep lately. None of us did.'

'Tell me about it. Cindy will be here like a rocket, when she sees that car parked outside. Where'd you leave it?'

'Down on the corner. I have the float with the horse on, too. It's a real worry, Monica. I'm going to have to find Jack another paddock, and there's no grass anyway, and they'll all soon be burned out. I had him in a paddock owned by an old lady for a while, but her little plastic gardening pots kept blowing over the fence, and he kept putting his feet through them? And she'd always fill me up with cups of tea, so my bladder was full on the rides? And, of course, if you have a dog, her cats never like your dog? It's always the same, with these old ladies.'

'We'll be old ladies one day. Nisi, you can't keep a horse in Paddington.'

'I'll take him round to the Showground later. They have stables in Randwick, too. Hey. I had a strange and beautiful dream the other night. May I tell you about it?'

'OK. Just so long as it doesn't excite me.'

'I'm sure it won't excite you, Monica. My dreams aren't like yours.'

'I dream of shopping.'

'I'll bet. Yes, I dreamt I was in this amazing Valley, that was just perfect for horses. I was riding down through this wonderful . . . '

'Oh my God, there's the front door. Excuse me. Is that Cindy home already? I hope not. Hold your horses, Nisi. Coming!'

'Hello there.'

'Hi. You guys are Mormons, I think it's a crock.'

'Nothing like that. Don't you recognise this man? What if I tell you he has a marihuana leaf tattoo on his right shoulder?'

'Oh my heaven, it's not . . . ?'

'Lo, Monica.'

'Eugene! It *is* you. But we heard you were missing in action, man! Since Tet. Do come in.'

'I'll be on my way.'

'No, please come in. I just made a pot of Earl Grey tea, Nun's Piss, as my husband calls it. Nisi, look who is here! My brother-in-law Eugene, with a friend. I didn't recognise him. Boys, this is Nisi.'

'Pleased to meet you, ma'am.'

'I'll go get extra cups.'

'Are you out here on R&R, Eugene? My husband is in camp at the moment. Since yesterday. Well, he's not really my husband.'

'Mmhuh . . . pooped . . . Mzz.'

'Hey, what's happening here? Has he collapsed?'

'Could I see you in private a moment, Mrs Ecks?'

'Oh, I had no idea. He can't stay here.'

'But he'll have to.'

'No, you take him back to where you found him. I have children living here, refugees from the bushfires! Do you think you did the right thing, taking him where he could bomb out on drugs? I don't think so. I think you're an opportunist little shit.'

'Please show the man some compassion. Who knows they're not all like him now?'

'Come on boy, this guy's a druggie from way back. Eugene is the family black sheep. He was born to be high. He hadn't dropped out o' college . . . '

'Oh my God, you're so heartless.'

'And you're just a good Samaritan, I suppose. Go on, get outta here and take your junkie pal along. I don't want either one of you round.'

'I see. Well, can I at least have your husband's work number?'

'No you may not.'

'Look, he lost his wallet, he's got no money, and you're going to turn him out in the streets? To be arrested?'

'Damn right I am.'

'Well, I'm not convinced this is what your husband would want for his serviceman brother. I demand to speak with him.'

'Who the hell do you think you are?'

'I am a journalist on one of the major papers, lady. Now would you like to see this story written up with your photo in it?'

'You don't scare me that way. I was a *Playboy* centrefold.'

'Sorry to interrupt, Monica, but Cindy has just come home from preschool, and your brother-in-law has been terribly sick all over the lounge suite. Can you tell me where to find the disinfectant?'*

'Oh God, I think I'll go back to bed.'

'Look I'm terribly sorry about all this, I really am. But I do think your husband should be here.'

'OK, I'll ring him now. You're right. I pass. I'm out.'

Balthazar, meantime, is in the classic crop-grower's bind: if he doesn't soon sell the heads he kept from last year's drought-declared crop, in order to fetch a higher price for them on the spring market, there's a chance he will smoke them himself, with his friends, and then he won't have the necessary for the fare to India. Or at least, he will have money enough for his own fare, but Rainbow—who has helped a great deal, by hiding four plants from him and holding out against his tantrums, the traditional winter role of the crop-grower's consort—will not be able to accompany him, and what is an addict without his Saki? Ask Omar Khayyam. Yielding, finally, to good sense, and feeling already the wellbeing and virtue you do feel, whenever you suspect you may have been smoking a little too much, perhaps, for slightly too long, and living in fear, with sore lungs and prostate and throat, but knowing now that your stash, if

---

* She would have used the diminutive; she would have said 'disso', for sure. But Monica wouldn't have known what she meant, and I needs must abbreviate my dialogue.

not your clever kick, will soon be converted to more widely negotiable currency, Beauregard is meeting an old friend, who does a little dealing on the side, and off the top, at times.

Shall we drink water and decline to assume female attire at the Dionysia? Is it such a crime to smoke the green weed? *Loripedem rectus derideat, Aethiopem albus*. Let the upright deride the lame, and the white man the blackfella. Juvenal.

Bear in mind that while Isaiah describes the Jews of his day as drunks, by the time of Clement those who use water in the Eucharist are proscribed as heretics. How do we get the toothpaste back in the tube, anyway? Statistically speaking, it does no harm, and has to be the hardiest herb know to man. Balthazar actually grew these plants on the fringes of a State forest—he's been visiting the North Coast for aeons—and they were never even watered, let alone weeded or fed. Wallabies took a few. Anyone can grow it, most anywhere. The police would be better occupied consulting their own credibility, detecting unregistered trailers and otherwise searching out the real crimes, and the real crims, and they should leave the citizens alone, to smoke as they please, and what they choose, in the privacy of their own homes, indeed, in public places, but I don't advocate decriminalisation: leegalize it, and you wipe out the rural economy.

'Time for a small fifty while we weigh this, man?'

'Sure. Oh you got the scales out. I already weighed it.'

'Yeah I know, but these deal bags are getting heavier all the time, don't you find? There'll be no problem.'

'I hope not. It's all sinsemilla. This is top dope, man.'

'Sure smells strong. Hey, you didn't come all the way from Central Station carrying this big garbage bag, I hope?'

'Yeah.'

'Oh no. Well, do you think that was wise?'

'Whattaya mean?'

'Oh Jesus. Anyone follow you?'

'Oh for Christ sake, relax. What is this?'

'You got off the North Coast Mail! Man, I can't believe anyone could be so stupid.'

'Whattaya mean? What are ya talkin about?'

'You been in the sticks too long. You dunno what it's like

now. Jesus Christ, John and Yoko just got busted the other day.'

'So? They jailed Dr Spock. What does that prove?'

'Ssh. I'll have a peek through these ven ... oh no. Who is that man? You know him? I don't ... oh no, he's crossing the street now. I want you to leave.'

'What?'

'Yeah go on, get out! Use the back door. Take it with ya. Take it all, take your bag.'

'Ar come on man, you're bein paranoid.'

'Get out, go on! Take the bag.'

'Farkin hell ...'

Even at the wheel of the Morris Oxford, with three on the tree and baldy boots, Barbara Byng is a fast, erratic driver. Her every departure, throughout life, will be accompanied with a crunch of gears and a flash of the reverse lights. Spotting Balthazar, who is strolling disconsolately along, inspecting a bandaid over the finger where his pet pygmy possum bit him, she pulls over, like a cabbie who has seen a fare, on a wet winter's Monday night. For his part, Balthazar finds this unexpected attention confusing, and unwelcome. He shrinks back against the brick wall. The car is full of gesticulating people, but the windows won't wind down, so it's hard to hear what is being shouted, above the hue of the horns, protesting, no doubt, the blockage of a city-bound artery during the late morning peak hour.

'Balthazar, isn't it? Balthazar Beauregard?' The future senator recalls all names. She has forced open the driver's side door, and is standing up on the brake pedal. We can see her winsome, freckled face, like a sunflower, over the roof of the car.

'You doing anything? Want to come on a sit-in?'

She makes it sound such fun. Well, I suppose they were a lot of fun, all the fun of a fun run, if you like parades, marches, vigils, strikes, pickets, deputations, public meetings, pamphlets, boycotts, slogans, songs and all that sort of thing. So this is how she musters the troops, picks them off the streets. And though you might have thought the car pretty full, with five people crammed onto the back seat, they manage, somehow, to make room for Balthazar together with his garbage bag, and they've not gone far before Barbara recognises someone else, and has both feet on the floor again. The brake lights don't work, so this whole exercise is fraught with terrible danger. But something in the combination of frottage with mortal terror, conducted in a Morris Oxford, is the ticket to enliven a devotee of the subcontinent, after a sleepless night spent sitting up on a permanent way. There are nine in the vehicle, by the time the greenhouses of Sydney University come into view, and Barbara could as easily fill up again, but this is her third run for the morning, and twenty-five people probably suffice to occupy a vice-chancellor's anterooms.

Waving blithely at the man on the checkpoint, a very good friend, Barbara Byng drives straight through, and heads off, around the number two oval, towards the Teachers' College. Here, she is confronted by a stern-faced Derek Frodsham, wearing his demo boilersuit, waving his hands like a car lot attendant, and side-valving like a guest of the governor at Long Bay Gaol, but in a Yorkshire accent. 'It's off' he announces. 'VC agrees to meet deputaation from Student Body, however still maintains right of faculties to appoint Seth Efrican citizens, and here we shall have to think very carefully about what action we propose, Barbara. By the way, could you come and have a word with a couple of the gals? They appear to have chained themselves to the front gate, I don't know why. Can't get the keys off them.'

So various the inequities vying for Frodsham's attentions at this point, he scarcely knows in which direction to lob his figurative Molotov cocktails. Naturally, he's involved in the turmoil in the local Communist Party. The Prague invasion has split the Communist Party of Australia to the point where the national executive fired off a stiff protest note to Moscow. That would have had them trembling in their boots in the Politburo. A meeting convoked by the CPA to protest the betrayal of Dubcek attracted over a thousand people to the basement of the Sydney Town Hall; better known, nowdays, as the registration bay for the City to Surf Fun Run (times change, if not the need to block the thoroughfares: ectomise *Medecins sans Frontières*, where's the *élan* of Paris '68?). But *Tribune*, in the interests of free speech, reprinted the Brezhnev apologia, and the Stalinist hardline old guard is fighting for survival, using kicks to the knees and blows to the balls. Elsewhere, on the local front, the first successful strike in the history of the Teachers' Union has just been organised, whilst overseas, the Lout from Austin, in a late *ukase*, orders a halt to the bombing of North Vietnam, to boof up the Paris Talks. In London, one hundred thousand drawing-room socialists march against the War, and they aren't even fighting the bloody War. This, of course, does not protect them from being beaten up in Grosvenor Square.

How bitterly Frodsham regrets his presence in the Colony, when he hears of the London march.

London! Paris! Prague! Oh to be in Europe, now that Spring is here.

In fact, Frodsham has scarcely time to spare for the local anti-War movement. Hasn't done any Physics in months, either. One must strike while iron is hot, and while Frodsham's preferred social dispensation closely resembles that depicted in the Heliopolitan mural on the wall of the wharfies' canteen, for the students of Sydney University, it translates as more say in what they are taught. To be sure, he still goes down to taps each Friday afternoon, and participates, as a member of the Vietnam Action Committee, in the weekly march, but it seems never to attract more than the same thousand or so stalwarts, which may, or may not, be due to the preoccupation of key activists, like Frodsham, with other concerns. It's coming to the boil, do you see? It's *all* coming to the boil. The impetus is shifting towards draft resistance anyway. *Save Our Sons*! Imagine the politicisation of all those apathetic housewives. The *soi-disant* liberal democrat would poo his pants in the parliament.

Is it possible Frodsham may live to take part in the first unFucked-up Revolution? The proletariat *will* rejoin its vanguard, the heart demands no less. Let the Peoples Arise! Let their Will be Done! Let them wipe the shit out of their purblind peepers, seize their Destiny in both hands, and accept responsibility for their own behaviour. And hip hip hooray say I, if this means, that when they have locked themselves out of their vehicle, they no longer demand of a passing postman, he should stop what he is doing to race home and fetch a coathanger.

'Anyone interested in buying some of this?' inquires Baltha-zar, opening his garbage bag. It's got a hole in it, he sees now.

Barbara Byng: early twenties, slight, fair, freckle-faced, braces on her teeth. Drives with the skirt of her dress aflap outside and beneath the driver's side door.

Now two of the three girls who have chained themselves to the front gate are tyros, quickly cut free with a pair of bolt cutters, wielded by a demonstrator from the Chemistry School. But Diane Zoshka has used a combination lock, purchased from a Jewish locksmith, of steel so strong, and hard, it needs to be sundered with a blowtorch; and as the lock is pressed against her throat, the use of oxy would seem impracticable. After discussion, it is agreed there is nothing for it but to cut the chain, and this will take time, because it's a length of railway safety chain, with links so big they barely fit between the apertures in the gate, and so heavy they are strangling Diane. Only the single exertions of several strong men in succession, holding off the chain, allow her to draw breath. There will be ample time for the media to assemble. Already, a crowd is gathered—students, bowlers from the nearby rink, swimmers from the nearby Olympic Pool—and many are voicing support of Diane's refusal to divulge the lock combination. When one brave man, in uniform, attempts to put his hands on the lock barrels, he is almost lynched: any attempted molestation, by a person in blue, of an enchained neck arouses in the citizens of Sydney the most atavistic of animosities. In fact, Barbara Byng and Derek Frodsham, looking on, while disapproving, are impressed. What a pity Diane couldn't have sought the sanction of older, wiser heads. Even the smock she has chosen to assume, one of her sister Paula's—diaphanous, preRaphaelite—is the kind of garment she would never normally wear, and demonstrates flair, and instinctive acumen.

'I wonder what she means to say,' says Barbara, voicing Frodsham's concern precisely. 'Is the press coming?'

'Yes,' replies Frodsham. 'Someone rang TV. They'll be here any moment, with the press. Have you, er, spoken to Diane recently? You know what this is about? I can't think it has any bearing on what we had planned for today.'

'No, but I do know she is coming up in court again soon. I

think it has to do with throwing the red paint over the veterinary surgery.'

'I hope this has nothing to do with that. You don't think it would, do you?'

'I don't know. What do you think?'

Balthazar, who's strongly built, shoulders of a chippie's apprentice, takes his turn holding the chain, in fact, he's the man holding the chain as the chain is being cut, and his hands are burning. And because Diane finds herself, when the moment of glory arrives, when the cameras are trained upon her and the crowd silent at last, utterly and totally speechless, incapable of uttering a word, he finds himself going back with her, in the Morris Oxford, to her sister's flat, because she is so very disappointed she wants only to die, and refuses to undo the lock, so there is this potentially lethal length of chain, about as heavy as Balthazar can manage to lift with one arm, while holding his garbage bag with the other, hanging from her neck, which is red and black and blue, by this stage, from dust and soot and bruises and burns, when Paula Zoshka opens the door, not only to her sister, whom she has recently evicted, and Balthazar Beauregard, holding the chain, but also Derek Frodsham and Barbara Byng, who have come along to proffer their wise counsel, and Brian Chegwodden, who, would you believe, was sent out to cover the story, and who has just determined he does love Diane's sister, after all, and can no longer deceive himself in this regard, because of his colitis; and later, during what is to prove an evening nearly as momentous as that on which was held the Wake for Martin Luther King, they are joined by Michael Ginnsy, who, having been contacted by Brian Chegwodden, at Balthazar Beauregard's request, by phone, decides he has a commercial interest in the contents of the garbage bag, and Eugene Ecks, who, when he woke, went straight back round to Michael Ginnsy's place, and Calvin Ecks, who went along to keep an eye on his younger brother, and later, Monica Ecks too, because Calvin Ecks, her husband, has to ring her to tell her where they are, and it sounds to her, over the phone, like a party going on, which by this stage, it is; and Monica's good friend Nisi Papadimitriou, who is staying with them, and who is anyway known to Barbara Byng and Derek

Frodsham from the Vietnam Action Committee, and dozens of other people, too numerous to mention here.

Balthazar Beauregard: the personal use of marihuana, now considered a misdemeanour, was seen as depravity on a par with sodomy, in '68. But in the twenty-seven years since elapsed, discrimination, from being a virtue, has become a vice, in the same way that enthusiasm, at one time a vice, became a virtue.

31. *Ginnsy invites Eugene and Brian to his pad.*

'Not bad,' pronounces Michael Ginnsy, 'but you should taste the muscat at *my* place.'

'Why don't we go round there now?' says Eugene Ecks, conspiratorially. 'Calvin passed out.'

'Do it,' commands a jovial Brian Chegwodden, who's had an idea for radio. Three muscateers, one in his top hat, leave the party, to commandeer a cab. They're soon outside the Royal Sydney Golf Course, close by the Wintergarden Cinema.

'*Entrez,*' says Ginnsy, escorting them up the stairwell of an old, postwar redbrick.

'Nice place,' whispers Eugene, 'like a womb. Feels safe. Dig the plush carpet.'

Eugene has changed uniform. His T-shirt inquires, 'Lee Harvey Oswald, where are you now that we need you?'

'Don't feel you're taking a risk, Ginnsy? I mean, a lot of people must visit.'

'Here we go, boys, come on in. Please excuse the mess.'

'Don't the neighbours get suspicious?'

'Look, I'm the best guitarist in the world. I don't think o' myself as a dealer, and if I was, there'd be more wisdom pushers than dope dealers roamin these streets and no one busts them.'

'Right on,' says Eugene, 'because if someone has something someone else needs, who's to say that someone won't have something the someone wants, at some stage? Guess what I'm tryin to say is, you dudes are the two best buddies I ever had. You showed me friendship in a strange land, man, and, you know, that's kinda heavy? I think I prefer tea to muscat at this stage. Where's this from?'

'Oh, ah, that big island to the north of Australia. You know the name of it. What's it called again?'

'New Guinea?'

'Nah. Doesn't matter. Here, smell this, man.'

'Wow! Smell this, Brian. I spent a fair bit of time in Nam, searching for a rare camellia.'

'Hmm! Delicate aroma, man. Should I make a pot of tea?'

'Yeah, we have just time for a pot of tea, then we must be gettin back.'

'I'll put the jug on.'

'So you're gettin engaged to this, ah, what was her name?'

'The gorgeous Paula. It was her idea.'

'Hey, dig the size of these leaves. So where'd you score this stuff, man?'

'Thirty-eight DD, 24, 35. Think I'm stupid?'

'Oh, ah, come in on one of those, er, one of those little, er, round things with wings. You know the name of 'em.'

'Gee man, this place could use a clean-up. What's with the greasy dumbbells?'

'Those are CV joints for a former Kombi. They go through 'em like you wouldn't believe. Yeah, I actually had a chick living here till recently. Go-go dancer. Nice chick, but it didn't work out.'

'Course it didn't work out. When did it ever work out? They only open their legs to have something to talk about with their girlfriends.'

'Don't let the tea stew, man.'

'No, no. Tea should be ready now. Taste this, boys.'

'Oh, this is beautiful, man, this is real tea. So what is it scented with?'

'Yeah, I do know, man, but I forget. I won't be able to tell you. Taste this, Brian. This is real tea. Yeah, she did a terrible thing to me, this chick, in the end. Got possessive and then, when I come home late from the gig one afternoon, she had moved out, but before going, she had taken my Twinings-

Teas—the Russian Caravan, Orange Pekoe, Lapsang Souchong, the lot—taken all my packets of tea, and she had dumped them in the tub, man, and you should see the tub now. I don't know what to do with it. Should have seen the bathwater!'

'Lucky she didn't find this stuff.'

'Oh she couldn't, because I had kept it hidden, for fear she might drink it, when I was out? In future, I'll keep all my teas hidden. When you think about it, man, tea is a drug, and should be treated with respect.'

'You know, in the old days, Ginnsy, when cocoa and tea and coffee were first introduced to the West, the Westerners got off their faces on cocoa, and Puritans deplored the tea shops?'

'They would do, Brian. Yet today no one takes any notice of the effects of tea, because it has become part of the culture, like booze. It'll be the same with pot, you wait and see. Notice how, already, pot has less and less effect? That's why I prefer smack and coke and peyote.'

'I thought you said this tea was smuggled in?'

'Oh sure, man, shit yeah. This tea is quite illegal. Enjoy. Indonesia! That's the name I was tryin to think of.'

That'll do for the moment. It's June '95 here. We'll end on the upbeat. I have to go down to the Valley, and select some crying wives, for the atrium of the Bangkok Oriental. That's *Telopea doliveresiana*, the world's most novel and exclusive protea. Grows nowhere else that we know of, and it's been a good earner for me. I get what I ask for each specimen, and we're talking Japanese yen. *Omnia praeclara rara*, everything precious is rare. Pruned, to buggery, by brush-tailed phascogales, but I just let 'em rip. Half a dozen plants'll see me out, at this stage.

Things don't look good for me. Back on the anti-metabolites. I won't be seeing the Blue Gum Forest again, and I used to climb from there to Perry's Lookdown in under the hour. Hand me that knitted beanie, and check with O'Rourke Funerals, Queanbeyan. See if they still offer the five per cent discount for Australian Postal Institute members.

Lousy five per cent. Used to get twenty per cent at Arthur Murrays.

32. *Diane loses heart.*

It's the week before the Wozzawunwun Rodeo of '68. Paula's party.

'Have a toke on this,' says Balthazar Beauregard to Diane Zoshka, who won't open her eyes. 'No hope without it.'

'What a fool you are,' replies Diane. 'Haven't the Black Panthers taught you anything?'

'I take orders from Babaji, Babe, and I don't intend to stand here all night. You're the one evading Reality. What if I just drop the chain?'

'So drop it. Who asked you to hold it in the first place?'

Conklita.

'It's OK, folks. Just means the monkey has to lie down. No big deal.'

'Thank you, Balthazar. You've been so patient. Darling, is it all right if I sit on the floor next to you? This is Nisi. Berenice.'

'It's all so pointless, Nisi. We're just not getting through.'

'Oh, I think we have made some impact. Just not as much as perhaps . . .'

'That's the point. There is no time! It's not just Nam, Nisi. It goes down deeper, and back further, and further and deeper, the further back and deeper you look. We're all going to die.'

'Darling, why don't we undo the lock? Your neck is beginning to chafe.'

'Cause I don't want to live in a world like this, and I can't seem to change it. We should all be free. Also, I don't want people enjoying this pathetic excuse for a party. It's so immoral.'

'Waste of time talkin to her. She never hears anything she agrees with. Always throwing stunts like this.'

'Yeah Paula, you would know. Turfed me out of the flat, Nisi. Ow! Don't pull my hair, Tart!'

'Fucking bitch! This was supposed to be my night!'

'Ow!'

'Paula! Paula!'

'You don't know what it's like, Nisi, having a sister like her.

She just absconded on bail money, cost me three weeks' wages. I hope she knows how to make hair curlers out of cigarette packets.'

'D'ya tell her your fiancé is a married man with two kids? So much for rings and roses. Ow! How pathetic.'

'You mean the police are looking for Diane?'

'Certainly.'

'Let me speak with her. Diane, this is Derek Frodsham. You recall the little chat we had concerning burnout? I'd say you just burned out, sweetheart. Wouldn't you agree, Barbara? Exit one anarchist. As Trotsky says, a theory very sweeping in its verbal negations, but lifeless and cowardly in its practical conclusions.'

'She be back. Always must be centre 'v attenshun.'

'Get fucked, Paula. Ow!'

Derek Frodsham: small, prematurely balding Trotskyite. Member of the International Committee for the Reconstruction of the Fourth International. He was the last abbot. I asked Kimbo how it could be a *bona fide* physicist got sucked into a religious cult. You know what he said? He said 'If you had seen what we seen, mate—if you had watched that writing appear on the trunks of all the trees, if you had seen that creek turn red, as though it were running blood, if you had heard the birds scream, the way they screamed that day, and it wasn't just because of the fire that threatened them—if you had seen the figure of a man you knew as well as we knew Att converted to a tree, with a flow of gum streaming from His groin, and a flow of gum streaming from His knife, and a flow of gum streaming from the cock and balls He held in His hand—a flow of gum flowing like blood and washing away the soil, and every gum tree on that plateau, oozing gum in great carbuncles—well you wouldn't be asking that question.'

33. *Diane attempts suicide. Maximilian. A search for the Erinungarah Valley. The Valley found. Crisis in the bush. Attis and Diane finally meet.*

'Why didn't you mention Diane had opened her wrists in the bath, Ginnsy? You went in there. You must have seen how red the water was.'

'Yeah, well, I been conditioned not to look at women in the tub, Paula. Comes from having had a lot of sisters.'

'But you must have noticed how red the bathwater was?'

'Oh yeah, well, I thought I saw what mighta been red bathwater, that is true. Outta the corner of an eye.'

'Then why didn't you say something?'

'Because I thought I mighta been imagining it, and I didn't want to cause a fuss and spoil the party. I figured a lot of other people would be using the bathroom after me, so if it was real, let someone else report it. Which they did.'

'Oh, I can't believe this man. Where do you find these weirdos, Brian?'

'Please don't call me a weirdo, Paula. Other people have feelings, too.'

'But my sister might have bled to death, because of your lack of concern. Can't you see how *serious* it was?'

'Oh, nothin's that serious, is it? Life, Death, don't get uptight. Your sister will pull through.'

'Yeah, she lost over a pint of blood, but she's expected to survive. No thanks to you.'

'Ar come on Paula, it's no big deal. I have known *heaps* of young women open their veins in the tub. As you say, it's just their way o' drawin attention to 'emselves.'

'He has a point, Paula. Diane knew someone would find her, and sooner rather than later. I mean, you just don't go taking a bath at a party, not when the toilet's in the bathroom. Not unless you lock the door first.'

'Well, it's completely ruined the evening for me, Brian. Could you ask these people to leave now?'

'"These people"! Ar, give us a break. "These people" are your brothers and sisters, Paula. Don't drive us away. Let us share the pain.'

'Get rid of him. I mean it, Brian.' And she storms off.

'She's a bit upset, Ginnsy. You understand.'

'Sure, I dig, man. And I feel terrible now. I shouldn'ta given Diane those quaaludes.'

'You gave Diane quaaludes! Oh no! I told the zambuck she hadn't even been drinking. How's it going, Eugene?'

'You sound henpecked already, Brian. Ditch the snatch, 'fore it's too late.'

'Could I ask you to move your brother, please Eugene? Get him off Paula's bed, at least. Please.'

'Now *he's* the one took the quaaludes, man. You want to talk about quaaludes, talk to him. He'll sleep for days, if he ever wakes.'

'Aw Jesus, Ginnsy!'

'Yeah, I know, man. It's a downer when a chick does a thing like this at a party. And they're forever doin it, ay.'

'I must try to look on the bright side. At least she took the chain off her neck.'

'Yeah, well I think I ought to go and visit her in hospital, now. What's that lady's name?'

'The one Barbara's talking with? That's Nisi.'

'I'll get her to come. She's a compassionate lady.'

'Please Ginnsy, no, don't do it, mate. Please.'

'It's no trouble. I really like Diane. I admire idealism. Diane is just the kind of girl we're gonna need, down in the Valley.'

'What?'

'Yeah, we're all movin down to the Valley, man. You should come. You know, where I lost the dog? You know that Valley I was tellin you about? Wasn't it you I was tellin about the Valley?'

'*Course* it was you. He tells everyone about the Valley.'

'Ah man, you should see this Valley. Anything'll grow down there. Blue meanies like you never ate. Yeah, I tell everyone about the Valley, but I don't think anyone believes me. I don't blame'm. *I* wouldn't believe me, and I'll believe any fuckin thing.'

'Go wake your brother, Eugene, or drag him off the bed at least. Please.'

'See that man over there? He's got beehives, and is lookin

for a place to put 'em. Him and me and Eugene are gonna look for the Valley this weekend, but you know, I have the feeling the dog is OK? Just a feeling, though. Can't justify it. Wanta come? You and Paula should come along, Brian. I really admire Paula. I admire practicality. Wish I was more practical.'

'Dunno, Ginnsy, we'll see. I guess it will depend on how Diane makes out.'

'I'm gonna suggest to Diane she should come too. We gotta get out of this *city*, man, it's a fuckin madhouse. It's drivin us all nuts.'

'What about your gig?'

'Yeah, I know. Fuck the gig.'

'And if that happens,' continues Derek Frodsham, bailed up by Maximilian Worboise, who can't keep away from him, 'if you, perceiving I might be about to kill *you* in self-defence, were perceived, by me, as about to kill *me* in self-defence, then I might feel I had no choice but to kill *you* in self-defence, and so you would be advised to strike first, or so it might seem to you. Strong deterrence predicates assured mutual destruction. Under a strategy of deterrence, my safety, so far from being threatened, if your nuclear forces attain parity with mine, is in fact guaranteed, because, if my forces are stronger than yours, then I might be tempted to use them, which would assure my own destruction, as the price of ensuring yours.'

'I *still* can't understand it,' says the interlocutor. 'Help. If, as you say, we have this parity now, why can't we disarm, bit by bit?'

'Max, we are holding knives at each other's throats. Now were you to perceive the slightest weakening in my apparent resolve to attack you, sooner or later, with all my might, you might be tempted to drive your knife home, and so we would both die, for I, though mortally wounded by you, would still have the bottle to take you with me, and every other bastard in this room as well. It is for your benefit, Max, and theirs, I cannot reduce the pressure of this knife I hold against your throat. My knife is your guarantee of safety, or so it would seem to me.'

'What an absurd situation.'

'Never fiddle with the Strong Force, Max. I think that's the moral of the homily. Not so easy to get loose, once you're held by the Strong Force.'

'Ah God. What can a man do?'

'Get upwind of the tracking station at Tidbinbilla, for a start.'

'There's a D.H. Lawrence happening at the Yellow House tomorrow night,' says Balthazar to Monica. 'Want to come? You know Aggy 'n Alby? Martin Sharp might be there. He designed the jacket on the *Cream* album.'

'Sounds like fun,' replies Monica Ecks. 'Happen I'll hop along, Cassidy.'

Maximilian Worboise: mid-twenties, overweight, anti-nuclear demonstrator. Christened 'Towtruck' by Darryl MacAnaspie, who felt he was close to a breakdown.

Paula Zoshka can think of few excursions less inviting than a weekend in the company of five weak personalities, but when she learns her pale, wan sister intends going south, she feels she must go too, as gooseberry, or duenna.

'What did you tell your wife?' she says, from the fluoro-orange kitchenette, to Brian Chegwodden, as together they pack a cut lunch for three, round 5 a.m. There's a wistfulness in her tone when she speaks of his wife he can't fathom.

'Oh, I just said I was going away on assignment. It's easy enough for me to get away. And who knows, if half what Ginnsy told Diane about this Valley is true, it might make an interesting feature, or radio play.'

'What, you'd tell the whole world about it?'

'Not in a radio play.'

'Don't worry. There is no Valley. I just hope the countryside looks pretty. It's spring.'

'Yeah, I think there's a drought on, actually. I really feel for Diane. She's the one believes Ginnsy, and I always thought she was so hard-headed.'

'She *wants* to believe him, Brian. She's on the run too, remember? And she's not hard-headed. Before she started mixing with the wrong crowd, she was the sweetest little girl.'

'They're all sweet, when they're little girls. Mha.'

'Oh come on, baby! Spare me. You must have known it wouldn't be easy, here. Put this tuna casserole back in the fridge. Is that someone at the door?'

'I'll get it.'

Michael Ginnsy, wearing a beret with his 'Stoned Again' badge on it, like a big datestamp.

'Good morning, Ginnsy. You're up bright and early.'

'Come straight from work, man. Ready for the big expedition? Eugene has a *Kombi*.'

'I thought Eugene lost his wallet.'

'I think he musta borrowed a gorilla from Calvin. Doesn't matter, main thing is, we have *wheels* now. Hi Paula! Where's Diane?'

'We let her sleep, till you arrived. You've overexcited her, man. All she can talk about now is this Valley. Freedom, with a capital Eff. So how many people are coming with us?'

'Well, there's you, and there's me, there's Eugene and Balthazar, that's three people from here, and we have to pick up Nisi from the stables. Eugene and Balthazar were at my place last night, probly still are. Hey, it's so good we got someone who knows about *horses*, man. And Bal is an expert on bees. It was meant to happen.'

'Seven people. Wow, it's going to be that crowded in the van.'

'They can handle it. Paula will just have to sit on your lap.'

'I sleep on the couch here, Ginnsy.'

'Sure you do. With a doll like her? Come on, let's *go*. We gotta get *started*! It'll take us around twelve hours, and I hope to get there before dark.'

'But I thought you didn't know where this place was?'

'I don't. But I hope to get there before dark.'

They're on the Hume Highway, and at this hour, the semis roll towards them. Picton. Tahmoor.

'She moves along, Eugene.'

'Not bad, for a 1600 engine with only fifty-seven horsepower. Eugene, did you replace that CV joint like I suggested?'

'Didn't have time, Michael. The military police were round at my brother's house last night.'

'Oh, that's a shame. Cause I can hear it knockin, whenever you turn a left-hand corner. It's a right CV joint.'

'Still accelerates OK.'

'Oh shit yeah! Don't panic. No worries, as yet. You see, the bearings inside the cage wear grooves in the cage, Paula, and then it gets all pitted, to the point it can cause a vehicle to shudder at low speed? But it's not hardly shudderin yet. Mine was really bad, hey. I was in second gear, goin *down* the hills.'

'I won't be comin back to Sydney, Ginnsy. I was due back in Nam, this weekend.'

'I beg your pardon? What do you mean, Eugene? How we supposed to get back?'

'You can have the vehicle. Just drop me off Someplace Safe.'

'So you're a deserter now.'

'Yep. I got no quarrel with the yellow man.'

'I so admire you.'

Eugene Ecks glances sideways at Diane Zoshka, who's a pretty girl, but acts so American.

'Think the Kombi's OK, Ginnsy? Or did I hot wire a lemon?'

OK, it's stolen. But no worries, this wouldn't register on straights, and no one else gives a stuff. It's *all* stolen.

'It's a good one, or was. Slidin door, sixty-eight model. Same as mine. Double-jointed axles. Maybe the gear linkages are a little worn. Who is it drives these buses, new, at max revs and ruins them? Italians? I notice we're having a struggle finding second gear on the way down. Does it pop out of reverse? Hope the transmission's OK.'

'Nothin to worry about. You comfortable in the sink back there, Paula?'

'I should have thought they had seats in the back, Eugene. I mean, had I realised you were fitted out for camping, my fiancé could have brought his car.'

'Eugene may have to live in this van, Paula. Did you consider that?'

'And you may have to join him, Diane. Did you consider that? You're wanted too, by police and social workers at the hospital, remember? Or have you forgotten, in the excitement.'

'You could get a bit more life out of it, man, if you dropped the whole joint out, and turned it around completely, but it's really not advisable, because if it fails completely, it could destroy the diff completely.'

'Oh don't fuckin worry me about that now, man! I'll ditch it, if need be. You have it. You drive it back, throw it away. What do I care?'

'Hoho. Throw away cars, yet.'

'Don't talk of throwin it away, man. Vehicles have feelings too. It's a great vehicle, really. Don't you agree they're great vehicles, Nisi, the way they just *roll* along there? Hand me my guitar, please. Ta. Yeah, they got a solid feel to 'em, ay. I have a theory it's because they got no proper chassis, as such. The belly pan is bolted to the subframe, which is just two rails that run under the car, and with all the panels bearing part of the load, that's why it feels so *solid*. Mmm, yeahh, hmmm, solid, woohh ...'

'You gonna play guitar now? Don't you want some sleep?'

'No, no, I rarely sleep. Where I live, it's noisy. You'd get more sleep at a slumber party. Anyway, it's a waste of time. I'll take more uppers, if I get tired. Tell me when we reach Cooma. Need more uppers Eugene?'

'No, but a small number wouldn't go astray.'

'Sorry, man. I'm out of that Lebanese blond, and I won't touch mull.'

'I'll take care of it,' says Balthazar Beauregard. To Paula Zoshka's consternation he proceeds, using licorice papers and heads, to roll a spliff that would shock a Dutch East Indiaman.

'We're gettin colder again. We shoulda turned off somewhere. Go back to Nimmity.'

Relying purely on instinct, Michael Ginnsy is not so much as looking out the windows. He sits instead, chin on chest, crumpled like a preying mantis. There's a bond between man and mutt passeth understanding.

'Didn't you have a map or somethin with ya?'

'Oh I would of, Diane, but they'd still be in the van. See, while I was stayin in the Valley, with this hip old couple I was tellin you about, there was this landslide? No, seriously. It's hard to believe, it's ridiculous, but the land chose just the time I was there to slide, and the road is now blocked completely. We're talkin about hundreds and probly thousands of tons of rock.'

'So how did you get out?'

'Walked. Hitched. Phryx and Gwen took me to a place you can scramble up a cliff. See, the Valley's surrounded with cliffs? Only other way to get out, is to float down the river. Then you wind up at some dam.'

'Oh why didn't you tell us that in the first place, idiot? Gimme that map. Jesus, I dunno. Some people.'

'Whattaya mean, Brian? Whattaya goin on about?'

'Didn't it occur to you, boofhead, we could work out where your Valley was, if we knew where the dam was?'

'Ar come off it, this is the Snowy Mountains, Brian. I did a project on it. There's dams all over the place.'

'We have to start somewhere. God, this country depresses me! Fences covered in tussock. Not a tree in sight.'

'Hey, wait!'

'What?'

'Did we just pass a turn-off back there?'

'Yeah, I think we did.'

'Go back and take it! I had a flash then, man. It's like the dog is trying to get through. Throw that fuckin map away.'

'No! I'd say we're lookin for this area here, Eugene. See this little dam down here?'

'And what road should we be taking, Brian?'

'Oh well. This one, as it happens.'

Two hours later, it's cool and getting cooler. Always need a fire at night, hereabouts. Every house has its firewood stash in the dead half-thousand gallon gal tank, and the bushfire brigade gets roasted, on a winter's midnight, in a gale, extinguishing many a chimney fire. Soaked with water, back in the shed, frozen.

'Can't we stop somewhere, have a meal and book into a motel?' Brian Chegwodden likes the sound of that.

'We're nearly there, Paula. I can feel it. The old couple said that if ever I wanted to come back, with friends, we'd be more than welcome.'

'What, we're going to climb down the cliff in the dark?'

'Oh shit, that's right. The road's blocked, isn't it. I forgot.'

He hasn't the memory of the shoe attendant at the Mevlana mosque in Konya, who takes your shoes without giving you a ticket, hurls them into a huge, disorganised heap, then, when you leave, without so much as a word being spoken, hands them back to you.

'I suggest we take the next left, Eugene. That will take us to the Erinungarah Valley.'

'That's *it*! That's *it*! Erinungarah, that's it, man. You just found it. Thank you, Brian. We got here.'

Twenty more minutes elapse, and the day is almost spent. The road past Wonderview winds through a canebreak of saw sedge, dagger hakea and prickly tea tree.

'This is an awful road. You sure it's not a firetrail? All these corrugations.'

'Gotta take 'em faster, Eugene. Gotta hare over corrugations.'

'Yeah, well we're too overloaded for that, and it's gettin dark.'

'Is it? I'm gonna open my eyes then. Oh shit man, the *lights* are so bright!'

'Whattaya mean, the stars? The sun? The moon?'

'No, no, the headlights. Did you bring a spare reggie? How long has the red light been on?'

'Look, there's a house down there. We could make some inquiries at the house.'

'What, the one with the bulldozers outside? No fuckin way! They'll have goitres and harelips, man. They'll be red-necks.'

'I think we should turn back.'

'You would. God, you're a gutless wonder, Paula.'

'Diane, it will soon be *dark*. If we get stuck out here in the dark, well, you know. Anything could happen.'

'Yeah, we might start living life to the full. Wouldn't that be dreadful.'

'Everything is just fine, ladies. I feel a pronounced Freedom from Fear. We're keepin goin. Hey, what's this coming up ahead now, Ginnsy?'

'I dunno. Hey, when everything gets really bright, it's a sign it's about to kark it completely. Keep goin! We probly got just enough luck left, to get to the Valley.'

'Are you *mad*? Turn back at once, Eugene! Oh Brian, we should never have come out here with junkies. They just don't *care!*'

'Don't panic, darling. We're bound to have a torch, and Ginnsy knows all about Kombis.'

'Yeah, keep drivin, fellow "junkie". What's with this "junkie", Paula, is that some kind of disgusting wild animal? Cause it sure sounds like one, the way you say it. It could be just somethin to be, well, you know, not exactly proud of, but relaxed about. Yeah, it's a little causeway, a little concrete ford, man. The creek runs over it, into the Valley. It's quite close to the Falls, actually. This is it, for sure. Oh thanks again, Brian. I could never have found it myself. Too thick.'

'Wish I could play guitar like you, Ginnsy.'

'I'll teach you sometime. Not a problem.'

'You *did* bring a torch, didn't you Eugene?'

'No.'

'Then shouldn't Michael fix the lights before it gets too dark to see?'

'It's probly not the lights, Nisi. They're drawin charge straight from the gennie. More likely the reggie, see, the reggie, which is in a small, silver box bout an arm's length behind the battery, when it fails, it causes the gennie to charge constantly at max amps, about fifty, which burns it out? Awkward to work on, too. In the '63 model they moved it from the top of the gennie to the side of the engine compartment. You gotta take out the air cleaner.'

'Oh shit, we gotta do something. Brian! Diane! Let's get *out!*'

'Where would you go, Paula? But yes, let's all get out, and stretch our legs. You can see the Valley, from just down there.'

'Oh fuck, I'm bogged now, mate. Can't move. Can't go forward or back.'

'You put a wheel in a hole in the causeway. Just leave the van here, for the time being, Eugene, we wanta make the most of this last light. Leave the ignition on. If the red light *stays* on when you turn it off, I don't want to know. Come on, folks! Take off your shoes and socks and follow me, and I'll show you somethin'll blow your minds.'

'Brian, aren't we in all sorts of trouble?'

'I really don't know, Paula. I'd 've thought so, but with so many contrary attitudes being expressed, it's hard to know. I guess there's always that house we passed back there. Country folk are friendly, and it's a clear night. Not too cold. I guess, for the moment, we just follow Ginnsy, go with the flow, I mean, what else *can* we do? We're in the middle of nowhere.'

'What did I tell ya? Look at that *view*, folks!'

Years later, it's the sound of this moment Nisi Papadimitriou recalls. A bush fly, buzzing along the Valley rim, has detoured for a short inspection. The Falls, because of the drought, are rather quiet; the creek is scarcely flowing. Currawongs and bell-birds and spotted pardalotes are standard East Coast fare, but you don't often hear a wonga pigeon here. Good tucker, they were shot, in their thousands, by the Moons and MacAnaspies. A plaintive, rapidly iterative call, like a car alarm, like a bull's cry, waxes on a current that is imperceptible on the Valley rim, where there's not so much as a breath of wind.

The west-facing cliffs glow in the last light of day. Where the Valley opens out, miles off, can be seen pasture and a wisp of smoke. Over the gorge circles, on motionless wings, a pair of wedgetail eagles.

'I *dreamt* all this the other night,' says Nisi. 'This has happened before.'

'I'm going to be here the rest of my life,' explains Diane Zoshka. 'Don't ask me how I know.'

'Whattaya reckon?' The insouciant Michael Ginnsy nudges the insouciant Eugene Ecks. 'This a good place for hidin out, or what?'

'Perfect. Sure it's not a hot shot? Ginnsy, I'm thinkin it's gonna be awkward, workin on that van, where it is.'

'Yeah. Need a timing light to be sure, but I'd say it's the reggie. Lights get dimmer when it's the belt, and the engine would be hot, because the fan runs off the belt. But the gennie will soon burn out. And the gennie's mounted in the sheet metal housing behind the motor, and because of the fan, it takes an hour to get it in and out again. That's on dry land. That's if you're not forever droppin it in the water. What, we got a snorkel and a spare reggie?'

'Why don't we take the reggie outta your van?'

'Ar, right. Good thinking, man. Though they have more than one kind.'

'Smack o'clock, Ginnsy. Did you bring a taste?'

'You kiddin? Is the Pope Catholic?'

'Don't worry,' explains Michael Ginnsy, teeth on the tourniquet. 'Once me and Eugene get down in that Valley, we won't *need* any o' this kind o' shit. In fact, we're lookin forward to givin it up.'

And they were, and they did. But Eugene Ecks is back on it, I hear, goes into Nimbin, for a hit. In '95.

'Where's the van? Oh shit, it washed off the causeway, look. How could that have happened?'

Eyes strain to make out the translocated van, in the twilight equivalent of piccaninny dawn. A fencer, struggling to finish the job, knocks off round now, cursing.

'No, don't go near it, Paula. Could be unstable. That rock is slippery. Shoulda left it in gear, man.'

The Kombi is maybe half a chain from the concrete, partway down a green sandstone sheet, denuded by water, which continues not much further, before tumbling just above the Falls into a pool surrounded by coachwood and tree fern, and what we call round here blackwattle, though we call green wattle blackwattle too. As they watch, the van's rear, which houses the engine, moves a little further down.

'We'll never drive it out o' there, man.'

'You're right. 'T's gonn'aft to be pulled out.'

'You mean we can't sleep in the van? Oh Brian, what are we going to do? I'm so scared.'

'Whattaya scared of, babe? Put things in perspective. No scorpions. No nogs, with AK 47's. Yer laughin.'

Brian Chegwodden doesn't like to hear other men addressing his Paula as 'babe', but this is not the time to remonstrate, and she is shaking like a washing machine.

Michael Ginnsy lights a ciggy. In the glow of the match, an idea comes to the astute Balthazar Beauregard, who starts methodically raking round, with his feet. Nisi Papadimitriou is quickly on the ball, and she's soon gathering firewood too. With her hands. They make a good team.

'T's gonna be all right,' exhales Ginnsy. 'Help is on the way.'

'What, you think the people back in that house will see our fire? In that case, maybe we'd better not light one. Could be on their property.'

They are. Someone sitting behind a desk drew up these sub-divisions, and the boundaries of the blocks run due north/south, in despite of the impressive natural contours. You wouldn't want to have paid the fencing bill for Total Goat Control. But this Ford is not part of Wonderview; to all intents, it is part of the Valley, for not till the grid runs over the cliff does the cliffline become the boundary, and that's a good four furlongs further south.

'Maybe a total fire ban. Either way, we're gunnew attract attention. Or are you thinkin of the people in the Valley, Ginnsy, could they see us from here?'

'Wouldn't be lookin, man. I was referrin to the dog. My dog will soon be on its way. Fats! Yeah, he's out there. I'm gonna whistle up the dog now. I gotta go grab me the whistle, which I think is in the guitar case. Form a human chain, come on! Grab hold of my wrist, Diane, that's the style. Gee, you got a nice, soft wrist. Oh, that's the bandage, of course. Yeah, lucky I thought to have brought along this whistle. They give us these whistles at the Dog Obedience Centre, where we did the obedience course. Fats is trained to obey a whistle, which only dogs can hear. Member how we heard that pigeon, which was miles down in the Valley? Yeah, well the Valley is like that. I never saw Fats more happy. You're singin in the bath, or barkin, all day. Full of reverb and runnin water. I'm sure the top of the Falls is one of those currawong calling sites, cause the currawongs were calling from there, weren't they? Yeah, the currawongs were calling from there, weren't they. From heaps o' places, you can be heard anywhere. Communication is not a problem. Phryx, when he needs to communicate with Gwen, he goes to the nearest calling site and bellows. You need strong lungs, though.'

'Privacy could be a problem.'

'We can't go back to the Falls in the dark, man.'

'We hafta. Remember the track down is somewhere on this side of the Valley, but not exactly where. I know it's not far from the Gap, and to get to the Gap, there's a short cut.'

'Why do we need this dog, which is just another hungry mouth to feed?'

'Wake up. Fattsy will know where the track is, cause he'll have come up the track, man. He can show us where the track is.'

'But we can't climb down in the dark, and we have to be back in Sydney tomorrow, some of us. Do we have the time?'

'"Do we have the time." Where is this man coming from? There's a cave in the cliff at the top of the track, Brian, where we could snugly sleep. S'posed to have glow-worms, though I didn't see any.'

'You only see glow-worms in the dark, dummy. When they glow.'

'Yeah? Well that accounts for it.'

'Hey, while you're lookin for the whistle there, man, can you grab us that orange juice bottle? See, if we filled the bottle with glow-worms.'

'Gotcha.'

'And some food, please Michael.'

'Right.'

The dog, responding to the whistles from his master, duly appears, in the company of others—semi-wild, the MacAnaspie pariah pack he's hanging round with—and the party, famished and exhausted, extinguishes the fire and having stumbled through the bush, after Fats, for an hour or so, dosses down, by 8 p.m. at the latest, in the cave, where the glow-worms create a glow like that from a jewellery shop in the mall during a blackout. By 8.10 p.m., were the glow from the glow-worms sufficiently bright, which thankfully it's not, Paula Zoshka and Brian Chegwodden could be seen doing that which they had promised not to, before they were married. Eugene Ecks, meantime, who reasons he should have sex, though doesn't really feel up to it, is mauling Diane Zoshka, with a similar end, presumably, in view. But she won't let him put his hands on her buns, or even her boobs. Nisi Papadimitriou and Balthazar Beauregard get caught up in the general, orgiastic vibration. Balthazar can now add the scalp of this former Miss Western Districts Charity Queen to his impressive tally. Certainly, the cave would have a cattleman jumping off his horse, thinking he'd found a cow who just calved: it sounds like an afterbirth being eaten. And it's all too much for Michael Ginnsy, because, when the others wake in the morning, he has gone, and taken the dogs with him.

'I must look terrible,' explains Paula, primping in vain at the moist rock face.

'Look great to me, babe,' asserts Eugene, whose own appearance would merit a thousand push-ups.

It is, in fact, after dawn, and a spring gale is blowing, roaring over the plateau, and making shiny the crowns on the silver-topped ash and the undersides of the swamp banksias. It's the kind of day on the postal run you can't decide whether to wear a jumper. The wind is cool, but under that wind can be sensed a warmth in the air. Maestro, a harpsichord arpeggio, if you would be so kind.

Tardy spring has come to the highlands. Brush cuckoos moan the desolate moan that assuages their guilty consciences, and a swordgrass brown butterfly flutters by, and the pink beardheath is turning white, as the tiny tubular bells open.

'Musta gone down the Valley,' says Balthazar Beauregard, 'we better see if we can find that track. Girls, spread out, would ya, but make sure you can find your way back here in, say, twenty minutes?'

The House that Glows, the kids called the cave. It stands, amid wiry coral fern, on a north-facing bank of a small creek. Overhung with rock, it's enclosed to the east by a slip, where the track winds down through the stinkwoods. Long abandoned by the time I saw it, it overlooks a big bush lemon, in a slope of golden tip and river peppermint, one of whose ironbarkish butts is close enough to grab from the cave floor. This must have been the one the kiddies climbed, when they wanted to expedite access. The House that Glows was a cubby, after fat Fiona died, then Balthazar Beauregard moved in, and it became the cell of an anchorite.

The tongued and grooved floor is still there, supported by piers of cemented bushrock, and, what would give a building inspector grey hairs, the bearers pass from these to the cave rear. Three cups and a blackened billy, all spattered with soil from thunderstorms, brood darkly. From the ledge, which harbours the cream Calvert's heath (my favorite epacrid, pandani excepted) steeps a stillicide which has rotted away the outermost part of the flooring. I note the patterns that the shadows of the leaves form on this floor would have enraptured a baby. The big footprint—that's the footprint of the bigfoot—a genuine antique this, monitors the cave entrance, touch of the Ancient Greece, and in the dirt, around the cave, are footprints going back 100,000 years, and ash, and cubic wombat turds. Two rusty old beds, each furnished with a damp mattress, remain, and there's a griddle, a car seat, a bent aluminium saucepan, and books.

Fiction by Castenada and R. Buckminster Fuller (ArBuckyEf). Metal Techniques for Craftsmen. How to Build Your Own Furniture. The Art of Blacksmithing. Knots and Splices. Home Handspinning. The Structural Potential of Foams. Plastics for Architects and Builders. How to Build Yourself a Concrete Boat. The Wilderness Cabin. The Indian Tipi. The Art of Building a Fireplace. The Fundamentals of Carpentry. The Techniques of Stained Glass. A Key to the Psilocybin Mushroom. Veterinary Notes for Horse Owners. How to Raise Rabbits. Goat Husbandry. A Modern Herbal. A Manual of Beekeeping. Organic Plant Protection. Compost Science. Concepts of Ecology. How to Be a Survivor. Someone has removed the forty-four the women boiled the nappies in.

While the three men spend half an hour trapping a goanna they have bushed up a turpentine, the women debate whether

Michael Ginnsy can be trusted to return. They conclude he cannot, and while someone can see on the far rim of the plateau what they think might be a man ploughing a field with a horse, no one can see what looks like a track down, and the women, sensibly, won't proceed unless they are sure they are on the right track. There is nothing for it but to walk out, in the hope of picking up the road in.

'I can't believe he'd do this,' says Paula, undulating through the bushy parrot pea, which is more prickly than the prickly parrot pea. 'We came at his invitation.'

'I think he's basically decent,' says Nisi Papadimitriou. 'We have to work on his love of animals.'

'This is rougher country than I recall,' says Eugene Ecks. 'We sure as hell didn't come in this way. I think we better head a bit further west, try to get out of these prickles. By the way, babe, don't let a branch go till you're sure it won't smack me in the mouth.'

'Why don't you go in front?' says Brian Chegwodden, who could happily smack Eugene Ecks in the mouth.

'Why don't you shut your face?' says Eugene. He'll be in a worse mood, by the end of the day.

The wind, by eleven, drops to nothing. The Fifth Brandenburg's cadenza gives way to Delius, *In the High Hills*.

'Oh no. It's the Valley again. We musta come round in a big circle.'

'Oh God, we're lost. Oh God, we're completely lost.'

'I don't think this is the Erinungarah Valley. Too broad. This must be some other place. From what I recall of the map. Hey! What's that over there, Eugene?'

'Looks like a settlement of some sort.'

'Where?'

'Look. See? Over there, Nisi. On that big flat.'

'I think it's a gathering o' some kind, man. Isn't that a circus tent?'

'See, Paula? Over there. Yeah, it's a tent. That's the road in. Hey, it's a little town!'

'Oh thank God. Oh thank God!'

'Oh don't thank Him yet. Still a long way off. Hard to say exactly how far. What do you reckon, Bal?'

'Least they have something to head for now, and I can see what look like cars and trucks and utes.'

'I think that house we passed last night on the way in 'd be far closer. Make more sense to head for that, wouldn't it?'

'No. Because from here they can see their destination. From here, they have something to motivate them. We have to consider the women.'

'Have you had a good look down, man? I mean, this cliff is steeper than the last one.'

'Oh. Then there's no way down, you don't think?'

'We don't have a rope.'

'Oh yeah, I see what you mean. Fuckin Ginnsy! Fuckin boofhead!'

'Please,' says Paula Zoshka, 'you're supposed to be men. Can't you come up with something?'

'Paula,' whispers Diane Zoshka, 'why do I keep thinking I'm Pookie at the Circus? Why am I so excited?'

'Ssshh. Listen!'

Straining their ears, they can make out the whistling feedback of a PA system, and wince as the final call is made for contestants in the Ladies Steer Undecorating. They have only themselves to blame, these contestants, if they didn't hear the final call.

'Rodeo,' laughs Eugene Ecks.

'Now I've done some climbing,' says Balthazar Beauregard, 'and this descent is by no means difficult. There's a pass. You would go down there, and then you'd go down there, and then you'd go down there, and then you'd go down there. More a scramble than a climb, but we don't have a rope. Sure you girls want to risk it? Anyone falling could knock you off.'

'This can't be happening, Brian. I don't want to have this conversation.'

'Tell us what we have to do, Balthazar. I have children depend on me.'

'It's quite easy, Nisi. It's not beyond anyone here's capacity. A child could do it. We can't afford to fuck up, that's all. Simple as that. Be mindful, don't make mistakes, and don't, whatever you do, stop, because if you lose your nerve and freeze, you'll have days, or hours, to think over your past life, and how you blew it, whereas, if you fall, it'd only be a matter of minutes, or seconds. I can't help.'

'Let's go!'

Diane, fully alive, leads, and the others, less fully alive, follow. It's amazing what you can do, when you think your life depends on it. Three hours later, they're cracking jokes as they wade the left arm of Wozzawunwun Creek, and head for the Rodeo Ground, where the third event of the Rodeo Big Five, the Open Calfrope, is due to commence.

Eugene Ecks: Calvin's younger brother, traumatised by service in Vietnam. What to the others was an ordeal here, was nothing but a pleasant outing for him. It all depends on what you're on and where you're coming from.

Act 4

34. *The Wozzawunwun Rodeo. Rastus, Rodeo Clown.*

If you're the second wife of a Burradoo futures broker, and if your idea of equestrian pleasure is to dress in a top hat and tails and ride a German warmblood in a circle, wearing your jewels and sunnies, while some old beldam, with a riding crop in her hand, keeps shouting at you, 'Push with your seat, he's looking sloppy!' or 'Keep your hands down, help him get on the bit!' or 'Goodness me, he's made you dirty, you must rug him in summer as well,' I advise you to give the Wozzawunwun Rodeo wide berth, which is easy, because it's extinct.

If you were just a little Pony Clubber, some wannabe who spends a sleepless night before a gymkhana, and who gets up before dawn to wake her sister and puts a tracksuit on over her joddhies and white shirt and a cap over her hairnet, then sets out to catch some stout little horse, who's all woolly from his shampoo from the night before, and slimy with grass and molasses stains that you will have to remove, while you French plait his tail and black paint his hooves and baby oil his nose and clip his whiskers before you set off, in the hire float, for the barrels and the Cavaletti jumps—if, as I say, you're just a little Show set tryhard, of the kind Nisi used to be, you're gonna get your rocks off and have your mind blown at the Wozzawunwun Rodeo, but ditch those jodhpurs, if you're only half-thinking of entering our novice campdraft, and get serious. Just as no self-respecting Harley rider would be seen, dead, in a full face helmet, or without his sunnies and denims, so a certain style is expected of members of the Australian Rough Riders' Association; forty-four-gallon hat, snakeskin boots, silver buckles, and a saddle with a saddle horn for starters, but leave your Arab and your thoroughbred at home, and bring along the Pinto or the Appaloosa, and your money too, because, let me assure you, the mouthwatering smell from that steak sandwich stand has been known to tempt stockmen from the booze tent—for we eat, like Homeric heroes, only bread and beef here, and with our fingers—and you'll be going through a carton of ciggies just catching up with old buddies, and what could be more very pleasant than shooting the breeze, half-tanked, with a dozy horse hanging off your elbow and a passing young lady giving you the glad eye, sounds good to me.

Besides which, entering a single event costs a spot, and it's over before it's begun, so to speak, but who knows? Ride hard, drink long, and if your hotted up U-beaut passes muster—be sure to be equipped with stickers, four on the floor, fire, fiddle, breeze, ease and fast glass—all your birthdays may come at once, Saturday night, after the ball. It helps, of course, if you comb your hair and straighten your nose first; it helps even more if you're Kimberley Moon, or some other star, or erstwhile star, of the Rodeo Big Five: Open Bullride, Open Saddleride, Open Calfrope, Open Bulldog, Open Bareback Ride. A motivated Darryl might have won them all.

Now you might be a Menippus, and might suppose, that if you've seen one rodeo, you've seen them all. Friend, I have a soft spot for you, so to you I reveal Wozzawunwun was different. It was always one of the more popular meets on the entire circuit, so I hear, but more importantly, if not unrelatedly, served as a kind of Saturnalia, for our hard-working, long-suffering, if not as a rule god-fearing, locals.

Not a true Saturnalia, because it was held in October, and not in those days that reflect the disparity between the lunar and the solar year. More a carnival.

A mountain man, during Rodeo, was authorised to stay drunk two days and three nights. His adult daughters could tell him what they thought of him. Tradesmen could mock his ineptitude in public. The Rodeo Clown, to his sons'-in-law delight, could shadow his journey from the booze tent to the urinal. More darkly, he could go home with anyone he caught, so he fancied, after the ball. Imagine it, which is all they ever did. Respectable CWA matrons disporting themselves in the hay with cowboys, while the more monogamous, if less well-endowed, repair to someone's house, to watch smutty movies on video.

And there was no recrimination and, such being the discipline of our rural communities back in those days of the manual exchange, none manifested; of course, no scapegoat was made available, to be put to death as Rodeo King first thing Monday morning, though there would have been plenty of volunteers, judging by the pleas for orange juice at the Club. We are, after all, democrats who don't believe in capital punishment, thus setting a poor example, I believe, to our immune system (as above, so below; and below, where nature *is* destiny, it is considered preferable that the innocent die, than that the guilty go free).

Wozzawunwun was the scene, Rodeo the pretext for the annual play-up, but it wasn't always thus, and the wowsers, in the end, had it put down, firmly, for it violated the Sabbath. I think the last Rodeo was held in '92, the year after I moved to Obliqua Creek. Subsequently, Wozzawunwun died in the arse, till only the store today remains.

Vale, Wozzawunwun! Vale Rastus, Rodeo Clown. We shan't see your like again.

I saw him only once, his last performance, October of '91, but I thought Rastus a great rodeo clown, though he only worked the Wozzawunwun Rodeo. Darryl MacAnaspie, his alter ego, is still with us, but Rastus is dead. Rastus was renowned for prestidigitations, not that he lacked conventional skill. Put him in a yard with a dangerous bull, he would take your breath away with his bravura. I maintain it's a shame he never went to the United States, but then, I maintain it's a shame *I* never went to the United States. They'd have loved him by the Rio Grande. Anywhere there's a touch of Spanish blood, he'd have gone over like a wetback on horseback. Make a toreador look a pajero, the way he could anticipate your bull's every move. Back in the days of the Aegean Civilisation, he'd have been a Cretan national hero. Never, before or since, did a man leap a bull the way Rastus did. Fairly put your heart in your mouth, to see those red braces tangle in the horns, after he had tried to dive over the bull's head or leapfrog the bull, as he had made it seem. He would just go limp, and the bull would toss him from side to side and thrash him round like a rag doll in the mouth of a cattledog pup, or a beetle in the beak of a dollarbird. Belt him into the dirt, smack him against the rails; you could see the newchums glancing sideways. Then, after a time, considering he had damaged his foe sufficiently, and losing interest, as male animals do when they sense absolutely no resistance to their will, the bull would saunter off, leaving Rastus lying in the dirt, prostrate, not moving, limbs at all odd angles, him being double-jointed; he could give himself a chiropractic workout *and* massage his own prostate. And then you'd see the little hand move up, half-Nelson style, to check out the billycock, and see if the billycock was still at its original, jaunty angle (which invariably it would be) and then the rusty dusty would be dusted off, the genitalia readjusted, and the little rascal'd backflip to his feet, and swagger off, in those oversized boots, using a jaunty little walk made perfect by constant repetition, at home and at work, and he'd front straight up to some old biddy, and repeat everything she had just said about him, word-perfect, and then he'd disclose some personal item of hers he had previously palmed, and pass some remark about that— he was wonderful at taking women's bras and corsets off, without their being aware of it—and then he'd waltz off to wrap the garment round the red ears of some reprobate, the kind who thinks it a joke, at the club, to hold a jug of beer in his hand like a glass and laugh! Begorrah, you'd be pissin yourself.

And he gave good value. He saw the pickin up, the ringwork, as one aspect of the job. He had licence for the weekend, Rastus, or so he deemed, and he used it to the full. You know those cattledogs, always rushing out at you from under trucks at rodeos, and pecking at your heels? If Rastus had nothing else on, he'd hide under a truck, and he gave a most brilliant impersonation of an individual cattledog. The tree-climbing type that can scramble up a tipper, the fence pusher-underer, the flattop truck-tray balance act; understood their idiosyncrasies to a tee, and you know, I've seen him taking off dogs when he wouldn't have known anyone was watching him? Had a genius, Darryl.* And when I think of all he had seen and done, by '91, I am flabbergasted. And I suppose I am envious.

Oh he despised animals, one and all, with Schopenhauerian hauteur, not excepting the third chimpanzee, and that's us, the aquatic ape with the subcutaneous fat. Of course, he did such

---

* The Estruscans, and following them the Romans, thought each man had a series of genii, who swapped shifts every seven years, cutting out entirely at age 70, which gives a new slant to your three score years and ten.

'There is this difference between us Romans and the Etruscans' says Seneca. 'We believe events have a meaning, because they have happened. They believe events happen, in order to express a meaning.'

That today such a statement makes no sense at all reveals what has happened in the West.

a great job pickin up, they never employed a second chimpanzee, nor thought to replace him, the year he did his boob at Cessnock ('88). Rastus wouldn't have worn that, and I don't think another rodeo clown would have enjoyed comparison with him. Most of them aren't clowns at all, they're Ronald McDonalds. Their gags are flat as a nightcarter's hat, they can't improvise. They're not funny. There's nothing quickwitted about them. They are cowpokes in whiteface, daredevils, stuntmen certainly, who've been on the rodeo circuit themselves, and who dress as clowns in a European circus tradition because someone at some stage did it and now it's part of the job. They have no understanding of what it means to be a clown. A clown has a wound that will not heal. A clown is too serious to let you get away with it. A clown is a paladin who spits on his gifts, Life is a clown. No clown dies a clown's death.

Darryl MacAnaspie: Rastus the Clown. The men of the Valley were not utterly isolated, during Autarky, and therein lay their downfall. The Autarky in that Valley was not complete and absolute. There was a perilous route in, through Fossicker's Flat, by Wozza's Camp. But this track was precipitous and dangerous, and the men would not tell the women where it was. It was by this track that Timothy Papadimitriou, Orion, made his way to the high school here. It was by this track that mules and motorcycles made infrequent journeys to the Wozzawunwun store. They had to get the marihuana out, for their women demanded conveniences. It was by this route that Kimbo and Fergus, till they did the deed, and Darryl, till he opened the Pass, and Attis, before his Passion, made their annual way to the Rodeo ground. I have heard tell of the fights they got in, with their outraged kinsmen, at these rodeos. Then first Attis stopped coming, then Fergus, then Kimbo, then finally, when Darryl pulled the pin on Rastus, the pin was pulled on the Rodeo. Because Rodeo just wasn't the same, without the incomparable Rastus.

These trips to the store and the Rodeo broke the Spell, I do believe. By the time the Gap Road reopened, the Cooktown rot had set in, and the Land of the Ever Young was fatally tarnished.

35. *Attis and Diane fall in love.*

Are we not programmed to seek faces in every feature of our landscape? In rocks and clouds and wallpapers and waterstains, from day one, faces—twisted, distended, grotesque, Dickensian dowagers, rather than the cast from *Neighbours* in my case, but be that as it may, when first appears before us the face we have been seeking, unbeknown to us, it seems we cannot recollect it, hours later, cannot recall it; yes, cannot recreate it, and here, perhaps, lies a clue; for of all the human faces that we saw, or thought to see, there was not one that was not manufactured by us, rather than provided to us, and so we kept up our ineluctable scrutiny of gnarled tree trunks, and the ominous patterns of cigarette burns on the carpets of lounge and saloon bars, seeking what only the gods can give, until, if at last we are blessed, he/she appears to us in the flesh (though the faces, portentously, still appear), irrespective of our self-perceived needs and fears and hopes, and indeed, always somewhat contrary to them, for just as an Aussie will not confess, on oath, the name of a man he truly envies, but will cite that of another over whom he is conscious of superiority in at least one trivial particular (and how very different our gallup polls would stand, how different our so-called social 'truths', our canons, if the data upon which these were based were amassed, not as the transcript of bald-faced ratiocination, but on the basis of the involuntary confessions of the autonomic nervous system; pulse rate, engorgement of the sexual organs, dilation of the pupils of the eyes—stand aside L. Ron Hubbard—so much of whose testimony we make it our perverse antipodean business to gainsay); so too, when Postmodern man finds his woman, or 'partner', to be more in keeping with his tastes (*dedit hanc contagio labem et dabit in plures*; the curse of poofterism arose through contagion, and is bound to spread further: Juvenal), if it be Love, that partner will differ somewhat from the one his mind and body would fain choose, and if there exists sweeter evidence than this for the soul's existence and lack of authority, I don't know it, or have forgotten it, or dare not adduce it here for fear of misrepresenting it. Because Romantic Love, as Manichaeus knew, provides the most common epiphany, and perhaps the sole epiphany still accessible to the urban Postmodern Last Man. Venus lives, and supplied by Her with irrefragable proof of our spiritual inadequacy, is it not unremarkable we cannot recreate the face of the twinborn creature who furnished it? Twinborn, because Cybele lives. Origen, a eunuch, gave the first allegorical interpretation of the Song of Solomon. Eunuchs love allegories, but eunuchs aren't allegories. The old and wise, the married and poor, book themselves on a cruise, if they fall in Love, or, if they cannot afford to get away, immerse themselves in the quotidian, confident that the *Donum Dearum*, Gift of the Goddesses, treated with contempt, will evanesce rapidly. But the young, the foolish, such as rise to the bait, for these True Love will take its indefeasible course, over the next fourteen or so years, and irrespective of the cost to others, and the cost to the planet. For Venus, the young wife, to this point has held the whip hand over Cybele the virgin, but this must change.

High time to confess Manichaeus understood the human heart better than Paul. In this tarnished Silver Age, where democracy in its purest form (Australian: we're as democratic as Rupert, and you can't get more democratic than Rupert) has all but dissolved the bond between man and woman, husband and wife, Christianity is a joke, while the sacrosanctity of Romantic Love is affirmed by all, and a myriad strident voices savour its social permutations, extend its limited carnal possibilities, and draw *schadenfreude* from the prominence of its role in the ruination of the rich and famous, whom we shan't be meeting in this *Saga*, through our protagonists. They had, however, money enough to book into the Terminus Hotel, that night, having hitched a lift in a cattletruck.

'What a dump,' says Paula Zoshka, prodding the threadbare

hammock-like bed on the bare boards, and it's a single room, not because she and Brian Chegwodden had agreed to sleep in separate rooms but because the publican's wife pretended not to hear when he asked for a double bed. Of course, if unmarried couples, with different surnames, want to sneak into each other's rooms, that's their business. We can all be broadminded, in the Presbyterian mode.

'These pubs are required by law to have a certain number of rooms to let, Paula. Otherwise, they lose their liquor licences. It's not as though anyone much stays here, as you can see.'

'I wonder what breakfast will be like? Greasy eggs and sausages, no doubt.'

'Are you still hungry?'

'Good God no! That steak sandwich at the Rodeo filled me up completely. It was so enormous.'

Grey eyes smouldering like hot ash, she glares at him and they embrace, as Diane enters the room.

'Sorry.'

'Couldn't you have knocked?'

'Sorry. Eugene's gone down to the bar, to try and find a mechanic. Bal and Nisi were wondering if you want to come out and eat with us at the Greasy Spoon. Apparently, they don't open the dining room Sunday night.'

'No thanks. I couldn't eat another thing. Anyway, I hate Greek cafes, though I wouldn't say that in front of Nisi.'

'Brian?'

'Town could be full of roughnecks from the Rodeo, Diane. I'd be careful, if I were you.'

'Hey, what about that boy on the white horse swept me off my feet, Paula? Don't you think he was cute? I can't get him out of my mind. I wish I knew his name.'

'Why?'

'So I can ring him up! I want to see him again.'

'Don't be so bloody ridiculous! Have you no sense of modesty? Aren't you in trouble enough?'

'I see. It's OK for you to screw round with married men.'

'What do you mean?'

'Oh come on, Paula, act your age. You think I'm stupid? You think I'm deaf?'

222

'Ears as big as yours, you couldn't be deaf, dear. We know you're stupid.'

'Yeah, well, I may go downstairs and have a drink with Eugene, girls. Room OK Diane? That's good.'

'What, the bar is open Sunday night?'

'No, but it would appear to be full as a goog. Can't you hear them? Full as a tick. House guests all.'

'Careful, Brian. You look the furthest thing from a country boy.'

Though Attis desires nothing more than to be left alone in peace, to think about Diane and hatch her out, as it were, he cannot furnish his reverie of the girl, as he heads for the caff with his brother, with a face. How odd. For the hair is there, that blue-black canopy of screwing curls so curiously mutilated, and the big ears, and the throat, so slender, and the hands, soft and bandaged at the wrists, and the faded and torn denim scungies, over the long thin legs and the neat seat, and the bosom, disappointingly small on any other girl perhaps, but here so wonderfully apposite, and no face.

No face, in the faceless figure, of whom his mind will not let go? Surely it was the hoyden's face, as much as her figure and fearlessness, which captivated him, as he grabbed her, and threw her, kicking and protesting, over the withers of his horse, while the calf she had been attempting to rescue continued with some kicking and protesting of its own, for we look for faces.

'This must be the caff.'

Diane throws her smoke in the gutter and, hands in hip pockets, knees open the swinging doors. The patrons by the till look her up and down, as Attis drops his large bottle of Coke, in shock. Fergus, swearing, surveys with a groan the damage to his chaparajos, and as he does, a half-dozen chips spill from the white butcher's paper he holds aloft.

Moistening her lips, Diane walks straight up to Attis and shakes him by the hand.

'We found each other again,' she exclaims. 'Good. We're the

223

only two real people round. Come to my hotel with me or take me back to where you live.'

'Turn it up,' grins Fergus, laughing with embarrassment at Con in the blue dustcoat. To Nisi he says, 'You better take her home to bed, Love. She's confused. Is she on drugs?'

'No,' says Attis. 'She was right. She was right in trying to protect that calf, and you were wrong, in laughing about her.'

'What? Don't urt 'em.'

'Too right it does,' says Nisi, and as she and Con argue the toss, Attis and Diane slip through the doors, with Fergus in half-hearted pursuit. They reappear, hopelessly in love, at the hotel for breakfast next morning, having walked round town all night, so they claim.

That's one good thing about Obliqua Creek. It comes into its own when the street lights go off.

36. Diane moves into Graceland. Paula and Brian split up.

Fergus MacAnaspie is dumbfounded to find the young woman now sleeping on the lumpy couch. He never could.

They're so pretty, when they're asleep. Fergus tiptoes to the fridge and quietly withdraws a bottle of beer. Nursing the beer, he sits, by the couch, to sip and stare at this strange girl.

Who is so tall she has had to curl, to fit on the couch at all. She is facing in, and from behind, you wouldn't know she was a woman. So slight, and so slender. Dark, but of that Celtic darkness goes with freckles. Most attractive. Her breath, as she exhales, lifts a curl that has fallen over her face. Her head is almost shaven, but her hair is long at the front.

She seems completely at her ease. Walked in off the street, like a cat.

All the dishes have been done. The whole flat is tidy. It has to have been the girl did it, because Mum doesn't come out till Tuesday. It wouldn't matter what day Mum washed, now Mum owns the vacuum cleaner, but Monday was always washing day at Wonderview. When you were a child, too young for school, your mother gave you a sleeping draught with breakfast. You woke around 3 p.m. and the washing would be hanging on the clothes line.

Kitchen never looked more neat. Even the dishrag has been folded, and placed neatly on the porcelain sink.

Ah well. When Attis gets home she'll have to leave and that's all there is about it.

Quietly, the screen door opens to admit—is it Cilla Black, who just opened at Chequers? No.

'Didn't mean to intrude,' says Nisi Papadimitriou, intruding.

Fergus, placing a finger to his mouth, indicates he will slip outside to speak. Pussyfooting in his burr-embossed socks, he quietly removes his stockhat.

'Not a bad sort of day,' he remarks, with the studious politeness of a drunken shearer, 'though we could use rain. Had some snow, a few weeks back, but didn't hardly wet the ground.'

'My word,' exclaims the woman, 'it's that dry where I'm from, we're expecting a bad summer. Gales. Already had a few fires.'

'Go on. And where you from then?'

'Blue Mountains.'

'I see. Which part?'

'Bell's Line o' Road. Know it?'

'Bell's Line o' Road. No, I don't think I do know that road.'

'It's very scenic. Heard of the Zig Zag?'

'Zig Zag? You mean the cigarette papers?'

'Old railway line up there.'

'Yeah, we don't have our railway line now. Bloody politicians took it from us.'

'Oh don't talk to me about politicians. They're all as bad as each other.'

'My Dad says no matter who you vote for, politicians get in. I'm Fergus, by the way. Fergus MacAnaspie.'

'Nisi. Berenice. Papadimitriou.'

'Pleased to meet you, Nisi. Didn't I see you in the milk bar? Were you at the Rodeo then?'

'Caught a bit of it yestey arvo, Fergie, but we were very tired. Been bushwalkin.'

'Oh I see. I spend a fair bit of time in the bush, Nisi, but I'm

225

goin too fast to look at it. That's my rig over there. Only did one run today. Bit of a headache.'

' "Simply the Best!" My goodness it's big. Yes, the flowers are lovely. Don't they say that means fires?'

'I think it does mean fires, Nisi. Lots o' them bush plants need those fires to regenerate. That's why we torch the coupes. Can I get you a cuppa? Would you like a cup of tea?'

'No, really, I mustn't stay, Fergus. The reason I dropped by is that girl on the couch is a friend of mine.'

'Ah.'

Meanwhile, back in the hotel.

'Where've you been, Brian? Did you go out?'

'Hmmm?'

'You just went out just now.'

'Oh. Yeah. Right. I'm on a high. I went out and had a look round town.'

'Did you ring Prim?'

'Hmm?'

'Your wife. Did you ring her?'

'Oh please Paula, not now please. Let's not spoil what . . . '

'What what, Brian? What might be our last, and only, dirty weekend? Is that what you were going to say? You cunt. You fucking bastard, you prick. I should have known.'

'Wow! Such language.'

'I learned it from men. Did you ring someone from the Post Office?'

'You don't feel worthy of happiness, Paula, so you punish yourself by opening old wounds.'

'Liar.'

'I beg your pardon?'

'Sorry, of course, you don't realise, do you. Liars never do.'

'Rave on.'

'Your whole life is a lie, Brian. Everything about you. Diane was right. And you did ring someone, because I followed you. I saw you go into the phone box and insert money and press button A. So don't tell me you didn't ring your wife.'

'OK, Snoopy, so I rang Prim. What of it?'

226

'I asked you not to, Skimpy, that's all. I asked you, just this once, not to. I saw you smiling as you spoke. Oh God.'

'Oh Christ.'

'Ahuh. Ahuh.'

'Is it such a terrible crime? Is it such a terrible crime to want to put a woman's mind at ease? I told her my hire car broke down and I was stuck somewhere near Yass, and I didn't know when I'd be back.'

'Ahuh. What made me get involved with a liar? And now I'm so worried about my sister, and. . .'

'Oh you and your fucking sister. How tired I am of you and your goddam sister! If ever I married you, it would . . .'

'Marry me? You wouldn't marry me, you never intended to. You're a con man. You don't consider me good enough.'

'I do so. Oh Paula, please. I had to ring home, OK? Please, baby.'

'No. No. Not OK. Take back this ring.'

'Please be sensible Paula. Don't get petulant, honey. Baby, baby, hey hey hey. Come here and let me lick the tears away.'

'Go and lick your baby's tears away. Go and lick your wife's twat. I can't handle liars, Brian. I've loved too many.'

'Oh yeah? So you lied to me. You said you'd never been in love. I suppose you were lying, when you said you loved me?'

'I don't love you.'

'But you said you loved me, Paula.'

'What, when you were fucking me? I'd tell anyone anything then. It's like being under torture.'

'Thank you. I think I'll leave. Do you want me to settle for the accommodation before I go?'

'Why not? I've paid for it. You've had so many bites of my cherry I'm coming down with cystitis.'

'How glad I will be to get on with my work and see my little girls again. You're not such a great screw anyway. What are you, frigid or something?'

'I can't turn it on for dud lays. You can't kiss properly. Goodbye, Brian. Liar.'

'Goodbye, Paula. Well, I guess it's better this way.'

'Sure it is. Nice and clean. Endings are so messy. We knew it couldn't last, Brian. Hey, it's been fun.'

'Sure we did. Diane saw to that. Goodbye Paula.'
'Goodbye, Brian. Take care.'
'You too. Ciao.'
Whew.

Venus offers Her devotees Eternal Life, as does Cybele. Is this why breaking up today is so very hard, so very easy?

Any Deity worth salt offers you Life beyond the Grave. Even my own tutelary Deity, Hermes. Think about it. Not so bad, dying, is it, when you still get mail. Old Cuth Cruikshank, he died in '53, but he was still getting mail when I retired. And how much better than Life beyond the grave, Eternity here and now, and they had it. They had it in that Valley, and they blew it! Monica Ecks, she must be fifty-two. I wonder if the new hubbie has any idea how old she is?

37. *Paula and Eugene visit Diane, to cadge a lift. Wozza of Ruffit Lodge. Short history of Erinungarah.*

After putting Nisi Papadimitriou on the bus in the town from which Brian Chegwodden has taken to the air, Paula Zoshka and Eugene Ecks call by at Graceland to visit Diane Zoshka. It is 8 a.m. but they find Diane at the non-rotary clothes line, hanging out the wash in her knee-length boots, a sprig of fast-fading kangaroo apple pinned to her bodice. Tough stuff, pegging out a pair of chaps with conventional pegs.

'Will you look at that!' says Paula, taking Eugene by the elbow. 'What in God's name does she look like?'

Eugene Ecks, who has the neck of a spirit bottle protruding from the front of his shirt, is not much interested in Paula Zoshka, or Diane either, by this stage. But confused by what he perceives as an ambivalent response to his American accent, he wants to get to the Valley as soon as possible. And for this, he reasons he needs Paula, as she's the kind of girl men listen to.

'Hi darl! Where's your curlers and bumper?'

'Hi Paula. Hi Eugene. I'm putting out the wash.'

'So we see. Never did that for me, Eugene. Well, what's happening, kid? You moved in here, or what? What's going on?'

'We gotta go out and get the van now, Diane.'

'Fergie's the one you should see about that, Eugene. And he's at work.'

'Who's Fergie, Sis?'

'One of the guys who lives in the flat.'

'I beg your pardon?'

'Don't worry. Att and he are brothers, Well, they're not really brothers. I mean, they're kinda more than brothers, and less than brothers? Would you believe Fergus actually found Attis on a sawdust heap at the mill? Apparently, he was abandoned there, by his mother.'

'Far out. So does Fergie have a truck?'

'Does he what. You should see it, man. Big Mack.'

'And he's not home? When will he be back?'

'Not till late tonight.'

'Shit. I don't want to waste another day. I think I'll wire my brother for more money.'

'I spose we could ask Att's opinion.'

'He's home?'

'Sure, he's studying. Examination starts soon. I don't like disturbing him, though. His mother'll freak out, if he fails.'

'This is rich. You were supposed to be doing your final exam this year, Diane. And you don't care about your own mother.'

'Att's mother is not bourgeois, Paula.'

'Look, I don't want to disturb the guy, but won't he be stopping for a cup of coffee at some stage? Christ, we gotta organise somethin here, Diane.'

'I was just gonna make him a cup of tea when I'd finished hangin out the wash.'

'Pardon me while I throw up. You never made anyone a cup of tea in your life, Diane. I don't think you know how to boil water.'

'I'm learning, OK? Look, I wasn't in love with you, Paula. Everything is different now.'

'Huh. If you "love" this guy so much, why would you disrupt him at this crucial stage? You're selfish as sin, Diane. And you've only known him a day.'

'Oh Christ, Paula, you're such a downer. You don't see it, do you. Everything is happening, it's all around, and you can't see it. Poor Paula.'

'Listen girls, can I rap with Att please? Hey, I gotta get out to this van.'

'... and so Attis, I would have to say, as I'm taking you into my confidence here, I cannot, in all conscience, return to Nam, and so I'm looking for somewhere to lie low, just till an amnesty's declared, or, in the event of an amnesty not being declared, somewhere to do time, I guess. But my needs are few, and because I have come to appreciate, in the tropics, the importance of cool climates, round here would suit me pretty good. So do you got any ideas on as how I might get out to the van?'

'Att's big brother's in Vietnam, Eugene. Enlisted with the Aussies.'

'Sorry man, stepped right in it. Goosed myself nicely. Didn't know the Aussies were there.'

'That's all right. We're Americans now. First Australian Task Force is under the command of the Second US Field Force. Now you say this Valley is somewhere round here?'

'Yeah. We forget the name of it, don't we, Paula? It was an Australian sounding name.'

'Can you describe it?'

'It was on the other side of that mountain range near where the Rodeo was held, man. You know the one we mean? Blocked off by a landslide, cordin to the man who took us out there.'

'Erinungarah?'

'That sounds like it. That was the name of the place, wasn't it, Paula?'

Balthazar Beauregard, running from a downpour, appears at the screen door, to confirm that was the name of it.

'My family own that Valley.'

'See what I mean, Paula? It's *all* happening, and all you want to do is talk about examinations, which are just another form of state oppression. Education is not where it's at.'

Herewith Diane, distaff Justinian, closes the Schools and severs the golden chain of the Colonial Platonic succession. 'I declare it in advance,' writes Spengler in 1920. 'This current century will not have passed without having seen the Western Soul outlive its will to win victories for Science. European science is on the road towards a self-annihilation through an over-refinement of the intellect.' And perhaps as well, or we'd be living today, as experts in the '60s predicted for us, in plastic, electronic cottages, interfacing from these with paperless Post Offices, when not taking holidays on the moon.

'Aw shit, man, where'd you get this honey?' Balthazar, deeply impressed, teaspoon in hand, from the pantry door. He had the munchies.

I believe Diane is correct. I think there is much to be said for leaving school at fourteen years ten months to work as a telegram boy. Many of us went on to higher things. In 1950 a black tie reunion was held, at the Australia Hotel, of fifteen former telegram boys, including Cardinal Sir Bluey Gilroy, Ampol Chairman Sir Stuart Thorpe, Governor-General Sir Billy McKell, Chairman of the Bradford Cotton Mill Sir Robert Webster, champion cyclist and cabinet minister Sir Hubert Opperman, and the Deputy Director of Posts and Telegraphs, New South Wales, Sir John Jensen. In his opening address, the Governor-General's Private Secretary, Sir Murray Tyrrell, said, 'You were given two and a half minutes to walk a city block. If you had to go further than four miles you were given a second-class rail ticket to your destination, and had to collect the fare from the recipient of the telegram. It was character-building.'

And salubrious to boot. Had Australia Snail Mail entered, as a nation, the 1994 Commonwealth Games, we would have placed fifth in the gold medal tally.

When he was young, I bet Wozza wanted to be rich and famous too. By the time he was my age I dare say he'd have settled on being rich and obscure. Today—what is today, by the way? Friday? I know it's 1995. I know it's winter, 1995. Anyway, he's in his nineties now, poor as a bloody church mouse, but so well known a creek, and a town, have been named after him, and he'd be the best known man in the district. What's a butterfly and a waratah compared with a creek and a town? Still, I can't speak ill o' Wozza. He rules lines on his envelopes. Served on I wot not what National Committees of Reconciliation. He's the sole surviving descendant of the Aboriginal inhabitants*, and when he scores this estate, under the Mabo+, he won't have to share it with a soul. Unless he marries it reverts to the Crown on his demise. His great-grandmother was a full-blood lady of the southeast Wun Wun people, though you wouldn't think so to look at him, would you, with his red face and blue eyes and curly white hair used to be so blond. On the other hand, if he did marry, who's to say the nipper wouldn't be black as a bucket of sump oil? But I think he's a confirmed bachelor.

All these confirmed bachelors, who should have offspring enough to fill a fridge door. You'd think we had a system of domestic slavery in place, as they did in ancient Rome, but we don't; it's just that we can see the superficiality of judging a man by the clothes he wears.

This'll be it. Ruffit Lodge, Good God, would you look at that chimney? Wonder the bloody ladder don't catch fire. You don't see too many corrugated iron chimneys nowadays. Still, I suppose if you've a corrugated iron house to match, albeit somewhat distinct in style from architect Glen Murcutt's

---

* 'It is a peculiar phenomenon, of which there are many examples, that states and peoples do not exert their cultural and spiritual influence effectively until after their own collapse.' A. Von Gall

+ Guilt. We English prefer, as a rule, to exterminate natives. As Toynbee points out, this is why, after the collapse of the Roman Empire, the Latin vernaculars survived on the continent, while in Britain, the barbarous English tongue took over, and has to be studied, in Oxford, to this day. Vandals, Visigoths, Gepids, Berbers were content merely to replace Roman officials. Angles and Jutes slaughtered the Roman population. We did the same thing in America, to the Indians, or rather, gave the job to the British and Irish Celts, as an alternative to being themselves exterminated, by us.

Moruya masterwork. I really don't expect to hear from Wozza anything I don't already know, but then I never expect to hear anything I don't already know, from anyone. I must be on guard against this attitude.

Wozza is certainly the one individual, not of the Valley, who knew a lot about it, and why I haven't spoken to him before this speaks volumes for my slackness. I've been a bit remiss, a bit dilatory. Jealous, perhaps.

We'll let him tell the story, as it comes to him, in his own words. Just check that tape recorder for us, would ya? One, two, buckle me bag and button me lip, yes it works. Needle's movin, any road.

'Ah Wozza! How goes it, old mate? Do you miss the old Rodeo?'

'What makes you ask that? I never went near the bloody Rodeo, D'Arcy. Never seemed to need other people, unless I was wantin to bleed me brakes. Only event might have interested me, they never seemed to have. I'd have liked me chances in the Open Pack Mule Tug 'o War. What, have you got a letter for me?'

'No. I've retired since last you received mail. Come out to talk about the Valley, remember? We confirmed it, over the phone.'

'I reckon you're like an All Night Chemist, you never shut up.'

'Ah, without words, what were we, Wozza? We humans have the larynx lower in the neck than other mammals. Must be for a divine purpose. I'll just switch on the tape recorder. Can I fetch you a cup of anything?'

'Very kind, D'Arcy. If it's evening a cup of hot chocolate, if it's morning a cup of hot tea. I'm like a bloody old wombat nowdays, don't know whether it's night or day. What, don't tell me you've joined the Alpine Historical Society? All they ever do is argue who should have the new streets named after 'em.'

'No, no, Wozza, nothin so pedestrian. This is a more momentous affair. Show us your famous vista before we commence. Where is it?'

'Go to the verandah and cast your eyes southeast. It's forgotten how to rain, D'Arcy.'

'It doesn't like being called it, Wozza.'

My word, will you look at that? I see the attraction of this barren ridge for the poor old coot. If he weren't blind, from using a chainsaw in the wind, he could see every lead and claim, every reef and pocket he spent his lifetime pannin, sinkin and drivin, from here. But there weren't enough gold, they reckon, to ram down the barrel of a muzzle-loadin shotgun. Deaf, from his stamper battery, to boot. See the metal detector in the hall, the one he painted white, like a cane?

'Erinungarah Valley. Only place you'd see the black-eyed susans *and* the chocolate lilies white. Yes well it was owned by the MacAnaspies, D'Arcy, but they did nothin with it, part from a bit of lucerne. Typical. There was a house there, on the flat, and they wanted to put up an inn, to take advantage of the passin coach trade, but then they opened that other road through to the coast, and that scotched that. Road through the Gap was prone to wash away, in heavy rain, so when old Mrs Cooper, member her? When she lived in that house, with her husband and sixteen children, this would have been, when? I think the 1930s. Anyway, she wouldn't go up the Gap Road, so they allays went down through to the coast, for their provisions. After the Coopers moved out, when she died—they reckon she was bitten by a snake, but that's what they'll always tell you, when they can't ascertain the cause of a death: a pity it weren't him, they wouldn't have missed him—an Irish couple moved in, and they was never married. They lived there, oh, a great many years. Could still be there. She had a private income. Put grapes on the Flat, and they used to grow a bit of lucerne, and, wait till you hear this, eat the lucerne themselves!'

'What, you don't mean to say you never heard o' sprouted alfalfa, Wozza? You're livin in the dark ages. Now before we go any further, can we speak of the Aboriginal connection?'

'What?'

'Your own people, mate. The Aboriginal connection.'

'Used to go up the bench to the Gap, and there's still a Diamond Python dreamin site, in that Valley.'

'Where? Tell us about that.'

'No, carn do. Now before the dam was built, I used to go down to my camp via the Erinungarah Valley, and I kept in touch with the Coopers, as she was most hospitable. But they'd gone, by the time the dam came creepin up, creepin up, and the MacAnaspies had cattle on the verandah. Oo, bloody disgraceful. They was just squatters too, you know.'

'When was this?'

'You work it out. Now my camp was at the foot of the Erinungarah Plateau, where it drops sheer away, in a place called Fossicker's Flat. It was there I had the *Golightly*, my stamper battery, and my Cornish boiler. They're under the waters now, hundreds of feet down, if not thousands.'

'Good Lord.'

'People think I was lookin for gold, D'Arcy, took me for a fool. Ha! Now I had thought to move to the other side of the lake what the dam created, which woulda given me access to the coast. In the event, I moved up the hill, but I could no longer use the Gap, as the Gap Road followed the eastern bank of the river, crossin back over to the western side before the conflux of the Erinungarah Crik with the left arm of my crik. So I had to come in through this valley, and then I knocked out the bridle trail from my camp, which come out here, and when I wanted to cross to the other side of the waters, I used a raft. Did most o' me fossickin over that other side.'

'I see. So when did the young people move into the Valley, Wozza, and had you anything to do with them?'

'Nineteen seventies. Maybe earlier, I never went up the Erinungarah Valley. Too noisy up there.'

'How do you mean?'

'Oh, you know. Motorcycles. MacAnaspies'd come down in trucks, to shift out cattle. Had a pack of half-wild dingoes used to hang round my camp. Had to bait one, from time to time. I'm a man who can't stand noise, D'Arcy, unless I'm makin it meself.'

'And how'd you meet up with the new residents?'

'Party of men turned up at my camp one night, said they was lookin for a way out of the Erinungarah. All had long hair and funny little caps like leprechauns, and sandals on just the one foot, but they was polite. They were a tribe, if you take my meaning. Yes, I'd call them a pack, or a horde. They had some artistic people in that Valley, D'Arcy, and some prominent people too. Zeno Zoshka, chairman o' Norwestern Nickel, his daughters was in that Valley.'

'So I believe. And these men turned up, and what happened then?'

'Peppered 'em with shot, then I told them of the bridle trail, and we agreed they could use it, in exchange for zucchinis. Apparently the Gap caved in, and they'd been usin a certain pass, but for some reason, could no longer use it. There weren't a lot of passes, out of the Erinungarah.'

'Any women with them? Anyone wearing women's garb?'

'Not that I recall.'

'How often was they comin through?'

'Never seen 'em for years at a time. Mind you, I was seldom home, so I couldn't really say. One of them come through every weekend there, for a bit. Had him loaded up.'

'That'd be Timothy Papadimitriou. Orion. They sent him to the high school.'

'That's right. Young Tim. Bright boy.'

'Stayed in town during the week. He was going to be the saviour, update the technology.'

'That's right. So he was. And then they started wantin to leave packhorses about, and fuel drums for the motorcycles, and even took some of my weepin gelly, once, without askin, so I had to warn 'em off. Two o'them bloody MacAnaspie louts went down and lowered the tone of the place. The young ones all spoke like Darryl, have you heard him try to speak? Married Valley girls I spose—well, likely never married 'em. It's old-fashioned. Shacked up with 'em.'

'Three actually. So had you any idea what was goin on in that Valley, Wozza? I mean, did they never invite you down?'

'Oh I might of, D'Arcy, and yes, they might of. But they was like me. Didn't exactly welcome intruders.'

'Oh? Why was this?'

'Because while we was doin it hard, you was up the club. Nervy lot, they were. High strung. Talkin, talkin, laughin, cryin. Couldn't shut 'em up.'

'And what kind of stuff would they bring in?'

'Oh, just the essentials. Razor blades, for checkin tappet clearances. Beer bottles, for feature walls. Rear vision mirrors, for solar cookers. Cathode ray tubes, for windows, bed bases for sievin soil. Wire nettin, for rabbit traps. Stockholm tar, for paintin mules' hooves. Second-hand roofin iron, an that's a bugger of a thing to carry on a motorcycle. Still, they was handy, some of'em. Watched 'em tossin sheets off one time, and not one of those sheets of iron finished overlappin another.'

'Pull the other one. Books?'

'Mebbe.'

'Circuit boards? We know they had some pretty flash electronic gear.'

'Yes, well someone took in a ghetto blaster once, and it come out next trip.'

'Any big 500 amphour batteries? You know they raided the telephone exchange and knocked off the batteries?'

'So I've heard. But you know, D'Arcy, it's an easy thing to blame an isolated group of individuals for every little thing goes missing. Before it was them, it was likely me. I do know they took the sleepers off the railway track, leaving only the scrap rail and the jewellery, but they was only goin to rot there anyway. May's well be put to some use.'

'And what come out of the Valley? They had no money, as we know, and you can't scrounge Stockholm tar at the tip.'

'Can't scrounge nothin at the tip nowdays. Bloody vampire couldn't scrounge a used tampon for a teabag, all taken off for recycling. Only free thing nowdays is kittens. See, I'm in a real pickle here. I need more bottles for me home brew, and the only bottles I have are filled with home brew.'

'Yes, it's wicked. Another mainstay of the rural life denied. In particular, Wozza, did you notice any strong, hardy, thoughtful-lookin plants o' Middle Eastern appearance?'

'No, but I didn't ask to look in the panniers. I'm not a customs official.'

'You knew the men emasculated themselves?'

'I did notice some of 'em had handbags, but that didn't mean a great deal, back in them days. Grow up, D'Arcy. I've heard the Wun Wun people were a peacful, gentle folk who lived in harmony with their surroundings. It was lucky for us they got access to the grog, son, at the same time as they got access to

237

flamethrowers and shotguns, or there wouldn't be a black duck
or a stick 'o rainforest left. Don't believe all you hear.'

'Whose side you on?'

'Any side I choose.'

'Is that right. I'll take that on board, Wozza.'

'Oh yes, I seen a ceremony once, one o' them bull-killin ceremonies, but I won't be speakin of that, not for the National
Library.'

'This tape is not for the National Library.'

'Don' matter. I'd need to know it would go no further, see.
Give'm me word.'

'Oh come on, man, they're all dead or brain dead. I'll hit the
pause button.'

'No. They tell me you've become a creature of one idea. If
you was a broody hen, we'd hang you upside down on the
clothes line.'

'Thanks for nothin, Wozza.'

'You're welcome.'

'Tassie tigers?'

'They're out there, and they never come from Tassie.'

Bloody old blowhard won that one. Can't tell branching grass
flag, an iris, from a chocolate lily. Think he really witnessed
savage rites? There are people in this town have been getting
mail from an acting primate.

But I was right about the bull's blood, and it seems the
eunuchs remained in the Valley. You see, they dressed in cast-
off women's clothing, according to the *Ballad*.

38. *Frodsham and Barbara discuss revolution.*

'What makes her think running away to the country is going
to solve anything?'

Balmain. Spring, '68. Barbara Byng has just conveyed to
Derek Frodsham what Nisi Papadimitriou has told her concerning Diane Zoshka.

'Would you mind if I clean this fridge before we leave,

238

Derek? It's my turn, but I've been that busy swotting I haven't had a chance.'

'No, no. Go ahead. Yes surely, Barbara, the challenge lies in the city, where people live. Here we can choose. I don't understand this mania for the countryside. Speaking as one who grew up in it and couldn't get out quick enough, it's the same, old dull routine, with never enough hot water. You spend your whole life doing the kind of work that's only noticed when you don't do it. The village in which I lived was unchanged from the thirteenth century to the eighteenth. The farmers had no idea of farming, and thought only to feed themselves. The roads were bad and there was no education. Oh, I know Rousseau thought Science undermines Virtue, but this returning to our "roots", Barbara, this revisionist fantasy of Robespierre and Tolstoy, has been discredited. We may not like it, but there is no way back for us, and just as well. We've no more chance of going back than the poor blessed Aborigines. Take this fridge. Can I give you a hand there, by the way? I don't like to stand here, pontificating and biting my nails, while you do the work.'

'No no Derek. It's refreshing for me to listen to a man as widely read as you. I always learn something.'

'Well, there you go. We met in a city, didn't we? As I say, has she any idea of what life will be like, without refrigeration? In the subtropics, everything must be kept salted, or eaten at once. And this means a vegetarian diet, with the toil that entails, or an unhygienic slaughterhouse close by, with time-wasting harvest feasts, and their attendant superstition. Where I'm from, a tub of lard would keep, without spoiling, one year to the next, but we spent our entire lives huddled over coal fires. In contrast, in the tropics, if conscience forbid as it must the keeping of servants, we tend to become lazy, Barbara, and end up smelling of spirits. Which is why it's all the more dispiriting to find Diane pulling the plug in a climate like this. We had a fresh chance here, in this beautiful harbourside city of Sydney, to build a society untainted by religion, inclemency of weather and the stench of inegalitarianism. No, I'm disappointed. Where Diane goes, others will follow. You watch.'

'Come on, Derek. It's not that bad.'

'It is bad and good, both. It is bad, because the disappearance of rational conduct is the first symptom, according to Spengler, of the final phase of the disintegration of civilisations, the final symptom of the final phase being the re-emergence of primitive religion, as a proletarian syncretism. At the same time, it is good, because not before the demise of Capitalism, can True Socialism take over. But those not with us must be deemed to be against. I quite understand the girl, as a member of the bourgeois intelligentsia, wishing to eschew the taint of money, but this is never achieved by lapsing to the level of populism, what Marx described as the idiocy of rural life. As Trotsky knew, the peasantry, precisely because of its petty ownership, its cretinous chauvinism, its geographical dispersion, its bourgeois aspirations, must yield, in the task of leading democratic revolution, to the urban proletariat. Better hammer than sickle. Couldn't she have found herself a job in a factory? Most of mankind have been peasants, Barbara, not just today, but from the time of the Agrarian Revolution of the fourth millennium BC—a political, rather than a technological, revolution in that instance—which saw the introduction of water reticulation to the swamps of Egypt and Sumeria (those lentils look off, I'd throw them out) right down to the Industrial Revolution of late eighteenth century Britain. You see, there were no peasants before there were cities, Barbara. Where there is money there are cities, and peasants, though strapped for cash, have money. Existing primitive types who do not have money are not peasants.'

'You don't think cities are parasitic?'

'Good God, you sound like a Red Guard. No, I certainly do not. I agree with Huxley. May I quote from his—that's Thomas Huxley—Romanes Lecture of 1893? "That which lies before the Human Race is the constant struggle to maintain and improve, in opposition to the State of Nature, the State of Art of an organised polity, by which, and in which, Man may develop a worthy Civilisation, capable of maintaining and constantly improving itself, until the evolution of our globe shall have entered so far upon its downward course, that the cosmic process resumes its sway, and once more, the State of Nature prevails over the surface of our planet."'

'Oh how very gloomy.'

'You think so? You mean the bit about the cosmic process?

240

Well, that's a few years down the track, unless we give it a nudge, through inadvertence. It is, of course, a worry that nuclear weapons have taken from us the security from extinction we have enjoyed, as a species, since the Neolithic Revolution.'

'And which revolution was that, Derek? You know so much about revolutions.'

'Imagine, if you can, Barbara, a world almost completely covered in ice. Primitive hunter-gatherers, clad in mouldy furs, huddle in frigid caves, picking their teeth with flints. It cannot be denied the Stone Age Mayans possessed a serviceable calendar, but by and large the level of stone age culture approximates that of the blackfellow. Do you realise it is thought there were fewer than 500 people in the whole British Isles, during the last Ice Age? And half of them were on St Kilda, which was free of the ice sheet. But in time, the ice retreats, the savannah becomes desert, the tundra pine, then later oak forest. People move south. The Holocene begins. Certain hunter-gatherers settle down in villages, in and about the Fertile Crescent, but they still hunt and gather, for the next fifteen hundred years. They have dogs, always have had. Then, around seven and a half thousand years BC, they domesticate grain, perhaps in ancient Phrygia. Certainly, level 7 at Catal Huyuk, on the Anatolian plain near Konya, Roman Iconium, shows a precocious development for a Neolithic site. The houses there are built of mudbrick and the walls are decorated with murals. The Great Step Forward! In fact, all they probably had to do, was clean their dishes out the doors. The emmer and the einkorn did the rest. Another thousand years on and they're still hunting gazelles, but are starting now to keep sheep and goats. Again, this may have been at the sheep's and goats' behest. But for the first time in human existence, we have an habitual sufficiency. We can multiply and become superfluous. They actually worshipped a Mother Goddess at Catal Huyuk, apparently. One of those squat little terra cotta jobs with the beefy hips.'

'Oh, that'll do Derek, we'll be late again. And do you think we're on the verge of another revolution?'

'I'm convinced of it. Something is coming, any road. Che lives. I look at San Ernesto's photo every night, before retiring. He thinks the Third World will seize from the Urban Proletariat the role of vanguard. In any event, the New Man will work, but not for money, Babs, because there'll be none, but through moral incentives, in a cashless society, where credit and debit are computerised. Mind you, it's hard to work with anarchists. "Idealistic Philistines" Trotsky called them. He was a Jew, of course, though very likely a Kazar. They were a Turkish horde became Jewish converts, around 750. You see, Liberty, and Equality, don't sit very well on the same committee. And that's where you come in, Babs, because Fraternity is what binds us.'

'Oh you can be sweet.'

'Yes, and though glad as I am, in many ways, to see the back of any anarchist, I want you to go down there and return Diane to Civilisation, for we need her. She has special qualities.'

Barbara Byng: I've done a foolish thing. I made the bad mistake of putting my address on the envelope of the letter I wrote her. I said I have the goods on you, Senator, concerning Dawn, your daughter. It's because of my failing health, I don't have time for diplomacy. I'm getting desperate. When I mentioned this to Kimbo, he says to me, Haven't you heard of Single Mother Chic, Sport? I had to confess I hadn't. I was cut off from the outside world, about the time they started mailing magazines in wrappers postmen couldn't open.

39. *A stroke of good fortune for Horrie.*

To the south, '68, the goodman sits on his arse, by the mouldering compost heap.

'What in Heaven's name you think you're doin?' Was a time the goodwife might have walked by, pretending not to have seen.

'Ello there, darl! Just want to see if the soil's warm enough to plant out those tomato seedlings I've had sittin, germinatin, on the front seat of the old De Soto doorslammer. It's true

242

what they says. Only way to gauge the temperature o' the soil, is to touch it with some part o' yer anatomy hasn't been desensitised through exposure. Turn yer back and I'll get up, if I can.'

'You seem cheerful. What's wrong with you?'

'Nothin's wrong with me. Can't a man appreciate his circumstances? Well, if you must know, I had some good news today. Goin back to ploughin that red soil has pleased God, I reckon. Bloke from the National Parks and Wildlife pulled me over.'

'Thought you said you wasn't gonna stop for them again.'

'Well, no, I wasn't. But I had cause to be glad I did. Way things are lookin, we'll be able to spend the rest of our lives in peace 'n quiet.'

'How do ya mean?'

'They've put a realistic price on the Valley at long last. They're flush and they're desperate. I can now approach Better Fritter Batter and make him an offer he won't refuse.'

'What if he don't want to sell?'

'He'll sell. There'll be some stick in with me carrot. I'll offer him better than market price, and promise to disappoint his expectations.'

'How will you do that?'

'I ave my ways. Sposin a brush-tailed phascogale were seen, right where he's plannin on levellin that site? That's his only site with a view. Only other site he's got, he's lookin straight at us.'

'Wouldn't we be better off usin the money to educate the boys? I mean, we don't need more property. You can't look after what we've got. Why do we need more property?'

'Because with the run, and a corridor of bushland between ourselves and Bunoo Bunoo, we wouldn't know we had a neighbour. It'll be like it was in the old days, only better.'

'Waste o' money. Have you spoken with Charlie?'

'No.'

'You'll need his consent, won't ya? He owns that Valley.'

'I'm confident Charlie will see his way clear to doin the right thing by us. You know how he hates the thought of goin off to some old persons' home.'

'You wouldn't.'

'Oh I might surprise ya there. My word, that's an attractive cardigan, pet. Have I seen that before?'

'Yer drunk.'

40. *Charlie visits the Lookdown. Iris remonstrates with Attis.*

'And your van is on the Ford?'

'Well, there's two vans out there now. One in the Valley, blocked in by a landslide, one, just a little off the causeway.'

'I hope it's still there. The creek rises quickly in rain. I guess we do have to go out and I wonder if we shouldn't take Charlie. He owns the Valley.'

'I do think we should get in sweet with Charlie,' says Diane, eyeballing them meaningfully.

'All right. My brother Darryl went to Cooma today, so he may have left his rig in town. He doesn't often take a day off, so he may be getting tyres fitted. Did you see it round? *Wasted Daze*, it's called. Shoulda heard Dad.'

'What, he doesn't fit his own tyres?'

'Not if he can help it. They are ten hundred twenties. I suggest we go to the garage, see if *Wasted Daze* is there, and if so, if it's ready. If it is, we'll take her out, and maybe pick up Fardy on the way.'

'What about your studies, man? Ten sixty-six and all that.'

'This is more important.'

'Brother won't mind us using his rig?'

'I don't think so. I have a licence.'

'Wow, you drive a semi and you're just sixteen?'

'I'm the son of a primary producer, Diane, and we can get licences early. They're not hard to drive.'

'You shouldn't need a licence to drive anything.'

Trembling, Iris draws Attis aside, and out of earshot of the others, says, 'Son,' she says. 'I don't understand. First Rodeo, now this. You can't afford to waste time, and who's this floozie? Where'd you meet her?'

'It's OK, Mum,' says the lad, with a smile. 'It's all right, just trust me. I know what I'm doing.'

'What about yer exams?'

'I was dux at the trials. Someone should go out and check on Phryx and Gwen. You can appreciate that.'

'I hate to see you wastin time with riff raff.'

'They're all right, Mum.'

'Oh one should be shot, his hair's that long, and the one in the crewcut stinks o' drink, and it's not yet eleven. What would your father say?'

'Where is he, by the way?'

'Went in to the cattle sales. Attis, I want you to promise me you won't do nothing you'll regret.'

'I don't regret things, Mum. Where's the point? No, that's not strictly correct. I'm real sorry now, for my penfriend. Should I write and tell her, do you think?'

'Tell her what?'

Enticed from bed, Charlie MacAnaspie pointedly ignores the strangers on his doorstep. He turns his back, and won't speak, and won't answer, when they do. Eventually, he snarls at his grandson, 'What you bring 'em out ere for?'

'They're in a spot of trouble, Fardy. Their van is bogged, by the ford above the Falls.'

'What they doin out there?'

'Oh, they was just lookin round. It is a public road. I'm going out, to retrieve it now. Want to come?'

'Why would I want to come? I got too much on ere.'

'Oh, go on with ya! You go out with Attis. You're only just under my feet. You go out and help the boys, go on. Girls'll stay with me.'

'No, we want to go too!'

Attis winks at Diane. 'We won't be long' he says. 'Stay here and have a chat with Mum.'

The van has been washed over the Falls. They see it the size of a dinky toy.

Charlie remains in the cab of the rig, looking straight ahead, the way old men will. When Attis reports the bad news, he takes it on the chin.

'Shit!' says Eugene Ecks. 'I'll have to wire my brother for more money, or rather, Balthazar will have to do it for me, cause it's likely the phone is tapped.'

'Want to check on your tenants, Fardy, while we're out here?'

'Nope. I'm not goin down there, now.'

'All right. Then why don't we drive to a place we can see the house, and check if the home fire's burning? Come on, Fardy, let's show the boys the Valley. Tell us where to stop.'

They can see Michael Ginnsy's multicoloured Kombi, parked outside the back door of the farmhouse.

'Hey, check out those grapes, man. Those are grape vines, are they, man?'

'What's that?'

'Where, Fardy?'

'I see a man, not a roo, scratchin round on the Flats, with a dog. Over there, by Jellybean Pool.'

'Oh yeah. I see them now. Over there, boys. Where the creek widens.'

'What's he doin, I wonder?'

'Lookin for mushies after the rains, man. Least we know he's still down there. Mr MacAnaspie, you know of any track goes down by a big cave?'

'Oh. You bin pokin round.'

'We didn't realise it was your private property, sir. But if you want our help in getting down there, we have no immediate plans. Do we, boys?'

'I'll go down when you're left town. Everyone got eyes on that Valley. Looks pretty good from up here, don't it? Down there, lookin back up, it's a different story.'

'How's that?'

'Too isolated. We built that house. Why do you suppose we walked out there and come up here, where it's cold? Never get a frost down there. That's a little piece of the coast. Up here, we're in the Alps. Look at that, boy, see that tree? That's a cabbage palm tree. Ever seen a cabbage palm tree up here? Figs down there, too. Cedars. Oo no, plenty of people want that Valley, but I'm not sellin, no way. That your old man up there on the other side, Attis, workin that red soil?'

'I don't believe you can see that far, Fardy. No, he went to the sale today. Nice try.'

'We was trained, as boys, to use our eyes. Raised on rabbits 'n pumpkins, and the pumpkins was all skin 'n seeds, back then. Warty little buggers, broke the knives. We used 'em for hand grenades. Plurry old fool, he's as good as two men short, why don't he buy himself some decent farming gear, if he's gonna go farmin? Anyway, that's our Valley. You've seen it, and now you can walk home. What, you American?'

'Yes sir.'

'Why aren't you fightin in the War?'

'Because we're in love,' explains Diane. 'But don't get upset, Mrs MacAnaspie. Love is Freedom.'

'Did you know that, Paula? Love *is* Freedom. It's true.'

Attis MacAnaspie: What would have become of him, without Diane? Theirs was a fateful meeting. We all know judges who think they're God— just ask Darryl MacAnaspie—but here was a man who became a god instead of becoming a judge.

41. *Olaf takes leave from Puckapunyal Army Camp.*

When Olaf Abernathy appears off the plane, clutching his greatcoat and swag, Nisi is impressed by the serge woollen battledress, surmounted by the black cavalry beret. He takes her tightly by the elbow, and they squeak and mince off to the cab rank, whence Rowe Street, in the city, for a coffee. It's only 10 a.m. A gusting nor'westerly wind is blowing, and century temperatures are forecast.

'I wish now I hadn't worn these winter clothes, but it was cold when I left Melbourne.'

'Olaf. Did you hear what happened?'

'About the fires?'

'My horse burned to death.'

'Shit. No way are we going back up there, Nisi. Stupid to live on the ridge. Boys OK?'

'They're fine.'

'Where are they now?'

'Mon's looking after them. The scene between her and Calvin is shocking. Calvin treats Monica like dirt, but lucky for him, her father did, too. Poor Cindy.'

'Let's not worry about them now.'

'How you coping, Olaf?'

'I dunno. All right.'

'Be honest with me, please.'

'Don't cry, Nisi, for God's sake. Your make-up will run down your cheeks.'

'I'm sorry. I can't hold it back. I need a drink. I need some loving.'

'Me too. Where can we go?'

'It's too early. Did you decide what corps to apply for?'

Olaf lights a Gauloise cigarette. The cabbie glances in the rear vision mirror.

'Will you apply to become a bandsman?'

'I haven't really decided what to do. I wanted to discuss it with you, first.'

Exhaling, he looks out the cab windows at the sights of busy Botany Road. His cock has been oozing prekum for days, and he can't wait to be alone with this hot chick. Preferably, in some sleazy dive, or even a luxury hotel would be good.

'Hungry? They feeding you properly?'

He lunges at her, pushes her head back, and rams his tongue down her throat. The cabbie concentrates on the road.

'Not yet. Not yet, please.'

'But we can't wait till tonight!'

'Maybe, but it's just eleven. I want it to last, I want the tension to build. Do you want to smoke some grass?'

'Oh. Have you got some?'

'I bought some for you. Let's go down to the Botanical Gardens and smoke it there.'

'You're going to smoke? Oh wow. Let's book into a hotel right away.'

'No, it's too early. It's not yet check-out. Look, give me space, all right?'

'Sure. Let's go to the gardens. Have you had enough cake?'

'Thank you.'

She knows now she wants to be rid of men, they're jerks. Four legs good, two legs bad.

They sit above the rosebeds, and surreptitiously share the joint that Nisi took, crumpled, from her make-up compact.

'Ah, that feels better. Gee, I've been so looking forward to this. Hey, where'd you get this stuff? It's blowin my head off.'

'Then don't smoke any more, because you haven't had a smoke in weeks, remember? I don't want any panic attacks.'

'Who says?'

'Oh. I didn't think you'd smoke down there.'

'I'm gonna pork your big fat butt off, baby. You look great.'

'Thanks. I wanted to please you. Can we talk, Olaf?'

'Sure. Shoot.'

'I can't stay with Mon any longer.'

'No worries. I'll be getting a housing loan. We can buy a nice house, with acres for the horse.'

'Are you deaf, Olaf? The horse is dead.'

'We'll get another horse.'

'Oh Christ, you're so insensitive!'

'Sorry. Being in the Army does that. Man comes out in a body bag, a man is sent in to replace him.'

'Look, I need to be with people I can trust, at a time like this. Understand?'

'Sure.'

'Must you serve in Vietnam, Olaf?'

'I don't want to serve in fuckin Nam.'

'But you will. You wait and see. You'll go, and you'll probably get wounded over there, too. In fact, I had a dream about it. It was a terrible, terrible wound.'

'Such concern is only natural.'

'I think it's obscene you want to fight in this war, frankly. I mean, what is wrong with you? Why would you want to fight in this filthy war? You're not proving anything. Why would you want to kill someone who's done no harm to you?'

'Oh come on, Nisi, you're forgetting about the housing loan. I can't get one as a small-time muso, and I don't want to have to go back and work as a builder's labourer again.'

'But you're a fine musician.'

'Bullshit. I never made it. There's nothing for me on Civvy Street, let's face it.'

'Oh come on, you're only twenty. You're only a boy. You're just a young man. You're too young to die, and you don't understand the issues.

I don't want to spend the rest of my life with a fuckwit who fought in Vietnam. None of my friends would ever speak with me again.'

'Huh! Great friends.'

'You may not like my friends, Olaf, but you admire one of them, at least.'

'Who's that?'

'Michael Ginnsy.'

'Oh yeah. Well Ginnsy's a great guitarist. Everyone knows that.'

'What if I tell you he just dropped out, and has moved to a hidden Valley on the far South Coast?'

'What?'

'That's right. You see, there's a Change in Consciousness occurring, Olaf, and you're going to miss out on it. The smart people are turning their backs on the mass consumer lifestyle in the cities, in order to become self-sufficient in the country-side and live in harmony with Nature.'

'You think Ginnsy would play with me?'

'If you were the only other muso round, he'd have no choice, would he. Come on, get smart, Olaf. Why don't we just piss off?'

'Because I'll be court-martialled.'

'You'd be a hero to the people that count. Hey listen, Barbara's going down soon. Why don't we get a lift with her?'

'Fuck it, Nisi, no! I'm on leave. I just wanta screw and smoke dope.'

'Don't worry, we'll screw. You won't last two minutes. You'd be taking leave of your senses, Olaf, to pass up this opportunity.'

42. *The Moody Valley Candle Company Co-op conceived. Barbara, Nisi and Olaf hitch a lift. Visit to Koala Kottage. Phryx and Gwen's disappearance. Ginnsy's ordeal.*

There is excitement concerning the prospect of establishing a new commune in the Erinungarah Valley. A few problems remain to be worked out: lack of vehicular access, the fact that the National Parks and Wildlife want to buy and Horrie wants to sell, and Charlie owns. But such problems are sent to be resolved, through collective effort of nisus. A name has already been devised for the new multiple occupancy: Moody Valley Candle Company Co-op. Discussions late into the night at flat three Graceland have determined on cooperative candle construction as a surefire means of establishing the commune on a firm financial footing. Once it is on a firm financial footing, money will no longer be needed. The plateau is alive, it seems, with bees, and Attis has developed an understanding with a pair of rainbow bee-eaters, who, acting as African honey guides, lead him to the site of a wild hive: whereupon, he breaks it open, and the bee-eaters feed on the larvae and wax.

Balthazar Beauregard makes a cogent suggestion: why not, now, move one step further, and domesticate, rather than hunt, these bees, seeing as how they're descended from domestic Italian stocks in the first place? Horrie MacAnaspie has stacks of old bee boxes he will never use again, and Balthazar knows of many more up north, sufficient to establish a huge apiary.

The bee-eaters can be recompensed for their efforts with drone comb, which is a nuisance, and a byproduct of these hives will be honey if not always the superb shining gum honey which so impressed Balthazar when first he tasted it.

The ancients, as we read in Virgil's Fourth Georgic, knew the value of honey: they had sugar, from India, but used it only as medicine. Honey, which can be sold or stored forever, pollen, a wonderful source of protein, propolis, with its antiseptic qualities, but chiefly wax, which can be moulded into candles, using Balthazar's highly original moulds, for which, in the markets of Sydney and Melbourne, is bound to exist insatiable demand. Insufflated with enthusiasm, Diane Zoshka is already spending much spare time calling by on members of the Country Women's Association to see if they have any old bee boxes. Those for sale she must reluctantly decline; those given freely she returns to Graceland, where Eugene Ecks, who is camped in the old dairy, spends hours tarting up and refurbishing them, cutting out rot, reassembling floors, painting the finished articles with a coat of pink wood primer, then one of undercoat and two of lavender satin gloss. Diane feels the white hive is bourgeois, and off-blue will better suit the moods of the Misty Moody Valley. Three hives complete, another on the way. No one has yet gone down to the Valley.

Paula Zoshka has returned to Sydney, but paid the bond on flat number three, and made Diane, her sister, put the phone on. It is true that having been bailed out by Paula, Diane failed to appear in court on a charge of indecent exposure, while presenting two uniformed cops with a pig's head on a platter. But surely no one is wasting time on such a petty malfeasance, when the State premier, according to Brian Chegwodden, is on the take in a big way. Brian has kept names from the papers. No one knows Diane is the daughter of Lady Zoshka of Darling Point.

Finally, Attis lands a job picking seed for the Forestry, and good as his word he's taking Eugene Ecks to the Valley while he checks on Phryx and Gwen. Diane wants to come too, but there's talk of Barbara Byng coming down from Sydney, so it looks like tomorrow at the earliest. As Fergus MacAnaspie explains to a dubitative Iris MacAnaspie, these blow-ins could be useful contacts for Attis, in Big Syd.

252

'I'm worried, son, I can't help it. I know that hussy's got designs on him. I just wish he didn't have to go away. To upset me further, your father's onto Charlie bout sellin the blessed Valley, now. They near come to blows last night. Darryl had to go between 'em. I reckon Charlie's shoulder's no better, he couldn't get one saucepan off the hook. So when you comin back out?'

'Dunno. We'll see what happens here first.'

Now a soldier in uniform, absent on leave, would be on a winner hitchhiking, you might have thought. But when, after ten minutes, no vehicle slows, Barbara Byng makes an impatient move forward.

'Let me have a try, Olaf.'

'Don't be impatient, Barbara.'

'Olaf, I'd like some sleep tonight, if we're going on a long walk tomorrow. Please?'

The minute he withdraws in Barbara's favour, an iridescent blue Ford Fairmont pulls over. The driver, wearing leopard skin tights, drives off again, after a brief exchange.

'That was Dinah,' explains Barbara Byng. 'Her son works at the Cockatoo Dockyards. She's only going as far as Camden. Her aunt has taken ill. I saw another acquaintance drive past too, but he'd have been visiting the Lawn Cemetery. Wonder why he didn't go out yesterday? Must have been at the races. Now wait. This car coming, can you make out the rego?'

'Want to take over, Olaf?' inquires Nisi, as the '64 Bellett screams to a halt.

'Don't stick your tongue in your cheek at me. I'll do it for ya. Get in the back.'

'You will not.'

Next day is the kind on which locals greet locals with the salutation, 'Back to winter, mate.' Overnight rain has ushered in an Antarctic air flow. Olaf is glad of his serge drills, and Nisi is wearing the greatcoat, as Attis drives them, dead tired, to the Valley, glancing from time to time behind him to check no one has fallen off the back of the ute, as the tailgate needs work. Beside Attis in the cab is Barbara Byng, racked with hay fever, and Diane Zoshka, studiously knitting a jocose pair of mohair bedsocks. Eugene Ecks on the tray, goose bumps below his T-shirt, makes light, if treasonable, conversation with Olaf Abernathy. Pink buttons (a kunzea), heathland mirbelia (a pea), heath milkwort (matchsticks) and Barker's boronia bemeasle the roadside verge, as the sky to the south becomes darker and darker, and finally headlight dark.

'Naa, it's nothin.' Eugene declines Nisi's offer of the tail of the greatcoat. 'Pisses down all night like this, in Nam. Half the time you're out in it.'

'Have you been in the Valley?' inquires Nisi. Attis pulls over as the rain becomes hail.

'Sorry about this weather, folks. Do we want to go on?'

'Yes please, sweetie. It's your last free day.'

'OK. Now about this track, I think I know the one you mean, but you know what might be quicker?'

'No.'

'Scrambling over the rockfall on the road.'

'In the ice. You're the boss.'

'It should have settled by now. The ice will melt.'

'Fine.'

'It's just some people are not really dressed for it.'

'Don't worry about me,' urges Barbara Byng, 'I don't need to come. I just need to speak with Diane, and I can do that anywhere. *Achoo*.'

'What do you mean? Did Paula put you up to this?'

'No. It had nothing to do with her. By the way, you know she could be pregnant? Apparently her period is overdue. *Achoo*. I only know because a friend ... Diane? Diane, are you all right?'

'Oh goodness. Oh poor Paula! Not again! Oh please God, no.'

'I'm so sorry, Diane. Me and my big mouth.'

'We must be free to speak the truth, Barbara. I have to cope as best I can. Let me get back in the cab, please. I want to lie down.'

'Oh, it's only gossip. Maybe just a false alarm.'

'I might take the soldiers down today, they're fit. Nisi, would you mind terribly if just the men came down today? I mean, that's a really nice outfit you're wearing.'

'Thank you. Attis.'

'I wouldn't like to see it ruined.'

'Of course. I hadn't realised we weren't going to use the track.'

'Well even the track won't be much of a track. And I mean, with high heels and fishnet stockings . . .'

'It's OK, really. You don't want women along, that's fine by us. We'll stay here.'

'No, it's not that we don't want women along.'

'We don't care, do we girls? We'll go back to Wonderview and spend the day there. What time you want to be picked up?'

'Oh, ar, what's the time now?'

'Oh eight hundred hours, man. And who's this other soldier, you refer to? You don't mean this guy who wants to see the war out playin selections from Cole Porter in a rotunda?'

'Get fucked.'

'Pick us up just on dusk where the road is blocked. Can you drive? We'll meet you there. By the way, this vehicle has Erinungarah registration only. Don't have an accident.'

'We might take it back to Graceland,' says Diane. 'We might decide not to spend the whole day at Wonderview.'

It's an arduous task, negotiating a route, if marginally less so where the collapsing sandstone has flattened a grove and left trees, slippery with ice and scattered like fiddlesticks, over and below what used to be the road. Halfway down the rock face, Attis resolves to return by the track, which means, tired and wet as they will be, they will have to walk back to Wonderview. Like many a honey hunter, Attis is a confident scrambler on rock, but he also possesses the leader's instinct that tells him what others are capable of. He can sense Eugene wouldn't care if he did fall, and that Olaf is mortified to be ruining his army boots. Finally, they make it to a formed earth road.

'Sorry about the scramble, fellas. It's a straightfoward walk from here on, promise.'

'Ginnsy was up here today, man, look at this. Fresh tyre tracks.'

'I guess he has to keep the battery charged. Probably drives up and down the Valley every day.'

'Where's he getting the juice?'

'Good to know he's down here. Hope he got the fire on. You're turning blue, Eugene.'

'Well, better'n turnin red. Hey, I'm not comin back out, you guys. I decided to stay down here. Fuck it.'

Descent of the Pass evokes an atavistic resonance in the teenage recruit. We have noted the prominence of valley views in Olaf's first meeting with Nisi. You will recall the sighting of a glade prepared him for the shock of seeing an arrow on a beer carton, which in turn convinced him his destiny lay in attaching himself to a stranger. Anglo-Saxons have an immemorial, and mystical, regard for forests, even if today those forests are half-dead with acid rain and Swiss in their mansuetude. Certainly, Charlemagne's eighteen Saxon campaigns bespeak a game of hide and seek. Canetti* goes so far as to suggest that Germans see an army in a temperate forest and trees as staunch, indomitable warriors of iron discipline, clad in barkish armour. Is it possible Olaf's recent military training predisposes him to admire what he sees? For he can honestly state, by the time he completes this arduous descent, he has had a positive experience in the Australian bush, an experience he always longed for, with renewed intensity, during periods of crisis.

True enough, the average dry sclerophyll forest contains nothing to detain the eye. Mere ochre road with the familiar drab trees, and the nondescript prickly bushes. But the coalseam by the Gap is almost at the surface, and though the collapse of the Gap has obliterated for the time being all trace of that cutting where the road descends through the coalseam under a copse of necklace heath that clings luxuriantly to the coal, having clambered over the debris of the sandstone rockfall on

---

* Elias Canetti, *Crowds and Power*, Victor Gollancz, London, 1962.

the talus—which looks as though an ice machine had been emptied over it, leaving clumps of half-fused hailstones, up to a foot deep—Olaf becomes aware he is entering a warm temperate rainforest of amplitude: not the customary, pitiful remnant, which has made a valiant stand in the narrow confines of a moist gully by deploying itself down a watercourse, so that you could virtually run through it, and out the other side, while holding your breath; but a rainforest broad and capacious, extensive, dominant and relaxed, with nothing to fear, for now, from the eucalypts, who keep a subdued, and respectful, distance. Not much in the way of understorey, but thick leaf mulch, with a touch of orange thorn, and everywhere rivulets, because of the rain, and a dank, forbidding darkness, tempered by the inviting wistfulness of wood pigeon wings in flight, and the brilliance of glossy green leaves, up to a foot broad in the case of the giant stinging tree. A monumental stand of coachwood, well south of its recognised range, descends from one bench to the next. Tall blackwood and pinkwood (mainland leatherwood) and cedars* pierce the canopy. Milk and passionflower and lawyer vines festoon the blueberry ash, while prickly little white starworts twinkle on the verges of the road.

'Don't you log this Valley?' inquires Olaf.

'We took the corkwood,' replies Attis, 'and we cleared the Flat, but we thought it would be nice to leave some old-growth standing somewhere, just so people would know what this country was like once. But it turns out this country wasn't like this at all. That's why the National Parks and Wildlife are so interested in the place. You wait till you see the eucalypts, boy, if you think these are big trees. There's even some old-growth red cedar under the Falls, only stand south of Milton. They'd be worth a fortune, at the mill. Over ten foot in diameter.'

'Wow.'

'Long-footed potaroo down here. Tiger quoll, sooty owl. Smoky mouse.'

'Fark.'

---

* Pencil cedar is not a cedar; bastard rosewood is.

The old homestead can be seen from afar, surrounded by attenuated fenceposts off which hang red loops of rusted, drunken, barbed wire. There's a glimpse from the tops, a sighting from this bend, a tantalising glimpse from that, another sighting from where a previous rockfall has cleared another gap in the Valley's defences and left a hole big enough to bury a bull in; all of which quickens the step and excites curiosity on a first visit. I made sure I walked in, when first I went down. But if smoke were rising from the chimneys, it wouldn't be noticed on a misty day, so long as the mist coming from the dam drifts and the silhouettes of the tree crowns ebb and flow, like promontories seen from a herringboat wheelhouse. How peaceful it is, how mild, down here, and with what resonance the birds' voices echo, thinks Olaf. A yellow-tailed tit's fast twittering cry no sooner ebbs in a flurry of demi-semitones, than a white-throated tree-creeper throws out a note which hovers like a nankeen kestrel in a gale.

'Can't see the van anywhere.'

'Mighta left it in the shed.'

'The cattle were down here, boys, look. Wouldn't you know it? Week-old cowpats.'

'I'm sweatin. Can't believe how warm it is. I could see my breath up top.'

'Very interesting. Take off your woollen jacket, for Chrissake. Yeah. It's a sweet Valley. Reminds me of upstate Oregon.'

'What? You got trees like this?'

'Californian blue gums.'

'I'll give'm a shout. Bad manners to sneak up, ay. Phryx! Gwen!'

'No smoke coming from the chimneys, man.'

'Yeah, and that's funny, cause they always keep the fires on. Gwen's like Fardy. Feels the cold.'

'Gwen? Phryx?'

Rough-cut weathered red stringy tankstand, sheds and chopping blocks. Antiques. Inside the house fence, an English garden, relishing this weather. Shunning kunzea and mirbelia, we have planted borage, hollyhock and honesty, well, fair

258

enough; no one's perfect. Brilliant, in the soft, wet light, the British mauves and pinks. No hailstones here. No shredded leaves.

On the verandah, only a pair of gumboots and a kero tin yabbi trap with a piece of fencing wire through it to hold the bait. If the verandah floor is a fountain, the rusted gutterings are faucets.

'Phryx? Gwen?'

Attis knocks gently on the doors and walls, while Olaf and Eugene gawk at the view. Seen from here, one of the Narrow Necks above flares into a great fat head, which seems to rear over the Plateau as a mesa, staring down upon proceedings in the Valley.

'Don't understand it. They wouldn't go out on a day like this, would they? Maybe they're chasin cattle further down.'

The Kombi can be seen, parked in the chaff shed, but no one answers the back door.

'I think we better check this place out. Eugene, would you go and check the van please? Olaf, could you check the loos? There are two behind the old chookhouse. They don't even keep chooks any more. I'll take a look through the house. If they are here, it will be less of a shock for them to see me, because they know me.'

Olaf and Eugene obey their orders, but can't focus their minds on what they do. When at last they enter the house, they are unprepared for what they find. The exterior, though shabby, could be any old widow's house. Inside, it's a museum piece.

A word of explanation: the four-gallon kero, or kerosene, tin, in the days of the pioneer, came to these backblocks in pairs, packed in a wooden box like a teachest. All the cupboards in this house are chests of drawers, made from the frames of these old kero boxes, with kero tins, one side cut off and the sharp edge bent, for drawers. There's a deck of eight, in a corner of the kitchen, and each drawer has a rusting metal cap in the bottom right-hand corner. The kitchen table is a blackwood plank, with sapling legs, and the chairs are stumps.

'Let's make a cup of tea. Then we'll go and look for this friend of yours.'

As Attis begins opening the kero tin drawers, in search of

cups, Eugene looks for a stove. Up the chimney is a set of black chains, and hooks, but the cinders in the hearth are wet.

'Bush stove outside the back door. I think that's what they use to boil water. It's just an old oil drum, with a hole in the side, so you may not have recognised it. Same principle as the timber tin heater in the bedroom. Seen the bedroom, Olaf? We shouldn't be snooping round, but go and have a look, mate, before they get back. It's a real old style bedroom. They aren't even married, but they sleep in the same bed.'

To be sure, the A/B hut at the training camp is a palace, in comparison with this. The oil drum heater occupies one wall, the kero tin chest of drawers another. A selection of brush-tailed phascogale pelts, sewn together with a saddler's awl, forms a rug for the floor, but the bedspread is just a wagga rug, corn-sacks stuffed with old items of clothes, on a bedbase of rawhide strips, under blanket. No pillow and no sheets. The bed smells bad, but there's a pleasing fragrance from a *pot-pourri* of lavender and rose petals under the bed, and a conch shell and a kero tin lamp on the kero tin chest of drawers, but no kero in the lamp. The lamp is a wide-mouthed dusty bottle with a cloth wick and a cork, and over this cork a lid from a syrup tin with a slit; but no soot, just dust. Apparently disused.

There is no artificial light here. No sign of any candle. On a cold night—and Olaf could see himself lying here beside Nisi, on a cold night—there would be only the glow from the embers in the timber tin, eyeing off the straining bodies through the knife slits in the side of the tin, but what is this? The cornsack curtains ensure Victorian gloom, but Olaf can see in the far corner what looks like an archery set. When he examines it more closely, he sees it's a musical instrument of some kind, with a single gut string and a kero tin with the front cut off to act as a sounding body. You'll have seen the same kind of thing played on the streets of Turkey, behind an upturned fez.

By the time Olaf returns to the kitchen, Attis has found three cups, but not in the drawers. Concealed with a teatowel, they were contained in yet another kero tin, bisected in this instance and folded in half to form a sort of washing-up dish. One of the resultant triangular cups, the one with the drainage cap, holds the water, while the other serves as a drainage rack for a number of metal utensils. To complete the trifecta as it were, another specimen of this utilitarian bush item has been sliced across the jowls to furnish the kitchen with a convenient pan. With a length of broom handle nailed to its back, together with an all-purpose twig brush, it stands by the door, next to the cooler, which is not in this case an icechest nor a kero fridge nor yet a Coolgardie safe, but would you believe a kero tin with the side cut out like a drawer, and inside this a smaller tin, ovate, perhaps a ham tin at one time, in which food can be put, the cavity between the inner and outer tin designed to be filled with wet soil. But the soil is dry and there is no food in the cooler.

'Now if we had tea, we'd be in business. The kettle's on the hob, we have cups. I don't think they slept in that bed last night.'

Wozza: I have ascertained, through my agents, that Wozza was sending large, registered parcels overseas for years, and describing the contents (which came, as came the Cornish tin, on muleback, to Massilia) as 'bones and stones' on the customs slip, as well as collecting cheques in return, from those few dealers who specialise in the buying and selling of fossils to private collectors. Which confirms what I suspected; that Wozza was prospecting not for gold but for bones and maybe feathers, the impressions of long-dead invertebrate and plant species in the shales and mudstones and coalmeasures of the southeast wilderness. Which would also explain why his steam-driven stamper could stamp with the precision with which a microtome can slice.

They find Michael Ginnsy, later that day, huddled dogless under a tree fern, trembling at their approach until he sees and recognises Eugene Ecks, whereupon he creeps out with a face so white and terror-stricken it makes Olaf laugh to see it.

'Hi, man. Good to see ya, guys. Terrible things are goin on down here, Eugene, Terrible Things! I'm involved in this Life and Death Struggle with Evil, man. That's why I hid, when I heard voices. I thought it musta bin that dude with the gun, comin back.'

'What dude? What gun?'

'Naa, can't talk about it, man. Can't make any sense of it yet. Gimme time.'

Act 5

43. *Diane visits Paula, learns of her sister's pregnancy. Barbara recounts strange goings on in the Valley.*

Diane Zoshka returns to Sydney with Barbara Byng the day Attis begins work. They stare through the grimy windows of their dogbox, taking in the countryside through dark glasses. Over the high Monaro, with its treeless, eroded creeks, flit flocks of sheep-like cumulus clouds as the low pressure system fades. Patterson's Curse (Viper's Bugloss), an import from the sclerophyll of the tideless Mediterranean, is reflected in the blue hills of snow gum, while the freshly shorn Merino wethers are reflected in the white cockatoos. In summer, there is often here the hint of autumn, yet so abrupt the ecotone between the high plain and the vast Far Eastern Gippsland Forest—a strip of bright green-crowned Alpine ash, streamers of bark bunched off the boles—that Diane is soon able to put her forest-bound lover from her mind. Though he is her first love, and she is happiest to be speaking of Attis, when not thinking of him.

In Sydney, the Xmas trees wink already from the windows of home units.

'I can't persuade you to come along? Oh Derek will be so disappointed. He has a high opinion of you.'

'No thanks, Barbara. I want to pretend I'm free, for a bit, just to see what I do with that freedom.'

'We're lucky, aren't we. Imagine if this were Czechoslovakia.'

'Have you been to Czechoslovakia, Barbara?'

'No.'

'Then can you be sure it really exists? I mean, don't you think we should concentrate on what we can be really sure of?'

'Can we be sure of anything?'

'Well, perhaps we should do nothing.'

'I'll bet a quid that's just what Olaf and Eugene and Michael are doing right now.'

Next day, Paula Zoshka invites her sister Diane to lunch at the Rib Room, where the decor has a colonial theme and the serving wenches wear miniskirt versions of nineteenth century costume.

265

'I'll have the chicken in a basket.'

'Does it come with chunks of processed cheese and rings of pineapple?'

'I guess so. I'm sorry, Diane, should we have gone to Beppi's? I didn't realise you were paying.'

'Don't be like that. I'll pay you back. Att's going to see if he can get me a job too. I was just making a point.'

'I didn't catch it.'

'Well, maybe it all starts with the food we eat. Have you thought of that?'

'I'm not sure I understand you. Is this Att's influence, or what?'

'Oh my God, you sound like your mother. Can't I have an original idea? She likes to blame the books I read.'

'There's no such thing as an original idea. I think we're ready to order, Diane? What do you want?'

'I'll just have some lettuce leaves, please, and a glass of water.'

'OK. I'll have chicken in a basket—make that coquilles St Jacques—and a bottle of sparkling burgundy. I'll eat if she won't. Thanks. Just *what* are you trying to prove?'

'Nothing. Why?'

'You don't shave your legs, you don't pluck your eyebrows. If your hair was any shorter, you'd be bald. If you get any thinner, Diane, you'll need to buy a whole new wardrobe of clothes, because they're all falling off your back. Where do you get your clothes, by the way? St Vincent de Paul? I spoke with Mum last night. Peter has to have his tonsils out, before Christmas.'

'Oh dear. Poor kid. Member how Mum always put sugar on the lettuce? Why did she always put sugar on the lettuce?'

'I don't know. I can't imagine. Maybe that's how her mother served it.'

'I wish I knew where this lettuce was from. I hope it hasn't been drenched with insecticides.'

'Diane, why are you here? Are you having problems with Attis?'

'Please. You don't understand me. Don't talk about Attis. OK?'

'I beg your pardon?'

266

'Look, I don't want to fight with you. I didn't come all this way back here to fight with you. Back off! Att is very special.'

'You think you're the only woman ever had it off with a guy?'

'Can I ask you something Paula? Are you pregnant?'

'Why do you ask?'

'Just answer, please. Are you?'

'Why would you ask?'

'You are pregnant.'

'I can't be ...'

'Oh Paula!'

'Shut up! It's easy for you. You probably don't even menstruate, you're that thin.'

'What are you going to do?'

'I don't know. I can't believe God would do this to me a second time. Why is it always me has to pay?'

'Make him pay. I presume it was Brian?'

'Of course it was Brian. Who else?'

'Surely you must have realised that what you were doing ...'

'Shut up! It was only my third day. Should have been perfectly safe. I can't believe my body would do this to me again. I hate my body worse than ever now.'

'You're very beautiful. You're just very fertile, and that's the trouble. Men smell it.'

'You wouldn't think I was beautiful. There's no hair under my armpits. I'm going to have it sewn up, Diane. Oh Diane, I'm so scared.'

'I'll stay with you, Paula. Will you go back to the same quack?'

'I can't go through that again. That's why I'm so scared. I still cry about my last baby.'

'Then what are you going to do?'

'Nothing. Let Nature take its course.'

'What? You're going to have the baby?'

'Yes, I am.'

'Why?'

'Because I want to. It would be nice to have a little baby, wouldn't it?'

'But how will you manage?'

'I'll manage. We manage.'

'You're probably not even pregnant.'

'I've been here before, remember? My breasts are swollen. I feel sick in the mornings.'

'Have you told Brian?'

'Not yet.'

'Will you tell him?'

'Eventually.'

'Have you seen him again? I mean, do you talk to him much?'

'I hate him. I detest him. He's everything you say and worse. Why would I want to talk to him? He'd only bore me shitless with this radio play of his. You see, it's about ...'

'Oh he's not that bad. He just wanted a fuck.'

'That's all they ever want. He's no different to Bob, or Frank, or Les, or Gerry, or Benny, or Royce, oh good, here's the food. That was quick.'

'Don't eat all that shit, Paula. Don't you care about your child's health? And you shouldn't be drinking alcohol.'

'It doesn't matter what I do now. It's too late.'

'Hey look! The sugar melts on the lettuce. Looks quite yummy, doesn't it.'

'He's going to marry me, Diane. This child will have a father.'

'You're so confused, Paula. You don't know what you're saying. Eat your battery food, and be quiet.'

'I *am* feeding two. It was good of you to come. You're the only one I can talk to. How like you, to have guessed.'

'Well, I didn't really. Barbara told me.'

'Barbara Byng!'

'She knows everything.'

'Oh she's such a pill. I wouldn't trust her an inch. How long before the whole world knows?'

'The whole world knows.'

'Thanks, Barbara. How could she have guessed?'

'Doesn't matter. They're all going to know eventually.'

'I might still choose to abort.'

'Oh please don't. Last time you bled for a week, remember? Have it adopted out.'

'I'm so ashamed. I'm so ashamed to have this body that

betrays me. And you'll be next. I hope you're taking precautions?'

'I don't need to.'

'Nonsense! You should go on the pill. Can't you learn from what happened to me? My life is ruined.'

'Oh rubbish. Anyway, I don't have sex with Attis.'

'Why not?'

'I don't know. We just don't. It doesn't occur to him. I'm happy just to be near the guy.'

'Oh Diane.' Paula takes Diane's hand and her eyes moisten with tears, and she quite likes Attis now.

'Maybe, in the future, we can all be good friends.'

'I doubt that. I mean, it's OK for us, but what would a radio writer have in common with a rodeo rider?'

'I thought he was going to be a lawyer.'

'I confess I don't understand this Henry Kissinger appointment. Nixon is known to be anti-Semitic.'

'Oh no more politics tonight Derek. Please.'

'You're right. So did you get down to the Valley?'

'Not right down to the Valley, no. The weather was bad. It turns out Diane's boyfriend's family is selling the Valley, to the National Parks.'

'Well, that puts paid to that little scheme. Storm in a teacup. Just as well, because they were moving in the wrong direction. The Great Blasket, an island off the coast of Kerry, continuously inhabited by a self-sufficient community since the Iron Age, was evacuated as recently as 1954, and why? Because the people, though beating off the linguists with a hurley, had no way of attracting a priest or a quack.'

'Besides, something terrible happened down there, Derek. Michael Ginnsy, do you recall him?'

'No.'

'He's that famous blues guitarist. He was at the wake for Martin Luther King. He wore a top hat, with stars and stripes.'

'Go on.'

'Well he's been down there for weeks, apparently, God knows why. They couldn't find a trace of the old couple he was supposed to have been staying with. At least, this is what Attis, that's Diane's boyfriend, told us. The others never came out. They decided to stay down there, including Nisi's boyfriend, Olaf, who was due back in Puckapunyal Army Camp yesterday.'

'Excellent.'

'So she's distraught, because she has no money, and her house burnt down in the bushfire. And of course, Eugene, Monica's brother-in-law, the American, he stayed down there. And you know what? Ginnsy told Attis the old couple were shot by a passing gunman. Shot! So he buried them.'

'Good God!'

'I don't know what to think.'

'You're better off out of it. Don't go down there, for God's sake. The police don't want to question you, I hope?'

'I hope not too, for the sake of Olaf and Eugene. I mean, I couldn't very well lie. I don't know whether Attis intends to report the deaths or not.'

'He has no choice. Clear-cut case of murder.'

'It's dreadful, isn't it. Shocking.'

'I do recall that man in the top hat now. He struck me as insane.'

'He's always on some trip or other, but I can't see him as a killer. He shouldn't have buried the bodies, though, should he?'

'Absolutely not. Destroyed the evidence, if, in fact, he is telling the truth, which seems problematical.'

'Attis says he claims it was what they wanted. Claims they ordered him to do it.'

'Oh, just keep away from these lunatics. On no account go back. Fancy a bit of dancing, take your mind off all this business? The Old Time Dance Band is on at the Trade Union Club tonight. That's always a good night.'

'No thanks, Derek. You've had too much to drink. I'm worried about Nisi. I think I'll go out and visit Mon.'

'Suit yourself.'

Paula Zoshka: Is it possible Mountain Gum is not the child with whom Paula is pregnant here? We know Paula had undergone at least one abortion, to this point, and Iris MacAnaspie had a few tricks up her sleeve, I've no doubt. All the old birds round here do. True, Iris never forgave the communards for taking Attis from her, and while it is unlikely she would have helped Paula, the sister of the scarlet woman, she may have given Nisi a few pointers, on such matters as procuring abortions, and preserving fruits, and Nisi may well have shared them. Women's business is not my concern, because I am a bachelor, and because my informant, Kimberley Moon, was never a ladies' man. There was, however, a child, Mountain Gum, born to Paula Zoshka, and Brian Chegwodden was the father of this child. How do I know? How do I know, when I'm getting too ill to move from the house and the phone's cut off? Because Orion appended a genealogy to the *Ballad of Erinungarah*, it was in the envelope, but it's come adrift, and I've lost the bloody thing. I've lost the blessed page. I spend an hour a day, on average, and have done for the past four years, searching for the missing page among my collection of householders, but as I invariably search the same heaps, at the same time, in the same order, I can't imagine I will ever find it. I like to think I do recall most of what I saw on that sheet, though I can still see the names as letterboxes.

44. *Attis calls by home. Horrie's new horse. Eugene reveals plans for a dome. Starvation averted. Eugene in despair. Phryx and Gwen: Attis' version.*

Early summer now, '68. Attis is promptly entrusted with the short wheelbase Landrover. Bright red, piled high with Storz adaptors, fern hooks and McLeod tools, it sits in the lane outside Graceland, to be woken with a faceful of jinker exhaust, as Fergus sips a second cup of coffee. No good trying to pick seed in the dark, so Attis leaves for work later than Fergus. But he gets up when his brother gets up, and reads the Bible, for something to read.

'Who's goin out with ya today then, boy? Who ya pickin up today?'

271

'No one.'

'What? Bludgin bastards got you doin the lot, on only yer first week?'

'I don't mind. Rather be alone. Way they see it, their job is fightin fires. They could be busy this summer. Anyway, they don't like picking seed.'

'Who does? How you likin it? Borin job, ay. Still, it's not forever. Can't see why Dad wouldn't let you dig some dams. He's been lettin the earthmovin side o' things slip. Mum reckons he's out there on the block most days, fartarsin about. Workin a bloody horse! Man's gone senile.'

'I don't mind picking seed.'

'Pays peanuts, don't it? Whatchy'on?'

'Thirty bucks a week.'

'Wot! An you're doin all the work. T'ain't fair. I'll put in a word.'

Some have the Good Book, others rely on that basic Australian sense of Fair Play.

'Don't bother. Don't worry your head. I'd rather be alone. Prefer it. Don't think I'll work the coupe today.'

'Why not? Best place for pickin seed. Can't get enough of that messmate, and there's stacks o' that, on the coupe. All them big messies are full o' seed. Easy pickin, too, tell you what. Find any shinin gum, stash it. Worth two hundred bucks a pound, they reckon. Well, better be goin. Where's yer girlfriend? Someone told me she moved out.'

'Went to Sydney, on the train, to visit her sister. She'll be back.'

'You hope. Won't see ya today then?'

'Reckon not. Can't stand the noise. Might go in and pick up the caving ladder.'

'Don't fall, for Chrissake. I wouldn't climb trees on me own.'

'I'll be right.'

'Reckon I should ask Nisi for a date?'

Why do spiders love Landrovers? You never saw a Series Two didn't have cobwebs all over the dash. Attis calls by at the depot, picks up a fifty-foot caving ladder, fishing lines, takes one look at the makeshift crampons, leaves them. You wouldn't need shoes to climb trees. With a few woolsacks in the back in which to collect the seed, and a thermos of tea, and a lunchbox, he drives off, out of town, at peak hour. Most of the crew, crack shots, would rather shoot off twigs, than climb trees.

After passing the by now very familiar succession of rundown farms, with their bus bodies, calf trailers and dilapidated haysheds, he turns off, hardly knowing why, from where he used to catch the school bus. He'll have to stop by and have a cup of tea with Mum, as she won't want him driving by without calling in. He may not appreciate the impact of his dereliction on a potential legal career. More likely, he's pondering what to say to his penfriend in his last, and final, letter to her, wondering why Diane Zoshka was born where he couldn't get to meet her, at school.

'Hello stranger! What brings you home?'

'Thought I might see what seed there was round. Too early for ya?'

'I bin up since five. Dad's still here, I think. Probly out with 'is pigeons. I do wish he'd sell them, but every time he does, they all fly back home again. You go and chat with yer father, while I fix yer some proper brekky. Norm and Fardy are still in bed.'

'Already had brekky, Mum.'

'I know the kind of brekky you would have had. I'll fix you a proper brekky. I'll make you an Ulster fry.'

The pigeons, meant to be confined to an outhouse used to be an old chook shed, have spread to the point where a cooing, revolving cock is to be seen on every elevated structure. Attis finds Horrie, a former district ring secretary, with an arm thrust to the elbow down a large bore coil of agricultural pipe, in the storage shed, bespattered with guano, to the rear of the truck workshop. He is standing on a sawhorse, by a pile of burlap bags, against a backdrop of ladders and fencing and trenching shovels. Beside him is a workbench, zealously indented, fitted with a vice and littered with drills, spirit levels, extension leads, muffler putty and belts of wood chisels. Tobacco tins spew splines, gaskets, blowlamp prickers, reamers and drifts. Next to the tin of yorkshire flux is a pair of punch pliers in a plastic pouch, and a big farrier's rasp, for preparing cockatoos for stews. Under the bench are tins of rustguard solvent, neatsfoot oil, DDT and lacquer thinner. Adjacent to the bench is a builder's barrow, and cartons containing stanley knives, cement working floats, trowels, a sleeper dressing adze, beekeeping smokers, redlead, insulating foam, woodsaws, soldering irons, gas bottles, U joints, ballcocks, emery paper, tile grout, and such items of engineering, fencing, plumbing and building desiderata as won't fit on the bench: ball hammers, scutcheon combs, shingle splitters, pinch bars, Stillson wrenches. Strung off the walls are coils of barbed wire, a dogspike puller outer, bull castrating rings, and a caulking gun in a gaff net. You weave your way in through a maze of sinks and bathtubs acquired, over the years, at clearing sales, and never used.

'Hello son! Thought I heard somethin in ere. I'll just gesture hypnotically.'

Gently, Horrie withdraws his hand, to produce a pigeon chick. It's at the unprepossessing age when the ears are big as the eyes and the nose still boasts a Hittite hump, but this one's future is assured; it is covered with stumpy white quills, which bring a smile to the old boy's face.

'Oh look here. Mealy's thrown a white chick. Wonder if the other chick is white? Just let me ... no, I don't think I can reach. Fancy her nestin right back in there, bloody swamp harriers, man'll have to take to 'em. So what brings you out here, son?'

'Pickin a bit o' seed.'

'Met your girlfriend, th'other day. She was out here with a couple of other lassies.'

'What did you think of her, Dad?'

'She struck me as highly intelligent. They *all* struck me as highly intelligent. Girls spent most of the day with me. Weather wasn't real flash, but I gave them a tour of the place. Even went down to the block with me, to clear the ice off the young spuds. They was taken with the new horse.'

'Oh? What horse is this, Dad?'

'Let's go in, have a bite t'eat. Got time? We don't see much of you, these days. Well, as you know, I dispersed the herd, and while I was at the sale, I got talking with Barry, that's the auctioneer's boy. Happened to say to him, just in passin, I don't suppose you'd know of any workin horse? Good Lord, look at the mess this shed's in! This tropical fish tank will have to go in the bathroom of the house. I keep thinking the water tank is filling. I shall have to do something about this mess too.'

Horrie picks up a pigeon feather and puts it in his pocket.

'That's a bit better. Well, he says, it's a remarkable thing you should ask, cause a woman come in the office just the other day, what had split up with her husband, and she's wanting to sell a number of donkeys and a Clydesdale.

' "Oo", I says, I never heard of a farmer's wife splittin up with her husband, but I could be interested in that Clydesdale. Could you take me out to see it? So we went out to see it— it's a gelding—on this little block other side of Johnson's Creek, and I couldn't believe my good fortune, Attis, as he turns out to be a fully broken horse, used for years to pull a stationery cart around the streets of Sydney. Quiet as the afternoon of a heatwave. Quieter than a meeting at the club, when they're askin for nominations for secretary. I opened his mouth, and as the sayin is, the groove grows out so he's over twenty, and his teeth are slopin plenty, but then, so are mine. The woman owned him even had the hames he'd worn his whole workin life. For some reason, these were hangin off an internal wall o' the house. But she was happy to throw 'em in, as a job lot. Minute I put those hames on him, boy, was he laughin. Mind you, Mum was none too impressed when I come home from the sale with a truckload of donkeys. Know anyone lookin for a donkey?'

'What, is the tractor broken?'

'No, there's nothin wrong with the tractor, part from the dreadful noise it makes.'

'Oh, do you think it's about to throw a leg out of bed?'

'No, I can't see it pushin a conrod through the crankcase. Nothin wrong with the big-end bearings. I just don't like the noise of the internal combustion engine, never did. What's more, I reckon I'm old enough to please myself what I do, at my age. I suppose, if the truth were known, I'm completely fed up with the modern world, and it was a pleasure to meet three young women who feel the same way.'

'So what are you doin there now, Dad?'

'I need a quart of chicken manure, to bate a roo hide, for Darryl. May's well get it, while me hands are covered in bird shit. He's gonna make himself a new stockwhip, I says, use cane for the handle this time. No, he says, I intend to use a piece of spotted gum from down the coast, as always. Man shoulda called him Egyptian god, he's that pig-headed.'

Meanwhile, back in the Valley:

'I think the dome should go here. Whattaya say?'

'What was that again?'

'I say the geodesic dome should go here, Michael. Next to the house.'

'Bullshit!' protests Olaf. 'The Flat is the best land in the Valley. It should be reserved for growing food.'

'Aw yeah, man. Wish we had some *food*.'

It's early summer, and nothing to eat in the Valley. Properly organised, there'd be beans, artichokes, broccoli, lettuce, leeks. There are self-sown wild parsnips throwing out a mass of compound umbels, and some wild potatoes off rotting mother tubers, the new crop the size of marbles. Herodotus, on the banks of the Araxes, found a people who smoked marihuana and ate roots, and black women dug in the dirt all day for bush tucker of comparable amplitude; but if you don't recognise a parsnip or a spud, no way would you dig one up. These city slickers have been reduced to consuming the munchies in the van and the cottage silverbeet patch, which boils down to next to nothing. There is a yabbi trap, but no meat with which to bait it; bunnies galore, but no gun; evidence of cattle, but no cattle. What did the old people eat?

'We are gonna have to go to town, boys. We are all out of Violet Crumble Bars. Who volunteers?'

They have spent some time acquainting themselves with the Valley, and that has burned up a few calories.

'No way I'm goin,' declares Eugene Ecks, selecting a fresh blue pigroot seed to chew, 'though under Section 10 of the

Visiting Forces Defence Act, the locals can't touch me. They have no jurisdiction. Ginnsy, you have to go to town for me, pal. Wire my brother for more money.'

'Eugene, I made an undertaking to Phryx I would never leave this Valley. He never left the Valley. In return, he entrusted his house to me. See, I know how to start the pump engine.'

'But we need supplies, man. Munchies in the Kombi are gone. We can't last another day.'

'Somethin'll turn up. You have to have Faith. One thing I've learned, since I've been down here, man, is the importance of Faith. Gwen was confident she would die, if she cut that tree, and it happened within seconds. That's the Power of Faith.'

'We're runnin outta gas.'

'I can go. I'll be safe. I won't attract attention. I never did.'

'Yeah, all right Olaf. Go. Go back to Wonderview, and ask for the loan of a vehicle. When you get back out, shout from a currawong calling site, and I'll meet you halfway.'

'Gonna be awkward, bringing stuff in. And it's gonna be hot today, when the mist lifts. Gonna be a scorcher.'

'Always gonna be awkward, man. But our isolation guarantees us safety.'

'Ah, come on Eugene! There is no such thing. Safety is a myth. I mean, you're on this speck of cosmic dust, whirling in a vacuum. Get real. But we do need people. Like I say, we gotta get ourselves set up, in this warm weather. Now's the time for action.'

'Pity we can't grow a bit of dope. Should do pretty well down here.'

'Oh I put a few seeds in. I had some left, in the van. See, when I'm tourin the countryside, I'm a bit of a Johnny Dopeseed? Always throw out a few seeds, it's the least you can do. And the grapes ripen eventually. But birds eat the crop, we shall have to watch the birds, with the grapes. No, we need animals, women, children, tools, gardens, livestock, all that. We need a thousand and one things. This place has never achieved its potential.'

'So how did the old couple manage, Ginnsy? There doesn't seem to be anything here. No tools.'

'In the beginning they had the lot, man, but in the end, they didn't need nothin. They had Faith they would be provided for, so they were. It's called the Law of Manifestation. Do the birds on the Flat worry about the next feed? No, they just get on with it. See, that's our objective, to get back to that. It only works, though, if you have Faith in the Cosmos. Aw man, their Faith was so great, they were wonderful people, *wonderful*. But in the beginning, they had the gear. Look! There's the chook-house. As time goes by, you need less. Which is lucky, because you *are* less. This will happen for us too, they told me. No sweat. But to begin with, we must fend for ourselves. Just till we have Faith in the Cosmos.'

'OK, I'm going up. Can I wear your clothes, Ginnsy?'

'Heaps of clothes in the Kombi, man, and would you mind taking the records from the Kombi? They're melting. Leave the tapes. Don't take the top hat.'

'What should I get?'

'Firearm. Cheap twenty-two. Wire Calvin for the money.'

'No! Absolutely not. There are to be no weapons of destruction, in this Valley.'

'Who says?'

'We'll take a vote. Olaf?'

'Yeah, I agree.'

'Good. That's settled. Two against one. Eugene, you have to trust me. I was given instruction, you forget that. I know how to start the pump engine.'

'Beers?'

'What is this? We came down here to escape materialism.'

'Olaf's right, man. You want booze, brew it yourself. I suggest flour, tea, sugar, jam, as much as you can carry, Olaf. And some petrol, and some power kero. No lentils or brown rice, please. That'll keep us going. Why don't you go and wait in the cave, Eugene? That way, you can help carry the gear down.'

'And what am I gonna do in the cave all day, Ginnsy?'

'Well that's entirely up to you. But if you feel, already, that Life has no intrinsic purpose ...'

'No, I'm just hanging out. But you kicked it, so I can kick it. Mightn't be such a bad idea. I was half-dead and you looked it. Anyway, Hollywood'll soon be back, and he'll have a good idea what to do, cause he's already living in a commune.'

278

'I presume you refer to Balthazar. He doesn't know how to start the pump engine.'

'Sure, Ginnsy. We dig. The point I'm trying to make is, we just need to hang in, till the others get down. Then we can formulate a five-year plan.'

'Ha. That's what I mean. It's not up to us. Pcheow! It's up to *Her*. Now I'm gonna take you to see Her, but not yet. When I feel you're ready.'

'Come on, Olaf. Let's go.'

They don't talk much on the climb up, for to need to stop would be disgraceful. Over the years the track widens and deepens, then the landslide and it disappears. I couldn't find it. But I do know the flowers they would have seen, hauling ass up the cliff face. Cockspur, blushing bindweed, wonga vine. Higher up, on the dry ridge, hickory wattle, cranberry heath, Swainson pea, slender bitter pea, prickly shaggy pea, leafless sourbush.

'Here's the cave. Someone may want to live in this cave, so what I'll do, I'll start cleaning it out.'

'What do you mean?'

'Oh just level the floor a bit. Need some piers, so I'll make a few piles of stones. You can't do much without power tools.'

'Well don't interfere with the worms, man. I understand this cave has Australian glow-worms.'

'Listen, you don't have to fuckin tell me what to do, OK? I'm sick of everyone tellin me what to do. I can't help I'm American!'

'What has that to do with the price of eggs?'

'Don't get smart, cunt. I would like to think everyone who came down here will put this nationality crap behind them. All this nationality shit, it's one small planet, man. Spaceship Earth. What is needed is a New Society, totally lacking in discrimination.'

'What, you ashamed of being American?'

'Course I'm ashamed.'

'I'm sorry, man. I didn't realise. I thought you were pretty full of yourself.'

279

'Look, man, I'm hip to the fact America is a fuckin bully destroyin the earth. I want out, that's why I'm here.'

'Oh.'

'And I get the feelin, I hope I'm wrong, you victimise me cause I'm American. Which I have no control over.'

'Of course not.'

'I regret it deeply. If I could change it, I would.'

'No worries, man. I'm hip.'

'And people don't seem to realise what I've *been* through, you know? I mean, *fuck*, man! The noise from those B 52s!'

'Relax, Gene. Take it easy, pal.'

'Excuse me.'

'You have a nice rest in the cave. Too hot to work today, anyway. Take it easy. Relax. You made it to the Last Paradise. Is there something I can bring you from town? Fifth of whisky? Quart of ice cream?'

'No thanks, buddy. I'm fine. I'll soon be able to sneak a few leaves off those plants, when they get a few leaves on. I'm a bit uptight, but that will pass. I feel like shit, but I'll be OK. Hey buddy.'

'Yeah?'

'We gotta get tight down there, man. Ain't gonna be easy down in that Valley, whatever Ginnsy may think. Lots o' work to do, an that's a heavy scene. Ginnsy's gone right off. Did you notice?'

'Oh yeah, some of the things he says are pretty bizarre.'

'He's tripping, man. He's off his face. Where's he getting it? Why won't he share?'

'Yeah right. I think so too.'

'I mean, what evidence do we have he did the right thing spreading this absurd story? How do we know these people are even dead?'

'Absolutely none, man. Absolutely none.'

'So how do we know we won't have the fuzz coming down, at some point, to investigate?'

'I think I better go talk with Attis today.'

'I think you better. No seriously man, we need to know the score here.'

As it happens, Olaf encounters Attis, just before Better Fritter Batter's grid. He sees the red Landrover and, freaking out, dives for the side of the road with an expert dive. But Attis has sharp eyes and, when he gets to where Olaf is hiding, stops the vehicle. Seeing it's only an avatar-to-be, Olaf emerges *dégagé*, shaking off gum leaves.

I don't mean to be blasphemous, Attis. You may have been what they claim. I've come to the unChristian conclusion the Mother of the Gods has more Sons than one. I've thought about you a great deal, and *pace* Mark, the saint with the Cybeline lion couchant at his feet, in whose Gospel (X, 18) Christ denies divinity, I believe the moment of Christ's baptism occurred at the moment of His death, posthumous apotheosis being the rule among the Hittite god kings and the Roman emperors, at least in Rome. So you wouldn't have been an avatar here, and I can allude to you freely.

Actually, I like Frazer's explanation of Christ: the prophet of a Hellenised Judaism, snared in a Babylonian Purim. Christ, the prophet of a Hellenised Yahwe, Mohammad, prophet of a deHellenised Christ, Mithra, prophet of a Hellenised Ahura-mazda, Attis, prophet of a Hellenised Great Mother, which is why I have styled you Attis. I hope You don't find that offensive. Enough.

'Hi Attis.'

'Hi Olaf. How's it goin?'

'Not too bad, but we ran out of food. I'm just on my way into town now.'

'Nisi's still there. In Diane's flat.'

'Yeah, I figured she would be. So what are you doing, mate?'

'Supposed to be picking seed. Haven't actually started yet. Thought I'd take a look at the cuttail on Fossicker's Flat, but it's getting late, so by the time I give you a lift back to the turn-off, I may go out to the coupe after all. Called by home. Couldn't get away.'

'Wouldn't take a day off, I guess?'

'Not at this stage. And Olaf, if you want to live out here, you will have to be very independent. Anyway, it won't be for long. Fardy has decided he wants to sell.'

'It doesn't really matter, does it? I mean, the rangers wouldn't even know we were there.'

'Oh I think they might. Hop in, and I'll take you back to the turn-off.'

'Thanks. Do you think I could borrow the ute from Wonderview?'

'Might be better if you didn't ask. I don't think Fardy would appreciate it, people living in his Valley rent-free.'

'We don't mind payin rent. It's just we got no money at present. Did you report those murders?'

'No.'

'You don't think Ginnsy could have made it up? That's what Eugene thinks.'

'No, I think he's telling the truth. From what I knew of Phryx and Gwen, it could have been something they organised.'

'You're putting me on. Someone shot them, man, or so we're told. And Ginnsy shouldn't have buried the bodies.'

'That is what they would have preferred. Petty considerations of justice would not have worried them at all. Gwen was a special person, Olaf. I knew her, since I was a boy. She always said that when she died, it would be like this. Unexpected. So I'm not fussed, besides, I think she may have felt she was past it. She was starting to repeat herself.'

'You expected this?'

'She always said not to be shocked by the way in which she would die, and she always said they would die together, and she always wanted to be buried next to Phryx, and never dug up. Never! No coffins! She emphasised that.'

'But that sounds like a suicide pact. This was murder.'

'My problem is that if I tell the police, they are bound to dig up the bodies. And I gave my word.'

'So where did they come from? Were they locals?'

'Gwen was Welsh or Irish or something. I don't know where Phryx came from. I only know he used to be a seaman.'

'Won't their families report them missing?'

'I don't think they had any. Gwen saw the doctor once in a while, but they never received mail. All they got was house-holders, for which they had no use, and Gwen's social security cheque, which came from the UK. I've checked. I arranged for the PO to return the cheques marked "Left address" with one of those big pointing fingers. I think that's fair.'

'Oh I don't know. Doesn't that implicate you? And two bodies, with bullets in the heads, buried in the vineyard. It's not an auspicious start.'

'Don't worry. My family intends selling the Valley, and the house will then be demolished, or rather, it will fall apart, as the rangers won't get round to fixing it.'

'No, man, that's not fair! We can make good use of the place. Can't we buy it off you? People in the commune will be earning money. We can pay it off. But what I really wanted to say is that Ginnsy is acting strangely. We're very concerned about him.'

'The old people's understanding of that Valley was hard for me to grasp at first. Does Ginnsy know how to start the pump engine?'

Balthazar Beauregard: Eugene called him Hollywood.
Ginnsy: I quite like Ginnsy's deflection (as recounted to me by Kimbo) of a lecture he was once about to receive, from Balthazar B. in god-bothering mode:

'Don't rave on about God to me, man. Of *course* anyone capable of designing a urino-genital system is capable of anything.'

Out of the mouths of babes and junkies. Our human ambivalence towards sex is, as Ginnsy observed, not culturally induced, and will not be cured by programs of public psychotherapy. It arises from the design of the human body by a demiurge that, in its wisdom, decided to make the male urethra serve a dual function, and put the arsehole an inch from the cunt in a creature the size of a large barramundi. So long as piss and shit are dirty—so long as it remains in our biological interest to regard piss and shit as dirty—then sex is dirty.

45. *Death of Charlie. Diane's plans for the Valley. Darryl meets his favourite centrefold.*

Death. It's on my mind, sorry. Skip this section, if you like. Resurrection. As Toynbee explains, the concept is Pharasaic, rejected by the Sadducees as having no authority in scripture, and instituted that martyrs could share in the (earthly) Messianic Kingdom. As Gibbon admits, the prime attraction of Christianity was its guarantee of immortality.

I'd rather have mine here and now.

Immortality, Salvation, Transfiguration, the Millennium, the Kingdom of God, the Virgin-born Son of Man, Ascension, the Last Judgement, the Devil—all concepts of Zarathustra's. Under the Achaemenian regime, they flooded into Judaism, thence into Christianity, thence into Islam.

Originally, the Jewish dead lived in a place like Hades, called Sheol. Well I can't go to church now, because I can't recite the Nicene Creed, if I do brook the *Filioque* and The Trinity made more sense without. I don't believe in the Resurrection of my own body.

> *Esse aliquos manes et subterranea regna*
> *Cocytum et Stygio ranas in gurgite nigras*
> *atque una transire vadum tot milia cumbra*
> *non pueri credunt, nisi qui nondum aere lavantur*

That there be shades of the dead, etc, not even boys believe, unless they're too young to pay their pennies at the baths. Typical Juvenal, from the second satire, the one against effeminacy. It'll be back on the banned list shortly, if it's not there now (*liceat modo vivere, fient, fient ista palam, cupient et in acta referri.* If we live long enough, expect to see poofters doing their thing openly, and wanting their 'marriages' recorded in the register).

I suppose there might be an egoless afterlife, which is no good to me. I want the kind I don't believe in. If I can't have that, I'll have nothing.

Oh, I've known a few like Charlie, cranky little ten-year-olds in their nineties. Some admire that, I don't. They haven't come to terms with their mortality, till one day it hits them, and they drop dead on the spot. People say, he died in his sleep, he felt no pain, lucky old bugger, I'm doubtful. If you're not souped up on opiates, I bet a quid you wake when you're dying. I suspect you undergo a searching moral judgement, at least, I hope so. It's all I have to look forward to, which is why I won't take my medications.

Back to '68.

'Phew, it's hot. Norman, will you go and see what's keepin Fardy please? Tell him his cup o' tea is gettin cold.'

It certainly came at the right time, old Charlie's dying when he did. Without old Charlie's dying when he did, our *Saga* might not have got off the ground. Might have been due to the oppressive heat, coupled with the power failure that rendered useless the bedside fan, who knows? I do know this: had he lived, he'd have likely sold the Valley, and squandered the cash on a cruise. He'd never been on a cruise, you see, except to Anzac Cove, and a certain person had been getting in his ear at the club, I understand. When Norman came in that fateful day, to fetch him out for his tea, he'd have looked across a veritable medico's mailbag swag of glossy brochures.

Charlie was forty-two when he fought at Gallipoli. Oldest man there, I should have thought. Put his age back, as so many of them did.

Cast a cold eye, on glaciers tumblin to the sea. Cruiser, Cruise By!

As Iris relates it, Norman reappears, dragging Fardy down the hall, by the crook shoulder. She turns, and there stands Norman, trailing the Fardy's body, as though for disposal.

Horrie hears the scream as he's walking back from the plasmolysing spuds. Can't make head nor tail of it. But his blood is frozen, and he stops in his tracks. It has that effect, the Celtic keen.

Good Lord, was that Iris made that noise? Has Barney been killed in action? Or has Darryl stacked the Firebird Scrambler, or what's going on? Breathless by the time he reaches the house, Horrie bursts in through the screen door—which, in this household of handymen, is in chronic need of maintenance, thanks largely to Barney's wombat, who can't reach the handle—to find the scene as we have described it, except Iris has now passed out, on the floor, and I don't think I mentioned the cockatoo in its cage, playing with the Swiss army knife to amuse itself. Norman, clutching his grandfather still, gives his father a crooked smile, in greeting.

The funeral service terminated out of town, at the Catholic section of the graveyard. Darryl, who hasn't been to Mass in living memory, hair slicked back with brilliantine, sidles up to Horrie and slips his arm round the shoulder of the older man, in the manner of a kindly grazier about to reprove a rouseabout. It's been the biggest local funeral in years, and they'll all go back to the house.

'What do you want?'

'Att says t'aask if them young women from Graceland can come back out to th'house. Should I buy more whisky?'

'Do as you like. Ask whom you please. I won't be there.'

'What? Won't be at yer old man's wake? Whataya made of? I'll be at yours.'

'Not if I'm at yours first. He had a good innins. I'm sure you can all speed him on his way without my assistance. And don't forget what I said to you about that biscuit of hay for the donkeys.'

'Where'll you be?'

'I have to speak with my legal representatives in Bega. Would you believe he died intestate?'

'Ah well, when ya git to 'is age, ya got no real need for 'em, ay.'

Attis MacAnaspie and Diane Zoshka slip outside, hoping for a bit of privacy, to be confronted by schooner glasses and china cups on the strainer posts and matrons prowling the garden in pairs pointing out this and that, while further afield some old soldiers in campaign ribbons admire the donkeys. Horrie, before leaving for church, yarded them, in the hope of a sale.

Attis has yet to speak with Diane, who's just back from the big smoke, and she looks a treat too, in her rust suede bell bottoms, Captain Hook hat and pheasant feathers.

'Do you want to walk to the spud grounds with me?'

'Won't that take too long?'

'They'll be here till midnight. Fardy being an old timer, his wake will last all day. Good chance for you to meet the locals.'

'Poor Iris.'

'She enjoys company.'

'Did I see Fergus chatting up Nisi?'

'Yeah.'

'What's going on there?'

'I dunno. He just likes her, I think. I don't think there's anything in it.'

'I hope not. She is so irresponsible. She left her kids with Monica, in Sydney, and is too scared to go back and fetch them now. So Olaf is going back with her, tomorrow. Then they're all coming back here.'

'He's taking his chances, isn't he? Wind up in the lockup.'

'He's at the flat now.'

'Have you spoken with him?'

'No. I had just time to freshen up, for the funeral.'

'He seems determined to stay in the Valley.'

'Well, of course he is. We all are. I know Olaf's keen as mustard to avail himself of Gwen's guidance.'

'Diane, I really don't think it's going to make any difference either way. Horrie wants to buy out the neighbour, so either way, the Valley will be sold.'

'Oh Attis, you must realise by now the Valley cannot be sold. It's too important for the future of this planet.'

'But don't you think it's a good idea to have it part of the National Park? I mean, they belong to the people.'

'At the moment, the people are so confused, they fuck up everything they touch. You must admit, Attis, Gwen would not have moved to the astral plane, for no reason. She knew, having passed her wisdom on to you, and to Ginnsy, her role here was over.'

'I can't buy that.'

'Oh darling, it all begins with us, remember? We began all this, by falling in love. Now you can't deny the importance of love. Everything starts with love.'

'Our love had nothing to do with Charlie's death, I would hope.'

'Can we be sure of that? Doesn't everything have to do with everything? I mean, I don't know, but things keep going our way. It's uncanny. Here, we have a chance to live entirely free of government. You will never have to go to Sydney now, Attis.'

'But aren't I going to university?'

'No. You can't go to Sydney. For a start, I won't be going there, and I can't live without your love. You wouldn't be happy there anyway, cities suck. Secondly, anyone failing to report a murder is guilty of a criminal offence, and anyone convicted of a criminal offence is not allowed to practise law, so where's the point studying law if you're never going to practise? In stipulating she not be exhumed, Gwen has saved you from a bourgeois fate.'

'Maybe they won't find out.'

'I'll tell them. I didn't want to raise the subject, as I didn't think it would be necessary, but Attis, Ll.B. from Sydney University, how bourgeois can you get?'

'So you don't think I should go to uni?'

'Of course not. It's a waste of time. The world, as we know it, including that uni, is stuffed, and has no future. We have to found a New Age, Attis, with a New Form of Consciousness. Now in order to do so, we must be alone, as the bourgeoisie would mock us. The Valley is absolutely ideal, even Balthazar and Eugene agree. I mean, with that road completely blocked, the bourgeoisie can't get in. They won't walk to the shops for a paper.'

'Then now we are delivered from the Law, Diane, that being dead wherein we were held: that we should serve in newness of spirit, and not in the oldness of the letter.'

'Something like that. Is that from the Bible? Hey, I so admire you, reading your Bible. Are those the spuds? They don't look very happy.'

'They didn't get rain at the right time. We have no irrigation here. Our piston pump is in the Valley, on the Flat. All we have here is the diaphragm pump, which connects to a power take-off. OK to spray with, that's about all.'

Olaf Abernathy, who gave the funeral a miss, is listening to Freewheelin Bob on the gram, when Monica Ecks knocks at the door of flat number three Graceland. He doesn't open up, but he knows it's her. She curses, in that groundbreaking way, and makes good to kick down the door.

'I know you're in there, bitch,' she screams, 'so I'm leaving your kids here, on the doorstep!'

Then off she stomps, dissembling, in her boots. Olaf hears the car start up. He opens the door, to admit the boys, and is feeding them half a crust of raisin toast each, when the crafty Monica reappears. She only drove round the block.

There seems no point now denying her admittance. The door is ajar, when she reaches it a second time. After a visit to the loo, she feigns cordiality, squatting by the gram to rummage through the stack of microgroove recordings. Singled out for her closer inspection is one of Ginnsy's favorite platters, *Smack Up* by Art Pepper, imported vinyl on the Contemporary label. If it's warped, that's only because it was left in the sun, in the van, in the Valley. And what's this? Ginnsy's solo album. And here's another copy of Ginnsy's solo album.

'May I sit down five minutes?'

She wears white lipstick. Her midriff is bare. No navel studs in the sixties.

'Feel free. I'm so sorry, Monica. I don't know what gets into her. Can I get you a cup of something?'

'Arsenic'll be fine. Where is she?'

'Had to go out. Went to a funeral.'

'Oh my god. What is it with this woman? Does she forget she bore these children, or what? Go get a breath of fresh air, boys. Now!'

'I'm not trying to excuse her behaviour to you, but we were meant to be coming down today.'

'You couldn't ring?'

'We have no money.'

'You couldn't ring reverse charges?'

'She was scared of what you might do. She is not as strong and tough as she makes out, Monica.'

'I don't think she's strong and tough. And don't try to defend her. I've had it up to here, with those boys.'

'Me too. Oh, you're a wonderful woman. She doesn't deserve a friend like you. How's Calvin?'

'Great company, if you like boredom. Who owns this dump?'

'Diane rents. I don't live here, I'm down in the Valley.'

'Oh? I had a visit from that girl with the freckled face. What's her name again?'

'Barbara?'

'That's right. She filled me in on what sounds like one hell of a stupid idea. Pull these boots off, will ya, kid? They're so tight. My feet swell in the heat. So do my boobs.'

'Sure. Agh!'

'Hey gently, gently, baby. Eugene down there too?'

'Yep.'

'Asshole.'

As she observes the young conscript's hand tremble like one of Horrie's pouter pigeon's throats, Monica's green eyes glance towards the window, as she checks to ensure the boys have disappeared. She knows they won't be coming back, till they see that vehicle safely gone.

'Would you do me a favour, kid?'

'Sure. Anything.'

'Oh my! Anything, he says. My hamstrings get so sore when I drive, and I have to drive all the way back, now is there any oil in the kitchen?'

'I'll go check.'

'Could you give my upper legs a rub?'

'No problem.'

'Is this the bedroom? I'll wait in here.'

It all happens fast, but that's Monica. When he returns with the cooking oil, she's lying, belly down, on Diane's bed, and her blouse is pulled halfway up her back, and her jeans and scanties are round her ankles.

Now this is a well-credentialled butt: back in '68 it featured on the wall of many a workshop washroom; in fact, later that

290

day, when Monica, with Olaf in tow, and he smartly melts away, joins the well-oiled throng at the wake, Darryl, in his grief on his second bottle of hooch, gives a disbelieving hoot, and makes straight over.

'Monica!' he says. 'It 'as to be you. I'd recognise that face, anywhere. You are Monica, from Alabama? Course y'are. What a blowout. Still workin on yer own car, Monica? Still prefer drinkin in baars, to cocktail lounges?'

Catching a glimpse of the tremulous Nisi, Monica flashes her a fulsome smile, while accepting a corned beef sandwich with fluoro yellow pickles. This, she follows with a cup of tea and a pink and white slice of coconut ice. All is forgiven, and Monica has defused the contretemps in a tried and tested way. For his part, when pride fades, Olaf wonders what it means in the broader scheme of things, for, sad to relate, there is no such thing as casual, meaningless sex. Would Monica put him so firmly in place a second time? Probably not. She would probably just put him in his place, firmly.

'You won't stay and visit the Valley, Mon? Oh, come on. Just for the day. Please?'

'No thanks, Nisi. To me, that Valley is the place Eugene is gonna rot in hell.'

Monica Ecks: it is asking a lot of any young man to resist the allure of a beautiful blonde. In fact, I think we gave up asking, around 1968. Perusal of Malory's *Morte D'Arthur*, the temptation of Sir Percival, in which the beautiful blonde is revealed as a hideous demon in disguise, underscores the contempt of the Grail Quest for ultimate carnal pleasure. I would not propose we view our male communards here as knights of the Grail: refusal to participate in unjust war, though courage of a kind, is unknightly; but we must address the concept of Courtly Love, because the failure of Attis to rise to its challenge precipitates The Passion in the *Ballad*. Men glutted with sensual lust, strive intuitively, to rise: the problem here is that Courtly Love, when misdirected, can go but down. We read where Lancelot, wounded in battle, lay with Queen Guenevere all night, but both denied adultery when sprung the next day. He probably didn't put it in. Who's kidding who? Women of the flesh get nothing from Courtly Love, except a good laugh, but Courtly Love is the only love a man can offer a Blessed Virgin. When Brigid appears in the Valley, all the men fall deeply in love with Her. It is painful, today, to see the tears in Kimbo's eyes, when he speaks of the beautiful Brigid. But they didn't know how to love Her, seen. They didn't know how to express their love, before Attis, in His grief at having defiled Her, both wed and joined His Lady, and showing the others what True Love means, in the Land of the Ever Young.

46. *Ginnsy reprieved. Nisi, Olaf and the boys arrive. The flat battery.*

Ginnsy, with difficulty, opens his eyes, which are full of sleep, and seeing the room around him and recognising after a spell, mercifully brief, the room as part of the house, thanks the Spirit of the Valley and emerges from his bed. All night he has listened to the song of the nocturnal cowpat salesperson (moo poo, moo poo).

Quis deus, incertum est; habitat deus.

Which god, we don't know. But there lives a god here.

The slightest knock of Ginnsy's arm against a door produces bruising. He is starving to death. It is so long since he ate a square meal his hunger pangs are abating, his hearing and vision abnormally acute. Eugene Ecks and Olaf Abernathy have both failed to return from the journey up top, and Ginnsy knows he won't make it up that track unassisted. He is too weak now.

'Fats,' he croaks, but there is no response from the ungrateful black mongrel.

The Valley stretches before Ginnsy, so pale and weak, as a metaphor. Chirping birds become his rumbling belly. A trickle of his own urine bedews the grass. The burbling creek bells in his ear.

Am I really here, he thinks, and can this really be happening to me? Or is it a dream, and shall I wake from Life, as I woke from sleep, a short while back. He stands, staring at the mythopoeic planet, overcome by its arbitrariness. For that the sky be blue, the grass green, is a prison of a kind, he decides. And that the one be due to Rayleigh scattering, the other to the quantisation of the energy levels in the labile electrons of the chlorophyll in the chloroplasts, proves, *pace Aufklarung*, not the key to the door we had hoped. Is it not more remarkable we find ourselves conscious here, and nowhere else but here, not more remarkable that others who were like us, judging by their writings, have died and gone before? Not more remarkable still, we have put this from our minds and carry on, as if immortal?

I am dying, thinks Ginnsy, through starvation; but he knows this cannot be, for one does not die. If one were to die, the sky might as well be green, the grass purple.

Eugene, meantime, scrambles down the track, concentrating on not breaking a leg.

In a sweat and a shake, each has kicked the habit, assisted, no doubt, through inanition. Inanition, the great staple of the Health Farm bill of fare: you won't catch me at a Health Farm. We take the psychotropics, in a psychedelic world, because we cannot live in a state of fixed content. But isn't it something just to be alive, albeit a bit of a joke—postmen, say, or postmenopausal? The sad fact is that Michael Ginnsy, once he has conquered his chemical addictions, has half a mind to reward himself the only way he knows, with more drugs. And so he is stepping over the Flat to see if he could find a coloured mushie—and even if he found one, who's to say he'd eat it? He sees himself, morally, within the pale—as Eugene Ecks, spilling cans of tinned tomatoes, sprints down the final, precipitous section of track.

'Ginnsy!'

'Adsum.'

'Give us a hand, man.'

It is patently clear the Spirit of the Valley prefers Ginnsy not to find a mushie. He is content.

Tinned baked beans on toast, with chocolate wafers and instant coffee. Eugene sips a Nescafe, smokes a Pall Mall cigarette.

'Aw man, this food tastes *great*. I never enjoyed a meal more.

Nother coupla days 'n I wouldn'ta bin able t'eat solids. Zgreat to be alive.'

'Yeah, the liquid diet's a bummer. Less it's a barrela booze.'

'What's happening with Olaf?'

'He's on his way down. Should be here soon. Got the old lady with him.'

'Oh?'

'Nisi. You recall Nisi.'

'Oh yeah. I recall Nisi.'

'And the two kids. The two boys.'

'Excellent. Oh that's really great, man. Things will start moving now. Is Nisi the girl with the gold teeth? Women and children around, it'll feel like a real community. It'll give us the incentive to get off our arses, start building the schoolhouse. So what do I owe, for my share of these provisions? Hey, we got flour? Nisi may want to cook some biscuits.'

'Nothin. I borrowed the money from Calvin. Hey, I think I hear voices. Let's get the Kombi out.'

The boys, loaded up with scout packs, sleeping bags, toiletries, all their clothes, all their comics; Nisi and Olaf, behind, staggering under the combined weight of the contents of an op shop; battered aluminium kitchenware and spoil from half an hour in the general store. Nisi bleeds, from where she fell, rather than accumulate potential energy.

'Well done,' says Olaf, when finally, all make it to the Valley floor. 'You did well. I'm proud of you.'

'When we go back, Mon?' inquires Aloysius. 'Where dis house we bin stay at?'

'Hmm,' muses Nisi. 'I wonder if a packhorse could make it down that trail.'

'Don't see why not. Attis says cattle go up and down there all the time. Sit on Yer Arse Pass.'

'Yeah, but we didn't see any meadow muffins. Only wombat spoor.'

'That's true. Well they didn't come to meet us and that was the arrangement, so I guess we have to walk to the house. Boys! Packs back up.'

'Can't we just leave the stuff here and get it later, Mum? My back's sore.'

'Please Tim. Don't spoil things by whingeing. This is a fresh start for us all. Don't spoil it, please.'

'Hi man! Hi Nisi, how ya doin. Good to see ya, boys. Just dump the gear there, man.'

'You were sposed to pick us up, Ginnsy. Didn't Eugene mention it?'

'I'm sorry. I couldn't get the Kombi to start. I'm thinkin maybe the timing is out, or maybe the carbie is dirty.'

'Or maybe the battery is flat.'

'Don't say it, man! Don't put your hex on the Kombi! I had no troubles, part from the insulation they put round the gas tank fell through the fan housing. Started every time, first pop.'

'Yeah, but we can't expect ...'

'*Course* we can expect, man! Course we can, and yes we must expect. Don't bring all that fuckin negative shit down here, I implore you. Leave it up top.'

'OK, don't get uptight. I understand you're upset you couldn't get the fuckin bus to start, but don't take it out on me and Nisi and the boys. We're tired and hot.'

'No, no, it's not a question of taking anything out on anyone. It's just that this was supposed to be a New Deal, Olaf, right? So let's not blow it, with these negative thoughts. See, what you don't appreciate, negative thoughts are more important than we realise? Than any of us realise. Because it's not just you, it's everyone. The whole human race has these negative thoughts, and that's why they have the problems. Don't even think about the battery being flat. I haven't cleaned the leads yet. That's all I have to say.'

'Good.'

'Over 'n out.'

'Right.'

'Course if the battery's flat,' adds Eugene, with just the hint of a smirk, 'we got no way o' chargin it.'

Silence.

'Who would like a nice cup of tea' says Nisi, rubbing her

hands briskly. 'And then, you must take us to the river, Michael, and show the boys the best place to swim.'

'Boys can swim in Jellybean Pool, but never on Christmas Day. Got that, boys?'

'By the way, Ginnsy, Balthazar rang. He'll be here tomorrow. He'll stay with Diane tonight.'

Michael Ginnsy: became a eunuch. Custodian of the Sacred Pump. It amuses me to contemplate those two old mystics' reaction to his irruption. Imagine Gwen and Phryx watching the multicoloured Volkswagen van bumbling through the Gap, followed shortly thereafter by a rockfall that cut the Valley off from vehicular traffic. The synchronicity alone would have left them in no doubt that here was The Harbinger. Here was a man to take over day-to-day maintenance, and let's face it, he was a good mechanic. What did they tell him? Who knows. How long did he spend with them down there? Two stints. Gwen still gets her social security cheque, and it goes back, sea mail, every time. You'd think they would have worked it out, twenty-seven years on, she's moved or deceased. I'm sure I could trace her, through that cheque, but you'll understand why I don't bother. I'd be the first they'd suspect of the murder, that's the way their tiny minds work. We know she had a feel for Celtic Myth. Oh give her her due, man, she was a great druid, she saw the God Crom. He spoke with Her. She found the meteorite, a carbonaceous chondrite predating the sun and the moon. As to Phryx, he was harmless, confused, a bit lazy, I think. Drank too much. Tch tch. I see Gwen as the force behind what happened in that Valley, and the Sacred Pump—that double-action piston pump, it was more the engine, really, that was sacred. They danced to the rhythm of the pump sure enough, but it was the handle that flew off the engine that smashed the bottle that emasculated Phryx. Gwen must have noticed a change in him for the better, after that incident, and it's not as though she was missing out: I dare say she was the kind of woman that has an orgasm in a thunderstorm. The pump is still there, on the bank of the creek. I can't get in, because of Darryl. He thinks I'm a nosy bugger, but from Sunrise Lookdown, equipped with a pair of high powered binoculars, I see that pump.

And the engine is a Ronaldson Tippett three-horsepower, they were a good pump engine. A man I play bowls with raked one, burning, from the top of the tip at Obliqua Creek, and it still functions.

47. *Horrie defers sale of the Valley. Diane camps in the House that Glows. Murder at the coupe.*

'Get the mail? Anything for me?'

Apollo Eight blasts off for the moon, but back at the farm, nothing much changes.

'You're still here. I thought you would have gone to work.'

'Can't a man take one day off in a blunny blue moon? Had a pair o' visitors, after you left. Want me to give you a hand there?'

'No thanks. I dare say it was Att and that hussy.'

'Oh, what makes you say so? I do think you're a bit hard on that girl. I'll have you know, she's very taken with this house, reckons it's got "character". I says to Attis, we should go into business, conferring character on houses.'

'So she was here.'

'Well, of course she was. When was you ever yet wrong about who was here while you were out?'

'You're hidin something from me, Horace MacAnaspie. Spit it out.'

'Oh, you're a hard woman. Sit down, rest your weary legs, and I'll fetch you a cuppa. Or would you prefer brandy, from the wake? There's still half a bottle, if Darryl hasn't found it.'

'Good Lord, what must you have done? I'll have a cup of tea, at this hour.'

'You mean ya don't know? You disappoint me. Now let's get one thing straight, from the outset. I am head of this house, am I not?'

'Don't use those cups, ya fool. Use those other cups.'

'What I'm sayin is, Charlie was my father, God rest his eternal soul, do you agree? I mean, he wasn't your father.'

'No, but I looked out for him, since I was a girl. No one else could be bothered. Where's Norman?'

'Att and Diane took him to town. Now that Valley has always been in my family, Iris, and my solicitor informs me that whereas you and I are joint tenants of Wonderview, Erinungarah Valley Koala Kottage is mine, and mine alone.'

'I don't want your blasted Valley. Thought you said Charlie left no will?'

'No, he left one. I found it. Had it in me bottom drawer the while. Just as well, or the Parks and Wildlife mighta made a grab. Take my meaning?'

'Spare me your confessions and get to the point. I've things to do.'

'Very well. I'm givin the use o' the Valley to Attis, for a bit. For a year. I won't sell it just yet.'

'Now what's Att gowan to do with it?'

'Well, there's a lot you could do with that Valley, Iris, if you was minded.'

'But he's gowan to Sydney. He's off to the university, he's gowan to be a lawyer.'

'Oh, you make it hard. See, he's not sure he wants to be one.'

'Yes he is.'

'No, he can't tell you the truth, because he's afraid of you. He's afraid of earning your disapproval. But frankly, I think that a young man, at his stage in life . . .'

'Oh you old fool. She's bin workin on you, the way she's bin workin on him. She just wants what she wants, and you're too big a fool to see through her. Her, with her big eyes and short hair, her smart ideas and city ways, she's more like a man. Well, she's not good enough for my son.'

'Not good enough for your son. I suppose you know who she is? Only the daughter o' Sir Zeno and Lady Zoshka o' Darlin Point.'

'Well, what's she doin out here then? What does she want with our Att? He'd have nothin to offer her. Oh, don't tell me she's serious with him. Anyway, they're both too young to know their own minds.'

'Fardy was married at their age.'

'That was then. This is now. What, is he gowan to borrow

298

money from her father to hire a team o' men to log that Valley? Huh. Cause our boys is flat out here, God knows. Darryl 'n Fergus have no time to go down there.'

'They don't want to log that Valley, Iris, to the contrary. See, you don't understand a thing. What we have in mind is a return to True Farmin Principles. We've forgotten the meaning of Family. When was the last time we did something together as a family?'

'We had dinner at the Bowling Club the night you won the Tombola.'

'And how long ago was that? See, Attis has a team of men lined up, ready and willin to work for no pay.'

'Hmm, I'd like to meet that team o' men. They can come up here any time. So he's not gowan to university.'

'Oh, he'll go eventually. We didn't expect you to understand.'

'I understand too well. She'll have her play at livin rough, last about a month, then go scurryin home to Daddy, leavin Attis with a broken heart and a team o' men he can't pay.'

'Look, if he gains admission to the university, he'll defer entry for a year, all right? Satisfied? He just wants to give farmin a go. I mean, he *is* a farmer's son.'

'He is not a farmer's son. No son of yours'd get to the university, unless he was drivin a delivery truck.'

'Thank you. He's as much my son as what he is yours, and he's free to do as he chooses. I commend what these young people are attempting and I applaud their spirit. In fact, if I was fifty years younger, I'd go down and lend a hand.'

'Oh, you'll be lendin a hand, Horrie, have no fear o' that. She got you worked out quick. Always was a fool for women.'

'You will look on the dark side. Always seein the worst in people. I don't know how in God's name a man's put up with you, all these years.'

'What about that road bein blocked? Who's gowan to pay to have that fixed? You said yourself, you haven't got the equipment for it.'

'I dare say Zeno will send down a posse from one of those big open cuts of his. He's got dumper trucks bigger than this house. They say he's a straightforward sort of man. I think him and me'd get on well.'

'Don't get your hopes up. The day his daughter marries your son is the day my sister writes me a letter that's not full o' propaganda, listen to this. "If only you could know the comfort."'

What wore away the track was traffic. Sheer volume of traffic caused the cap of the ridge to subside, cutting off the Valley all but completely, as a result of the second rockfall, May '79.

Summer '68–69. Having failed in an attempt to locate the wrecked Kombi—there's a stretch of sheer cliff upriver to the Falls—Eugene Ecks has spent a Sisyphean morning lugging out the flat battery. As has become increasingly apparent, the cave is an essential locus of operations, and Diane Zoshka will need to live in the cave whilstever Attis keeps going to work, and Attis will need to keep working whilstever capital buys commodities, as no one else in this commune, Michael Ginnsy excepted, has a brass razoo, and Ginnsy has forgotten his assumed name and could never write his signature the same way twice: his will become one of those tantalising unclaimed bank accounts. A vehicle can be handy too, when resorting to the *pis aller* of a purchase. The cave, however, is an hour's plough through the tantoon from the firetrail, which makes it a good three hours' hike from the Flat—and only a Mac-Anaspie would deem this firetrail negotiable. If Attis means to live in the cave with Diane, he'll be getting up when Darryl goes to bed, as the coupe that is now being logged is an hour's drive the other side of town. In other words, as anyone could see, the whole enterprise is impracticable. As for having the Pass reconstructed, forget it. When Darryl finally got through, May '86 (International Year of Peace), he had a team from the Forestry, and the Department of Main Roads, working for a month.

These beautiful mountain fastnesses survive in pristine condition for a reason. For the same reason, they are always cheap, should ever they come on the market. Thus, they tempt the unreasonable folk whom Zablocki ('81) has so eloquently categorised as 'classless, white, urban, liberally, but not professionally educated, and insulated both from any real danger of slipping into poverty, and from any real prospect of becoming absorbed into a demanding, and worthwhile, career'.

'How's it goin?' inquires Eugene Ecks, dumping the twelve-volt battery on the floor. You can still see where it landed. His garb, where the acid has chewed through the cotton, exhibits the characteristic arabesque of the battery bearer.

'Attis and I have been working out who should live in the Valley, Eugene. Anyone down there now can stay, and anyone is welcome who was at the Wake for Martin Luther King, with a partner. I happened to mention I went to Barbara's Wake for Martin Luther King and it caught Att's imagination. He envies me, I think, that I was living in the city, and able to attend.'

'Cool. Because King was about equality, Diane.'

'Right. And in the Moody Valley Candle Company Co-op, Eugene, everyone is free and everyone is equal.'

'Way to go, Diane. Do they have a battery charger at Wonderview?'

'What's a battery charger?'

'Never mind. Is there a piece of paper on which I could write a note?'

'No. We're not properly set up yet. All we have is this metho stove and these sleeping bags. Attis should be home early. He didn't go to work, as he wanted to fetch some more stuff for the cave. We're going to have to stay up here while he's working, but it shouldn't be for long. Just so long as we need money.'

'He's a groovy guy, Diane. You did well.'

'Eugene, it's his Valley. His father just handed it over.'

'I hope that doesn't make him 'n you King 'n Queen, or nothin.'

'Of course not. You wouldn't say that if you knew us. We're not like that.'

Compelled to call by at the hardware store to pick up some bits for the eggbeater drill, Attis sees Fergie's jinker outside flat 10 Graceland and it's not yet 3 p.m. Didn't Fergus score a second load? Does he know he has to pay the rent?

'That you, Att? Come in, mate. Door's unlocked.'

Fergie, feet up, belching his way through a bottle of Corio whisky, and that's not Fergie.

'Siddown. Drink?'

'No thanks.'

'Beer in the fridge if yer change yer mind. Fuck, mate! Whatta day.'

'Somethin up?'

'Reckon. 'Knoath. When I got back for me second load, coupe was crawlin with coppers. Been a murder.'

'Yeah?'

'Know that young bloke just started? 'Parently Smitty put him onto that huge big grey gum up top.'

'What, the one they were going to leave?'

'Right up the top o' the coupe. Shoulda left it too, need a week to drop it and a low-loader to shift it, anyway, the kid's barrellin in, last thing anyone sees, come smoko, just the sound of the saw, on idle. You'da known 'im, wouldn't ya? Woulda played footie against him, wouldn't ya. Come from down the coast.'

'What happened?'

'Smitty goes to check it out, finds him cold motherless dead. Ar, ya shoulda seen it, Att. Shot through the head, .ate. Farck.'

'You saw the body?'

'Coppers'd only just fronted. Smitty's there, spewin his ring out. Wasn't done with a slug gun, neither. Didn't know what had caused it first, thought he mighta broke a chain, but the saw's there, 'n no blood on the saw. Well, I mean there was blood on the saw but it wasn't *swimmin* in blood. Blood every-where. Turned him over, and there's this neat entry hole mate Faarck. What kind o' cowardly cunt does a thing like this, Att? For all we know, coulda been personal, mighta been some sheila involved, but mate, what if some lunatic's creepin round, usin people for target practice? Crew went home, thing like that upsets ya. Who's next?'

'Could have been a stray shot? Someone shooting seed?'

'Not up there. Tell ya straight, I'm not goin back, not till someone's charged. Man's a sittin duck, in a jinker. You wanta be careful too, so how's Nisi? Seen her lately? Got a nice personality, Nisi.'

'How far into the tree was the cut?'

'Dunno. Never noticed. Why?'

Fergus MacAnaspie: killed himself, June '87, by cutting his throat with a chainsaw. Kimbo says he was upset with Darryl for re-opening the Gap Road. And Horrie, who refused to eat from the day Fergus died, was dead within the month, which made Darryl hard-hearted: see, Darryl must have thought he was doing the world a favour, but the jury is still out.

48. *Nisi in Koala Kottage. Attis takes a solitary stroll.*

Summer '68–9 still.

'Good afternoon, Ginnsy.'

'Good afternoon, Nisi. I couldn't get to sleep last night. The Forces of Good and Evil were battling over me again. Where is everyone?'

'Eugene left early to carry out the battery. Would you care for brunch?'

'Ta. You're spoilin me. Where are the boys?'

'I don't know. Went off somewhere. I had to fetch the butter from the creek.'

'Great, isn't it. Such a healthy lifestyle. Great to go to sleep and wake up, rather than pass out and come to. I been spendin too much time in the sort o' place you can always get breakfast. Think the boys appreciate it here? You tell 'em I found this place?'

'Oh I think they love it. Of course, they do get bored at night, with no electricity.'

'Yeah, I like TV. Well we're all gonna have to learn to play cards.'

'I'm so glad there is no TV. One of the reasons I came here, Michael, was to get the boys away from it. I believe it

303

alters the brain in ways we don't fully comprehend, and it's not just the illusions on the screen. Did you k ow they emit microwaves?'

'Oh sure. TV has its good points, but as you say, we abuse it. You comfortable on the floor?'

'Not really. I find it odd a house this size has only the one bedroom.'

'Yeah, well it probably wasn't always like this. And even the bed in that one bedroom is not so comfortable, let me assure you.'

'It doesn't bother you, being in that big bedroom all by yourself?'

'No. I'm not scared, if that's what you mean. I just wish my fuckin dog would front. Only reason I'm down here is because o' that mongrel. Has he been seen this morning? Wish I hadn't lost the whistle, but I'd lose my head if it wasn't screwed on.'

'No. And that's not what I meant. You take milk in your coffee?'

'Yeah. You think I'm selfish, don't you, but I'm just obeying orders, Nisi. I have instructions to live in Koala Kottage. You guys have to build your own houses.'

'Oh Michael, really! You're unmarried, you have no children, and the house is far too large for one.'

'I know. I know. It wasn't my decision. It was Phryx and Gwen's decision.'

'Hmph. That's easy to say.'

'How do you mean?'

'Well, we never even met these people! You could claim anything you liked and we wouldn't know the difference.'

'Ar, give us a break, Nisi! I wouldn't purposely mislead you.'

'I hope not. Here's Eugene back. Did you see my boys on your travels, Eugene?'

'Nope. They're not on the track. Hi man, I left the battery with the trogs. Attis would like us to be in the house, so when the boys get back, tell 'em to stick around.'

'Well I'll tell them, Eugene, but that doesn't mean they're going to do as I say. You know what boys are.'

'Yeah, I don't like takin orders either. What's with this fuckin givin people orders shit? Thought th's was democracy.'

'Come on man, it's not like that. It's just Att has some heavy news and wants us to be here to hear it. That's all. I wouldn't know if we all sleep in the house.'

'Where else would we sleep?'

'I don't know. I sleep on the verandah. And lookit, I think we *do* need a meet. We need some organisation.'

'Absolutely. Got to start to care 'n share, gotta get that schoolhouse built, fore school goes back, but I must live in this house, man, cause I know how to start the pump engine.'

Paula Zoshka sends a telegram to flat three Graceland. It's handed to Balthazar Beauregard as he wires Calvin Ecks for money. Olaf Abernathy, in his typically irresponsible manner, has disappeared. They can't find him. It seems Paula Zoshka and Brian Chegwodden will soon be down, to start a new life together. They may live in flat three, for a while. Then again, they may not.

Diane is so excited by this news, Attis cannot get a word in. She babbles all the way down the track, to the point he feels he needs to be alone.

He's still thinking of his poor Noumean penfriend. Did he do the right thing there?

'Go to the house,' he tells them both. 'I'll be along later.'

'Where you going, darling?'

'I have to check on something. I want to look at the cedars.'

'Let's think,' says Balthazar Beauregard, thinking. 'I haven't been up there yet. What about you, Diane? You been up the Sacred Grove?'

'No.'

'Is that what they're calling it?'

'That's what Ginnsy's calling it. It's upcreek, near the foot of the Falls. Ask Eugene.'

'I don't need to ask. I really need a walk.'

'Bet you do, but it takes a while to get there. You won't make it by dark, Attis.'

'Doesn't matter. There'll be a moon.'

'Wow, you're a real bushman.'

'It couldn't wait till tomorrow, darling? That way I could come too.'

'He wants to get his head together, Diane. Come on, gimme the battery, kid.'

'Diane, I'll take you some other time. Tonight, see if you can get some feeling for what the people want to do. Some may wish to be building, while others will prefer to get the gardens established. But please emphasise the stronger men will have to help me, for the time being. We'll be bringing the gear down, though I don't quite know how we're going to do it. Especially the Silent Knight refrigerator.'

'The answer will come in the Sacred Grove, man. And don't hurry back.'

'Thanks. I won't.'

You can push a thumbnail into red cedar. Bugger of a wood to strip paint off. In contrast, cutters of railway sleepers tell of iron-barks too hard to work, and take your file and your file brace too, when you're sawing yellow box for firewood.

Within thirty years of colonisation, the best red cedar was plundered, gone. Down the cedar getters' snig trails arrived free settlers. Allocated a clearing lease of fifty acres or less, they were obliged to clear their plot of trees, by axe, within five years. Under-standably, they preferred to clear the softer woods on the richer soils, though the country was mostly open woodland, according to Charles Darwin in 1836. The dense forests of today grew later, bespeaking the dispossession of the Aborigines, who never extin-guished a cooking fire, and burnt the country to keep it open.

A man purblind could find his way from the talus to the bracken bulrush and blackberries. Harken to the friendly wings of the grey fantail, the reverb of the whip bird. Flies are bad, and as Attis breaks a sprig of hickory wattle to serve him as a cowtail, he glances at the house, below him on the Flat, and sees what must be a gladiolus, by the tank. That tank will need to be mended, which means cement and wire netting, maybe a new tank.

Barefoot, he moves silently, taking the most rapid route upriver. Where the Flat peters out, in brush kurrajong and a cairn that would well have been a stab at a drystone wall, the creek is low, poached by cattle, obscured by brambles, but clear, if shallow. Moss-covered dead kanooka, water gum, sprawls over the stream, makeshift bridging. Much mistletoe in the manna gum: the splash round the bend could be black duck or platypus. No big fish, because of the dam. Growing among the riparian stones, *Lomatia myrcoides, Dodonea triquetra.*

The sun sets early in this Valley. The sky is clear, so there'll be a moon, but time of darkness, before it rises. How few are the forests in which man can sit, by night, without fire or fear. No boar inhabit this Valley, no bear, no buffalo, no big cat.

When the moon rises, to frog chorus, Attis can see the Shining Gums above him. This is the lowest growing stand anywhere. They are found, as a rule, on the deeper soils of the sheltered siltstones higher up, in the cool temperate rainforest of blanketleaf and southern sassafras. Gleaming, the tall straight grey-green trunks and thick streamers of bark, emerging from an understorey of soft tree fern and Christmas mint bush, accentuate the vertical crowns, from which hang leaves twice the length of a man's penis. So vertical a tree, so quintessential a eucalypt—the genus is still rapidly evolving, as shown by the wide prevalence of hybridisation among the species—so semi-abstract, so calligraphic a tree (one wonders what Monet might have made of one), so antithetical to an English oak's out-stretched horizontal crown; yet, regarding wildfire and light-ning strike, which the more ripe for conflagration? Which tree more sacred to Jupiter? Which vector more prefers fruit, hard and wooden as a gumnut? The Shining Gum canopies entice Fire Squirrels up and away from lignotubers, so that, beckoned on with flaming streamers, seduced with flammable oils, they leap, and the seeds, unscathed for up to ten minutes at 500 degrees, shower from the capsules, from the fatal Gasp of the Embrace, to germinate in the ash of luckless rivals.

What willing Nature spoke. In the sky above, Apollo Eight orbits the rising moon.

Attis finds he need proceed no further than the Shining Gum. Because he recalls something good that happened in the Shining Gum Grove. It happened when he was a boy of eight.

He had been asleep—they often slept in the Valley, when the men were mustering scrubbers—away from his big brothers—everyone likes to find his own posse for a swag (this in the days when each MacAnaspie kept a rawhide headstall in his pack, and his horses, when there was no night yard, wore a pair of light rawhide hobbles)—and all he could hear was Barney snoring, the pop of burning logs, and the horses, as they shuffled off in the direction of the Flat. He can't remember why they were here, doesn't remember what he was dreaming, but something happened that night and he woke before or as it happened. Then, feeling safe and beatific, he drifted back to sleep, but not to dream.

Come dawn, he couldn't properly piss. His stream was blocked, with a plug, but his brothers, when he complained to them of this, tears in his eyes, roared laughing.

Attis MacAnaspie: A man's first experience of sexual pleasure seldom involves a woman. We are so designed that our first experience of sexual pleasure is bound to a time, and a place, and a dream, and a Mystery. Women come later, if at all.
Barney MacAnaspie: snores something fierce. I wouldn't like to be in prison with him, sharing the same slot. The sort of man who attracts friendly fire, during time of war. You only get five minutes of silence, every half-hour, when he stops breathing entirely.

49. *A meeting of the co-op. Rude Boy. Annunciata and Fiona. Olaf's admiration for Ginnsy. The Kombi won't start.*

'Are we all here except for Olaf? Where is he, by the way?'
   'Stayed in town. I think he's up at Graceland.'
   'Could the meeting please come to order? I think we need Barbara here, just to chair these meetings.'
   'She'll be down, don't you think? I think she'll come. She'll be here eventually.'

'Order! Order!'

'What's with this fuckin *order* shit, Ch-erist! About the last thing we need. Order is Death. I thought you were supposed to be an anarchist, Diane.'

'Grow up, will you, Michael? It seems we all want to play silly buggers. Well, I want to say this to you all, before we start, and I hope you're all listening.'

Two that aren't, Nisi Papadimitriou's boys, Timothy and Aloysius, are meant to be in their sleeping bags. In fact, they have sneaked out, through the window, and are presently hiking over the Flat. Eerie shadows, where the trees grow, and the plovers give you hell, but Aloysius reasons tonight's meeting may prove a torrid affair, which may prompt Nisi to neglect her routine checks on the wellbeing of her offspring. It's worth a try.

'You scared, Rude Boy?'

Rude Boy—a nod in the direction of the early reggae men of Jamaica—is the name by which Aloysius O'Looby now insists on being addressed by his younger half-brother. Alexander, Monica's eldest, was ahead of his time, in this regard. But anyone living in the Brixton/Clapham/Balham part of London will understand the argot. I thought for a bit there might have been an element of Rasta to the Erinungarah Cult, for the psychic components were certainly present—the Bible, the Galliambic metre, a sacramental use of marihuana—but I now feel superficial resemblance (dreadlocks) is bound to be convergent evolution. I shouldn't be surprised if Finn MacCool and the White Boys boasted dreadlocks, for they hang naturally from Irish heads that are never washed, combed or clipped.

'What me be scare of, Little Bro? Me don' see no consooma, don' see no happy marry couple, don' see no man in suit. Be notin' here scare I.'

'What about bulls?'

'Dem kin see. Dem be eatin. Better be scare you snake.'

'Snake?'

'Oh yeah. Better you don' tread de hole. Snake by de River o' Babylon, him swallow boy like you, one gulp.'

'I want to go back.'

'Go, Boy. Run.'

'But you have to come.'

'No. Radio! Rude Boy want fe hear Bunny, Jimmy, Jethro Tull. Chum Poww! Dum Poww!'

'Don't be noisy, Rude Boy. Mum will hear.'

'Her not hear elephant fart, him fart in she face. Dem be out of it by now, Boy.'

'But you said they haven't got erb.'

'No. But dem have mooshroom. Dem be eat de blue mooshroom.'

Olaf Abernathy walks into Koala Kottage round 9 a.m. next morning. Accompanying him is Sister Annunciata, who was at the Wake for Martin Luther King.

'Anyone up? Looks like they're all still asleep.'

The sun is high and the flies in the kitchen busy. Diane Zoshka's tangle of short-cropped curls spills from under a blanket on the floor. Attis MacAnaspie, in the style of Darryl MacAnaspie, sleeps on a chair, head on the table.

'I'll just go see if Nisi's round' whispers Olaf, heading down the hall. He pauses, and his shoulders assume a Brian Chegwodden-like asymmetry, to indicate he's lighting up. It's a legacy from days on the breezy building sites in the city, but any breeze here is imperceptible. During the past half-hour, beads of sweat have formed on Diane's forehead.

Attis stirs. He stares at the table. He doesn't remember who, where or what he is. But hearing a breath he turns and, seeing an unfamiliar female face, smiles in greeting.

'Hi' he says, 'I'm Attis MacAnaspie. I'm sorry, seems we all slept in. Would you care for a cup of tea? I'll get a fire going. Could be quicker to do it outside.'

Hastening immediately out the door, he lights the oil drum fuel stove.

Nisi Papadimitriou could do with some coffee and she could do with some eyeliner. She's wearing what looks like Selim the Grim's kaftan, red, with big yellow soccer balls.

'Who's Attis talking to?'

'Sister Annunciata. Fiona is still up the track. She sprained her ankle somepin bad.'

'Wonder you didn't offer to carry her down. You obviously spent the night with them.'

'As you keep sayin, we're all the same Family. I don't have a problem with that, and I'm sorry you do. Anyway, it's a job for two men. She's a big girl, Fiona. Hi, Diane.'

'Oh you're back. Listen, next time you plan on using my flat, would you mind telling me first?'

'OK, but I don't plan things. You won't be hearing from me. Want a smoke?'

'Why not? You owe me. Is someone looking after breakfast? Oh wow, it's so late.'

'Att's outside with Annunciata. I think he's getting the stove going.'

'Who's Annunciata?' Diane yawns. How can this flat-chested woman be so sure of herself, thinks Nisi.

'Well, she *was* Sister Annunciata. I think she just did a flit. Oh man, it breaks me up to see these fascist institutions crumbling.'

'Fiona is on the track, Diane. Fiona? You'll know her when you see her. Hey, would you believe my boys are still sleeping? They must have totally exhausted themselves.'

Olaf Abernathy is avid to accompany Michael Ginnsy when, half an hour later, Michael Ginnsy goes to fetch the Kombi from the Gap Road. The Kombi will need to be driven to the foot of the track, to collect Fiona. Balthazar Beauregard and Eugene Ecks have gone up the track, though it's been decided, if Fiona's ankle is broken, they'll take her to the cave, for prompt evacuation. But Olaf thinks it's likely just a sprain.

'Big woman like her, I dunno what you were *thinkin* of, man, bringin her down that track. We got no food here. No one thinks o' bringin nothin in. Everyone just turns up empty-handed, and I don't have the Faith to cope. How'd these women hear about the place?'

'You were the one telling everyone in Sydney about this Valley, Ginnsy. Now Barbara knows where it is, what can you expect? And why'd you leave the Kombi at the foot of the Pass, stead of in the chaff shed?'

311

'So as to be able to clutch-start, without flattenin the battery. See, in theory, we got two batteries, but in practice only one? That's why we gotta get that other battery, from the other Kombi. ASAP.'

'Oh, you haven't done that yet?'

'Well, of *course* I haven't done it yet. I haven't had the time, man. You get involved in these Cosmic Struggles, you got no time for anything. I'm totally exhausted.'

'But don't you want to fetch what's left of the acoustic? I was hopin we could have a jam. That's what I bin doin. I went to look at a PA advertised in the paper, but they wanted cash. Hey, I'm so lookin forward to playin with you. You're a legend.'

'It'll be smashed to matchwood, Olaf. Shame, cause it was a Gurian. Anyway, if we were to play, what kind of music could we play?'

Michael Ginnsy plays just slightly flat. That's where he hears it, cause that's where it be.

'Country rock'd be fine by me, but I don't mind if you prefer blues.'

'Oh no rock 'n roll, man! That's the Devil's music. You got sympathy for the Devil, what does that make you? No, we can't have that kind of music down here. That is what creates these killers. Did you know that, played right, a gut-bucket blues can cause a drunken man to kill? I got a lot on my conscience. But how would you feel about goin upriver and gettin that other battery for us? Let's hope it wasn't damaged, in descent. Eugene went up, but he lost his way, or somepin.'

'OK. Settle down, Ginnsy. Don't make these rash decisions, man.'

'Hey, there's Kombi. Near that tree. Too many eucalypts here, man, they're bastards. Like the paintwork? I actually paid someone to do that. If you think it's too brash, we could camouflage it. See where I backed into a tree? You're forever backin into things, with that tiny ridiculous back window. Actually, mightn't be a bad idea to paint it with khaki and green roof paint, cause I think they spot Kombi from up top and that's what's bringin 'em down? You stay here, man. I'll roll it and clutch-start. Hey, we lucked out with the choice of vehicle, though it's easy to cross-thread the plugs on alloy heads, and they lowered the clearance on this model. Fourteen-inch wheels. The old ones were even better for the bush, with the big fifteen-inch wheels, and the diff stepped up on account of the final drive reduction. Good traction, too, with the weight over the drive wheels. Pull most anything. It would be difficult to bog such a vehicle.'

Michael Ginnsy: Gwen Bletherstone Mayall and Phryx Pfingstl hated eucalypts, and passed this on, as Wisdom, to Michael Ginnsy. I'd say they were just expressing the fear every farmer has of eucalypts. Eucalypts are thirsty beasts, and they love firestorms, which farmers don't. When they were introduced to India, the Indian farmers rioted against them. Eucalypts thrive on global warming. They are the tree of Siva. They are the tree of the future. They are the enemy of the farmer, the friend of the hunter-gatherer. 'Your days are numbered,' they say to us, but we can't revert to hunting. There are too many of us, we lack the skills, and we crave modern conveniences. Oh yes, there are men, to the north of Australia, who spear barramundi in the shallows of the mangroves, with the aid of aircraft landing lights hooked up to truck batteries, but they trade the fish that they spear, at the store, for cans of beer and shotgun cartridges.

Kombi won't start.
'Like, I don't understand. I don't understand anything really.'
'Is the carbie clean? Maybe you left a rag in the intake manifold. Did you time it on idle or static?'
'Ar, don't keep goin on about that. I told you, I spent a day on the tuning with what was in the van, Olaf. I did the fuel screen, the air cleaner, checked the coil, did the valve clearances cold, I checked the timing, put in new plugs and points, new condenser, new oil screen gaskets, even new rubber seals for the plugholes, man. I tightened the front wheel bearings. I cleaned the pressure relief valve. I did everything but split the fuckin crankcase. I actually threw away the lights, so as to save the battery.'

'Then what are we gonna do?'

'Dunno. But it's no good you pushin any further. Save your strength there, Pal.'

'You don't suppose the battery could be flat?'

'Now how could the battery possibly be flat? We just had it charged. It was holdin a charge. Come on. Gimme one more push.'

'Steer away from that bog.'

'Fe sure.'

Bogged to the Dayglo Peace signs, the Kombi provides the men with a focus. Pushing through a clump of three-vein cassinia, they gather round in gratitude. Balthazar Beauregard, naked under bib and tucker overalls, hair drawn back in a ponytail. Attis MacAnaspie, with his short back and sides, blue shirt, moleskins, bare feet, stock hat. Olaf Abernathy, in granny glasses, serge woollen battledress, army boots, no shirt. Eugene Ecks, T-shirt and jeans rags now, riddled with battery acid burns. He evicted the spiders that came with the gumboots that came with the house, and he's wearing those. Michael Ginnsy in dark glasses, mauve poncho, platform heels, checkerboard flares, Uncle Sam hat. Mud-drenched.

Now one way of telling the eunuchs from the men was all the men were bearded, except for Attis, who grew no beard, according to Kimberley Moon. And Eugene had just one of them little wispy Uncle Ho jobs, but the rest were the full Jim Morrison. Blast! I should've mentioned this to Wozza.

'Whattaya reckon?'

'Reckon we got no tractor, man. D'ya hear me, Kap'n Kaos? Got no tractor here, man.'

'What if we all got on the end of a rope?'

'There's a problem. We don't have one.'

'Got a tow rope in the van, Ginnsy?'

'Do I look like a negative thinker?'

'Before we do anything else, we ought to sit down and take stock. Write an inventory, here and now. What we got. What we need.'

'I don't think a rope is going to help. Look at it! Up to the doors. And that mud's like quicksand, man, it sucks the gumboots off of yer. No way can we dig those wheels out.'

'We may have to drain this bog at some stage. Can't we do it now?'

Olaf catches Attis' eyes, and they're smiling. Thank God. Not everyone here is a compleat fool.

'Just needs a new battery. This would not have happened, if the battery was holding a charge. Where's that torch and piece of mirror to check the water in the battery?'

'Who says the battery's flat? Horn sounds OK.'

'Maybe the starter gear is hung up on the flywheel. Put it in third gear, man, and push it backwards.'

'Ha ha. Come on, we just had the battery charged. It was holding a charge. It's not the battery.'

'Maybe the solenoid. Give it a smack with a hammer.'

'Why'd you steer in the bog for, fuckwit?'

'Oh. I get to speak. Thank you. Now you see, I think Kombi is trying to tell us something here. You must always take note when a vehicle won't start, or wants to go into a bog. This vehicle has a protective attitude, which has saved my life on numerous occasions.'

'OK. So what's it saying?'

'Ar, but it's not mine any more, dig? I gave it to the community.'

'So what's it saying to the community?'

'That is for the community to say.'

'No good to anyone like this.'

'Maybe it doesn't want to have to move the fat lady.'

'Don't be like that, man. Fiona's OK, she's a doer. She pitches in.'

'Where is she now?'

'Left her in the cave, but she's fine. Just a bit sore.'

'Want my opinion?'

'No.'

'I think Kombi's sayin, no more people here for the time being. We gotta get organised.'

'Absolutely. But where do we start, man? What are our priorities? We couldn't agree on anything.'

'That was only our first meeting.'

'What's going to change? We don't have time for all this wrangling.'

'You're the man with the experience, Hollywood. What work do you think should be done first?'

'I told you last night, Eugene. Where things are done for their own sake, there is no such thing as "work" only "art". Of course, this may take time, but food must be our priority, because food is our first and most basic need. Houses you can build in winter. But you must plant when the time is right to plant, and the time is right to plant. In fact, it's getting late in the season.'

'It's midsummer!'

'That's right. Like I say. Midsummer is late in the season.'

'I don't see why we can't do both.'

'That's because you don't understand what's involved in either.'

'Hoss shit, I don't!'

'We're going to need a few basic tools. Dad said he would lend them.'

'That's generous. What a kind man. What does he have to spare?'

'About ten of every tool ever invented and some he invented himself. He's a real hoarder. Plus, he's always losing things, so he buys another, and when the first turns up, that makes two.'

'I hate to say it, but this is wrong. *All* wrong. We are going about things the wrong way.'

'You're a loser, Kap'n Kaos. Anyone told you today?'

'What are you saying, Michael?'

'That we should go to the Sacred Place, where we should meditate calmly and pray for guidance from the Spirit of this Valley. Because unless things are done in the correct spirit, we are wasting our time, and this is not just my opinion. This is what Phryx said.'

'OK. Let's do that.'

'We wouldn't have a chain block?'

'I know what you're thinking, Balthazar, but that's a hell of a business.'

'Yeah, takes too long,' adds Olaf. 'Using a chain block, you only got ten foot max, and then you're gonna have to rechock the vehicle and extend and reanchor the wire rope. Besides, what's it gonna hook on? But I have another idea. Att, has your Dad got one of those old Donald wire-strainers? The ones with the claws?'

'I'm sure he has.'

'OK. Now suppose we use the Kombi as one strainer post. You see, if we tie the loose end of the wire to a tree up the Pass, then roll the wire roll back down, we wouldn't even have to cut the wire. We tie *another* wire to the chassis of the Kombi, then we put the Donald strainers on the join, and we probably need a length of pipe to slip over the handle for purchase, but then we can walk the Kombi up the hill, with people pushing and digging as required, and we have up to a thousand feet of wire we can play with.'

'That's a great idea, Olaf,' says Attis, after cogitation, 'I think it'd work. Long as we use the old eight-gauge wire, the Donalds don't like high tensile wire. What do you guys reckon?'

Michael Ginnsy: called Kap'n Kaos by Eugene Ecks, who, like Darryl, had a penchant for demeaning nicknames. Eugene and Darryl were the men who, far from becoming eunuchs, acquired, by force, a harem. Must we conclude a vibrant, abundant masculinity is indispensable to us? To the contrary: by this time, procreation had ceased. The Rites of Brigid were being observed, in the Land of the Ever Young, and while such men as remained grew old—and old, perhaps, before their time—eunuchs and women and children had been released from the ageing process. Thus, Barbara Byng has denied she has had a facelift, to the Senate. But I wonder if the Great Mother intended this *Saga* as more than a brief flourish, a demonstration of what She could do, if She chose, whenever She chose. I cannot believe She could forever isolate a group of human beings, under the Melbourne-Sydney flightpath.

50. *Xmas. Monica visits Calvin and Frodsham, Cindy's illness. Fergus visits the Valley.*

'In the end, Calvin,' concedes Derek Frodsham, 'and it can't be far off, you'll find liberal democracy the government, by those least fitted to govern, of a complacent bourgeosie. And of course, as a scientist, I am concerned by the liberal democratic abuse of science.'

'Ain't gonna be easy educatin' em,' agrees Calvin, scrubbing the turkey dish. 'Mentality of that female vote has got to be a worry. More 'n fifty per cent o' voters, and you tell me how they judge a man.'

'Oh, by superficial appearance, I should have thought. By his clothing, by his hairstyle, by the wealth and reputation he commands. We can't all be Kennedies.'

'I guess you're right, but hell, Derek.'

'Apart from that, how's work?'

'Hopeless, on the immunoassay front. That's what women do to ya. One thing happened, though, kinda bizarre. My assistant broke a thermometer in a guinea pig nest and stumbled on a new mercury catalysed reaction. We think we may have found a way to make a halfway edible paste from gumnuts. Is there life after science, Derek?'

'There was for Pascal and Socrates. That the doorbell?'

The only other house resident with nowhere to go Xmas Day stumbles off, in dentate paper crown, to open the front door. On returning, he catches Frodsham's eye.

'Calvin's wife.'

'Oh no.'

'Want me to get rid of her for you, mate?' Frodsham flourishes the carving knife.

'No thanks, Derek. Tell her to wait in the front room. She alone?'

'Hi Monica.'

'Hello Calvin. Merry Xmas to y'all.'

'Can I get you a slice of fruit cake? I guess you'd prefer a drink.'

'Calvin, I really don't know why you're here, stead o' bein home with your family.'

'Then you must be forgetful as well as suppliant. I'd rather not discuss it. How's Cindy? Give her my present?'

'You don't consider Alex a member of the family, do you, Calvin?'

'What family? I did the best I could. I'm sorry it didn't work out.'

'I will have a drink, thank you.'

'Would you prefer Coolabah Claret or Resch's Dinner Ale? It's all we have.'

'Mix me a cocktail o' the two. Calvin, I'm concerned about your daughter.'

'Why is that?'

'Cause she won't eat 'n she won't sleep 'n she won't talk. She's frettin. I know we agreed it might be better not, but could you come round to see her, please? For Xmas Day?'

'Alex! Turn down that West Indian music. Was his father a cricket player?'

'We didn't do a lot of talking, in the short time we were together. Cindy! Daddy's here, sweetheart.'

'She in bed?'

'I told you she would be.'

'Hello Cindy. How's my gal?'

'I'll leave you.'

'No, I prefer you stay. Guess you miss yr Daddy, do ya, darlin? What's this photo you got here.'

'That's Timothy. Nisi's boy.'

'Don't you dare touch it! Don't you dare touch it!'

'I won't touch it, sweetheart. But why would you want a photo of this little boy next to your bed?'

'So she can look at it, night 'n day.'

'Mommy tells me you're Mommy's girl, you spend a lot o' time in bed, but you don't sleep. Is this true? You take her to a doctor?'

'That was a cheap shot.'

'What did the doctor say?'

'Said she may need a tonic, way she's losin weight. Wanted to know if you and I had thought of seekin marriage guidance.'

'Want to tell Daddy about it, Cindy?'

'No.'

'Cindy, if you don't tell us what your problem is, how can we solve your problem?'

'I want to be with Tim.'

'But Tim's gone away, sweetheart. You understand you cain't play with Tim now.'

'But I love him.'

'Sure you do, honey. I bet you love all your little friends, but sometimes people need to move. You're a big girl. Cain't they write each other?'

'Silly Daddy. He don't understand, that where Timmy's gone, they don't have a mailbox.'

'Cindy. Sweetheart. I know how you must feel.'

'No you don't. You could never understand.'

'OK. I could never understand, but I do know people get over things.'

'They were close, Calvin.'

'Sure they were. But I know Cindy is a sensible girl.'

'I cain't get her t' eat. Doctor says, she don't soon eat, she may need to go on a drip.'

'Oh to hell with that. Get me some custard and a spoon.'

'Don't cry, baby! Look at that, Calvin. I believe this child has a broken heart.'

'You wouldn't know a broken heart if it jumped up and bit you on the ass, Cindy! I may have to get tough here. You want Daddy to get tough wit' you?'

'This is punishment for us, Calvin. This is God's punishment for what we have been.'

Cindy Ecks: The love Cindy felt for Timothy was, like Darryl's refusal to be gelded, a destructive stress within the commune that guaranteed its demise. Guilt-stricken, having broken Cindy's heart—I won't dwell on this, it provides the subtext to the *Ballad*—Timothy, a mind they could ill do without if they hoped to maintain the technology, abandoned the Valley in his mid-teens, and turning his back on everything it stood for, demonstrated to the younger generation there was life outside the Erinungarah; or, to phrase it in the context of Spaceship Earth, to phrase it as Max would phrase it, you'd have to be mad to live off the interest when you can squander the capital. Attis, who took no part in the orgies of the early seventies, exempt from the guilt of promiscuity, must have observed the sufferings of his fellow men and women and lamented greatly. But typically, the gods choose Attis, the only upright man in the Valley—*vir optimus Obliquae*—to tempt and to transmute.

Or maybe Brigid just prefers men without beards. She wouldn't be alone there.

Late summer, '69.

'I see what looks like a mauve box coming,' proclaims Annunciata. 'Maybe two mauve boxes.'

'That'll be Fergie.' Attis MacAnaspie glances, before speaking, towards Olaf Abernathy. 'He said he might come down with the supplies. He must have brought a hive down.'

'Reckon we'll rob any honey this year?' Balthazar is keen to get stung. It's addictive.

'Too late for swarms. Have to shift a colony. Lucky if we're not feeding sugar syrup by May. Only reliable nectar source we have round here is the rough-barked apple. Sometimes get a big bloodwood flow, but I wouldn't consider this a top spot for an apiary. No ironbark. You want to be on the coast, in the spotted gum, or out on the western slopes, in the yellow box.'

This intimation the Valley may not be perfect in every respect stuns the company. They stare about them, dumbfounded.

'Ah well, it's the wax we want. You plannin on stayin down here, Attis?'

'He owns the Valley.'

'I know that, Diane. I'm just inquirin if he's gonna live in the Valley or up in the cave, like you said. And we must remember those top honey eucalypts he cites produce the best honey anywhere. We'll do better than a Scottish beekeeper.'

'I only ever hunted honey. I don't know what I'm doing. Diane thinks it's a good idea to keep working and live in the cave, but Fiona seems happy in the cave now. Wouldn't you say so, Diane?'

'I think the bees will drive away the honeyeaters.'

Wrong, Nisi. Golden dagoes were introduced to this country in 1822. It's the black cockatoos who compete with the bees for the holes in the trees that are feeling the pinch.

Attis' inevitable appeal to Diane Zoshka makes Diane *de facto* leader, and to establish a commune of any kind you need a charismatic leader. Such, at least, is the view of Peter Caddy, guru of Findhorn. Mother Ann Lee's Shakers, older than the First Fleet, are still going, if not strong. And what killed the Happy Valley Candle Company Co-op on the Upper Duck Creek, in two months? Group leadership.

'I sure would,' replies Diane, 'but how come Fergie's not working today?'

'He'll want to tell you that himself, and issue a warning at the same time. I'll only say it seems to confirm what Ginnsy told us, about what happened here. We have a problem.'

'Scuse me.' Annunciata, remorse-stricken, rises from the step and heads off towards the sacred pump. Mounted on three-inch redgum bedlogs, it boasts a crank handle, a grimy toothbrush and a canvas cover. Christ will surely comprehend why Annunciata finds it impossible to pray, but life without prayer will guarantee problems, continual problems, endless problems. The godless life does not bear scrutiny, to the detriment of our Postmodern literature.

Contrary to what some people may think, Annunciata is in pursuit of Jesus. The *real* Jesus.

'I could go and meet Fergie,' muses Michael Ginnsy, 'or I could see about gettin that other battery in, or I might just take the dog for another stroll. Folks, will you look at the condition on this dog? What's he been eatin, I wonder?'

'Is it such a good thing,' inquires Diane Zoshka, once Michael Ginnsy is out of earshot, 'that men cut down the trees in the coupes and the dogs eat the wild animals?'

'But isn't this the price we pay for being civilised?'

'I don't buy this everything has a price, Olaf.'

322

'Neither do I,' adds Nisi, 'because we sure as hell don't need dogs. We don't need a dog *pack*.'

As though on cue, her younger son dashes by, pursued by a cute pup. He would beg to differ.

'We need this, we need that, what we need. Self self self.' Isn't anyone game to tell Olaf what Nisi did with Balthazar Beauregard in the cave?

Now they watch Michael, who with maladroit movements, throws sticks in the creek for Fats to fetch.

It was thoughtful of Fergus to bring down a hive, but what the Moody Valley Candle Company Co-op needs right now is tools. Eight-gauge wire, the Donald strainers, but more importantly, a minimal kit for clearing the garden and erecting temporary dwellings; bars for digging postholes and grubbing stumps, pliars, axe, bushsaw, shifter, mattock, hammer, nails, brace and bit, tinsnips, hacksaw, with some second-hand roofing iron, and some shovels, and some forks and spades, and don't forget the leather gloves for the blackberries. There's a shed, behind the chaff shed, which could be used for a dwelling; regrettably, it's covered with blackberry canes to a depth of feet.

Who was the clown walked through here, spreading blackberry seeds?

Baron von Mueller. In his own words, 'The blackberry deserves to be naturalised on the rivulets of any ranges.'

But he wasn't a compleat fool. 'No settlement, however princely, no city, however great its splendour, brilliant its arts, enchanting its pleasures, can arouse those sentiments of veneration which, among all the grand works of nature, an undisturbed noble forest region is most apt to call forth.' 1871.

1969. 'Where you bin, Darryl? We shoulda called you the Loch Ness Monster, you're seldom seen. Why you walkin so slow?'

'Can't run when you're carryin a beer, Dad. Spray all over ya.'

'Pon my soul, you're gettin lazy as the next-door neighbour. I seen Fritter Batter today stroll along his boundary line with a

323

transistor radio pressed to his lughole. They come out of their cities, but they cannot exist without these transistor radios.'

'Naa, he's tuned just off a station lookin for shorts in 'is electric fence. Reckons he couldn't take a shower, when first he come here. Drain in the old hut was a better earth than the water pipe.'

'What, you talkin to him?'

'Not really. He was talkin to me.'

'I'd be careful who I spoke to, with this killer about. Reckon it might just be him, someone from outside the district. Where's Fergie? Thought he was comin out today.'

'Said to tell ya he was takin supplies to yer Valley.'

'Oh I see. Cause I was hopin for a bit of help get them few spuds lifted.'

'They won't be ready for claampin yet.'

'Thought I might shake a few off the sides of the rows and hill the rest back. My mouth's waterin for new potatoes. They're recovered well, now the drought's broke. Of course, we need the follow up.'

'I'd give y'aaand, cept I ave to go to town.'

'You go to town every day and night of your life. I wonder you don't move into Graceland and be done with it.'

'Wouldn't feel right, leavin you oldies alone, with no one to caare for yez.'

'Oh you're all heart. Ever thought o' gettin married, Darryl?'

'Plenty o' time for that. You never married till you was older 'n me.'

'No, but times have changed. I didn't speak to a woman that wasn't a member of my family till I was haired in the lug. See, them days, you stayed put and went to bed when the sun went down. Knackered, from clearin timber, and if you'd stepped out of line during the day, you spent the night draggin your paillasse up and down a flight of stairs. I went to the coast once a year, but the rest of the time I remained here. Now what's this electric fence, son? Sounds to me downright dangerous.'

'Trains an animal to respect yer fencin. When they touch it they're supposed to get a boot, but it's not properly workin yet, see. Somepin shortin it out, and the goats keep climbin over and gettin onto the Run. You want somepin in town?'

'Nothin you'd carry on a motorcycle less you was Chinese. Say, how would you feel about diggin a dam, while you got nothin much on? Gettin very dry again. Mother's complainin the soil in her flowerbed rings when she hits it with a shovel.'

'Caan't. Leased yer sheepsfoot roller to the DMR.'

'What!'

'Meant to tell ya.'

51. *Brian receives a shock. Fergus recounts the killing at the coupe. A journey to Obliqua Creek. Annunciata names Orion. The manhunt.*

The single rail line to Obliqua Creek was closed in the early sixties, rendering the biweekly rail motor defunct: a pity. Brian Chegwodden should be stepping off the train, not stepping off a bus, in shock. More Freudian, the dusty rail motor throbbing by the big cabbage rose in the forty-four. The door pushes out, pan to the wild eyes, dishevelled hair, a goosestep, he lunges into space, misses his footing, falls arse over head to the platform. And give him the old cardboard suitcase, held together with baling twine, and Paula, in a crinoline.

Brian is distraught. He has just learned Paula Zoshka has been pregnant to another man. But as he gazed out the window, having received the news, was the countryside not whispering, 'Come to me, My Darling?'

'Brian!'

She runs up the street, wanting to explain, because it wasn't as he thinks, it never is. But he strides ahead of her, purposeful, solitary. The solitude is genuine, the purpose illusory. Brian has no purpose now, other than getting to the bottom of this matter, so he turns in his stride and demands more answers from the passionate beauty with whom he is entangled.

'How many times did you fuck this guy? I can't believe this. How many times, Paula?'

'I don't know. Four, maybe five. Ten. Who knows?'

'But I asked you before we got engaged if you had been

325

involved with someone else, and you assured me that you hadn't. It seems you're a liar.'

'No I'm not. I didn't mean to lie to you, Brian.'

'But you did lie to me. So what was the big attraction with this guy. Eh?'

'There was none. That's why I said I wasn't involved, because to me involvement means liking someone and having something in common with them.'

'Oh you're incredible. I suppose you told him you loved him?'

'Yes I did, and I remember feeling terrible about that, too, because I didn't love him at all.'

'So you're a hypocrite.'

Paula's grey eyes fill with tears at the slur, and she looks more lovely than ever. And Brian, when he's angry, or jealous, he looks so handsome it's a crying shame.

'I told you I couldn't cope if you had been involved with someone else.'

'Yes, but you've been involved with someone else. You're married to Prim and I have to live with that.'

'Ah yes, but that was above board. It wasn't deceitful. Anyway, you knew, and it didn't bother you or you wouldn't be here.'

'It does bother me, but what can I do about it? What can we do about the past? We can do so little about the present. Haven't you done things you regret? We're all here together now. That's what matters to me.'

'Ha! I told you I couldn't cope if you had been involved with someone else, and you deceived me, and now I can't cope. See? I'm not coping. I don't know what I'm going to do now. I don't know if I can go ahead with this venture. What was the name of this guy?'

'Benny.'

'Benny! And does he fart and shit and belch, this Benny? Does he piss?'

'I suppose so.'

'You suppose so. And you let such a person take off his under-daks and put that thing with which he does piss, into your body. Oh, you filthy disgusting creature. Why would any woman do such a thing?'

'I don't know. I wasn't behaving rationally.'

'I'd say not. Was his penis like mine?'

'Aren't they all the same, or similar? I didn't see it, because it was dark in the carpark, but I had to guide it in. You guys like to be guided in.'

'Oh God. If you can't see that I'm unique, Paula, what hope is there for us? Was his bigger than mine?'

'Much the same. I don't know, Brian. Maybe just a bit bigger. I didn't actually measure it.'

'You didn't actually measure it. I'm surprised. You realise he had an arsehole?'

'I presume . . . '

'You presume. You *presume!* I put it to you, Paula, you knew. I put it to you those pretty painted nails have been close to Benny's filthy stinking arsehole. Don't smirk, because it's not funny.'

'And do you find my body disgusting?'

'No. Actually, I find you very beautiful, but your arsehole particularly so, which makes it all the worse. Because that lovely body has now been contaminated, and you should hear the way these characters talk about women like you, they brag, Paula. They skite to other men. Got lucky with a barmaid the other night, they say. Shoulda seen the norks on it. Heav-ee.'

'I didn't go out with men I could respect, because that might have been dangerous to me. I could have got involved. So I went for sleazebags and set myself up to lose. I was just using Benny, Brian.'

'Ha! You were using *him?* Ho ho. Pardon me. Can a hole use an object? Can nothing use something? Come on.'

'Anyway, why do you deserve a virgin? You've told me you've had fifteen women.'

'Yeah, but I'm stuck with you now, aren't I. A woman other men have screwed. When they see us in the street, they will gloat to themselves, I screwed that chick. Benny scored with you, Paula, yet you admit he's a sleazebag who didn't deserve you, whereas I gave up my marriage.'

'He knew he meant nothing to me, Brian. He cried, when I wouldn't have his baby. But down in the Valley we can make a fresh start, we can put all this shit behind us. Don't you want to make a fresh start? Don't you want to learn to love others? You're so full of hatred, Brian. I never knew an angrier man.'

'I never wanted anything so much, but do you love me, Paula? Not that it means a thing, coming from you. Probably not, because you still refer to me as a typical this, a typical that.'

'Of course I could love the father of my child. You think I would go through with this otherwise? I can be so good for you, Brian. I only did those things I did because I was screwed up from childhood. But you must give people credit for change. People can change. People can grow. Everyone who lives in this Valley will change, you wait and see. Diane assures me of it. You and I will change and grow. Isn't that what it's all about? Personal growth?'

'I'm just a bit sh-sh-shattered. You understand.'

'I try. Here we are at Graceland. I don't want to stay here.'

'Me neither.'

'Let's go straight out to the Valley.'

But they remain at Graceland, they have no choice. Someone has to give them a lift out, and no one can be found.

Brian Chegwodden: the pain he has caused other men by sleeping with their wives-to-be is now repaid to him, in trumps, courtesy of Paula. Thus, there is justice to it, which is why he cannot release himself. The pain he feels, though irrational, is underscored by the premium placed on a virgin wife, in those societies where pyjamas are worn during daylight hours, and stems from the habit the male of our species has of revisiting in idle moments—often first thing in the morning—the sexual conquests of his past life, to review them with complacency. No matter they came to nothing; for that is what they did come to, in a biological sense, if the mating were unproductive; and Postmodern women go out of their way to ensure such matings remain unproductive. No matter that men understand, more fully as they grow older, that women, too, will often copulate with men they despise and detest, through convenience, for fear of the consequences of falling in love. No matter that, as Brian has learnt, those who make tallies will be tallied against: there is no possession more fundamental, to a man, than the body of his woman. No matter that he can never possess her; she is his only possession: no matter than he can never know her, there is no knowledge he is more loath to share. To share a woman with another man is to experience diminution: but to copulate, within a closed, promiscuous society is to be annihilated.

Fergus MacAnaspie has the nascent phalanstery engrossed as he recounts the killing at the coupe. He has reached the point where the body is found, when he stops, and pulls out his tobacco pouch. His line of patter owes much to his father, who grew up in those enviable days when bushmen took their yarn-spinning, as part of bushcraft, seriously. If you couldn't hold a mate's interest in the pub, or over a campfire, or whiling away the hours spent walking next to a dusty dray, or slumped in a sodden saddle, you missed out on work, being deemed selfish, or stupid. So you talked to yourself, till you had your own style, your own range of proverbs and one-liners, and you knew the value of a pause: you knew when to air a speculation, as you took a sip, or bite, or drag, or went to check the hobbles. Fergie's in the habit of rolling a smoke, which takes time, as he does it one-handed. And while thus engaged, he might field a query, but he won't be drawn as to what might happen next.

'Wasn't done with a slug gun, neither,' he says, his tongue eventually free. 'Didn't know what had caused it, at first, thought he mighta broke a chain, but the saw's there and no blood on the saw. Well, I mean, there was blood on the saw but it wasn't *swimmin* in blood. Blood everywhere. Reckon the wattles'll be jumpin from the ground, ever seen grass where a cow's bled to death? Nothin beats blood for fertiliser. Had an old bloke used to order blood from our abattoir, just to put on his roses.'

'Sounds like our man, Ginnsy. Gotta be the same guy.'

'Coppers are on the job now,' concludes Fergus. 'Made the regional news and the front page of the local paper.'

'Hard to believe,' sighs Diane Zoshka. 'How things change in a day. We come down here to evade a police state, and now this idiot, this murderous fool ...'

'Hang on, Diane,' objects Michael Ginnsy. 'Gwen manifested

329

this gunman. Which is why, upon reflection, I wasn't all that upset. Member how you kept askin, Nisi, why wasn't I more upset? You all thought I made it up, but that's cool. Yeah, that's cool. I forgive. See I thought that gunman mighta been a phantom, who disappeared when Gwen passed on.'

'Get a look at him? I gotta get back to work, mate. I got payments on me rig.'

'I saw what I thought was a purple demon on the Flat. Do we believe in demons?'

'Really,' says Nisi. 'It's apparent we can't have Michael giving evidence.'

'Ar, the police won't listen to me anyway, Nisi. I got busted by 'em not long ago. Sposed to be reportin to 'em now.'

'Is anything missing from round here?'

'We wouldn't know what to miss, man.'

'If this character's living rough, he nicks what he needs from somewhere. Speakin of which, you wanta come back to the house now and grab the gear, Att? While I'm free?'

'Right,' says Attis. 'And maybe these guys would like to come and we can make a push on the tools.'

'Hey, where's the flour?' Nisi checks through the order.

'Left it up top with Fiona. She kind of twisted my arm. Wants to make a batch o' pancakes, boys!' Fergie winks. 'Knockin her up a shelf later.'

'I beg your pardon? You left half our provisions in the cave? Oh really, Fergus. We have no flour.'

'I don't mind runnin ya back to town, niece. Your credit is good with me. We'll drop these boys at Wonderview, then duck into Orbost, and you can buy all you need. Cheaper in Orbost.'

'What is this' inquires Olaf. 'We don't need a commissariat.'

'I'll come,' says Diane.

'I'll stay,' avers Annunciata. Only Annunciata observed the glance Aloysius flashed Tim, at the mention of someone living rough. Her years in the classroom have taught her the significance of such a glance. Those boys know something.

'Saw ya comin,' laughs Fiona, from the cave, as she shoos the flies off the flapjacks. 'Water's boilin. Introductions later. Hope yez're hungry. Siddown 'n eat.'

She's counting, with a fat finger, hoping there'll be chipped enamel plates and cups enough to go round, but there won't.

'Now we know where the flour goes. We hope you don't hurt the glow-worms, Fiona. They don't like methylated spirits.'

'Well, stuff 'em,' opines Fergus, 'cause a woman's got a right to cook. My word, these are lovely, Fiona. Never liked damper 'n cocky's joy.'

To her credit, Diane simply grabs Attis' hand and laughs, hilariously. The cave has been taken over. Fiona, though limping, has swept it out and cleaned it out, and obviously sleeps on both makeshift beds.

'I haven't any lemons left. Will you have ants?'

'You shall ave a lemon tree,' replies Fergus. 'I shall buy you one. Meyer or Eureka?'

'This is what it's about, man,' confides Michael Ginnsy to Balthazar Beauregard. And where it's at, they've been forced to share a billy lid on the lip of the cave.

Balthazar is bound to concur, because the thought was there. Refined flour, sugar and tea is rubbish tucker, but the thought was there. Fiona is an asset to a commune. Good vibes. All she needs is education.

'Ever smell kibbled rye hand ground in a stone mill, Fiona? We'll get you some honey, too. When I was back up north, Att, I could hear the drones buzzing, man. *Love* to hear the drones buzzing. Made some drone jewellery once. Reckon wheat'd grow in this Valley?'

Balthazar Beauregard: speaking as one who was once fool enough to try to make a living from 50 hives, I find it hard to conceive this fancy that twenty-plus people could live off ten. No way in the world could twenty-plus people live off 2000 hives, today. It's your overheads. The day of the small beekeeper, like the day of the small farmer generally, is gone. It was gone by 1968. I pulled a trailer, with my Jowett Javelin, from one end of this country to the other, chasing the flow, I didn't live extravagantly. I dossed down in my portable

331

extraction caravan by night. I requeened religiously, I never employed labour, yet I was back at Australia Post, begging for my old job, within two years, because I couldn't make a quid. There are queen-breeders making money today, but that's like teaching jazz studies. Still, we have our dreams.

The *Ballad* contains a reference to mead. Like the medieval monks, the communards wanted wax, so must have made mead from the honey they robbed. It's like a blue vein cheese, mead, you make it without hardly trying. You just extract your comb uncapped.

'Who's this cat?' inquires Eugene Ecks, who is riding in the cab with Fergus and Olaf. They zip along, Fergus priding himself on his four-wheel drifts through every corner. Communication between cab and tray is facilitated by a lack of windows.

'Got a guitar on his back and a frisbee in his hand. Kap'n Kaos! Who's this guy, man?'

'Looks like Grainger,' sighs Nisi. 'Yeah, I'd say it was Grainger for sure. Pull over, Fergus. He was at the Wake for Martin Luther King. He's at all the protests. Is there room in the Valley for Grainger?'

'*Course* there's room in the Valley for Grainger. *And* his blanket and his bunsen burner. Grainger! Stoked to meet ya, man, I'm Michael. This is Eugene, Balthazar, Olaf, Fergus, Nisi and Diane you know. See you got a guitar there, Grainger. Do you play guitar?'

'Grainger can't talk,' explains Nisi. 'He will not talk or cut his hair till US Forces leave Vietnam.'

Nor wash his coat, its furry vinyl lining vitiated by knots congealed round lumps of hardening liquids.

'No worries,' continues Michael Ginnsy. 'I prefer to speak uninterrupted. Since you're into guitar, Grainger, why not buy a copy of my solo album? Pcheow! I'll even give you a discount.'

'I didn't know you made one' says Olaf. 'When do we get to hear it?'

'Cut it in Memphis, man, but they didn't promote it, I haven't seen it in one shop. Jazz is death. Why is it people prefer shit, when they have the choice? I don't understand.'

'Hey, come on, man, don't dud democracy! Just buy more 'n more of everything. Anyway, what's the good of albums in the Valley, when we got no power to play 'em?'

'Oh we'll get the power on, Eugene. We have to have the power.'

'What? Power lines?'

'No, no. Mills. Water mills. Windmills. Turbines, man. We'll generate power.'

'We don't need power,' insists Nisi. 'Power was the beginning of the End. This idea machines can do everything better than people is bullshit. All you do is create machine-like people and make the Valley look like shit. Besides, ever since the world was draped with these high-voltage power lines, the human population has exploded.'

'I thought that was because of Chilean nitrates.'

'People think electricity runs through the cables, but it doesn't. It forms a field around them and we are literally *bathed* in it. Who knows what it does to our gonads? Who knows what it does to children that play near electric heaters? I have actually lived in a house where the light tubes glowed when the switches were *off*.'

'Far out. Got the address?'

'Ar, but we will just have low-level, non-ion ...'

'I want this matter cleared up now. No harmful radiations in the Valley!'

Fergie's eyebrows rise. 'Wot? Yez are goin to bed with the birds?'

'Not at all,' explains Nisi. 'We will purchase kerosene lamps to supplement our beeswax candles.'

'Ar, stuff that, Niece, everything'll taste o' kero. Ya can't see what you're eatin less they're right next to yer tucker, and they always leak. Darryl was forever gettin belted for fillin 'em on the breadboard. Cher-erist, who's this comin now? Looks like the law and we're unregistered.'

'Pull off the road.'

'Too late. He's seen us.'

'Got brakes?' Eugene, calm in a crisis. 'Hit the brakes and make dust, man. Olaf 'n me gotta get goin. Comin, Michael? Diane?'

'Stay cool,' advises Balthazar. 'Hang loose.' He pins Eugene to his seat, gagging him with a forearm.

Rude Boy like fe sit wit de feet pon fireplace, covered mit de blanket. No matter what de weather, he like to sit so. He's in the bedroom, covered in the wagga rug, feet in the chilly oil drum, when Annunciata, Tim tagging behind, clutching two lousy pups, locates him.

'Rude Boy!' Annunciata speaks in a soft brogue, but she holds her own in the classroom. This is the first time an adult has addressed Aloysius by his preferred name. Nonetheless, he hangs loose, and if surprised or pleased, doesn't speak, or move.

'Rude Boy! Would you take off that carpet from your head a moment please? I'd like to speak with you.'

Slowly, the wagga rug parts to reveal a tousled head of hair and a pair of compressed eyes. A sandy fist comes up to rub the eyelids, but the eyes don't open. Not even when a pup yelps.

'Oh Timmy, you hurt that little pup, would you put him down this instant?'

'But ...'

'Don't argue with me. There's a good boy. I'm to be your teacher, boys. Did you know that? Are you glad?'

'Dem want fe trick your mind.'

'Oh what nonsense, Aloysius. Anyway, whatever you may think of me, you're still to be taught by me. The others have gone up top, so we can have our chat. Boys, I want you to know that some of the things we'll discuss today will be confidential. Now who can tell me what that word means? Rude Boy?'

'No.'

'It means that God alone will hear, beside ourselves. Do you believe in God, Rude Boy?'

'Yes.'

'Good. Very good. We know that God will hear us, don't we, because God always hears us. We know we're not alone.'

'Yes.'

'That's right. We can never be alone. Now boys, I'll be straight with you. I have the feeling you have seen a stranger in this Valley, or you know someone who has. Am I right?'

334

Careful scrutiny of Tim's response is spoiled by the remaining pup suddenly wriggling free. Annoyed, Annunciata turns towards the elder boy, but as feared, the rug is back on the froward head.

'Rude Boy! Take off that carpet from your head. I want to speak with you this instant.'

'Me don' care fe talkin.'

'Oh what kind of talk is this, from a young man? Speak properly, Aloysius O'Looney! How old are you?'

'You can't give orders,' explains young Tim. 'We do as we please down here.'

'Do we indeed? Well, you've heard there's a bad man about. A very bad man, and do you suppose you can stay in this Valley, doing precisely as you please, when your mother could be shot dead at any moment, because you won't speak out?'

'We don't die,' insists Tim.

'No go a burial,' confirms Rude Boy. God knows where they got this notion. Rastafarianean, perhaps.

'I see I was wrong. Yes, I was wrong to have spoken at all. I think I'll just tell Mister Fergus you know more than you're letting on, and he can get it out of you. You work it out with him. Do you prefer that? And while you're thinking it over, I'm going to give this pup of yours a name, young man. See the way he walks behind you? Well, that reminds me of the dogstar Sirius, which walks behind the Hunter, in the night sky. Only out here everything's upside down, so the Hunter—that's the constellation Orion—He looks a bit like a saucepan, doesn't He? So we call him The Saucepan. God can take something plain, like a saucepan, turn him upside down, and he becomes a proud Hunter.'

Late summer '69. Police swarm over the countryside from far afield, but the Moody Valley Candle Company Co-op's luck is in. The car that decelerates till the driver's elbow is the regulation six inches from Fergie's, contains only the local sergeant of police, who has been assigned the Erinungarah region.

'G'day Fergie,' he drawls. 'G'day Att. When you boys gonna register this ute?'

335

'Any day now, Sarge. Still waitin for the parts.'

'Yeah and I'm still waitin for that miniskirt I ordered for me maiden aunt. Takin this team in for a haircut?'

'We just been out the Pass, Sarge. Landslide.'

'Yeah, someone told me it was blocked. Wasn't there an old couple livin out there?'

'Ar, that woulda been a while back now.'

'I see. So there's no way down, ya don't reckon?'

'No one's been out this way, Sarge.'

'Didn't think so.'

'These are friends of Att's, Sarge. From Sydney University. Lookin for a bit o' casual seed pickin.'

'Oh yeah. You still pickin seed, Att?'

'I would, but they closed the forest.'

'That won't be for long, son. We'll get our man.'

'I just wanta get back to work, Sarge. Got payments to make on me rig.'

'Bit of a wild goose chase, Fergus, just quietly. He'd be long gone from here. They're speakin to some kid down the coast, dunno what'll come o' that. Ar, it'll blow over. Just a stray shot, wouldn't you say? Can't have murder without a motive. You was there, wasn't ya?'

'Got there after you, Sarge. An' I don't think it was a stray shot, no.'

'Ah well. Suit yourself. So you reckon there's no point me proceedin?'

'Not really. Can't get down the Pass, and the firetrail hasn't been graded since the year dot. Peters out past the Ford. Covered in grevilleas.'

'You wouldn't take this vehicle on the main drag, would you boys?'

'No way, Sarge! This is just a bush basher.'

'Good. Then I'll spin round, follow you home, make sure you go.'

'Nice to have met you, Sergeant.' Michael Ginnsy is almost in tears. Some of these bush pigs seem human.

'Nice to have met you too, son. Behave. See yez, boys.'

'Thanks for the chokehold, Hollywood. Guess I owe you one.'

'He's blinkin his lights,' says Fergus, staring up and to the left. 'He wants me to pull over.'

'Pedal to the metal, man.'

'Owe me another one, Eugene. See what he wants again, Fergie.'

Reprise. The sergeant reapproaches them, and leans on the ute as if to issue a ticket.

'Just heard on the radio they found a camp other side o' Johnson's Creek, and it looks like the man we're after. Might head out there. Bet a quid it's that Yank.'

'Come again?'

'Yank in town recently. Shot through from R&R. Bet a quid it's him.'

'Yeah?'

'Ar, stupid war this Vietnam War. If you can't attract yer best young men to yer regular army, yer society's in trouble. See they're only conscripts, Fergie. Can't handle the stress, poor little bastards, so bein kids, they crack. They're none of 'em warriors. All the warriors are in the gaols. They won't take 'em in the army.'

Slap on the roof.

'See yez round like a record. How's Barney goin over there? I don't mean him, of course, he joined up. Be due home shortly, wouldn't he?'

'Reckon. See ya, Sarge.'

'Yeah, see ya boys. Have an enjoyable stay, kids. You should be right to go pickin seed, shortly.'

'You know what this means, don't you?' says Diane Zoshka, a little later. 'We're going to have to go out and pick seed.'

Seed picking: the only local work to be found was picking seed for the Forestry. The communards couldn't get into Obliqua Creek, on a daily basis, and there's not much work in Obliqua Creek. We read in the *Ballad* that Barbara was picking seed at the time of the second rockfall, and the *Ballad* locates the second rockfall during an 'Indian Summer', autumn. I've checked with

337

Barney MacAnaspie, and he remembers those girls picking seed. Loggers don't like greenies, but they don't mind pretty girls. So, typical of our modern world, there was no work offered the menfolk. Fergus and Attis and Darryl MacAnaspie were like a Loch Ness Monster, seldom seen. But when they showed up at the Rodeo, to do their annual picking up, in Phrygian caps with their hair in matted dreadlocks, wearing riding boots on just the one foot, and smelling like eucalyptus lollies from the Green Munga they ate when they were starving, then the pent-up resentment towards them in the district exploded in terrible fistfights, for there wasn't a cattleman or logger hereabouts didn't hate them, or envy them their debauchery. So that Darryl, by the time he donned his clown suit, was often black and blue from the resentment of his peers.

52. *Paula and Brian disturbed. A party at Graceland. Attis takes an irrevocable step.*

Shoulder healed, Kimberley Moon is visiting Wonderview. He'll be able to take the girls to town to shop. The men scout through the sheds, throwing what looks at the same time vaguely useful and useless into a heap. But it's only manners to give Horrie the final say on what can go, and he's ferreting round on his block, and it's getting late in the day, and as the journey back to the Valley takes hours, it's decided they will meet at Graceland, enjoy a last takeaway and some beers, then spend the night in flats 3 and 10, before heading off, at first light, with tools, provisions and fresh resolve.

If Nisi is worried about her boys, she is able to conceal her concern. On the way in she talks nothing but donkeys and ponies to stockboss Kimbo. Diane Zoshka, though not much interested, sees already the sense of using donkeys, and not the Kombi, for the transport of materials. The van, despite its payload, is the province of the men, while the donkeys fall under Nisi's jurisdiction, and women less incline than men to waste time standing round before work.

'In Ireland, they're usually pulling a cart. The ones I saw in Turkey had saddles of wood and stuffed rags, with just a girth strap. You fit baskets either side. If you train them properly, you only need a halter. I've seen them transporting bundles of lucerne each as big as a haystack, as well as a moustachioed Turk with his feet trailing the ground.'

'Only way to stop 'em, ay. Bit like my old scooter.'

'Could you suggest some tack, Kimberley? You've seen them up north.'

'Shoot 'em for pet food, there. Those bloody things o' Horrie's are s'posed to have come from a circus. One of 'em opens all the gates.'

'Yes, well that's our advantage, Kimberley. We don't need fencing. Our Valley is enclosed.'

'That's what you think. I'd probly try those military saddles, know the ones I mean? Those old Indian military saddles?'

'Now where would I get one of those?'

'My old man's got heaps. You can have 'em. Strip off all the leather bits. Fleecy skin for your saddle blanket. Probly get away with canvas webbin for your breechin.'

'Gee, thanks. Everyone's so generous. Iris has a sewing machine, so if we can buy some waxed thread and a leather-working needle today, I could run up some saddlebags from nylon mesh, or something like that, oh this is so exciting! We can use them on the track, you see, Diane. They're ideal over rough ground.'

'Great. Would you mind stopping at Graceland, Kimberley? I want to check on something.'

Paula Zoshka and Brian Chegwodden were balling. Paula has just time to pull on a pair of jeans, and is heading down the hall towards the loo, when Diane opens the door of the flat and the sun hits the formica.

Kimberley catches a glimpse of Paula's charms.

'Sorry, Paula,' says Diane. 'I didn't realise you were here. How'd you get in the flat?'

'Found the window unlocked. Excuse me.'

'I always leave a window unlocked. Is Brian with you?'

'Yeah, in bed. We were just having a nap. I won't be long, Diane.'

Brian, flushed in the face, emerges from the bedroom, exhausted by his struggle to get a purchase on the brass door handle. But what could he expect? This, after all, is Diane's flat. She has a right to entertain.

What to wear for that weekend, maybe lifetime, in the country? Brian has opted for Bermuda jacket, cravat and grey tailored slacks. His wife took all his safari suits and gave them to a derelict.

'Brian!' Diane rushes over to embrace the new member of the Family, but Brian wants none of it, and pushes her off, but not before she has smelt his must. He must share in the blame for what ensues.

'Good to see you again, Diane. So much has happened since last we met. Are these your friends? Do you think they could give us a lift out to the Valley?'

Kimbo's close-set black eyes smoulder, as they still do, when he's had his roids. He'd like to challenge this siss to a contest. Instead he snarls, from the corner of a thin-lipped mouth, 'You girls goin shoppin, or wot?'

'Let's just you and me go,' says Nisi. 'These are Diane's rels. They're going to live in the Valley.'

'*Wot*!'

'Oh?' Brian, a deferential stranger to incivility, sends out the journalistic riposte. And can he be hip, this surly, bow-legged, all but cross-eyed hoon in the stockhat? If so, he's not laid back.

'Ya gotta be *jokin*. Never seen a softer pair o' hands. You a facecream salesman?'

Fighting talk, ignorant too: Tai Chi masters have softer hands still. 'Hey, come on,' says Diane, 'that's enough of that. Don't act like kindergarten children, boys. Who knows, Kimberley? You may decide to live in the Valley yourself, one day.'

'Huh. How long yez reckon yez'll last? I'm busy this weekend. Gotta ...'

Mouth fallen, agape, aghast, Kimberley steps back, as though from a taipan. Paula returns up the hall from the loo, hands clasping naked bosom.

'Hi,' she says, with a grin, 'so this is where the rent goes. It's a bit of a hole.'

Brian would fain remove his jacket to shield Paula from Kimberley's gaze, but one brass button defeats him. By the time he's got the damn thing off, Kimberley has gone. They hear him drive away.

'What got into him?'

'Diane, he's a country boy. They're not used to this kind of thing.'

'What kind of thing?'

'Topless barmaids.'

'I'm sorry,' says Paula. 'Oh dear. It seems I've done it again. I thought, because of my hands, you know?'

'Fool,' shouts Brian. Upbraiding Paula, he storms off, to seek out the pub in which it started, his kismet. There he will find himself ordering jars from the same underemployed barman as Kimbo.

Kimberley Moon: father-to-be of Turpentine. You know what keeps most long-term marriages afloat? Joint tenancies. The fear of loss of assets. No assets, no fear. By the time Kimbo, a virgin when first we meet him cadging an inner tube, emasculates himself, he has slept (by his own admission) with Paula Zoshka, he has slept with Smitty's widow, Breda, to whom he was betrothed. But Breda wouldn't live in the Valley, she felt out of place there. He has slept with Monica Ecks. He has slept with Balthazar Beauregard, though claims nothing happened, and with Nisi Papadimitriou, for years, before she bore him his son. He claims he slept with Barbara Byng and Annunciata at the same time—but this being physically impossible, he must mean within seconds of each other. He could have fallen asleep on one, as it were, then dozed off on the other. Nor was his case peculiar. Excepting Attis and Diane, the communards of Erinungarah behaved as we behave in our dreams, but you see, there was no escape for them. When at length, they opened their eyes, they saw they were naked, and felt shame. Their Paradise had become a Hell. They felt the way a Rolling Stone feels, at a London party. Reduced to helpless laughter.

Sixty nine.

You think the contretemps might bring Diane to her senses? You'd be wrong. It has the opposite effect. It's a wonderful night for a Van Morrison moondance, as Grainger, the man who won't talk, has pot, so later that evening, in flat 10 Graceland, where the Family mills around, stoned—Bob on the gram, conciliatory beers, through Brian Chegwodden's generosity, and here, in this flat with them, members of the self-same Family, an American; and Michael Ginnsy, a blues legend who has lived and worked in the US, and spoken with Bob, which lifts your Aussie self-respect, makes you feel you rate; and Darryl MacAnaspie making Brian Chegwodden laugh, when, after his first taste of pot, he straightway cuts a fag in Fergie's mouth to pieces with a concealed stockwhip; and Kimberley Moon, legless drunk but able to relax, now he knows Paula Zoshka is pregnant; and Balthazar Beauregard dancing, alone, and Grainger dancing, with his guitar, and Paula falling about, as Attis tells them what happened back at Wonderview, earlier, when Horrie, in philanthropic mood, and suggesting the Sunshine Portable Engine could be useful in the Valley, if and when the Gap were cleared, to power the portable chaffcutter—purveyor of feed for the donkeys—actually got the damn thing going, though it hadn't started in fifty years, and couldn't stop it, to the point it came within inches of demolishing the shed, even though there was no water in the radiator; and Olaf Abernathy, when he tried to short it out with a screwdriver, he got an electric shock, and after the fuel was turned off, it kept running on oil from the sole remaining drip-feed lubricator, quite as though importuning them for a piece of the forthcoming action—it is then, because everything is going so swimmingly, that Diane Zoshka pulls sister Paula aside and says, I want to be alone with Attis tonight, I want to do it. And Paula replies she understands completely, and where does Diane want to do it? And Diane says, in flat three, in the bedroom where you and Brian did it. So Paula conspires to keep everyone else at flat ten, and Diane takes Attis to flat three.

When it is over, Diane needs to be held, but Attis wants to go for a walk; or maybe Diane wants to be held, but Attis needs to go for a walk. In any event, Diane remains unheld, Attis goes for a walk. He walks all the way to Wonderview, arriving on dawn. He walks, successively, through the town, the pasture on its outskirts, the wilderness. Who, in these Last Days, was not more attracted to the first than to the last?

Attis, however dimly he may realise, has forfeited the right to bypass All This. Through what he has just done tonight, with Diane, he has lost the right to hang loose. He cannot now view the World as it is, but has a stake in the World. He must fight for his rights, must maintain his lust, must defend his turf, must protect his child, his child's child. He has earned a life lagging. The Book of Wisdom, the Philosophical Rose Garden, has effectively slammed shut.

'Make Love, not War,' says Grainger's guitar sticker, but you can't make love and not make war. Wise up, Grainger.

No one can be hip who is sexually alive! O Feminist, O Christian, O Buddhist, hear this Truth. Stop torturing us.

As Attis leaves town, he feels pride in his new manhood. As he walks through moonlit pasture, he savours the prospect of Valley life. But as he enters Wild Nature, he is filled with remorse at the blood he has provoked, and the white limbs of the snappy gum shrink in horror from his tentative approach.

Better, no doubt, to marry than burn: but to enter the Kingdom of Heaven, one must cut the Gordian Knot. Celibates ooze.—Gordias, a Phrygian.

Brian Chegwodden: Christened 'The Commodore' by Darryl, on account of the Bermuda jacket.

53. *A debate, concerning the purpose of the co-op. Sister Annunciata sets a trap for the battery flatteners. Ginnsy's meeting with Mehmed.*

More receptive souls are stoned still, and they're all fuzzy as the conifer *cryptomeria*, when they reach The House that Glows next day. It's mid-morning; lugging the gear from the trail to the cave was a chore and a half. The kero fridge has been put, for the time being, in the too-hard file.

Paula Zoshka and Brian Chegwodden smooch as selfless Fiona serves them a snack of rancid fare, as the butter cannot be kept cool in the cave in the absence of a Coolgardie safe. Down below, it's kept in the Creek and the boys trot down to fetch it out.

This is the cave in which Paula conceived. It didn't happen in a sordid pub.

Some of the Family, covered in sweat, scratches and flies, haven't been to bed. But what would go down even better than a dip in the Creek, or a sleep, is a surf. Not far off, as the pigeon flies, holidaymakers relax, in droves. There are times in the Valley you can smell salt, but you never hear the sea.*

'Why is she always ravin on about *donkeys?* Know the first thing we're gonna do? Olaf 'n me goin up that Creek to fetch that other battery down.'

'Yeah?'

'Yeah. I had trouble acceptin we have a phantom battery flattener, but I say someone sneaks out at night to listen to the radio. I destroyed the tapes.'

'Aha! The radio.'

'Well we'd hear them, if they were blastin the horn. I, too, have known the thrill of groovin all night to the AM tuner, as it drifts in and out, but I don't like the Beatles. I prefer the real thing. Makes you feel less lonesome in the countryside, a radio, but we must have charge in the battery, boys, or we got no clean clothes, or radio. See we wash clothes in the back of the

---

* On the day of Attis' Passion, the *Ballad* says you could hear the sea in the valley. But that was a very strange day.

344

van, by putting them in a can with some soapy water, then driving over rough terrain?'

'Wouldn't be us, man. Must be the kids.'

'Don't blame my children! That's too easy.'

'Never mind, Nisi, we have two batteries, we can swop them round, so one's always charged. We lucked out that we lost that other bus over the cliff, when you think about it. I'll take the radio out, and put it in my room, for safekeeping.'

'But you don't like rock 'n roll! You don't like the Beatles!'

'There is Dead People's Music on the ABC. Classics. I wouldn't mind listenin to the news, either, see what's goin on. I could never hear it at home, cause my grandfather clock always drowned it out.'

'Ar, that's not what's goin on, man. *This* is what's goin on! People smile, and make love, and throw frisbees, but that never makes the news.'

'Now we have hives and foundation,' says Balthazar, 'Att and I grab the bees. Right, Att?'

'Just so long as someone else makes a start on the garden, Balthazar. What about you, Diane?'

'I feel like punching you on the nose, you fucking *deadshit*. What's wrong with you? How could you treat me like this, after what happened between us last night?'

'But you didn't think he could respect you, Diane, after what happened between you last night? Hey come on, you guys, lighten up. You're bringin everyone down. Better the second time.'

'I am a gardener,' explains Brian. 'Why don't *I* oversee the garden?'

'You could oversee the garden from here. We want someone to work in it. Well, I guess Grainger 'n me get the job haulin Kombi outta that bog. How we sposed to communicate? I got outta Nam, Grainger. Won't that do?'

'Guess Fergie'll let us know what happens with that other business.'

'He was in his rig, glued to the citizen band when last I saw him. Maybe Diane's right. Maybe we should all go pickin seed. We're gonna need money.'

'Only till we're set up!'

'I'll be gettin guidance in the Sacred Grove this evening. Olaf 'n me gotta pass through it to fetch the battery down. We won't get back tonight, so can we take some pancakes, Fiona? Thank you very much. You know, I think we're a bit inclined to forget the reason we came down here in the first place.'

'And what was the reason *you* came down here in the first place, Michael? I'd been meaning to ask.'

'I'm a bit inclined to forget, Nisi. Could be I got lost, lookin for a way through to the coast. I still remember how blown out I felt, when I came through the Gap and saw the Valley, though.'

'Did you think then that only a few months later you'd be down here playing a part in all this?'

'I *do* remember this incredible feeling of elation, but I often get that, when I'm flashin DMT. Now I'm straight, all I can see is the amount of work I have taken on. Oh man, I don't see how I'm gonna get through it in a lifetime.'

'Depends how long you live.'

'Depends what we're about. We tryin to create another LA? I thought the idea was to get back to somepin more environmentally friendly.'

'Right on, man. Good call.'

'But already we're settin up these hives. Why aren't we huntin for wax?'

'I dunno. Hollywood? That was your idea.'

'It's a question of survival and management. Honey, salt, powdered milk, wheat, keep forever, if you store them properly. Add a few sprouted beans and seeds, you have the survival diet. Plus, I thought wax was going to provide the commune with a small cash flow. See, if you want to go on the dole, they're going to know you're down here.'

'But some of us are cleanskins!'

'That's not the point. If we're gonna pick seed for a cash flow. . .'

'You don't need to earn a living, man. As ArBuckyEf teaches, the living has all been earned for us, forever. We're all on welfare, whether we like it or not. We all depend on the air, the water, the plant life, on every other human being, and every dollar in that dole is one less dollar for makin napalm.'

346

'I don't think I can get you a start anyway. The Forest is pretty much a closed shop. And frankly, I don't know of anyone else hunts honey. I just didn't know any different. I didn't realise you could keep bees in boxes. I mean, I'd seen lots of hives, but none of them had bees in. They were always stacked in sheds.'

'Now that's gotta be tellin us somepin.'

Attis smiles. 'I remember Darryl used to keep his silkworms in the hives at home.'

'That's it!' exclaims Paula. 'We can make silk! We can grow mulberries and keep silkworms!'

Eugene rises, shouldering the sack of eleemosynary spuds. 'Settle down,' he grins. 'Aim o' this game is a dome 'n a dope crop. Let's keep it simple.'

The characters in general: Kimberley Moon said a funny thing to me once. He said there were times, in that Valley, you felt the basic human identity. There were times you felt you were on the trippy eccy, you couldn't tell one person from another.

Annunciata, in Fergie's absence, divulges to Attis her concerns over the boys. The instinctive need to confide, *sotto voce*, in a man is a legacy of convent life, but it causes Diane Zoshka, who would have been unfazed by it yesterday, annoyance today. To show this, she belts at the ground with her mattock till the Valley resounds to the blows, but Annunciata ignores her, and Attis has no clue, ever, as to why Diane behaves as she does.

'The boys know something,' confides Annunciata, whispering, so the others won't hear. Attis, having shown Eugene Ecks how to work the strainers, leans on the defunct tank, contemplating the frisbee. 'I believe they have seen the killer in the Valley. Do you want to speak with them now?'

'There *is* someone else in this Valley. I have felt that for some time.'

'Then you must speak with the boys, Attis. They need a man's approach.'

'Michael thinks they sneak out at night to listen to the van

347

radio. That's why the battery is always flat, oh well. They wouldn't go further than the van. If they have seen someone, that someone is in the van, at night, or somewhere between the Pass and the house.'

'Is food missing?'

'I do recall them telling their mother they lost some perishables in the Creek. Mind you, that's easy done. But seeing they're her boys, maybe we should involve her in this discussion.'

'I have to tell you all boys are less truthful when their mother is present than when she is not. You're a boy. You know what I mean.'

'I do try to be honest, Sister. At times I think I succeed. Let's go to the house. Diane! We're just going to the house, to talk to Nisi.'

'Could you bring us back a drink, please?'

'I don't think so. Fiona took the cups. She struggled down the track while we were away, according to Annunciata.'

'Oh Attis, you are going to have to call a meeting.'

'Is Attis in charge?' Brian Chegwodden wipes his brow on his silk cravat. 'I don't care, as long as I have a vote. I mean, I was a member of the advance party.'

'God, you're an arsehole, Brian. Isn't it obvious, even ...'

'Don't call me a journalist, again. Would you like to be called a schoolgirl? I don't care who's in charge, just so long as I have a say.'

Diane hurls down her mattock. Her fingers are blistered and the blisters broken.

'Why the fuck *are* you here? Is this material for a feature? Exposé! Correspondent speaks! My life with the carefree hippies.'

'Oh what's your problem, Diane?' says Paula, barely missing her foot with the fork. 'It's supposed to be all Love and Light here, and you're like a bear with a sore head.'

'Hi,' says Brian. 'How bout this? I propose we form a circle, before returning to work, and quietly think some positive thoughts and share some warm fuzzies.'

The noise is Diane, choking through tears. But Grainger, who forgot the length of pipe for the strainers and is passing by on his way back to fetch it, mimes enthusiastic acquiescence, and pushes them together, till they do form a circle.

Nisi Papadimitriou watches from the kitchen window. They hold hands, as Balthazar leads them in a chant, the words of which are unimportant here. Round and round the nascent garden they weave, holding hands, heads held high.

Olaf is holding Paula's hand. How beautiful that woman is, thinks Nisi.

'Sanitary *napkins*! Oh Nisi, you must be joking. What is this? A kibbutz?'

Eugene Ecks groans. 'Shit,' he says. 'We're gonna talk about sanitary napkins now. Aren't there more important things, like, for example ...'

'The issue of napkins,' contends Nisi, 'raises the issue of sewage in general. And frankly, the existing toilet arrangements here are totally inadequate. *Is* there a septic system? Does it need pumping? Has anyone so much as looked? I strongly suspect, from the stench, that people have been ... oh Grainger? You want to write something down.'

'How's he gonna know when the Vietnam War is over?'

'He'll hear it on the radio, same as you.'

Attis looks at his watch, but it can't tell him the time till he unclips the chocolate leather hood, as it's one of those ex-service jobs, common in pawnshops, in the mid-60s. When he does look up, it's at Annunciata, and this is the final straw, for Diane.

'And when do we get to hear what's going on between you and her, Attis?'

Annunciata looks at Nisi. 'It's OK,' says Nisi. 'You can tell them.'

'I didn't want to raise the matter,' says Annunciata, 'till the boys left the house, but I think they're leaving now. Yes, there they go. I can see them.'

'Keep away from the window,' warns Attis. 'Just keep talking, please. We think we know where the boys go, but we must give them time to get there.'

'It's not like them at all,' explains Nisi. 'Someone must have threatened them.'

'There *is* someone else in this Valley. I knew it the moment we crossed that Ford.'

'Just a moment,' objects Brian Chegwodden. 'What evidence have you for this?'

'Att's a bushman,' explains Balthazar. 'He knows about these things. A true bushman has the intuition of a yogin, or an Aborigine. Even *I* know when a campsite has been used, though I couldn't tell you how. And don't forget, this is the man who uses birds to find wild hives. He knows this place.'

'Then what do we do?'

'Why, just keep discussing the toilet arrangements, for the time being. Give them ten minutes or so, then we'll go out after them. They're going to the van. They listen to the radio.'

'That'd be right. Fuckin little *bastards*, selfish as sin, the pair of them.'

'Olaf, I have to tell you I can no longer think of you as someone special. Understand?'

'Suits me, Nisi, great. Terrific. It's been a downer, for too long.'

'I'm so relieved you feel the same way. I want my boys to think of all the men here as their fathers now. I don't think anyone should have exclusive rights of any kind. Does anyone?'

'I don't want to raise yer boys,' says Eugene. 'Makin 'em's the only fun in the whole process.'

'Don't be such a fascist, man. Can't we break the endless chain?'

'Hey,' says Diane. 'I think it's *marvellous* Nisi and Olaf have shared this moment with us! If only we could all be so honest. It can't be easy, but OK, here goes, I'll try to be honest too. I was jealous, Annunciata, because of the way you look at Attis. He is so handsome. You see, we had sex for the first time last night, and I think he was disappointed.'

'With himself, probly.'

'I'm sure he wasn't disappointed with you, Diane. You may be straight up and down, but you have character, kid, you have spunk. Now your sister's got a lovely pair of knockers there'd choke a mule, but she is not as pretty as you, why? Because she has a mousy personality.'

'I wonder how Annunciata must feel about this? People screwin outta marriage 'n stuff. I have to say I feel uncomfortable around ex-nuns. I was brought up to hate Tykes.'

'Oh this is *fantastic*,' avers Diane. 'This is marvellous. We're making real progress at last.'

Diane Zoshka: all for honesty. Saw no reason why people should not have sex, or defecate, in public. But the only people outside the Valley who ever did were Eskimos in igloos.

More than a mile of sheer cliff demarks Fool's Dope* Flat from the Sacred Grove. Even so, the cedar cutters would have got through, had they exploited this Valley. They got to the cedars before the roads came. From the Shoalhaven to the Daintree, they left no cedar brush untouched. Ergo, this is Spaceship Earth's southernmost stand of *Toona australis*. It is well concealed, can't be seen from up top, and yields to pencil cedar, south to the Howe Range.

The scramble to the foot of the Falls would have been a daunting rock climb, had not Phryx Pfingstl constructed a path, on the west face of the Gorge. About a hundred feet above the Creek, it consists of footholds cut in the rock and a rope to which you can cling, if you feel like a tear on an eyelash, as they say in the Pamirs. Gwendolyn Bletherstone Mayall could negotiate this traverse, so it can't be all that difficult to do, but there's one part where the rope has snapped, and this gives pause, like glass at an intersection. A bridge, consisting of a gum log, about two feet in diameter, spans a gap too far to leap, thirty feet from where the path sets out. Gwen had faith enough to stroll over, Phryx could stroll over too. But Michael Ginnsy opts for caution, and scrambles across on his hands and knees.

It's twenty-three years since he did any serious crawling. He'd be safer walking, ay.

The thought occurs to him midway, how would you carry a battery back?

He glances down. It's hard to see; a mist has blown up, in

---

* *Lycopus australis*.

the wake of a southerly. Cold too, almost dark, he hadn't realised how late it was. He might turn back, he should, but he
can't, he won't. Gumption: he has it.

Glancing down was a mistake. Ginnsy wonders how deep's
that water? What happens if you *do* slip? He sees he must
straightway return and spend the night among the Shining
Gum. But about to swing round, midlog, he sees a sight puts
his heart in his teeth: a man in a jean jacket, with the arms
ripped off at the shoulders, and a red felt cap, wades upstream,
holding a gun over his head. Ginnsy, in haste now to get off
the log, slips, and while able to correct himself, dislodges in the
process his top hat, which plummets to the Creek, hitting it
with a thwack. Petrified, he observes the subsequent motion of
the red, white and blue artifact. Will it sink?

The man in the red cap turns round now. Ginnsy can see his
face; not distinctly, because of the hour, but well enough to
recognise him.

Having noted the topper, the killer makes for it, but the hat
is heading for the sea. One shot, however, fired from over the
head, rips an exit hole big as a fist. Grabbing the now mutilated
topper, pouring water out the hole, the killer looks up, towards
the log. He points, deliberately, his rifle at the log. But his
purpose is just to get a better view of proceedings, through the
telescopic sight on the barrel. Laughing, he heads back
upstream, renouncing the red felt cap for the topper.

'Have the police found my other camp?' he shouts, of a
sudden.

'How should I know?' replies Ginnsy.

'Because you went out. You know.'

'I know you're a *maniac*, man, to have shot that old couple!
I recognise you. Why'd ya shoot the old couple for, man?'

'Because I had a contract to fulfil. Did the police find my
other camp?'

'You better believe it. You should turn yourself in.'

But the gunman, scorning further response, disappears round
the bend.

It's dark now, too dark to move. Ginnsy spends the night on
the cliff. He reviews his entire existence. If he had one J and
the roach to eat, he could make less sense of it than usual.

At first light, he presses ahead. There's no trace of the gunman in the Sacred Grove, or in the Kombi, which sprawls, like a native bear in the clutch of a leatherwood tree. But thankfully, as if to prove the encounter was no acid flashback, the red felt cap has been left, abandoned, at the terminus of the Cliff Climb. It's not a bad cap, as caps go, and when your hair is three feet long, you've lost your hairnet, how ya gonna get your gennie brushes sparkin with the engine runnin?

Thus it was the Phrygian cap first found its way to Erinungarah, though whether of French, Phrygian or Roman provenance we cannot venture. And from Erinungarah it spread, in modified form, to Wozzawunwun, and thence; to the ski slopes.

Mehmed Contramundum: hailed from the Caucasus, the ancient world's recruiting ground for elite soldiery. It was here the Mamlukes, and later the Ottoman Janissaries, undertook their raids for boys. Both these great warrior sects were celibates, who reproduced by seizing the best efforts of the 'breeders'— for whom they felt a contempt on a par with that of the Postmodern homosexual. We read in the *Ballad* that Mehmed, against Diane's wishes, adopted Attis; thus, Attis had no biological father, but was twice adopted.

Warriors, priests, and *a fortiori* the Crusading Orders of Knighthood, fear the debilitation of sex, to circumvent which, they reproduce through recruitment. But Mehmed illustrates graphically the temptation to which the Templars succumbed. As the Greenbrown man, he repents him of his crimes, and Cybele honours him, Defender of the Grove.

The red Phrygian cap Mehmed wears is a cap that signifies Freedom. And they sought, and were granted, Freedom in the Valley, but a Freedom premature and ineffectual.

54. *A journey to the Seven Sisters. Dialogue with Mehmed. Eugene*
reveals the meaning of the dome.

When Michael Ginnsy returns round midday the next day, he
finds the Family in the kitchen. Having listened to his account
of his journey, they grow belligerent, in their confusion.

'Did you get to the Grove?'

'Yeah.'

'What happened?'

'Nothin.'

'You receive Guidance?'

'No.'

'Why not?'

'Didn't ask. Didn't like to hang round, man, I figured that
guy could be anywhere.'

'He woulda shot ya back at that log bridge, if he was gonna
shoot.'

'He could change his mind. In my experience, people are
unpredictable.'

'Michael was brave to have done what he did.'

'Can I look at the red cap, please Michael?'

'Yeah, it's a beauty, isn't it, Paula? Shame I lost the topper,
though. Shot dead. That was the only hat I owned, fitted most
of my hair in.'

'So he admits to three shootings.'

'Four, including the topper. Well no, not exactly. But he did
ask if the coppers found his other camp, so he must know the
police are after him.'

'We have to talk,' says Attis.

'What about Cindy?' inquires Eugene Ecks. 'We take her
into town, there's every chance she'll come straight back. She
got her mother's personality. A determined child.'

Cindy Ecks it was, in the van with Nisi's boys, Aloysius and
Tim. When the boys, having sneaked to the van to flatten the
battery through the radio, were surprised, taking in Mary
Hopkins singing 'Those were the days, my friend,' Cindy Ecks
was with them, and the boys admitted they were hiding Cindy,
and feeding her.

'Let her stay. What harm can she do? I still can't fully

comprehend how she got down here by herself. What a story.'

'Gonna write a feature on it?'

'Shut up, Diane, leave him alone. Christ, you're a bitch.'

'Takes one to pick one.'

'Sister! Sisters! Less honesty.'

'Poor Monica. She will be distraught. I must contact her at once.'

'And while you're doing that, Nisi, would you mind askin Calvin for more money?'

'How does that guy get out of the Valley? Is he climbin a cliff, or what?'

'Not hard to do. But he'll be stayin here now. Where else can he go?'

'Gotta get rid o' the cunt.'

'If only we knew who he was.'

'Oh, I know who he is. I recognised him. He was at the Wake for Martin Luther King, that big, tough guy, with the beard and the tatts. You know the one I mean. The Arab.'

'Oh *no!* Oh my *God!* Attis, you don't suppose?'

'I don't suppose, Diane. I just look up and listen to the trees. And I had a dream, at this table, last night.'

'You sound like Martin Luther King.'

'Yeah, don't lay your dreams on us, man, we beg. Last place I lived at, that's all they ever did.'

'Shut up, Hollywood. Take no notice, Attis. What did you dream in yer dream?'

'Hey, I see Fiona struggling down the track,' says Annunciata, who's always staring at the track. 'She has a big tray of food with her. She's such a dear. Someone should help her out.'

'Where are those boys? They should go help.'

'In disgrace. Battery flatteners.'

'I shall ignore that. Cindy wanted to see the swimming hole. I thought it would be safe.'

'Poor Fiona. She was working with delinquents, you know, and it's so very hard. They don't like people who are too fat, or too thin, or too young, or too old.'

'I dreamt I met this man you mention in the cedar grove. He means no harm.'

'I said to him, Attis, I said, ya should'ta shot that guy for cuttin that eucalypt, cause they're bastards, right? They're the enemy. They are what Gwen called Friends o' the Fire. We gotta get *rid* of 'em, fore they reduce us to the level of primitive savages, which is what they will do. But he just said, he's such a loser, ya gotta accept these things as they are.'

'Oh, what a heapa shit. I don't pretend t' understand his thinkin, but we gotta parley with the man. We gotta persuade him to hand himself in, cause we don't want the fuckin pigs down.'

'Someone should be working in that garden. Come on, Diane! Let's you and I go do it.'

'Are you joking, Paula?'

'No. I suspect there'll always be some terrible crisis occurring here. In the meantime, life must go on.'

'Far out, Paula.' Here's a girl with the right attitude, thinks Balthazar.

'I'd like to see those cedars, man, if you're goin up that way.'

'We all would.'

'Then why don't we *all* work in the garden, just for a bit, then all go up?'

'But what about first telling Monica Cindy is safe here with us? Shouldn't someone do that first?'

'Nisi,' explains Attis, 'I'd have to drive all the way back to town just to do it. See, we don't have the phone on at Wonderview. It may seem hard, but you must accept the fact of your isolation here. We can only deal with one crisis at a time. I'd be happy to go back and speak with Monica, but first I must speak with this man.'

'You don't know for sure he'll even be there, Attis. In the meantime, Monica's in agony.'

'I'll back Att's intuition. Hey, we're runnin out o' paper, Grainger. Use the same piece twice.'

'Mehmed Contramundum,' muses Balthazar. 'Who would have thought it? I made him a penis ring.'

'Let's not prejudge the man,' says Attis. 'In my dream he means no harm.'

'Fuckin murderous *cunt*. I don't want him in the Valley.'

'But you made the rules, Diane. He may not want to stay.'

'They say up north he's a mercenary. He's away all the time. Always overseas.'

'Great.'

Now Fiona doesn't feel that she can make it up the Creek, in the wind, so she remains at Koala Kottage with Cindy. A cool wind has blown up. Unbeknown to the adults, the boys have been up to the Falls many times. Michael Ginnsy and the rest of the gang follow Attis best they can in the wind, although Diane Zoshka has to tell him several times to slow down, so they can catch up.

'I can't go any further,' says Nisi P, catching sight of the log bridge. 'I shall have to go back to the Flat.'

'Course you can do it,' says Eugene Ecks. 'If old ladies can do it, you can do it too.'

'You don't care if I come or not. You *hate* me. You hate me and my boys.'

'Oh God, Nisi, did you have to make him *cry*? You know Eugene's been through Hell.'

'Let him raise two children alone. Then he will know what Hell is about.'

'You're so stupid, Nisi. You think you're so hip, yet all the things you look for in a man begin with "non".'

'Men? Where are these men? Oh, I'm sorry. I'm sorry if I made you cry, Eugene. I guess I *am* expecting my period, and I have run out of contraceptive pills.'

'Put your first foot in that hole up there, go on. You can do it. You know you can do it.'

'Meeting this guy will bring it back to us, see? If she was a soldier, she would understand.'

'Ladies before gentlemen, Nisi, go on. You go first. That's right.'

'So what do you think of Attis, Olaf?'

'He's OK. Why?'

'We three were the first down here, man. Don't forget that. Apart from Ginnsy.'

'So?'

'You hear him say he looks at trees for Guidance? Pretty spacy thing to do.'

'I've seen him do it.'

'Yeah?'

'Up top. The scribbly gums.'

357

'See, the point I'm makin, he's taken over. Which may, or may not, be a bad thing.'

'Well, it *is* his Valley.'

'Sure it is. Sure it is. But it's gotta be more than *that*. Oh wow! She crossed the log no worries! First try! Fuckin bitch.'

'Att knows this Valley, Eugene. His family are the only friends we have. We need them.'

'He's not claiming that, though, is he. No. He's claiming Guidance. And it's true. When you're alone, and you're in trouble, you *do* read trees, I've done it myself. Ah well, we'll soon know how good his Guidance is. He's stakin his judgement on this one, man. This'll make or break the guy's credibility.'

'Oh my God!'

'Unreal.'

'Faarck.'

It is hard to believe there were trees this size up and down the whole East Coast, so thickly on the Hawkesbury River— today a bright green drain—the pioneer had to work with a torch in his non-axe-bearing hand. But then, there were sperm whales in Sydney Harbour, and they didn't long survive the advent of the outcast. Cedar getters were just whalers who didn't want to wet their feet. These river dolphins were blue whales, sperm whales, relics, up for grabs. Any convict wanting to turn over a new leaf had them for minimal effort. What wouldn't they have been worth? Won't warp, cut easy, float, durable, branchless boles. Gone, within the century, but only the best parts of the best, and biggest, trees. What remained was left to rot, and crush the sapling growth.

'Att, these trees are *unreal*. Thank you so for bringing us.'

'Any camellias here, man?'

How to convey the UnReality? What a copse! Bastard rose-wood, grazed low by cattle into shrub on the plateau, fifty feet here. Lilly pilly and sassafras, which, together with the roaming blackwood, constitute the canopy of the bastard brush on Bunoo Bunoo—where rainforest and wet sclerophyll contend with each other, and rabbits and cows—big trees, in the absence of the frosts and winds, that kill the first seasonal shoots. Sassafras, of the fragrant leaf, seen on the red hill as a wanderer, sprouting, trampled, from a dozen suckers, where Angus steers scratch ornery hides and rip off all the leaves in spite, just to spit them out again: here, although close to its recognised range, a hundred feet tall. Who would dare fall one of these boys for golden deal, to be milled as mousetraps? Lilly pilly, commonly coppiced by cows, two feet high on the headlands of Wilson's Promontory, fifty feet tall here, five feet broad.

How many staves for a beer barrel could you knock out of this blackwood? You'd need a pair of binoculars just to see the crown. And the same holds true of this pittosporum, one of our esteemed native daphnes, an ornamental hedge in the Southern Highlands, often seen by letterboxes. Keep the Ventolin handy, when this bloke buds up. And above the decomposing logs, the stinging nettles, the kangaroo apple, above the filmy fern; lianas, the diagnostic feature of the warm, as distinct from the cool, temperate rainforest. Anchor vines, and here, interloping from the sclerophyll, the running postman, dusky coral pea, wonga vines, thick as a man's tattooed arm. Caving ladders, or the skill of a Tarzan, needed to find the leaves. All you can see from the gloom of the ground is a mess of tangled rope, like a drunken deckie's effort to throw a springer over an A-frame. And we could go on, we could fill books. Huge man ferns, and you would call them man ferns here, in the Tasmanian mode; coach-woods, one of only two native timbers to meet specifications for aircraft construction; logged here, so smallish, and suitable only for shoe heels and sewing machine bobbins, but with black wattle and Christmas bush, gum vine, native crab apple—all found here, or hereabouts—comprising the Cunoniaceae family, confined exclusively to the East Coast. And what can we say of these leatherwoods, except they make the best honey in the world? How the television botanists, the sawyers of the soft-wood mills, how the apiarists of Mole Creek, the backpackers from Stuttgart, how the organic chemists of Sydney Uni, the freelance photographers, how they would all like to get their mitts on this magnificent freak of Nature. But it can't happen, not while the local member is a mate of Horrie MacAnaspie's.

The Seven Sisters—for so they are yclept—grow touchingly close to each other. No lianas obscure them, no other species grow between. They grow straight up, and their canopy is a hundred and fifty feet above the Valley floor. The trunks measure twenty feet in circumference ten feet off the ground. The only comparable softwoods remaining on the island continent would be the bull kauri at Lake Barrine, on the Atherton Tableland in North Queensland, or maybe one of the twenty-three surviving adult Wollemi pine discovered by a canyoning abseiler in the Blue Mountains as recently as 1994. Check out the big bull kauri, multiply them by two, put them away, last of their kind, in some sacred, secret place; now you understand why the Family join hands and hug each other and weep and scratch deferentially the grey bark, to smell the red heartwood, sweet with ancient wisdom. Now they know why they came to this Valley, and are blown away that they came before they knew why they had come.

'Shoulda told us about these trees, Ginnsy.'

'I tried to, man, but words can only do so much.'

'Then ya shoulda written some music.'

'Come on! Is this a fit subject for a blues?'

'Beautiful, yaa, but it's all Maya.'

'Wake up to yourself, Balthazar.'

'How old would you say these trees are, Attis?'

'Bout a thousand years old.'

'Lie down and look up, Diane. Wow! Just lie down and look up at *that*. Great to see a trunk that size, swayin to and fro in a breeze. And listen to the creaking of the ship's timbers. It's like being on a ship.'

'It's more like a man and a woman making love.'

'Woohh! You got a leech here.'

'Wah! Get it off of me!'

Red cedar today abounds, but *diminuendo*. In the Kangaroo Valley, on the benches and gullies of the foothills of the Wollongong scarp, it may still be found a hundred feet tall, but never more than three feet wide. Can it, will it, grow again ever, as it grew in pre-European days? Until a thousand years, or more, have passed, non-scientists cannot tell. But the prospect of a fine cabinetwood maturing a millennium must be deemed remote in a world where the human population doubled over the past fifty years. World population, about 500 million in the time of Juvenal—David Suzuki says one billion, Paul Ehrlich about a third of that: I'd say they were guessing—was only one or two billion by the time of the Industrial Revolution. By 1990, it was five billion.

And yet in the 1790s, when the cedar getters were doing their ugly thing, it was found, back home, that coke could be used instead of charcoal, to smelt iron. Thus was preserved the pitiful remnant of England's native forest. You wouldn't have wagered much on the future of English oak, in 1700.

Estimated to have covered a mere one per cent of the Australian landmass in 1788, and back to maybe a quarter of that by the time of which we speak, the rainforest in the absence of fire is advantaged by the Greenhouse effect. But if climatic instability precipitates as some think it may a new Ice Age ...

The plant species of Australia survived well the last Ice Age. This was not the case in Britain, where more extensive glaciation caused many, if not most, plant species to become extinct.

But let's look on the bright side. See the tiny seedling that waits so patiently in the gloom of the forest floor for a gap in the canopy?

The mood in the garden later that same day is somewhat subdued. Attis has gone to town, and were it not for Paula Zoshka cracking the whip no one else would work, for what a day of contrasts it has been. Mehmed has ruined, with his wicked deeds and candour concerning them, the most beautiful experience. Moreoover, his implied presence in this Valley, down the track, forecloses what was open ended. These *Sagas* are meant to end with a Charles Manson, not begin with one. And he is still there, in the Grove, no doubt of the opinion he has every right to squat. Someone should have put him straight.

'I wish he'd just disappear, man, retrospectively. Know what I mean?'

Eugene Ecks yawns. 'He's raisin issues you don't want

to deal with. I back Att. He ain't no threat. Guy's seen too much combat. I seen plenty like him. He won't last long, in boob. Someone'll kill him. You don't last long with those attitudes. They make sense, only in theory. I seen plenty like him, in Nam. Nature works against 'em Hey! Know what I'm thinkin?'

'What are you thinkin?'

'That cedar tree that's dyin, man. We got the makings of a great dome.'

'Hey, what's going on here? You guys swinging the lead?'

'Oh hi Paula. We're just discussing where to put this fence.'

'Come again?'

'I'll tell her. The fence must go, Paula. See, what's the first thing you notice about this garden here?'

'Well now, Eugene, let me think. It's overgrown?'

Mehmed, guilefully representing himself as Defender of the Old Growth, had the Family half-disarmed by quoting Aldo Leopold at them: what he had done was 'right', he maintained, in that it tended to preserve the integrity, stability and beauty of the local biotic community. All the more, when Attis, shooting down a yellowing cedar leaf with seventeen leaflets—using Mehmed's point three-oh-eight assault rifle to do so—confirmed what Mehmed avowed; that the tree into which Phryx and Gwen had barely cut was moribund.

'Not a problem. Anything else?'

'No veges?'

He had said he had shot Phryx and Gwen, when he saw their assault on the Sacred Grove. And he had shot the youth who attacked the grey gum, only after having issued warning. Smitty, the ganger, present in the pub, had witnessed this warning, and now Mehmed was looking for Smitty. Having dealt with Smitty, he would turn himself in. He had made a gesture—token, because he now understood he could not persuade others to cease idle talk and join him in righteous action.

'No veges, but we can plant plenty, once we get the seeds. C'mon!'

'Soil needs lime?' Brian Chegwodden intrudes. He can't bear Paula to have a private conversation.

Paula Zoshka openly accused Mehmed of wanting to kill

362

Smitty, but Mehmed maintained he would not do so, provided he received something in return; namely, the right to retire to the Valley, which he preferred to any other place he knew, when once again he was free, possessed of a licence to be at large. He would not hide, it was not in his nature. But three concurrent life laggings could see him paroled in as little as fifteen years.

'Why'd you get involved with the Peace Movement?' Diane Zoshka, hoist with her own petard. 'Thought you'd be all in favour of war. I wonder you're not in Nam now.'

'What? And serve supremacists, who strip the leaves off trees?'

Back in the garden.

'I dunno bout that. Soil looks good to me, Brian. Nothin wrong with these roses. Hey, I'm talkin about *shape*, man. What shape would you describe this garden as?'

'Well, with the fenceposts falling down, it's a bit of a parallelogram.'

And Mehmed's last words? 'You will find, if you remain in this Valley, your thinking will change, Because it will need to.'

'It's a square, man. It's a *square* shape. Nature abhors the square. Ever grown dope in a square garden? And veges grown in a square garden, while they nourish the body, they don't nourish the spirit. They don't nourish the soul. What Ginnsy and I got to do here, is pull down this fence completely. We can't have our garden the same shape as that hideous fuckin square house.'

'You surprise me.' Brian has been waiting for the diatribe to manifest ironical intent. 'I didn't think, you know, that you thought along these lines, Eugene. So to speak.'

'Took me for a straight, did ya Brian? You're the revisionist here.'

'Oh I get it,' says Michael Ginnsy. 'The tree dying, like, that's an offering from Gwen.'

'Could be. See, we know what you're thinkin,' continues Eugene, his cold, hard eyes on Brian. 'You're thinkin this hippy bit is a heap o' crap, but that ain't so. The fools know, man! The fools know. Read Shakespeare, then spend a week in a dome, or better yet, read Shakespeare *under* the dome. It's a revelation, Paula. I was straight, well, sort of, and might have remained straight, had I never encountered the thought of ArBuckyEf. You see, conventional critical path conceptioning is linear and self-under-informative. Only spherically expanding and contracting, spinning, polarly involuting and evoluting orbital-feedback systems are both comprehensively and incisively informative. Reshape environment! Don't try to reshape the self-balancing, twenty-eight jointed, adaptor-base biped. And it's true, because it's realistic. Domes have a subtle influence. They change your thinking, cause you can't think square in a dome. See, Bucky's geodesic dome, it blends with Nature, man. It is constructed through triangulation, like Nature is constructed, and they're cheap, and you can put one up in a day. Dome building is easy. Girls can do it.'

'I do think we should blend with Nature,' says Paula, looking at Brian, in hope. He, in turn, is inclined to sneer, but he's not prepared to martyr himself in the cause of the Australian Federation bungalow. To think he picked this bum off the streets; he could have walked by, purchased a pie and a bottle and returned home.

'I don't understand what you're saying here.'

'OK. It all goes back to the *plough*. Where is the straight line in the human body? Why are curvaceous women so gorgeous?'

'Hey, you're right, man. The earth is round.' Ginnsy can dig this curvature rap.

'The earth is round, the sun is round, the moon is round, space is curved. People who live in harmony with Nature live in round houses. Yurts, igloos, beehive huts. I guarantee the native peoples who lived here had round houses.'

'Hey, that's right,' says Paula. 'Gunyahs. Isn't that what they're called, Brian?'

'They're called willy willies.'

'Sorry.'

'Friend o' mine wrote a book once, no one wanted to publish. It was called, *How Square Thinking Is a Terrible Accident*, that came about through the plough being Invented before the mouldboard that turned the furrow, with apologies to John See More. The early farmer had to plough his field at right angles, man, to break the soil. So next thing you know, he's got square fields, he's fencing square, building square, cities are going up on square grids, and we're startin to *think* square, like; we're not part o' *that*'—Eugene waves an arm—'cause that's unstructured. That's not square like us. Any wonder we feel cut off from Nature, when you never see a square in Nature?'

'Tessellated pavement?'

'You a city boy, Brian? Hell, I'm sorry for you. Why would a man want to live down here, who's hankerin for pavement. You belong in Drop City, man. Luke Cool and Peter Rabbit, they make panels from car tops. Buy 'em fifteen cents apiece in the US of A. Chop 'em with axes, caulk 'em with tar.'

'So you want to build a dome? Is that what you're trying to say?'

'Yeah, because rectilinear buildings are structually unsound. Gonna build us a dome here, then we'll tear down that ugly square farmhouse, with its unsound square rooms and square windows. But till we do, let's get this garden right. It must be circular, and all the plots should emanate from a point, here. Lemme draw it for ya, Paula, with a crooked stick.'

'You *are* a hippie, after all. So we're gonna help you build your house. You gonna help us build ours?'

'What's with this "yours and mine" man? He don't understand us hippies, Ginnsy. Poor guy! Lived all his life in a square house, went to a square school, writes square thoughts, on square sheets of paper, to be read by squareheads. Man, we're a *family*! Gonna build us this huge big dome, and we're all gonna live in it together. Right Paula?'

'Yeah, I'm not so sure,' admits Ginnsy. 'See, I promised Phryx I'd take care o' this place.'

'Best way you could take care o' this place, Kap'n Kaos, would be to tear it down completely. Then we relocate the materials in a more harmonious manner. After all, we're gonna need a floor for the dome. Gotta get into it somewhere.'

'We'll see what the community has to say on this. Michael?'

'Call him Kap'n Kaos.'

'No! I think it's cruel, Eugene, the way you call people by these cruel nicknames.'

'What did you want to ask me, Paula? And don't worry,

names mean nothin. They reflect on the people that give them. It's like giving a piece of *music* a name, you know? Man, the Namer.'

'I don't intend to be cruel. I just hate straight names, Paula. C'mon. Give *me* a name.'

'No! Give yourself one. I wanted to ask about the pump, Michael. Can we irrigate the garden, using the pump?'

'Oh. Irrigate the garden using the pump. Hmm. I don't know about that. I suppose you *could* irrigate the garden using the pump. Yes! Why not?'

'Is there a problem?'

'Not exactly. It's just the pump. Well, it's kind of that the pump.'

'C'mon. Spit it out.'

'It's a sacred pump.'

Even Eugene smiles and Brian has hysterics.

'What do you mean, Michael?'

'I know it must sound silly, Paula, and everything is sacred, when you're hip, but the rhythms that you hear, in the delivery pipe, when you put your ear up against it—the triplets from the engine, the slap of the valves, the counter-rhythm of the pump shaft gears—that is the rhythm Phryx and Gwen used for dances when they conducted ceremonies. Know the sound a bus makes, idling at a bus stop? Mind you, I can't see why we couldn't water the garden, at the same time.'

'And that's another thing about the geodesic dome. They are *amazing* in the rain.'

Michael Ginnsy: christened Kap'n Kaos by Eugene Ecks. As well as being tagged by Eugene and Darryl with these reductive sobriquets, the Moody Valley Candle Company Co-op communards adopted nicknames, to signify rebirth. But, after thought, and through fear of creating confusion, I have omitted these from my *Saga*, except in the case of those children born in the Valley, who had no other appellation.

55. *Letter from Barney.*

Late summer '69. Attis is sidetracked on his way to town, round dusk, by a low-loader blocking the road. There has been a letter from Barney MacAnaspie, which Horrie, over the past week, has surreptitiously memorised. Darryl pins Fergus to the stump-mounted pipe vice, as Attis drives up in the red Series Two.

'Why did you block the road? That thing has no reflectors. I might have hit it, in a fog.'

'Looked at all like a fog, my son, we would not have parked it there. Had enough for today, cunt? I'll let you go, then. Dad was keen for ya to drop in, Att. Got a letter from Barney.'

'You don't need to block off the road. I always call by anyway.'

'Don't keep goin on about it. You pickin tomorrow?'

'No. Have to make a phone call.'

'Here they are! All the boys are here now, Dad! Come inside, boys. Dad's got somethin he wants for ya to hear. Don't laugh, if he mispronounces words. Where you off to, Attis?'

'Have to make a phone call, Mum.'

'Oh. Who to?'

Attis looks at Darryl and sighs.

'Monica.'

'Monica!'

'Her daughter turned up in the Valley.'

'Phoor! Monica.'

'Now this won't take long, if yez keep quiet.'

Mudwasp, looking for keyhole, exempted. Charlie's slouch hat in Charlie's old chair, rising sun badge burnished with Brasso. Horrie, wearing his own campaign ribbons on his cardigan, dons reading glasses. 'Go change that shirt,' he snaps at Darryl. 'Take your places,' he instructs the others. 'Fergus, have the kindness to shut the door. Mum, you going to stay and hear this?'

'I should think so. I'm his mother, aren't I?'

'Darryl! See what's holdin him up. Pity it's not a rope round the neck. We should have called him the late Darryl MacAnaspie.'

'Oh that's a relief, Dad. I know now Barney can't be dead, or you wouldn't have made a joke.'

'I might of. Good God, is that you in a striped shirt with polkadot sleeves now? How dare you. Go and change again.'

'This is the only clean shirt I can find, at a moment's notice.'

'I won't have my brave eldest boy reportin to a man in a clown suit.'

'All right if I wear me football guernsey then?'

'You know your mother don't like the smell o' mothballs. Oh all right, under the circumstances, but hurry.'

'Were you thinkin of going by without callin in on me?' inquires Iris.

'No,' replies Attis, 'I was going to call by on the way back, Mum. Phone call is very urgent.'

'Ow many's down that Valley now? What's bein done about the road in?'

'Ssshh!'

'Right' says Horrie, 'we can begin. I received this from Barnaby. Goodday, he says. It may be of interest A Company, 3 RAR, all in APCs, cleared 1400 D445 NLF from an ARVN CP, in the town of Ba Ria, Phuoc Tuy Province, in recent days. The fire fight went on all night. Counting Long Dien, my regiment has now lost twenty killed, eighty wounded, but I remain fit. I am looking forward to seeing you all again, God willing. How's my wombat? Your loving son etc. Wish to God he'd put a date to a letter, and what happened to that wombat?'

'Ad to get rid of er, Dad. Comin through the screen door.'

'You wouldn't know when this was written. And the envelope's been trodden on, with a boot.'

'That'll be the postman.'

'This is the only letter we'll receive. Never a letter writer, Barney. You a letter writer, Attis? I hope so. Now the postscript. We have reason to believe that Long Dien, he says, which we are supposed to be protecting from the D445 is in fact their principal recruitment centre. You are not being told the full story. No, I don't suppose we ever were. That's it.'

'What's he tryin to say?'

'Search me. Main thing is, he saw action and survived. He can now consider himself a man. A real man.'

'Don't seem to know 'o he's fightin. Don't seem to know much.'

'Would you want to live in a communist world, Darryl? Would you be prepared to slave out your heathen guts on land you could never hope to own?'

'Might be a fairer system, ay.'

'Fairer system, my eye. You know what communism is? It's takin Christ out of His manger, and dumpin Him on a production line. Chairman Mao as Son of Man versus the moneychangers, minus the miracles.'

'Oh don't be blasphemous in front of these boys.'

'I'm not bein blasphemous. The early Christians were the first commos, Iris. Well, fair enough, I suppose. Don't much matter how you live, when you see yourself as only just bidin your time. Just waitin for that Last Trump says you can drop your bundle.'

'God and Mary forgive you, Horace MacAnaspie. You will be judged for that.'

'Don't waste your time preachin at 'im, Mum. Clear he don't believe in a Better World.'

'I have to go now,' says Attis. 'Excuse me. I have to make a phone call.'

Horace MacAnaspie: without his support, in the form of tools, advice, and so forth, the commune could have languished, and Horrie was legal owner of the Valley, during Autarky. When he died, he left it to Barney. Barney, like Horrie, is a good mate of our undistinguished local member, who quashes periodic moves to incorporate the Valley into the National Park by pointing out that the Postmodern Valley has little conservation value and that any attempt to seize it would so alienate the electorate as to prompt them to change their vote at the next election. By the time Horrie died, of a broken heart it seems, following the death of Fergus—and Kimbo tells me Horrie was never made privy to what went on in that Valley, though I do wonder at times to what extent Kimbo tells me 'the truth' and to what extent, like Clever Hans the counting horse, he reads my mind and gives me what I want: see, he needs to keep me coming back, I toss him a lump of sugar, I buy a second-hand book whenever we meet—Darryl had reopened the Gap Road, and Darryl began logging that Valley, following the illegal seizure of his sons, as he saw it, by the State. He logged the cedar. He made a lot of money in a short time, enough to go to gaol and buy a rig each for Harley and Norton, who, in due course, rejoined him. Those boys must be eighteen to twenty, by my reckoning, but they look ten or twelve, too young to drive. Darryl lets them take their rigs as far in as Wonderview. They sit up on a heap of cushions, nursing a two-litre bottle of Coke each. Only allowed to drive as far as Wonderview. Mystery men. As to the rest of them down there now, those ferals, they're in some way associated with Darryl's new wife, the girl with the buck teeth works at the bakery alternate Mondays. She got the sack from her job in the library, talking television all day. I had a hand in that. She was still at the library, though, when I moved here, August '91. The *Ballad* depicts her as driving off, each morning, in Darryl's F 100.

Harley and Norton only go to school alternate Mondays now.

56. *Barbara on the buses. Calvin's lair. Cindy located, Monica's remorse.*

Derek Frodsham, smiling as he scrawls some comment on a paper he is marking, is shocked to hear the door to his cell being bashed, as if by police. But, thank God, it proves only to be Barbara Byng, dressed as a bus conductress.

'Barbara!'

'Derek, you must help. I thought I'd call by on Mon, you see, but the place was deserted. In the middle of the school holidays! I found a key under the mat, so I let myself into the house. On the table, I found a note from Monica to Calvin, saying she was going away for a few days—a few days!—and would he look after the kids. Well. I could hear West Indian music coming from Alexander's bedroom, but when I got upstairs, I noticed that Cindy's room appeared to have been ransacked.'

'Oh. Was Alexander home?'

'No. But he can't have been far off. Anyway, Cindy has pulled all the clothes from her drawers, and strewn them about the room. I decided to wait for someone to come home. I waited almost an hour, Derek. Nothing. Then, looking about, I saw from a calendar on the fridge that Calvin was supposed to have been taking the children the day Monica wrote the note. But I don't think he could have turned up. Has he been at home lately? At your place, I mean.'

'No, I don't think I've seen him in weeks, now you mention it.'

'This could be serious. You know his work number?'

'Not offhand, but we can find it. I think he's in the Med School, isn't he? Where's that phone book. Still on the buses?'

'Oh yes. I was hoping they'd put me off at Christmas, but they always want to keep me on. It's a bore.'

'I'm not surprised. Ecks. Ecks. Strange name. Probably an Anglicisation of Ecksowicz. Here we are, Ecks, Dr Calvin C. That'd be him.'

'I could always go back and see if Alexander has come home.'

'Can't you ring?'

'He'd never hear the phone, Derek. I could hear his record player from the bus.'

'There's no answer.'

'You're quite sure he hasn't been at your place? Oh dear. It seems Monica left before he turned up, doesn't it.'

'That'd be her. We can go round to his lab. You want to leave your satchel here?'

'Oh no. My tickets and takings are in it. I can't leave it anywhere.'

'Suit yourself. I'll just finish marking this paper. It won't get any marks, it was due last November. You know much about Boltzmann? He was the first to formulate entropy in terms of probability, and he committed suicide. Anyway, see what you think of what I say here, I thought it rather wicked. Oh. I can't read it myself.'

'Derek, please! There's no time to waste. We must locate Calvin at once.'

'He should be somewhere about. Of course, these medicos don't keep the same hours as ordinary mortals.'

'I thought he was at the hospital.'

'Yes, but his lab is somewhere here. Let's take a walk in this direction. Poo, what a smell! What's the story with this Jan Palech burning himself in Wenceslas Square?'

'I haven't had time to think about it. Look, Derek! There's Calvin's name.'

'Dr Ecks. He should get himself a job at Brand X University, Brandeis. That's a joke. The door is locked.'

'Put your ear against it. Oh dear! Monica's told me he sometimes locks himself in his lab, for months.'

'Does he? Oh yes, I can hear running water.'

'He's in there. Go on, Derek, knock on the door. Break it down.'

'Calvin, this is Frodsham, old mate. Need to speak, cob. Urgent!'

'Hear a voice?'

'No.'

'I'm sure I hear a voice.'

'I'm not entirely convinced we should disturb him.'

'What? Oh don't be bloody ridiculous, Derek. His family is at risk.'

'Yes, but any man who can settle to work in Sydney, in January, Barbara.'

'I don't believe what I hear. From you, of all people.'

'I tell you what. Why don't we get a cab back to Paddo, where we can speak to this boy, what was his name?'

'Alexander.'

'He'll be able to tell us what's going on.'

'So you won't disturb Calvin.'

'We can't be sure he's in there. If he is, yes, I'd feel more comfortable with something to report.'

'What I've told you is not enough?'

'Who am I to judge? It *is* compelling. I appreciate your concern. Furthermore, if there is a problem, Calvin would wish to be informed, as he is very fond of his daughter. But against this, must be weighed a possibly irremediable disruption to his researches, specially if we disturb him for what proves to be no good reason. I mean, he could be on to something, Barbara. He might be inventing the morning after pill.'

'What, in this dump?'

'Oh you're so Australian.'

'I may lose my job over this, Derek, but I have a feeling about Cindy. Do you believe in woman's intuition?'

'Come come. What is science about? Oh no, you won't lose your job. You told me yourself you know the name of someone on every bus.'

'I hope she has come to no harm. She is such a lovely girl.'

'I'll buy all your tickets. How about that?'

They arrive back at the Paddo terrace to find another note on the table. This time it is from Alex, stating he has gone to stay at the beachhouse of a friend. No address, no phone number, no mention of Cindy, or when she'll be back, or when he'll be back. And the record player is still playing, thumping over a scratch.

'Seen Bob Gould lately, Babs? Someone told me the other day he's a former postal worker. That may well account ...'

'Derek, I did the wrong thing. I should have stayed here and waited.'

'It's all very strange.'

'Monica should not have had children, Derek. I've actually heard her abuse Cindy for ruining her figure.'

'Well, it wasn't ruined that badly. I never heard a woman get so many wolf whistles.'

'It's only because of the way she walks.'

'I see. Does her note say where she went?'

'I know she belongs to a tennis club. But she's been gone now for three days.'

'Mixed doubles, I dare say.'

'Derek, what are we going to do? Shouldn't we contact the police?'

'I'll pretend I didn't hear that. What's the time?'

'Oh dear. The phone. Shall I answer it?'

'I think so. Under the circumstances.'

'Hello? No, it's a friend of Monica. Monica's away. Who is it speaking please? Attis! Oh Att, it's Barbara here. Barbara Byng. No, we don't know where she went, and we can't contact her husband, *or* her son. Good heavens! Good gracious! No, keep her there for the moment, Attis, just for the time being. You have put my mind at ease. Goodbye.'

'Who was that?'

'Attis MacAnaspie. Ringing from Obliqua Creek. Can you believe Cindy was found in the Valley?'

'What Valley? Oh *that* Valley? Damn! Phone's ringin again.'

'You answer it this time. It may be Alexander.'

'Hello? Frodsham here. Oh, Monica. It's Derek Frodsham, Monica. Yes, I dare say you are surprised, I tell you what, I'll put you straight onto Barbara and she can explain things. No, Calvin's not home.'

'*Coward.* Hello? Yes, but have you any idea where your daughter, son, or husband is? Yes, that's right. Yes, I think you should, and the sooner the better. You're a disgrace.'

'Sorry.'

'Oh she's a bitch. And after all I've done for her. Such language! Did she tell you where she was?'

'There she is now, at the front door.'

'You talk to her, Derek. I'm scared of what I might say.'

But no need to be scared. Monica is now determined to prove what a good mother she can be, which means putting her offspring first, and perhaps even going to church. There is nothing Barbara could say that Monica doesn't thoroughly agree with.

'You're right. I'm all you say 'n worse, cos always I got to hide from someone, if it's not my mother, it's my daughter. Guess I bin needin somethin like this to bring me to my senses, Barbara. I thank my Daddy, for dyin, and Calvin, for bringin drugs into this house.'

'And where does the wealth come from? Eh? Think of that. You're a travesty.'

'Leave her alone now, Derek. The question is, what do we do now?'

'You tell Calvin, when next you see him, Derek. Ah'm gone. He can tell Alex.'

'No, you tell him yourself, Monica. When you get back here with Cindy.'

'Oh no, Cindy is where she needs to be. Ah don't want her becomin like me. Ah won't be comin back heah. I cain't survive in a city. And you're right, Derek, this is all *shit*.'

To illustrate her newfound contempt for material possessions, Monica takes up and smashes a number of cheap, breakable items.

In the meantime, Frodsham and Barbara are fully prepared, should it prove necessary, to break down the door to Calvin's lab. But to their surprise, he opens up, to the smell of ether, a smile on his face and in his hand a petrie dish of the first ever preparation of Green Munga.

'Taste this,' he insists. They recoil.

Monica Ecks: given the fact that, though born in the South, she was educated on the West Coast, and spent years in New York, Britain and Europe before moving to Australia, small inconsistencies of speech as revealed in her dialogue are not the result of ignorance on my part; to the contrary, they have been painstakingly reconstructed.

Eugene Ecks: by coming up with the Green Munga, he puts

375

the evergreen eucalypt on a par with olive and pine. It is a fit object for worship now, because it can now be eaten. But not with relish, by other than koala bears or the spitfire larvae of the sawfly wasp, unfortunately. It was unpalatable, and a great deal had to be consumed by human beings for adequate nutrition. And there being no ether in the Valley, power kero was used in its preparation. Kimberley pulls a terrible face, when he speaks of the Green Munga. A *pis aller*.

57. *Attis meets with Smitty. Calvin and Frodsham return to Paddington. Paula and Brian move from Koala Kottage. Diane accosts Attis. Darryl's perilous descent. The Energy Question. Brian broods over Paula's past.*

Late summer '69. In town to buy a bottle of Porphyry Pearl wine with which to celebrate the result of his school examination, Attis providentally happens on Smitty, who's buying a carton of longnecks in the bottle booth. No one is yet back at work in the forest, and the publicans are laughing.

'G'day, young Att.'

'Hi Smitty. I was going to ring you. Can I have a word?'

'Feel free. But if ya wanta know when ya can work.'

'No it's not that. Well I guess it is. Oh. Can I have a bottle of your best Sparkling Starwine please?'

'Starwine, eh. What's the big occasion?'

'I did OK in my school exams. Mum gave me money to buy wine. You doing anything right now?'

'Av a few things I afta do in town.'

'How bout we go back to Graceland? We could talk there.'

'What's wrong with the public bar?'

'I'd rather talk in the flat, if it's OK with you.'

'You gettin on with the other blokes all right, are ya?'

Monica, with more clothes than can safely be carried, is heading, meantime, for Graceland. She took the car from the

Medical School carpark, which means Calvin can no longer offer Derek Frodsham a lift to school.

'What did Barbara think about it all, Derek?'

'I don't think they get on too well. Did you see the note she wrote?'

'What note?'

'Oh. I thought she was going to write a note. Didn't leave it on the fridge door?'

'All I know, man, I know through you. Ain't nothin on that fridge door, ain't nothin in that fridge. Oh. There's the phone. That may be her now.'

Calvin, who just slept eighteen hours straight, is rolling a small number to celebrate the historic breakthrough. As he speaks, in muffled tones, Derek Frodsham studies the patterns on the pressed metal ceiling. Derek's thinking of the Shearers' Strike of 1891, when one hundred striking Australian shearers, financed by trade union funding, formed themselves a rural co-op at the Alice River in Queensland. Barbara wants Derek to visit the Valley, but he hasn't yet mentioned this to Calvin.

'Well fuck you too, buddy!'

Calvin resumes the chore of removing twigs from the album cover.

'Who was that, mate? The missus?'

'No, my bank manager. I'm funding Utopia, Derek. First through my brother, now through my wife. She just emptied the joint account.'

'She means business.'

'She may have taken off with a lover. She has done that before. Or she may have found something she simply cannot live without in a sale. But I am inclined to believe she went to the Valley. I can believe Cindy went there. In fact, I wouldn't mind betting they're all down there. I bet Alexander's there, too.'

'Would Cindy have told Alexander where she went?'

'Who knows what goes on in the minds of non-scientists? There we go, my friend. Derek?'

'Yep.'

'Let's get totally ripped.'

Smitty, having just received what may amount to a death sentence, sits on the lumpy couch, sniffing. He pulls a tailormade from a pack, then wrenches open the carton and seizes a longneck. No can, no pull ring; the tale remains to be told of how Australian scientists will invent the pull ring *and* the cardboard winecask.

'He wants me to bring me own axe?'

'That's right. I don't think we should meet, though, do you?'

'No choice. Coulda done without this, but. Only seen him once in the pub. Don't remember too much about the man. Do recall he drank lemon squash. Give him a bit of a razz about it.'

'I thought I should speak with you first, Smitty, fore I go to the police. He's giving himself up.'

'So he says. Ya done the right thing, but don't go to the police, mate. What sort o' man 'd want to be a copper? Stuff the fuckin police. This is between him 'n me.'

'Ar, don't be silly, Smitty. I want to lure him out, that's all. We just need your cooperation.'

'Whattaya take me for? Think I'm the kind o' gutless mongrel backs off from a blue? No way. Think I'm the kind o' coward goes runnin to the cops? Fuck that. We'll do it his way. You tell him I'm lookin to even the score, though, Att. He killed one o' my crew. I haven't forgotten.'

'He's dangerous, Smitty. Professional soldier. Big and strong.'

'He may be big and strong, mate, but is he fast and clever? No good bein big and strong if you're slow and stupid. You say he won't come outta that grove, all right. I'll meet him down there. We'll do it quick, make it next Wednesday, say, midday, we'll get this over and done with. Tee up Fergie 'n Darryl, will ya? Don't wanta to be shot in the back like poor little Roger. Att.'

'Yeah?'

'Promise me you won't say nothin to the police, mate, whatever happens. I mean, ask yourself what kind of man'd want to be a copper. Eh?'

'If that's the way you want it, Smitty.'

378

Paula Zoshka: 'Oh what's the good of *talking* to you? I can't seem to get through to you I'd changed by the time you met me, can't you understand? I was a decent woman by then. Why must you persecute me so?'

Brian Chegwodden: 'I do understand. You are getting through. I just need to keep hearing it. I said I couldn't cope if you had been involved and ...'

'Oh I can't stand any more. It's not going to work!'

'Yes it is. Yes it is. I'm sorry, Paula. I see I shouldn't have spoken. I apologise.'

Paula and Brian are camped far from the farmhouse, the first couple to break away. Brian is not prepared to let other men perve on Paula, but he daren't say as much. It sounds selfish, put that way, and subject to endless scrutiny and reproof, we have the best possible chance of growing conscious of our manifold shortcomings.

Eugene Ecks is still raving on about the dome, how spacy and groovy it will be, but Michael Ginnsy, as Brian Chegwodden notes, is silent, on such occasions. Ginnsy, for one, means to stay put, while the others, through their very lack of comment, betray their own uncertainties. Nisi Papadimitriou now contends that exclusive fucking, like exclusive friendship, threatens communal survival. But Brian Chegwodden is not yet ready as she to embrace this quasi-Shaker conviction. Of course, no one could object to a meeting hall, in which to be together as a Family, some pleasant space in which to party, to parley, to solve the world's problems. Consequently, plans are afoot to fell the sick cedar and float it to the Flat.

Dawn comes late and night early to the Flat, surrounded by tall trees and towering cliffs, and such is the resonance of sound produced here you can tell where anyone is and what they are up to.

Nine a.m. on a late summer's morning. Grainger and Balthazar Beauregard play with the pups and the frisbee. Eugene Ecks paces up and down, checking sites for the Dome, though Michael Ginnsy, still fast asleep in the only bed in the Valley, insists it must shade the grave of Gwen and Phryx, that their spirits may fortify it. Annunciata and Nisi wash dishes in the kitchen of the cottage, laughing spasmodically. Cindy Ecks, Aloysius, Timothy, splash truant in the Creek.

Attis watches the colony of bees he just hived head for the messmates. Predominant, atop the talus, but spilling over the Pass to the ridge, and down the wet gullies to the Creek, with impeccable prescience they put out blossom a week before the drought broke. The bees will get good pollen from them. The honey, though, is poor and dark.

Diane Zoshka comes sneaking up behind Attis and flings her arms round his waist. She feels him stiffen to her touch, before he throws a playful headlock round her.

'What do you want?' he says, wiggling her curls beneath his fingers.

'Stop it! Let me go! I don't want you looking at my hair. It needs a wash.'

Conditioner, another item for the list everyone adds to all day long. Wrangles over its every accession consume much time at nightly meetings.

'Whatcha doin?'

'Just hived this colony, Diane. It's in the top box. The bottom box is full of foundation. I'm waiting to see if the workers will work, and hopefully the queen will move onto the new comb, through the hole. Really, we should have done this in spring, when the brood nest was expanding.'

'What's with the grass in front of the hive?'

'That's so they have to fight their way through. It will dispose them to take note of their new position.'

'Don't they know where they are?'

'They forget. Lots fly back to the old site. I took them from a tree not far from the Ford, so we need to be sure that enough remain here for this hive to be viable. But we won't be seeing bees all over the boxes this summer.'

'Is the old colony still functional?'

'No. They just fly round it till they die.'

'Crazy critters.'

'Yeah, but they work so hard, they're so fierce, they remind me a lot of you.'

'Bzz. Can we go sit and talk somewhere? I had to get out of that kitchen.'

'How bout here?'

'No. Somewhere downstream. I want to be alone with you. I want to be out of earshot.'

He has not asked to make love again, so has a fair idea what she wants to discuss. He conducts her, by the hand, to the southernmost edge of the Flat, where a sagging, sunken bridge of flood damaged logs conveys the indistinct remains of the road to the bracken-infested far bank. Their banter disturbs a few black ducks, who take to the air, wheel and settle downstream. The air is humid since the rain, and cumulus clouds mass over the Gorge. Diane's nape gleams with sweat as she buries her head in her hands. Most every day there's a late storm about, but the Valley has so far missed them all.

'What's the matter, Diane?'

'Don't you know? Can't you guess? I had you picked as special. I can't believe you can be so insensitive. Was it so horrible, making love, that you can't bear for me to touch you now? I mean, do you want me to leave?'

'No. Of course not.'

'You did so well in your exams. You don't need me any more. I don't care. What I mean is, I don't think I can stay here, if it's going to be like this.'

'Diane!'

'Do you want to talk about it with me? You want to tell me what I've done wrong? I know it wasn't very nice for you. I bled a lot, I'm sorry. That won't happen again. That doesn't happen any more. I mean, it was just the first time, Attis. You can't expect it to be any good, the first time. Paula says her first time was awful, and all the guys say their first time was awful, so don't be afraid to come near me, OK? Did I offend? Have I got bad breath?'

'Diane, please.'

'Why don't you talk to me about it? You've hardly spoken to me since. I've been waiting and waiting for you just to say something, do something, but you ignore me, and I can't stand it any more.'

'I'm sorry, Diane. It's not your fault.'

'Do you still feel the same way or not? I mean, you told me you loved me.'

'I do love you.'

'Tell me again how it was, for you, when we met for the first time, Attis.'

'At the Rodeo?'

'During the calfrope. When I rescued the calf.'

'Well, I was surprised, because you weren't at all as I had expected. I didn't think much about what happened then, till Fergie started joking about it later, with Kimberley.'

'Where you surprised that I did what I did? I mean, did you think I was very brave?'

'Oh sure. You're very brave, and that's what I like about you so much. You're so very brave.'

'Is that all you like about me?'

'No. You're very honest too. You may appear rude, but that's because you are honest, and others aren't as brave and honest as you are. I told Mum that.'

'Am I like the girls you knew at school?'

'Oh no, you're very different. You have more experience of life. I feel you understand more.'

'Does it bother you we come from different backgrounds? I mean, are you scared my family won't like you? Don't worry. They are just bourgeois.'

'I don't think of you as having parents. Besides, I can't see myself meeting them. I was thinking, as I shifted that colony, I don't ever want to leave this Valley. I feel strange about the place, now I've worked over the mountain.'

'That's what I love so much about you. We all want to live down here, but we can't do it, without you. Most Australians wouldn't feel at home here.'

'You weren't born here, Diane. Most of the people I know work in the bush, same as me.'

'They don't love it the way you do.'

'They love it but they hate it as well. They're probably a bit afraid of it. Whereas, because I spent my childhood running round in it, I guess I'm not.'

'No, you're special. I got talking with Balthazar, and he was saying, how just the way you walk through the bush is unlike anything he ever saw.'

'Yeah, well his hair is unlike anything I ever saw.'

382

'He meant it as a compliment. How do you feel about sex, Attis?'

'Weren't you afraid? It must have hurt.'

'My love for you took away my hurt. I think you're just the most beautiful guy. Did you used to masturbate?'

'Sorry?'

'Jerk off. Wank.'

'Oh no. Nothing like that.'

'Most guys do.'

'They say they do, but I doubt it.'

'I guess for me, desire aside, it's my knowledge that our love made all this happen. See, if we hadn't fallen in love, Attis, I can't see how this commune, and Att, it's going to be the most *amazing* . . .'

'Diane, I know I have to be with you, but I felt so sad, after we'd made love, and guilty. I don't know why, but I can't ignore it. It overwhelms me. I just can't seem to ignore it. Nothing seems the same any more. I feel shut out.'

'Shut out of what? Hey, come on, you're being oversensitive. You've gone from being a child to being a man, it has to happen. Oh mate, I was lucky when I found you. Paula must be so envious, she has such an arsehole in Brian. But they have good sex, she says. Can a good thing be the reward for a bad thing?'

'I'm not very good at sex. I can't seem to get into it.'

'You'll improve. We both will. Do you like my body?'

'Very much.'

'Touch me here, then. Come on! Here, on my inner thigh. Feel how *soft* I am, Attis. Stroke me.'

'That's really not you, Diane. I have to be with the real you.'

'Then enjoy me, for Chrissake! Am I so awful? I bet other guys would like to screw me. Oh Att, it's all for the good of the world. Others may come and go from this Valley, but you and I will *stay*, man, and we will demonstrate how people can live together with *no rules*.'

'You think everyone should screw everyone else, the way Nisi says?'

'She's just scared of being left out. We'll talk her round. Take off your clothes, Att. Come on.'

'Is this Wednesday? I've got to be back at the house by twelve. The fight is on today.'

Attis MacAnaspie: had he grown up in Sydney, I could see him as homosexual. In the case of passive individuals, I think it's a question of who gets in first.

Activity on the Flat, and in the Valley generally, ceases around eleven, as the unmuffled throb of Darryl MacAnaspie's larger offroad bike is heard, wending its way through the scrub. Fiona awaits Fergus in the cave, and that's got to be Fergus now, half a mile behind Darryl.

'Come on,' shouts Rude Boy to Timothy, and together with Cindy, they dash from the classroom. Annunciata berates them, to no avail. Nisi watches from the kitchen window. She's making a start on the kero tin cupboards, rank with rodent coprolites.

Horrie and Iris dread it when Darryl has no paid work to do. He always ends up in hospital, or the courthouse.

Wearing no helmet, gunning the throttle to stop the carbies choking on the rich mix, he is slouched over the tank, talking to his pillion, when eventually Fergus catches up with him. The arrangement was that they should take their bikes to the top of the track to save time, but this is not the top of the track. Darryl sits on Sunrise Lookdown, a piece of all but naked sandstone rock that juts over the Gorge, the place where Kimberley Moon discarded his hand-tooled saddle. Sunrise Lookdown commands a view of the Flat, and a fair view of Sit on Yer Arse Pass, or as good as you will get from anywhere. Darryl is shouting in Smitty's ear and tapping the air with a tailormade, as Fergus hits the kill switch, and kicks the stand down on his own motorcycle.

'Come on,' shouts Fergus, 'stop fartarsin round. No time for sightseein.'

Smitty, who's nursing an axe, has it in his favour that Mehmed will be forced to listen to the roar from the bikes for a good hour.

'Come on,' shouts Fergus, kicking Darryl's tyres now. 'Shift yer fat arse!'

'Shut yer ugly face, Daddy's Boy. Can't ya see I'm thinkin?'

Two minutes pass. Darryl removes his shades and wipes the sweat from his eyes, grimacing.

'Reckon I could just about git down that track. You stickin with me, Smitty old mate?'

'Why not?' A man must determine to savour his last moments on earth. Fergus just shakes his own head, and leaves his own bike with fat Fiona.

Adam Lindsay Gordon once leapt a horse over the fence on the edge of the Blue Lake, Mount Gambier. Jim Barron, of Grassy Gully, took a horse down Ettrema Gorge, from Barrons Pass to Cooee Flat. But no one yet took a motorcycle down Sit on Yer Arse Pass, which is unusual in that it follows a dry ridge, not a moist gully. The little rodeo clown, fag in mouth, dwarfed by the thing between his legs, commences descent, with Smitty sitting bolt upright on the improvised pillion seat. Smitty is under instructions to anticipate Darryl's every move, but when he falls off at the first bend and Darryl doesn't so much as look back, it's clear Smitty has no choice but to scramble up and rejoin Fergus.

The noise Mehmed hears from the Grove is that of a souped-up six-fifty, unmuffled two-stroke, with sharp fistfuls of full throttle jabbing over meaningful silences. A big mob of reptiles, goats, birds and wallabies flees before Darryl, as if from wildfire. The noise is terrific, the loudest noise heard on the Flat since the Gap collapsed in the rockfall.

Haring across the Flat, Aloysius and Timothy thrill to every stutter of the groundbreaking bike, as, two thousand feet above, Darryl, standing, eases his way over the loose stones. Often, as he feels the rear wheel let go, he spins round, fast, then creeps uphill a bit.

When he arrives at the steep middle section of the saddle, from which he could see the rapids if he looked straight down to his left and if he looked straight up, the looming face of the mesa above him, he dare not use his front brake for fear of falling arse over head, and he dare not use his back brake for fear of locking up and moving sideways, interesting. What might he do? Fergus had the notion he would lay it down and shove it along on the tank, but instead, feeling himself crabbed, he goes, being Darryl, for the doctor; guns the throttle, to give himself grip, and then he's off the track, hurtling through the blackboys. Pretty much out of control, dealing with each obstacle as it presents itself, he is, momentarily, released from the miserable boredom of his quotidian existence. Death reaches out hands innumerable: inorganic, and vegetable.

Below, they hear the protest of the underbrush at the passage of the plummeting vehicle, the thunk as it glances off a tree and, miraculously, survives the impact; poignantly, the roar from the engine as Darryl makes unexpected contact with the track, and fights, in vain, to retain it; but the further he descends, the faster he is going. A root, catching the heel of his left boot, rips it clean off the sockless foot, which is anything but. Finally, he's in the clear and, leaping a ten-foot wattle, hits the Flat and spins to a standstill, in a shower of sods and a spray of fuel. The astonished assembly, which includes by now Nisi and Annunciata, and Attis and Diane, and Balthazar, but not, as Darryl sadly notes, Monica, accord him silence.

'No matter 'ow 'aard I try' he complains, addressing Timothy 'I cannot seem to drop it.' Then he collapses, trembling, as he tries to dismount, and has to be assisted in lighting a cigarette. He is still sitting under a native peach, smoking and chatting with Aloysius, when Fergus and Smitty reappear. Then the mountain men move off, skirting the Flat, and Balthazar is told to piss off when he attempts to join them.

Before dark has fallen, the three MacAnaspie brothers are back on the Flat, horror-stricken. Fergus and Attis support Smitty, who is wearing a bloodsoaked sling. His arm is deeply wounded, almost severed. The crotch of his moleskins is red with blood, too, but he can walk, though it hurts. Darryl, sore from his morning's efforts, sobs as he reaches for his bike, which won't start, and he's still sitting on it, retching, when Fergus and Attis begin the slow ascent. Attis stops to pick up a note, sitting on top of the cairn. It's a request, from Eugene Ecks, for a box of plastic drink straws in four different colours.

'What happened, Darryl?'

The women have learned about the fight from Diane, who was under strict instructions not to mention it. Darryl just shakes his head.

Mehmed is soon seen, making his way towards the plateau via the track, his tent on his back. He holds Smitty's blood-stained axe in one hand, and the Uncle Sam topper is on his head. The topper he tosses, contemptuously, at Darryl, as he passes the cairn, and Cindy rushes in to grab it.

'I'll be back,' warns Mehmed.

If Darryl can't speak of what went on, Paula and Brian didn't even look. So shattered are they by the loss of Mehmed's tent, for which they have been hanging out, they move back to join the rest of the Family that evening, that very night.

At the next plenary meeting, the topic set for discussion is 'Energy'.

No mains in the Valley. No power, no water, no sewerage, no phone, no gas. No access. No street lights. It's dark.

'We have two sound batteries, so we keep one charged by swopping them round and we leave the Kombi parked up the Pass.'

'Yeah, 'n I bet I know who gets the job carrying the batteries up 'n down.'

'Yeah, well your clothes are already ruined.'

'A donkey could do it.'

'Yer tellin me. But could he install the battery in the Kombi?'

'We're lucky that other battery wasn't completely stuffed.'

'Some of the fins are cracked.'

'It is just so impractical, man, to use the Kombi to charge a battery. I mean we got, what is it, fifty horsepower there?'

'Fifty-seven.'

'And we're usin a donk that big to charge a twelve-volt battery, it's ridiculous. Think of the wear and tear on the van, not to mention the fuel. Fuel *costs*, man! It costs the planet.'

'All we got is what was in the tank, and luckily, it was full, plus the reserve jerrycan, which I filled, but which is now empty. How much is left in the main tank?'

'Not much.'

'A donkey could bring in the fuel.'

'But could he *pay* for the fuel, Nisi? Cause we got no money.'

'I'm with Nisi. What's with these batteries? Doesn't it matter what women think? You men just wanta create your stupid problems and play your endless stupid games. Paula and I are more than happy to use kerosene lamps. Right Paula?'

'We don't got no kerosene lamps, Diane. And where's this kerosene?'

'There are so many lamps at Wonderview. Horrie said we can have them on loan.'

'Aladdins. They're not too bad. One hundred watts. Nice soft light. They break, of course, and they leak and they smell, but they're OK. We used to use them at home.'

'But we don't produce kerosene, Att. Is this kerosene shale in the Valley? I think not.'

'So much for wax candles.'

'We won't have wax for twelve months.'

'I don't like Aladdins. They flare all the time and they must be dead level. You can't carry them round. You can't take them outside. One flick of your wet hands from the sink and the glass cracks. They coke up and they put out so much heat from the mantle I've seen them blister paintwork. What we need are storm lanterns, Tilleys. Those, you can carry round. True, they got a metho preheater. That just means when we buy the kero, with the money we get for our wax candles, we buy a little metho as well. No problem.'

'Got any Tilleys, Att?'

'Are they the ones from Nashville? We have the ones from Nashville. Aladdins, I think.'

'OK. I guess that takes care of your suggestion, Hollywood. We have no Tilleys we can borrow.'

'I don't *believe* this. Wasn't the whole idea of living down here to make do with what we can produce? Coal! Wood! OK, so it's hot, sitting here in summer with just the fire to see by, but I don't hear any complaints. And later, we have our candles, and they produce a lovely glow.'

388

'Yeah, flatterin to older women. Anyway, let's be honest and admit it's not the light we need the batteries for, it's the cassette player. There is no *music* here. It's drivin me nuts! I can't live without music.'

'And so say all of us.'

'See, I thought Ginnsy would play his acoustic, at least, but he won't even play Grainger's guitar, and Olaf and Grainger can play, so they claim, but they won't play in front of the great master, so what is the end result? Silence.'

'Yeah, it's dull without music.'

'Dull? It's a fuckin bummer. I think if that radio was still in the van, I'd be a phantom battery flattener.'

'Where is this radio, Ginnsy? Bring it out immediately and put it on at once.'

'I thought we just decided we don't want the bus runnin up and down the Pass all day and round and round the Flat. No, there has to be a more efficient way of chargin that battery. I agree.'

'Nisi? Hello. Nisi? When do your donkeys move in?'

'Just as soon as I have had the chance to finish making their saddles.'

'I'm sorry. Diane! We were supposed to be helping Nisi with the cupboards today. I feel so squeamish, Nisi.'

'You are both too busy getting yourselves pregnant to be of any help to anyone.'

'I wish there was some way to put the van on blocks while still enjoying the luxury of music.'

'*Necessity*, man. Necessity.'

'OK, necessity. Plus, there is all kind of modern twelve-volt appliances you can get for caravans.'

'Oh, you make me *sick*. Why don't you go back to the city where you belong?'

'There's that pump engine, which I know how to start.'

'Why don't we ask Darryl to drive the Sunshine Portable Engine down?'

'Great idea. But why not a brand new combine harvester? See, if we fall behind with the payments, who's gonna repossess?'

'What size is this pump engine, Ginnsy?'

'Ronaldson Tippett three-horsepower.'

'Great! That's a bit better than fifty-seven. You work it out, man. What's a good fast idle on a Kombi?'

'Oh, bout nine hundred.'

'OK. Nine hundred revs per minute, puts out forty amps or so of charge, hundred amp hour battery, that's a hundred over forty, that's two and a half hours. Two and a half hours! Not counting charge for the coil and solenoid. Two and a half hours of drivin up and down the Pass each day, and round and round the Flat, just to charge a battery. But using the pump, we can irrigate the crops, fill up the tank, water trees. Think about it.'

'Nothin to think about. He's right. It is utterly inefficient fuelwise, to use the bus. And do we need a bus?'

'Ar, give us a break! It's my bus!'

'I wonder how fast the pump engine turns? Probly bout three and a half thousand revs, OK. Let's assume we have fifty-five amps output from the gennie at three and a half thousand revs, just hand me that paper, please Grainger.'

'Paula. Do you want to come and help me with the coffee and tea please? Come on.'

'Can we grow coffee and tea in this Valley?'

'OK. So for fourteen volts, that's twelve volts plus charging, that's fifty-five times fourteen, that's 770 watts, which is approximately one horsepower. But we have three horsepower, so we can charge both gennies! And it's only going to take a hundred over fifty-five, that's two and a half hours, oh well. You'd agree it is more efficient. I'll check out the pump engine tomorrow.'

'Yeah, I know how to start it.'

'Yeah, he knows how to start it.'

'You gotta be careful startin it, man, or you could have a terrible accident! You *will* have a terrible accident! Phryx had a terrible accident. Only it wasn't an accident.'

'But we must have our Kombi on the road, man! He's our *mascot*. He discovered the Valley.'

'I think Att had an idea it was here.'

'And before him, there was Aborigines. Don't forget the Aborigines.'

'I won't. I have the feeling I'll be thinking about them, more and more.'

390

'OK. That just means someone gets the job of pullin the battery and the gennie and the reggie in and out of the van all the time. Wasn't the reggie in that other van OK?'

'Stuffed.'

'Oh come on, this is enough of this meeting! I take it we're all in favour of what Olaf suggests? Good. Now can we listen to some music please?'

'We could, if I hadn't destroyed the tapes, cause I can't handle that diabolical shit. Forces of Evil, man. Ya got to keep watchful.'

'There is no doubt about him, is there? *Why*, man? *Why?*'

'I'll settle for the radio.'

'Reception is bad, cause we're down in this Valley. It fades in and out, which is actually kind of interesting.'

'How did the plants do today, man?'

'Good! Two more little leaflets on Eric. I'm pretty sure he is a male.'

'What a bummer.'

Brian doesn't understand how Paula's past can fill him with such existential horror, but it does; and, just as a bright druggie, intrigued by the insights he fancies himself to be gaining into the Nature of Consciousness, will have acquired, by the time he is no longer intrigued by anything, the habit of regarding his vice as a form of legitimate scholarly inquiry, so Brian, on rare occasions able to disengage from endless eidetic recitation based on Paula's most intimate disclosures, is drawn to scrutinise his jealousy, as a pathologist might contemplate a knife with which he has been lacerating himself.

What is the nature of this obsession? Why does it exist? What, if any, is its biological role, and how does it create the pain it creates? If only we knew.

According to Freud, and Lamaic Buddhism, jealousy is the key to rebirth.

Paula, repenting her guileless honesty, now engages on extenuations: but the specious process by which fornication is reduced to the level of a failed takeaway meal is undermined, in virtue of its paradoxical impact on the memory. And if acts that expose the most private bodily parts and words of endearment mean nothing, what can be said to have any meaning, that happens between man and woman? A semantic outrage. What reason has Brian to feel the process ends in himself, necessarily? He does, of course, feel the process ends in himself, necessarily. His jealousy, concerning other men in the Valley, is now under control, so he thinks. But, given he does feel 'special' to Paula, is he not perhaps deceived by this perception? If so, what has deceived him? There is nothing now Paula can do with any man she hasn't done before, no words of endearment that can be uttered that would come, unfamiliar, to her lips. And is it not by our words and deeds we exist for others, if not ourselves? If God is extrinsic to us, shall we not be surprised on Judgement Day? But, if He is always within us, how can we not be vindicated?

Why should it matter, any of it? Is Time illusory? Do people not change? ''T's only he who loves not that is fettered by compulsion' (Mevlana). Brian can often see the logical strength of Paula's contention that what she did before they met is none of his bloody business, though, in a real sense, that he was not there is cause sufficient for despair. He has observed that, unlike men, women waste little time brooding over their partner's sexual past. But Reason's pretence of being a prime mover, scoffed at by Love, is confuted by Jealousy. The pain a man feels, as he contemplates his beloved's illicit sexual history, is not, on the whole, generated by fear she may lapse again into promiscuity; no, it has no such rational premise. Would a man who has never suffered passion have any interest in the adult past at all? Would he not rather prefer to revisit that magic realm in which Eros stirs, those years from fourteen to nineteen, say, when the world is bright and beguiling?

That was the best time, thinks Brian. This need to disburden ourselves of past loves is a prime motivation in acquiring new ones.

'Brian? Are you asleep? I feel you're awake and brooding again.'

The characters: I strongly suspect that eunuchs have not the interest in things mechanical that men have. So, as the men aged or became eunuchs, Technology, in the the Land of the Ever Young, was doomed.

Today, in the Valley, no such problem. Darryl is on the grid. He has a microwave, and a big TV antenna. Bugger the windmill, the photovoltaic self-tracker's hooked up to the battery bank.

58. *Falling the giant cedar. The drought breaks. Smitty's dire fate.*

After inspecting the doomed cedar, checking it from every angle, Darryl admits it's a job for Smitty to fall, precisely, a tree like this. And Smitty won't be dropping this tree, because Smitty is leaving the district.

'Yeah, they got his plumbin workin again, but now he can't piss standin up.'

'I'm not surprised. What about Dad's big crosscut, Darryl, the one that reaches across the roof?'

'Gotta know what you're doin with it, sport. Don't wanta bring this whole grove down.'

'I'll talk to Dad.'

'I wouldn't. What makes ya reckon he'll let ya do it? Oh, I know he spoils ya rotten, but what would this timber be worth? Few superfoot in this baastard. Probly just about pay a man t'hire a helicopter and lift it out.'

'Oh no, this has to be the timber for the meeting hall.'

'Sez oo? I can't see how you'd git *this* one out, without gittin *that* one out.'

'What if I climb up and lop the crown first?'

'Yer jokin. Plenty of good, accessible timber here. What about that stand o' blackwood? What, yez scared o' workin hardwood?'

'Won't be a nail in the entire structure, according to Eugene, Darryl.'

'All mortise 'n tenon?'

'No. Probably use an adze to get the angles on the dome

393

struts, then finish off with a plane. Can't use power tools anyway. No power. Pity we can't get a generator in, it's just the Family feel this is the right tree for the hall.'

'Why must you do everything for 'em?'

'It's just till they've settled in. You think Smitty'll be OK? I feel a bit guilty over that.'

'I hear he don't wanta know us. Must blame us that everyone heard, but you can't keep a thing like that quiet, even if ya don't press charges. What a thing to have happened, ay. Rather be dead. I get nightmares about it still, ah well. Time to visit Monica. Let's have a pleasant dream, for once.'

'She's a married woman, Darryl.'

'Never said I was gonna pay her bills! She asked me to show her round the Valley, Attis. Ah, 'slike a dream come true, seein her down here. Beats the pants off a shithouse door.'

'I beg your pardon?'

'Next time you're up in the workshop, ask to use the convenience. Big picture o' Monica, back o' the door. I should know, I put it there. Got the mag at home too, though the pages are all stuck together. Naa, she's always bin me favourite centrefold. I was in love with her for years. And to think I'm seein her today in the flesh. Why can't *we* produce women like that, stead o' these bats with hunched shoulders, that live alone and keep a hundred goats 'n a gun? Not sure I wanta go back to work. Might be a danger to meself 'n others, ay. Bit cuntstruck.'

'You've always been a danger to yourself and others, Darryl. I think you always will be. I might ask Dad to come down and take a look at this tree. He's been saying he means to come down.'

'He'd do anything for you, after your exam result. Walkin round town all day, he was, just acceptin congratulations. Must run. How do I look? Wish I ad me other boot and some clean clobber to wear. Duds got a bit knocked round, while I was bringin in the bike. Lost me dark glasses, too.'

'When will you take the bike out again?'

'Dunno. Might leave it down here yet. Reckon the old Studebaker'd make it down?'

'Don't even think about it, Darryl.'

Darryl MacAnaspie: wearing just the one boot. Wozza says the men on the track wore just the one sandal on the foot. They borrowed boots for the rodeo, and the eunuchs went barefooted.

'What are we *doing* here, Diane?'

'Picking mushrooms.'

Paula and Diane Zoshka range the Flat, seeking field mushrooms in the cowpats. The guys have carefully garnered the goldtops and the blue meanies. Both girls are barefoot, Diane in jeans, Paula in a cheesecloth kaftan.

'I mean, what are we doing with our lives?'

'Conducting an experiment. Trying to live so what we do with our "lives" seems less momentous.'

'What if it doesn't work?'

'You can leave. No one has to stay.'

'But do you think we have the right mix here?'

'What do you mean exactly?'

They hear the kid bleat. Cindy found a kid, near the rockfall, and brought it back to the house. But there is no bottle with which to feed the kid, and no milk to put in the non-existent bottle.

'The people in the Family. I worry that, you apart, no one seems in the least idealistic.'

'Everyone is idealistic. It's just most of us are Australians. Some people show their idealism. Others can't.'

'I don't see Monica as idealistic. She strikes me as an opportunistic bitch. See the way she couldn't look at me? She must have been flirting with Brian.'

'It's a fresh start down here, Paula. Who gives a shit what people used to be? Hey, there's one!'

'That's a puffball.'

'You can eat puffballs. You just can't eat toadstools.'

'Put it separate.'

'We need a nice old cow, Paula. Mushrooms without butter, yuk!'

'Diane, I'm getting so fat on the mashed potatoes we eat for every meal, I feel I am being fattened for slaughter. I should see an obstetrician.'

'Why? You feel unwell?'

'No, but I should be eating a wider range of foods, surely.'

'Mushrooms tonight, fresh from the field. What's wrong with fresh mushrooms? I bet they're the best you ever tasted. Won't be like those ones at the greengrocers that look like they're off the top of someone's compost heap. I think it's great we can't take food, and stuff like that, for granted now.'

'I don't want to give birth on the ground, under some wrecked vehicle.'

'I guarantee you will give birth in the very best place to give birth. You'll probably do it in the Creek, squatting. They say it's best if you squat.'

'Aren't you ever depressed, Diane?'

'I don't let myself get depressed. I am sustained by a vision.'

'How's it going to be, for you, if things don't work out here? You'll soon be pregnant.'

'I will see they *do* work out. I see all the people here as unformed, with the exception of Attis, and I still have to talk to Attis about corporate profit in regard to woodchip. It doesn't worry me everyone's fucked up somepin fierce, what would you expect? The *lives* we have led, Paula! Barbara told me Malcolm Muggeridge says Armageddon is close. He has to be right, for once. We're born in these awful, sterile cities, condemned to these horrible square boxes, dedicated to mass consumption, spending our lives, if we're men, going off to senseless wars, or if we're women, reading shit. Look at the garbage our mother reads! If only we could get someone like Richard Walsh to run the *Woman's Weekly*. We know Life shouldn't be this way, but we lack the guts to challenge things, because no one can bear to hear the Truth, Paula. This is just an attempt to Change the World. People are doing it all over the place. If we can make it work in one place, then we can spread it everywhere.'

'But everything is going so slowly.'

'Be patient, Paula. It takes time to destroy an entire civilisation. But there are compensations. Look around you. Isn't this just the most beautiful place?'

'Yeah, but I worry ...'

'*Don't* worry. Release that worry. Ask yourself, what does worry achieve? Paula, are you happy with Brian?'

'Oh, we're getting on not too bad at the moment.'

'Because if you're not, you should ditch him. You'd be better off alone. You're part of this community. It's not important you have a man. There are plenty of men down here.'

'Oh no, we'll give it a bit more time. I want to have a baby in the Valley, whatever happens. Wouldn't it be great to be able to say to someone, you were born down there? But I will see an obstetrician, I think, just to be sure things are OK. What do you think this weather will do? I don't like the look of those clouds.'

'It's going to piss down rain soon. We better get a move on.'

'Good tomato soup weather, boys. Pity we got no tomatoes.'

On the third day of torrential rain, the dawn glows primrose yellow. The Friends of the Fire look thoughtful, the peppermints sombre, the gums apeel. The Gorge roars, the Creek is wide, brown, and bearing huge tree limbs. The sacred pump, which Olaf hadn't yet got round to looking at, is underwater. The verandah is soaked and slimy. Everyone sleeps, at night, in the house, with the pups and the starving kid and the snail trails. No work can be done. The grape crop is ruined, the seeds in the circular vege garden drown. And the house leaks, but the waters are caught in a myriad glass bottles, from the Fowlers Vacola bottling kit Nisi found in the chaff shed.

'Oh my,' says Monica, 'that kid o' yours is drivin me *nuts*, Cindy. Why'd you bring it home for, child? We got no milk it can drink.'

'Spose I could always go an fetch yez a tin o' powdered milk.'

'Would you do that, Darryl? And could you ring my husband, to see if my son arrived home? Did I mention Barbara turned up at Graceland, as Fergus and I were leaving?'

'No. Where is 'e now?'

'Up in the cave, with Fiona.'

'Likes 'em fat, ay. Better 'ave a word. Attis! Comin for a swim?'

'Not in this. You won't get over the Ford, Darryl. Which is a shame, because now would be an ideal time to float the cedar to the site.'

397

'Where's Eugene?'

'It was his turn to check on the plants, man. I did it through the night.'

'How they copin?'

'They'll make it. No sign of the Cooktown Rot.'

'This is the last of the dry wood. Don't let that fire go out.'

'If the fire goes out, the house will fall down. That's an Irish proverb.'

'Mention this weather on the radio, Michael?'

'Wouldn't know. Daren't use the battery.'

'Why?'

'Too dangerous to drive Kombi in this, man. Sides, we have no petrol.'

'Shoot yez a killer, if yez like, but have to go home first, fetch me three-oh.'

'No guns in the Valley!'

'Fetch me shanghai then.'

'Children, there are cattle, see? Over there. By the trees.'

They hear the lowing of the disgruntled, half-drowned herd. But cattle blame people for all their problems.

'Listen? Is that someone shouting?' Nisi cradles Timothy's head. Rude Boy, his own head covered in a blanket, sits with his feet on the kitchen embers. Over the sink, on which are stacked unwashed mushroom-and-spud-smeared platters, a tiny silvereye battles its own reflection in the steamy window.

Thank you, Mother. Thank you, Cosmos.

A few reluctant comments on Smitty. Subjection to being castrated then buggered, by a victorious and, necessarily, sword-wielding opponent, was a not uncommon fate of the wounded *retiarius*—gladiator who fought in jocks, armed with net and trident, in the Roman Imperial arena*. The practice is alluded

---

* Seneca, *Quaestionum Naturalium*, V11 31 3 '*cotidie comminiscimur per quae virilitati fiat iniuria, ut traducatur, quia non potest exui: alius genitalia excidit, alius in obscenam partem ludi fugit et locatus ad mortem infame armaturae genus etiam in quo morbum suum exerceat legit.*' Quoted by Housman. Some things are best left untranslated.

to in Juvenal (Satire VI, the Bodleian fragment never found in schoolboy texts), who goes on to tell us that these unmanned creatures were favoured sexual toys of society ladies. From which we may deduce that the wounds so received were not invariably fatal. It is perhaps of interest that the urethrorectalis muscle, surrounding the anus, butts up with the bulbocarvenosus of the penis, both areas being under the control of what is known in Yoga as the muladhara chakra. Sodomy, we should say, is as old as man.

Formation of the eunuch by wholesale penile and scrotal testicular amputation was out of favour in Sydney, in the 90s. During the Postmodern sex-change operation, much penile tissue is reserved, for subsequent construction of an artificial clit. During a radical orchidectomy, as indicated in the treatment of testicular and sometimes advanced prostatic cancer, the operation is invariably performed through the inguinal canal. An incision having been made in the groin, the testicle is mobilised upwards, the gubernaculum divided, and the spermatochord cut, with subsequent ligation of the vas deferens. The sacral route, slicing off the bag, is reserved for punishment of spies in Iraq—there achieved by scrotal suspension using piano wire—and surgically, in cases of sacral haematoma, a rare trauma which may arise from a kick to the balls on a football field. I say rare, for the balls, though descended, are relatively well protected; indeed, that is why they are located where you cannot politely reach them to scratch.

Not so, for the penis; erect, it projects from the body up to a foot, according to *Cleo* magazine, virtually inciting its tormented owner to excise it with a sharp object. Consisting, as it does, of a sponge of capillaries that fill with blood on tumescence, a loss of blood must invariably follow prompt and traumatic removal; happily, a man who has just had his cock cut off inclines to detumescence.

In cases of surgical penile amputation without simultaneous orchidectomy—as indicated, for example, in treatment of cancer of the penile stem—the suspensory and fundiform ligaments which support the penis are cut and a vertical elliptical incision made to the base of the penis, which is then extended over the anterior surface of the scrotum, in the midline through the skin and the Dartos fascia. It is then a matter of dividing and dissecting the two corpora cavernosa (the spongy bodies that inflate, prior to intercourse) while transposing the urethra in the corpus spongiosum (this being the tissue opened, with a razor, during Aboriginal subincision) to a hole manufactured in the perineum, just below the scrotum.

Then follows a deal of fiddly tying off; the profunda arteries, which run through the middle of the corpora cavernosa, the urethral arteries, the bulb arteries, the dorsal arteries, and the dorsal vein, which is the big one you can see pulsing, just below the skin, must be ligated. We may imagine that in the case of amputation by sword—or axe, or flint, which Catullus describes as the method favoured by priests of Cybele (*devolvit ile acuto sibi pondere silicis*, he cuts off his weighty groin with a sharp flint: Carmen LXIII 5)—much attendant bleeding might occur. When John Bobbitt, ex-US Marine, was deprived of his penis by his wife, in '93, the urologist assisting at the operation performed to reattach the severed member—which was thrown, by his wife, from a car window, and later recovered by the fire brigade—described the existence of a huge clot, where the penis used to be.

In the absence of prompt medical attention, this clot, specially where amputation included simultaneous castration, would pose, as well as a risk of infection, problems of urethral stenosis. An Indian youth, Mohammed Hanif Vora, initiated into a sect of eunuchs in the city of Baroda, woke in pain six days after the event, he reckons—which occurred in the 1980s, and which was performed, under opium anaesthetic, by a crone armed with a dagger—with a full bladder which he was unable to empty through a blocked urethra. This was salubriously unblocked, with a kick or three.

So common once were eunuchs in the East, they all but constituted a third sex. Concerning the trannies of Rome, Gibbon says: 'The use and value of those effeminate slaves gradually rose with the decline of the empire.' Elsewhere, he describes them as 'that pernicious vermin of the east, who, since the days of Elagabalus, had infested the Roman palace'. They survive, to this day, in India, as many as a million, not all of whom have access, as they do in Sydney, to synthetic hormones. On the subcontinent, their vulgar blessings at weddings are considered indispensable, while in Sydney their flair for cabaret enlivens many a dull suburban life in the closet. In Rome, the castrati of the Sistine Chapel Choir were not banned by the Pope till 1903. One of their number, Moresci, who died as recently as 1922, made a sound recording which reveals the fatuity of striving, using boy soprano or countertenor, to replicate the voice of a Farinelli in a Handel oratorio, written for eunuch's voice.

Castrati, however, retained penes. A theological inquiry, devoted to the issue of whether or not they could marry— because they sometimes fell in love with women—concluded they could indeed 'satisfy' women, which makes an interesting commentary on the role of the eunuch in the Ottoman harem.

Two surgical procedures, though irrelevant to our purpose, are nonetheless worthy of passing mention, in tribute to Post-modern surgical ingenuity. The creation, from a man, of a tranny capable of undergoing female intercourse is, as we might suppose, a procedure dear to the heart of many a Post-modern inner-urban democrat. The correlative procedure, microsurgical reattachment of the severed penis to its stump, had been performed (by '94) at least six times in Sydney, eighteen times in Bangkok and as long ago as 1929 in Weimar Germany. Reconnecting the urethra, to restore urinary func-tion, is straightforward; re-establishment of erectile capability requires great surgical skill. Thoroughly bloodtight reconnec-tion of the three corpora is essential. In addition, during an op which may take up to eight hours, the inner (Dartos) fascia, and the outer (Bucks) fascia must be reconnected, along with the skin, arteries, veins, urethra, and as many nerves as may facilitate subsequent erotic satisfaction, which tends to be partial. For up to a year following the op—according to Jill Margo's 'Man Trouble' column in *The Sydney Morning Herald*—jogging, weightlifting and diving into swimming pools are strictly contraindicated.

Nor is recovery of the detached member in itself crucial to success. In 1985, Dr Earl Owen, of the Sydney Microsurgery Centre, fashioned in Shanghai an artificial penis for a man who had had his eaten by a pig as a child, using skin, blood, tissue and nerves from an inner arm, over a piece of the cartilaginous twelfth rib. Hooked up to the femoral artery, this obscene devil's artifact did the job, apparently.

Not all who cut the Gordian knot, though, later repent them of it. Some cannot. In Japan, penile amputation forms an adjunct to the honourable self-mutilation of hara kiri, and reattachment of the penis to a corpse would serve no useful purpose.

And some, like the Corybantes of ancient Phrygia, and the communards of Erinungarah, according to Kimbo, buried theirs in chambers, or the soil, that trees again would bud in the spring, while others gave them to benefactors as keepsakes. Lucian tells us the great festival of the Syrian Goddess was held in Spring. Multitudes flocked to the city of Hierapolis, from all over the East. To the wild music of flute and drum, man after man would step from the crowd, intoxicated by the atmosphere, and seizing one of the swords that stood ready for his purpose, strip, and unman himself on the spot. Clutching his severed genitals, he would then run through the streets, and the house into which he hurled them had the honour of furnishing him an outfit of women's clothing, which he wore for the remainder of his life.

Ever seen a Christian priest? Frauds, in women's clothing. There was, however, a sect in eighteenth century Russia, called the 'White Doves'.

59. *Calvin and Frodsham discuss the Valley. Building the dome.*

Late summer. Early Fall. The hail of acorns, courtesy of King parrots, under the oaks of Obliqua Creek has ceased, and Horrie has lifted his main crop, mostly chats, as the haulms, weakened by drought, died early. He forked a good few, but was relieved to find he hadn't transfixed a single local frog, as they have magnificent golden eyes.

Back in Sydney, Calvin Ecks has been dismayed by lack of interest in Green Munga, while sedulous work in physics, in the humid weather, has proven beyond Derek Frodsham. Frodsham spends his days in Bob Gould's bookshop, though he seldom buys a book.

'You get the mail for me, Derek? Any reprint requests?'

'They won't give me your mail.'

'The hell they won't. I'll write you an authorisation. Here.'

'Calvin, I form an impression they'd like to see you at work more often. It's true I don't go in myself, but I'm only a post-graduate. My sole responsibility . . . '

'Don't lecture me. I just did the best piece o' work ever came outta that fuckin hole.'

'That was a month ago, or more. I must confess, Calvin, I'm a trifle concerned about you myself. I mean, you stay in bed all morning, you go to bed never later than eight, and when I come home early, as I did this afternoon, I find you watching *Rin Tin Tin*. You seem to have no interest in helping the Third World. Have you finished *The Wretched of the Earth*?'

'That is just not true. You realise the political potential of an edible gumnut and gumleaf preparation? Those fuckers grow anywhere.'

'I cannot seem to prove, to your satisfaction, that simply improving productivity, Calvin, without prior reformation of global political infrastructure . . . '

'Shut up, Derek. You sound like a cosmologist. No one is listening to you. You weren't cut out to be Trotsky, you lack a common touch, now listen. I gotta get down to Utopia, man. I gotta get my access sorted out. When is Barbara coming back to school? Weren't you going down there with her?'

403

'I was, but I should have to say, with Trotsky, the country leaves me cold, Calvin.'

'Jesus, man, all you talk about is peasantry, and you don't know the peasantry from fuck. Y'owe it to yer soapbox. What is going on in that Valley, Derek? My daughter hasn't written me once.'

'My family were peasants, you see. That's the difference between us. Barbara claims a great deal is going on. An adventurous construction program, and they found a meteorite, and one of their number, a former nun, is smitten by it. Saw a Vision of the Virgin. I've asked Barbara to bring me back a piece of the meteorite, so I can have it analysed. It may be a carbonaceous chondrite. They predate the Solar System.'

'That should solve the problem, Derek.'

'Yes, I hope so. Calvin, I do take note of what you say.'

'Hey man, look at this little guy on TV now. He got a nose like Spiro Agnew. Fuckin Muskie! Americans will never elect to high office a candidate who blubbers on the boob toob. That is what cost us the election. Not that I give a shit, from here.'

'Yes, I think you're right. I've become sectarian. I ought to go down to the Valley and acquire some practical knowledge of the problems that face subsistence farmers. I no longer expect Australia to be the first capitalist country to undergo Revolution. To the contrary, it seems perfectly content to remain a British colony.'

'They don't subsist on these communes. That is just a myth.'

'I'm aware you send them money.'

'You know my problem? Know what is the problem with me? I hate to admit it, but Monica was my source of scientific inspiration. She put my mind in such a spin.'

'But you're always splitting up!'

'That was just our thing. This is different. This time I think I lost her, man, probly my brother. I wish I knew. If I thought something was going on there, they wouldn't *both* be getting an allowance from me.'

'You're too generous, Calvin.'

'I don't mind her screwin other guys. Well I do, but you gotta put up with that, with Monica. Generally, it doesn't interfere

404

with what is cooking between her and me, but this time something serious has happened, Derek. I feel totally numb.'

'You don't care if you never see her again?'

'I don't care if I never see her again.'

'You'd better go down.'

'Yeah, I better go down.'

Stumps, today, the Seven Sisters, but one stump taller than the rest, and you'll find on it none of the tell-tale teeth marks indicating use of a chainsaw. It was felled by hand.

First, Attis, wearing spikes, climbs the tree and tops it, using ropes to guide down the bare limbs. No tower, no cherrypicker. All the leaves have fallen off. Then he and Fergus, working off planks, using axes and a crosscut, drop it, old style, within a foot of where they had hoped it might land. They are assisted by Darryl, who stands at a distance, bawling instructions.

Regrettably, no one thinks to keep a piece of branch, to forward to plant pathology.

As there's not much room to spare, the whole operation proceeds slowly. To general relief, Attis proves able to throw his axe left-handed.

Eventually, down comes the Seventh Sister, a gift, as the Family now sees it, from Gwen. Someone has a notion of spearing the great log, one hundred and twenty feet long, into the Creek on rollers, but the idea is abandoned, as retrieval of a log that size, should it jam, would be difficult. It could even raise the water table. Nor is it apparent how it might be snigged, even supposing there could be made available a bullock team. Indeed, it is now obvious why the Seven Sisters have been spared. They couldn't be floated out, because the Gorge is too narrow; they couldn't be hauled out, because of the sheer nature of the Gorge; and they couldn't even be dragged up the cliff, because of the trees growing from the cliff face. But to let stand and rot this freestanding dead Australian red cedar! Unthinkable. The world's most expensive building timber, according to Barney, when I asked him recently, and he would know.

So we cut such wood as we need, and float down the 'bolts'— to use a timberman's term—with someone hanging off the back.

Sixty-nine. Eugene Ecks, using beeswax foundation and the cobbler's awl, with which Nisi Papadimitriou has been sewing saddlebags, and the plastic straws—A struts colour-coded blue, B1 struts clear, B2 struts green, C struts barberpoles, white with red stripes—has whipped up a model dome, by wiping the awl, dipped in hot wax, through the straws, at the ends, to form hubs. This model dome, on its breadboard base, has become the cynosure of nightly meetings.

And by March, the farmhouse is crowded; Nisi Papadimitriou and her two children, Monica Ecks and her two children, Paula Zoshka, Brian Chegwodden, Balthazar Beauregard, Michael Ginnsy, Diane Zoshka, Attis MacAnaspie, Eugene Ecks, Olaf Abernathy, Grainger, Sister Annunciata—though she spends most of her time with the meteorite—Fergus MacAnaspie, though he often gets no further than the cave—and Darryl MacAnaspie, who has abandoned his job as a truckie, or so it seems, and lives in the Kombi van. Kimberley Moon visits Darryl, Barbara Byng visits everyone. Horrie, *de facto* patron, likes to be kept informed, though he can't scramble up and down the Pass, because he is past it: indeed, construction of a larger dwelling, or a second dwelling, is urgent.

Eugene Ecks: 'The idea is, ya use what ya *got*, man! That's where we lucked out, with this Valley. First Drop City dome used two by four second-hand lumber struts, over plywood hubs. For skin they had tarpaper, covered with chicken wire and stucco, with bottletops holding the wire to the tarpaper. Car glass windows. Tarred over the stucco.'

'Shit. That must have looked awful.'

'It did. But the point is, Diane, that by using these materials, they proved you can drop out of the system in the world's greediest nation. You don't need an income. You can build yourself a fine home and it needn't cost a fortune. Needn't spend the rest of your life in hock to some fuckin bank.'

'Anyone had any further thoughts on how big the dome should be?'

'What you see before you is a scale model for a twenty-four footer.'

'That wouldn't be anywhere near big enough.'

'Don't you listen? This is a *scale model*. Suitable for yer mommy and yer poppy, yer brother and yer sister and you.'

'I thought we were tryin to get away from all this nuclear family shit.'

'You were right, Brian.'

'How many people do we need to house? That, surely, is the question.'

'We have twelve to fifteen adults here at present, and four children, not counting visitors.'

'Visitors are a fuckin hassle, man. Sorry, Barbara, but that's the way I feel.'

'What's wrong with having visitors?'

'They don't always dig what you're into. People from the city who may or may not wish to contribute, and supposin they wish to contribute, may or may not be able to contribute.'

'I try to contribute.'

'Don't be paranoid, Barbara. We don't mean you.'

'Why can't they stay in the farmhouse, once it's empty?'

'Ah no, man. *I* must stay in the farmhouse!'

'Let 'em stay in the fuckin cave, fuck 'em. They're just gonna bring in all that News o' the World, all *that* shit.'

'Fine. We need a policy on visitors, but can we please address the topic at hand for the moment? Otherwise, we will go back to standing orders and that's a promise.'

'Why should she chair the meetings? She is not prepared to live here full time.'

'Right. We're getting sidetracked again. We never get anything done. So how big a dome are we gonna need for fifteen people? That is the question. I don't think we'll ever have more than fifteen people down here. Do you, Diane?'

'Who can say how many kids we'll have?'

'We could cut these struts a hundred foot long, man. We could build a *monster* dome.'

'That's right. Go for the big ego trip. Build something we don't really need and waste precious resources.'

'Got a radius of one hundred and forty-four inches.'

'Yeah, but can't it be varied? You said it can be varied.'

'Of course it can be varied. Don't you listen? I'm using Clinton's computerised figures, look. This is for your three-frequency, icosa alternate breakdown. Remember how we discussed that triangles are the strongest structures in Nature, which is why we use a crosspiece in a gate? See, this dome is based on a regular polyhedron with twenty identical equilateral triangular faces and twelve pentagonal vertices, right? So in a three-frequency breakdown we have nine faces for each icosa face, so that F(L) here equals nine. And if you count the number of vertices on each icosa face, you have, well let's do it. Let's count them. One, two, four, six, eight, ten. Which means V(L) here equals ten. And eighteen edges, are you with me? So that E(L) equals eighteen, now for the dome as a whole, V(G) is 92, E(G) is 270, F(G) is 180.'

'I'm going to make the coffee and tea. You want to come help me, Paula? Come on.'

'This is all the data you need for any five-eighth dome, man. For example, take this chord factor here, point 40354821. This, multiplied by the radius, gives you the length of the strut with vertex 1.1 at one end and vertex 1.0 at the other, only, as we found last night, there are actually two kind of B struts.'

'Sounds easy.'

'Course it is. A girl could do it. So we multiply this by the radius.'

'Where'd you get these numbers, man?'

'Paid Calvin to look them up for me. Of course, we need to make a slight adjustment, so as not to have the struts butting hard up against each other, and then we also need to know the axial angle, which for A struts is ninety minus eighty, near enough ten degrees, and for struts B and C, ninety minus seventy-eight, near enough twelve degrees, and the dihedral angle is not a real problem, with wood, because it bends. Specially softwood.'

'Did you ever actually build a dome, Eugene?'

'No, but it's easy, man.'

'Maybe girls *should* do it. Girls! Come out of that kitchen for a day.'

'This is a twenty-four foot dome and you say that's about right for an old style nuclear family. So we need something three times that big at least.'

'Could be. OK. Seventy-two foot, why not? That sounds like a good size dome to me. Let's check it out with Clinton here.

B strut for a seventy-two footer, that's thirty-six foot radius, point 40354821 times thirty-six times twelve, that's about fifteen foot, man. They'll all be round that size, see this one has struts fifty and a quarter, fifty-eight and an eighth, fifty-nine and three-eighths, and we need a total of 165 struts, all about fifteen foot long. Sound OK to you, Mountain Man? Attis? That's for a structure, I might add, of thirteen thousand, two hundred cubic foot volume.'

'Farck.'

'You could hold an auction in it.'

'Twelve hundred and ninety-six square foot of floor.'

'Faarck.'

'We'll have wood enough for that *and* the cedar shakes. Did Darryl find the maul wedges?'

'Cindy! Don't bring the puppies inside, darling. They should be outside, eating the goats.'

Narrative Pace: I have made a bad blue with narrative pace, as no way am I going to finish now. I'm going far too slowly. That's where inexperience tells, and of course, you never know how long you've got, in my condition. I must have thought I was going to live forever! They haven't even got the dome up! Kimberley says discard what I've written, start again, but I haven't time. All I can do is to keep going, at what I feel is an appropriate pace. I'm sorry, but I am very unwell. I'm all the time nauseous, know what I mean? Can't keep anything down.

60. *Life in the Valley. The Sacred Site. Working Cedar. Brian gets a Glimpse. The dome goes up.*

'What are you doing, Brian?'

'Just lying here, looking at that eagle floating by up there, Paula. He hasn't moved his wings in half an hour.'

'Neither have you.'

'Oh don't be hard on me, Paula honey. You know this isn't my scene.'

'How so?'

'I'm not like other men. I'm not mechanically minded. I'm not a good carpenter, I can't fix a battery. I can't play a musical instrument. I don't know how to build a fence.'

'Yeah, but they'll teach us. There is nothing mysterious about these trades. Everyone is going to help build the dome, which is why the dome is such a great idea. There will be no specialisation in the Moody Valley Candle Company Co-op. Everything that needs to be done can be shared, and people that have acquired skills in the past will pass them on to other people. We will all cook, will all wash the dishes, all build the kitchen. Our lives will be so rich.'

'Yeah OK, how's the tum? How's bub?'

'Fine! I'm glad I'm eating fresh greens at last. That young spinach is *so* tasty. I can't wait until the lemon tree has lemons. What a pity Phryx and Gwen hadn't thought to plant a lemon tree.'

'I think the spinach is going to seed, and it's not spinach anyway, it's silver beet. When is this cow coming down? When are we getting this house cow?'

'Just as soon as Fergus gets to a sale. I want to milk the cow, Brian. Can't you see me milking a cow?'

'No. No way. Surely, we should all get to milk the cow.'

'Don't tease. Girls should milk cows. I don't want you pulling someone else's teats.'

'Hey, come here, gorgeous. Don't you just love this kind of weather?'

'No, I hate it. The sun is out in the mornings, and you think it's going to be so warm, and then it turns cool and cloudy. Mon has such a great selection of sweaters, though. Do you think this sweater suits me?'

'Sure looks good. Only you and Monica have the tits to wear that kind of thing. They look ridiculous on Diane.'

'And I have the belly now, too. So what do you like about this kind of weather?'

'Hey, you're amazing, you know that? You are the only person I ever met interested in what I think. Oh, I dunno. I guess my name should be Commodore Autumn. I get off on autumn weather. It is sad and beautiful both. It makes me restless. The sun is pale. The air is smoky from the burn-offs. Reminds me of Balmain.'

'Poor wittle fewwow. You have a smoke with Ginnsy? You hit that reset button again?'

'Just a small toke.'

'I can smell it on you.'

'So? Last deal I bought was grown in an abandoned mineshaft, under a kennel on a hinge. This has got to be more healthy. Next year I'll make wine. Promise.'

'How will you keep the bowerbirds out of the grapes?'

'Ginnsy is gonna have a word with them. Explain the situation to them and try to get them to see reason. Seriously, they're bastards, aren't they. I caught one in the silver beet this morning. And that awful noise they make! The lyrebirds get them down beautifully.'

'Horrie says that when he was a boy, one little girl would have the job to shoot them and make stew from them. Yuk! Did I tell you I found a wittle bower behind the tank? You want to come see it? Dey have bwue stwaws and some pwetty scwaps of paper. It is so cute. You can't hate them.'

'Maybe not. I'm just sorry they exist.'

'You're not sorry we came down?'

'Not when I'm stoned. But I do need to see my kids soon.'

'Why?'

'Because they're my kids. That's why.'

The Sacred Site is on the east wall of the Valley in the coal measure above the talus. And Balthazar Beauregard likes a walk, in the light of the moon, if it's a clear night.

'Annunciata! Do you mind if I join you?'

'Balthazar! You scared me.'

'I'm sorry. Beg pardon. You don't mind if I visit?'

'Are you here to meditate?'

'No, not right now. First, I must get my head together.'

Balthazar has made three bad blues with women over the past year, and this could be a fourth.

411

'Can you feel a presence, Bal?'

'I feel a presence of some kind.'

'What are the others doing?'

'Building a big dome.'

'Did you ask them to come with you?'

'Sort of.'

'Why does nobody come?'

'It would require a special general meeting, and they're flat out with the dome.'

'First things first.'

'Please don't be hard on us. We all feel your prayer is on our behalf. Is your vision still strong?'

'No.'

'Too bad. Here, I brought you some food. You should eat. It's just potatoes and greens. Won't taste very nice cold.'

'Is the garden doing well?'

'Very well! The pumpkins have started and the cabbage moth are easing off. We should get broccoli soon.'

'Balthazar, the Virgin appeared to me. Just over there.'

'Yes, I know. You're lucky.'

'Tears were flowing from Her eyes, but She was smiling at the same time. Do they think I'm mad?'

'Of course not. You see this thing in the coal here? There's a guy coming down here soon, a friend of Barbara's, who is a scientist at the university. He thinks it may be a meteorite. Would you mind if he took a small piece of the stone back for analysis?'

'Oh, I should have to ask Mary. I don't want the area spoiled.'

'He wouldn't be spoiling it, Annunciata. Just making it a bit bigger.'

'Do you believe in the Mother of God, Balthazar?'

'Not by that name, perhaps.'

'You know, I thought I was looking for Jesus.'

'You looked for Him. But Mary found you.'

'You understand. Are the children being taught?'

'Not really. I did tell them to watch the way the goats cluster in the paddock every morning, and study each of the trees, noting the way the leaves shine, or fail to shine. Who can say these matters have no relevance? Patterns emerge, to those who watch. Michael wants to start the sacred pump engine, but he can't do it till everyone is there.'

'Does he still wear dark glasses? Tell him they're a sign of the Beast. And tell the children to read their Bible. I'll be back in a few days.'

'Did you see the native passionflower's in flower?'

'Oh, so *that's* what it is. Then it's true, Balthazar.'

'Dog's not big enough, Darryl.'

'Well, fuck the fuckin dog. Kick it to the shithouse.'

'Did you bring the wedges?'

'Get it on the block first, boof'ead. Worry bout your wedges then. You'll need another pulley.'

'Can't find the left-handed broadaxe now. Seen the left-handed broadaxe?'

'How do we work it? Score from the butt up or hew from the top down? Wish Dad was ere.'

'Cut with the bevelled edge to the outside.'

'We've gotta get a move on, Fergie, hundred 'n sixty-five slices to chip. I wanta get this dome up for Kimbo's reception. We want it held in the dome.'

'What? Kimberley Moon? Is he gettin married?'

'We thought it best if he married Smitty's widder.'

'Oh? And what does she have to say about it?'

'Don't worry yer old grey 'ead, son. They've known each other for yonks.'

'You sharpen the broadaxes, Darryl. I'll go sharpen the sleeper dressin adze, and the plane, and the draw knife, to champfer the tenons. We want seven ten-be-fives, for the foundation piers. That's ten foot long be five foot in deeameter. Most of the cedar will go in the foundations. The struts can be thin as paddlepop sticks.'

'All held up by 'ot aair, ay.'

'So if you'd like to saw us off seven ten-be-fives.'

'Did it earlier. Floatin 'em down now.'

'You reckon the bearers'll span thirty-six foot?'

'Take five foot outta that. Thirty foot. We can cantilever six foot. Twenty-five foot.'

'Still a big span. Need big bearers.'

'Something substantial, I'd go for two-be-twos. Two foot be two foot, that should do for bearers. Mountain grey gum, ay, cut 'em to size. They always used mountain grey gum for buildin bridges. Peerless bridgin timber, too. Good wharfin timber, off turpentine piles.'

'What about floorboards, Darryl?'

'Grey gum again. Polish up a treat.'

'How's it gunna slot in though?'

'We could mortise and tenon the bearers. Use oak for trummels, I'll nick a bit from Memorial Park in town. We'll need the boardwood seasoned, though, to slot it in precise. I think I know where there's some ringbarked stuff, courtesy of Fritter Batter's goats. I'll get you to put a tongue and groove in all them boards, me boy.'

'Usin this thing?'

'Come on! How do you think they built the woolshed on Bunoo Bunoo? No sawmills, back in 1800, either. All timbers was handhewn, all joints notched and pegged. We'll notch and peg every joist and nog, then peg the floorboards onto 'em.'

'What size pegs, ya reckon?'

'Two inches. You can drill the two-inch holes, usin the hand crank drill, Fergus.'

'Thank you very little. Two-inch holes into hardwood!'

'Ar come on! You was at the meetin. You heard what Monica said. All to rest on cedar poles, everything to be done by hand, and not a piece of metal in the entire structure, now watch your leg with that broadaxe. You'll find the closer you cut to your leg, the cleaner the cut you will get.'

'What if the dome's not ready for the wedding?'

'Breda don't want no flash weddin. Reckons it's too soon.'

'Hey, here come the girls with a cup of tea, Darryl. We better put our shirts on.'

'Look at them, Paula! Just look at what they're doing now! Aren't you freaked out by the skills of these mountain men?'

'To tell you the truth, I find them crashing bores, Diane. They have no conversation.'

In order to arrest the ten-be-fives and stop them floating by, a boom has been slung across Jellybean Pool, but none of the bolts float against it, as the song of the broadaxe now resounds through the Valley. Because one log is snagged, and the others can't push past. Owing to a failure in communications, all seven were pitched, from the rollers, on the stream before the first was removed. The bed of the Creek was cleared of debris, sufficiently, it was hoped, to give them clearance, but now there is a logjam with which to contend, that no one knows how to deal with.

'Go get the mountain men. Fast.'

'No! We don't want them thinking we can't do anything properly. Grainger, you were supposed to be guiding this log. How did this happen?'

'There was a surge. He lost control.'

'I guess I could dive under it. Maybe it's snagged below.'

'Careful, Monica!'

The men watch thoughtfully as Monica's naked nipples harden. That water is cold.

'Hey, why don't we all just stop what we're doing and pray for Guidance, or better yet, Help? According to Phryx and Gwen, one's prayers are answered in this Valley.'

'It's either that or gelignite. Do we get to hold hands?'

'Balthazar, go fetch Annunciata. She's been praying for days.'

'Yeah, but she's praying to the Virgin Mary, man, and I can't handle that.'

'Eugene doesn't believe it will work. And while anyone among us does not believe it will work, it won't work.'

'I won't get in your way, though. I'll stand over here.'

'*Fuck* you, man, this is your project! This is your dome, Eugene. Don't you care?'

'How would you feel if it did work?'

'You're a bunch of superstitious fuckwits. Don't bother fetchin the nun, I hereby call on the Spirit o' the Valley to release the logs forthwith! I undertake, if this be done, I will henceforth believe in the Spirit o' the Valley.'

No sooner has Eugene's voice ceased, than a grumbling is heard, and the grumbling becomes a rumbling. But the twisted smile never leaves his face as the ten-be-fives break free. Sheer coincidence. Monica whoops, Diane shakes her head, but Brian experiences a mystical sensation, and let there be no doubt, the religious sense has to do with the concept of Entropy, which in its raw, undogmatic state, expresses itself as a search for omen.

Michael Ginnsy, scrutinizing the assembled faces, seizes at once on Brian's.

'You saw it, didn't you man? You got the *Glimpse*! I could see it in your face. You gonna lose it again, man, because we do, but that doesn't matter. Hey, just imagine *livin* there, man! That's where Phryx and Gwen were comin from. Now we gotta go find the Power Spot. You should do it, man, cause you just got the *Glimpse*.'

And so the most useless man about the place gets the single most important job in the entire project. Colitis or no, Brian will detect the Place of Power on which to site the centrepole.

'See, there's a *ley* line runs through the Valley, man, and it comes out on the summit of Glastonbury in England? I buried Phryx and Gwen somewhere near it, but I coulda been out by, who knows? I was shittin myself. Very unrelaxed.'

'I believe I can find the right place for the central pier, Paula.'

'Yes, I believe so. I'm sure you can do it, Brian.'

'Better sharpen that fencin bar, man, if we're gonna dig seven holes, four foot deep by five foot wide. We need a forge and an anvil.'

'Let's use coal from the Sacred Site. Or charcoal, from the Sacred Grove.'

'But the bar needs to be cherry red.'

'We'll hold our evening meeting round it.'

'Here he is. I see 'e got a scorch height of at least six foot, judgin by 'is eyebrows.'

'Someone put pure petrol in my drip torch. No, we couldn't get a burn going. Had to give it away.'

'Back on the seed, Att?'

'They don't want me on the gang, Darryl. Because of you, and what happened with Smitty, our family name is mud on the coupe.'

'Fuck 'em! We can't be blamed for what happened to Smitty.'

'They're not real impressed with you either, Darryl. They can't find anyone to take your place.'

'No other driver could ever take my place. You tell 'em I'm sellin the rig. Tell 'em I caan't approve o' takin the old growth for chip.'

'Tell 'em yourself. How's it going, Fergie?'

'Not bad, Att. I'm puttin in the angles, and polishin up with the leaves off a sandpaper fig. See, this is a B2 strut, twenty-eight and thirty degrees at both ends. We need thirty-five of these, each 171 and seven-eighth inches. Did you see Diane?'

'Isn't she helping Paula finish those caps?'

'She won't thank me for tellin you, but she's been sewing your initials on a shining gum leaf, to make a bookmark for your birthday.'

'Why?'

'Because it's your birthday tomorrow, Attis. Easter Sunday! Happy Birthday! You don't hold it against me I told you the truth, I hope?'

'What, about the bookmark?'

'No. About the sawdust heap.'

Derek Frodsham enters the Valley Easter Monday, accompanied by Calvin Ecks and the nuclear activist Max Worboise. It would have made better sense, to have arrived sooner, on the Friday, but none of the newcomers intended to venture into the Valley over Easter, although the urge grew stronger in them as the holiday period progressed. Calvin knew that Cindy had wanted to visit the Royal Easter Show, and so he is laden with sample bags. He actually ducked out to the Show, with Derek, on the Thursday. They were watching what might have been the Hytest Trophy at the woodchop, at the same time sharing a surreptitious joint, when Derek Frodsham suggested a visit to the Valley. But Calvin Ecks, dreading Easter traffic, scotched the notion, firmly. On the Saturday, Maximilian Worboise drops by to discuss the situation on the USSR/Chinese border, putting the wind up Calvin. Thanks a million, Maximilian. Most of the traffic was coming the other way by Sunday, anyway. Once at Obliqua Creek, they called by at Graceland, but strangers answered the door who had never heard of Diane or Fergus. Luckily, Barbara Byng came by, that afternoon, with Darryl, to Wonderview, to see what she could scrounge in the way of 3/8-inch zinc-plated carriage bolts, to add to the 431 Fergus purchased on the Saturday. And Calvin Ecks, Derek Frodsham and Maximilian Worboise saw Barbara Byng from the road. Such was the Valley's attraction in those days, the problem of visitors proved illusory: no one who had been at the Wake for Martin Luther King who went in went back out. Derek Frodsham would later speak of his first sighting of that Valley, as St Kevin might have spoken of Glendalough. Maestro, could we can a touch of 'Dawn' please, the first of the four interludes from Peter Grimes? Ta.

I remember that Easter. The rain coming late had made it *seem* like Easter. All the spuds Horrie had missed were back in flower. Still warm, when the sun came out, and the grass growing a treat. Possumwood on the talus making a deal of rubescent new growth. Spears, emerging from blackboys. They'd been there since Mehmed left the Grove. Pumpkins laughing, no downy mildew. Clouds scudding over. Barbara Byng sneezing. Currawongs in chorus. Cardigans, indeed shirts, going on and off all day.

And the farmhouse, with the welcome swallows flitting around the verandah. Here is a house can be pondered and reflected over an hour before you meet it. Hobby farmer's dream home.

'There she is! There's *Cindy*, man, look. There's my daughter! I know the way she runs.'

The circular garden, plots laid out by Annunciata in mystical format, fenced by large, bent hoops of iron. The scraps of square mesh fencing. The goat-ravaged remains of a vineyard, host to a couple of lavender hives, furiously working. Behind the house, what remains of, and what was found within, the bramble-covered shed, once Olaf took to it with a five-foot pry bar and catspaw. Lengths of four-be-four and two-be-one and six-be-two hardwood, nails projecting; quantity of roofing iron; couple of four-foot concrete pipes; a cage, about five-be-five-be-five, maybe once part of a calf trailer, but which, inverted, could be useful in keeping the wallabies, wood duck and brush-tailed phascogale out of the dope; a black, malevolent-looking iron cross, female fittings on all extremities; a pair of car wheels on a chassis built of welded lengths of six-be-two angle iron; a disc plough, spotted like a common seal, with brown rust flaking off the seat; some chicken wire; some wire rope; a decorative wooden cupola, with weathervane at thirty degrees; the tailgate of a truck; an open bag of cement, rock solid; some steel quad, a steel wheeled farming implement, of which remains only the wheels and a seat support; a grey chicken grain feeder, suitable to feed about 2000 birds; two internal house doors, rotten with white ant; a wrought-iron gate; a red jerrycan; a set of railway scales on wheels; some pantry doors with bakelite knobs, and so on, and so forth, all of it brown, grey, blue grey, white. Just a touch of colour in the garden pots and conduit.

Further off, beyond the hives, the building site, furiously busy. Seven huge cedar posts as piers supporting a massive hardwood platform, upon which swarm a baker's dozen of Caucasians in Phrygian caps. The best of Bob blares forth from the cassette of an open-doored Kombi. Certain women and men mount scaffolds and ladders, while others scurry over the deck, and others still gingerly climb a lattice, emerging from the deck and towering over it; this huge, triangulated woodwork skeleton, like the micrograph of a snowflake, that teeters and rocks, as it rests at five points only on the deck below. While certain workers direct the positioning of 165 colour-coded struts, others secure these to sixty-one half-inch plywood eight-inch diameter hubs. A man in faded bib and tucker overalls—for twin sets spun in the grease and gear flung off at the start of the City to Surf have not yet replaced cheesecloth kaftans, army fatigues and bell-bottom flares—undulates over and about the site, weaving his way through dogs and goats and dancing, while periodically pausing to fling holy water at workers from a conch. No sound of hammer, only the ratchet being tightened over a bolthead. Attempts to circumvent the use of metal in the structure were abandoned, when the whole thing fell down, twice.

'It looks great up, though, doesn't it Darryl? This time it should stay up, too.'

'Somepin different.'

'Is there any way into this Valley, apart from this one track?' inquires Maximilian. 'If law and order collapsed in the cities completely, can anyone get in?'

'We're on the verge of nuclear war' explains Calvin. 'Big standoff between Russia and China.'

'Oh yeah. Are they comin in vehicles?'

'They could be running. They could be crawling. They will be desperate. Many may be armed.'

'Wouldn't worry me 'ead. We can easy defend this dome.'

'Is that farmhouse on the map?'

'Yeah, reckon it might be. See that plane in the sky above ya? That's the Melbourne-Sydney flightpath.'

Barbara smiles. But does she smile, when a front bencher and frequent flyer, forever travelling between Melbourne and Sydney and Sydney and Melbourne and Canberra, she glances from the window of a jet plane to find herself looking down on the Erinungarah? Or does a bleak look come over her face, as her hands hang heavy on the laptop.

Derek Frodsham: christened 'Trotsky' by Eugene Ecks.
Calvin Ecks: christened 'Nostradamus' by Eugene Ecks, in recognition of his vatic tendency.

Epilogue

A valediction.

Sorry.

Can't hardly lift the pencil, don't see a lot of point writing on, Nurse! Top of the bookshelf in the kitchen you will find a tape recorder, may I have it please? Ta. Sick of this paperwork.

Have to prepare. Have to prepare *now*. Community nurse sitting by the bed twenty-four hours per diem. Country Women's Association said they would do it, the boys from the club have been very good, very kind, mean well, but won't shut up, as they're embarrassed. So I've been anti-social to them.

See this thumb? Got that from a twist-top. No strength left in the hand. I says to the Maori, I says, 'I forgive you for givin me the onion from the pig's arse at the hungi.' He burst into tears.

A huh a huh a huh! Pardon me.

Didn't get to where I'd wanted with the *Saga*, but have made a codicil to the will, and you will segue into the *Ballad*, if you can be bothered, no worries. The pathetic fallacy. Should it see the light of day. Regrets? Yes, I'm sorry. A huh.

Would I smoke another fag? A bit of mull? Yes, very likely, have you got some? Just joking. A huh a huh.

Driftin in and out. Given me something, I don't know what. Something to make me go quietly. A huh.

What was it Dylan Thomas said? Memory's gone.

Bad writer anyway. Had the postman opening mail.

You have read about it, you have watched it on the box, but it can't happen to you, it won't. You're not ready.

Regrets? Yes, a few.

Mother, is that you? *Mother*! It is you. I'm off to join the Majority. Sorry, make that the Minority, since the Living now outnumber the Dead. Come for a walk with me, dear. Regrets? That carded parcel, back in '59, I did see it. I told a lie, I took it out. I don't know what became of it, may have bounced out of the bag, could have been stolen, who knows? But I shouldn't have lied. But I was afraid.

If only they would tone things down, people wouldn't have to lie to them.

And the dog registration renewals. I have, on occasion,

delayed them. And the message in the bottle from Cruiser McCoy, his last will and testament, I shouldn't have taxed it.

Mother! You're wearing your ermine gown.

Regrets? Yes, I'm sorry I didn't go back home when I was well. I'd have gone in the European summer, that was when I always went, and I broke a few hearts, here and there, and I'm sorry about that, and I'd have stopped in Istanbul, because I'd have stayed at Sultanahmed, a room with a nice view of the Marmora, just so long as to recover from the flight. Listen to the gulls. I probably wouldn't leave my room. I just want to hear the Call to Prayer one last time. On the loudspeakers. A huh.

Good Lord, I hear it now.

Listen to that! Call to Prayer, oh *passionate* cry, that fills the Postmodern, PostChristian ear with envy. I'm well placed here, I hear a dozen minarets. One's very loud, must be the local. Yes, that'd be the one next door, and that one, that's the Blue Mosque. Coming from over there.

They're all coming in now, Suleymaniye, Beyazit, all charmingly out of sync. Oh, this is a real pleasure.

What's that you're saying, dear? The roosters are very loud this morning, do I want the window down?

No thanks. Leave it up.

Yes, they spent that first winter in the dome, but it leaked something fierce, as the pitch at the top wasn't steep enough for shakes, and the vinyl windows turned yellow and collected dust, and it got too hot in summer and attracted flies, and there was too much noise and no privacy. Great place for a party, though, when Life was a bit of a Party. All the women got pregnant, those first few years, which is very important. Kimbo says he'd sign a stat dec on it, and he knows I'm a Justice of the Peace. Everyone changed partners, except Attis and Diane. In the late seventies, they nicked the sleepers off the railway line, leaving the scrap rail and the jewellery, and started building the mudbrick houses, using clay slip and strickle stick and sleeper size brick frames, nine-be-five inch, the lintels tied in with barbed wire, and that took years, and some aren't finished yet, and all this time, spattered in creosote and mud, they traded, in marihuana, mostly. Ate the Green Munga in Koala

Kottage, but only to avert starvation in spring. Yet nothing of real interest occurred until they were completely cut off from the outside world, by which stage Orion, he would have been— fourteen? Sixteen? He married Cindy and they had a child, Passionflower, and it was Orion, Timothy Papadimitriou, going off to high school that brought the place undone.

But only indirectly. See, they wouldn't cut that umbilical cord completely, and paid the price. I mean, what in God's name had made the men suppose those women would want to live in poverty forever? And what had blinded the parents to the fact the children would be gettin out, as soon as ever they could? To use a phrase of Gibbon's, they found themselves beggars, because their parents had been saints. I don't think they even realised they were living in the Land of the Ever Young, until it was gone. Mind you, a few newcomers drifted in, recently, friends, or rels, of Darryl's new missus. The pet rat, Doc Marten, nose-ring mob, the ferals. They're as good as two men short. And Mehmed came back as the Greenbrown Man. He never did go to gaol.

Time to check out, we all do it. Billet for the light rail, get the light rail to the Topkapi. Run the gauntlet in the Otogar. Poor bastards, Ataturk gave them a stone in lieu of bread, you see. I'd be happy to never see another portrait or statue of him.

What's that, dear? Shivering? No, I'm not cold. Hot if anything. It's that hot wind blowing. Meltemi, they call it. Off the Russian steppe.

Grab a Kamel Koc. Off to Cannakale. Dur Yoldu!

I must make the effort, yes this time round we must make the effort to visit Gallipoli. Be more patriotic.

Look here. Juniperinus oxycedrus. Ever eat a vine leaf stuffed with juniper berries?

'I fancy I could eat one of Bellamy's veal pies.' Whose last words were those? I should know.

Wait a bit. This is not Anzac Cove. This is not juniper. This is prickly parrot pea, had me fooled. We must be on the Asian side of the Dardanelles. Yes, of course. Patterson's Curse, see? Woody mullein. Over there.

What's that? Would I go back to bed? Oh. We're up on the old railway track. *Illic heu miseri traducimur*, that things have come to this. You'll laugh, but I thought I was in Turkey. Looks like I'm the turkey here.

We played our role in the Heroic Age of Turkey. We were the barbarians, from beyond the Pale. Everyone kills someone, at some stage, dear. Here we are, names, on this War Memorial, of men who killed other men, during the Great War. MacAnaspie, C.

No, I *don't* want to go back to bed, I want a last walk round Obliqua Creek.

Here we are. Kaz Dag, ancient Mount Ida, sacred to Cybele. *De testem Romae tam sanctum quam fuit hospes numinis Idaei*, front in Rome with a witness as upright as the man who was given charge of the numen of Ida, Juvenal. *Ego viridis algida Idae nive amicta loca colam*, must I live rugged up against the snow in the freezing cold of green Ida? Catullus. *Hanc varie gentes antiquo more sacrorum Idaeam vocitant Matrem*, She it is the various peoples, in their ancient ritual, call the Mother of Ida, Lucretius. The things that stay in your mind. We caught the dolmus to Bayramic, through the ripening wheat and the Cerris oaks, and now we're trudging uphill in the heat, through the rock-rose, and bugger me, it's hot. Ask that old bugger if we could have a drop of the cool spring water.

There's a St John's wort. First we've seen today.

Come on, keep going, don't stop! I know the view won't be much. We must do something to reduce emissions, wait: I hear Syrian pop music. Must be a shepherd up ahead with a ghetto blaster. Keep an eye out for those Sivas Kangal dogs! I was attacked by three of them mongrels once. Fair near shit meself, but luckily, had the presence of mind to show aggression.

There are times you must show aggression. I can't think this is one of them.

Sheep bells! By Jove, they take me back. Women in the shalwar, men in the cloth cap, bringing the flocks back to town around 4 p.m. You could sit in the pub with no beer over a tea, under the portrait of Ataturk, and you'll marvel how the flocks can mix at the trough and then separate again.

Pessinus, I'm talkin of, are you stupid or deaf? Balhisar they call it now, they changed the name. They change all the names. Oo, it's a dry, dusty ruin, same as this. Hot wind. Got a name,

426

what do they call it? Meltemi, that's right. Off the Russian steppe. A huh a huh a huh! Lucerne flats. Poplars by the streams, turtle doves and tractor engines. Dry bed of the Gallos runs through Balhisar, and there are broken Byzantine column drums, of the whitest marble, lying in the sand. Just lying there. Imagine that, in Molong. Imagine that at Black Springs. I should have gone to Turkey, instead of coming here, but who'd be a Turkish postman? Locals drive donkeys in, but you can't see Dindyma. 'Gunuyuzu Dag' they call it now. Got a transmitter tower atop. Sacredest peak to Cybele in the whole ancient world. Power spot now. Transmitter tower. Shape o' your boobs, darlin, like the hills behind ...

I shall have to have a spell. I'm pooped.

White limestone, and behind the houses, the big yellow New Holland harvesters. Where am I?

Feel a bit queer. Think I'm going to have to shut up.

Oh. You put me back to bed. A huh. You're very kind. If you should go to Selcuk, stay at the Aussie and Kiwi pansyon, it's a barrel o' laughs, and visit the Artemisium, do. It's next to the boulevard with the mulberries. Only the one column left now, and a stork's nest on that, but they planted river red gum by the altar, as they did at the carpark in Miletus. You'd like to see those. And they're doing well. Friesian cows, on the tether. Great was Diana of the Ephesians, Who started Life as a Meteorite, and wound up as the Virgin Mary.

Listen to those tour buses! Shut the window please, a hhrrgh.

Isn't today the last day of the millennium? Oh. You know I thought it was. I want my ashes thrown in the bush today, dear, have you got that?

Today. Go to the museum in Selcuk. They have a fine head of Attis. *Has* something, know what I mean? Second century. A huh. Only decent Attis you ever saw. A hrrgh. Mostly propping up a table leg in his Phrygian cap, figure o' Christian fun, but here he is transfigured, dreamy, relaxed. On top of the situation we're all in, stranded here on Spaceship Earth. Sensuous. Dionysian. That's the way to be. That's the way to go out.

See that peasant woman picking berries off those wig trees?

Ask what's she's up to. Tell her to come over here. They know a lot, she may have something she can recommend for me. I can't draw breath.

No no, get *him* away, please! I don't speak the language!

Open the curtains. I want to look at the cross on the window of the building site. Did you know the Virgin Mary started life as a meteorite? I think we all did.

Uh oh. I can barely look at the cross on the window of the building site. Jesus Christ, He was a chippie, a carpenter, He's going to ask me a few hard questions, shortly. He'll think I've let Him down.

Mother! Oh Mother! It's You again, You're back. You must have read my worried heart.

Mother, would you intercede for me with Jesus Christ? Think You could put in a kind word? You're His mother too. Thanks. I've wasted my life. I see it now. Sorry.

I'll die. I'm glad this life is over. And it's not as bad as they say, I don't feel as if I'm going to sleep. I just hope I won't be serving the public ever again.

TAMAM

Bibliography

Among the volumes failing to fetch a reserve at the D'Arcy D'Oliveres dispersal sale will be:

G. Harden (ed), *Flora of NSW*, UNSW Press, 1990.

D. Freney, *A Map of Days*, Heinemann, 1991.

G. Langley, *Decade of Dissent*, Allen & Unwin, 1992.

E. Gibbon, *The Decline and Fall of the Roman Empire*, Strahan, Cadell & Davies, 1797.

J. Frazer, *The Golden Bough*, Macmillan, 1911.

A. Toynbee, *A Study of History*, OUP, 1939.

I. Howe (ed), *The Basic Writings of Trotsky*, Secker & Warburg, 1964.

A. Bloom, *The Closing of the American Mind*, Penguin, 1987.

C. Driver, *The Disarmers*, Hodder & Stoughton, 1964.

J. Schell, *The Fate of the Earth*, Picador, 1982.

Fitzroy Falls and Beyond, Budawang Committee Press, 1988.

J. Sturgiss, *The Man from the Misty Mountains*, Budawang Committee Press, 1986.

M. Quick, *Green Crowns*, Juniper Press, 1955.

S. Lloyd, *Ancient Turkey*, British Museum Publications, 1989.

J. Seymour, *Self Sufficiency*, Faber, 1976.

R. Kantor, *Commitment and Community*, Harvard UP, 1972.

Faces of Findhorn, Findhorn Publications, 1980.

P. Manly Hall, *The Secret Teachings of All Ages*, Philosophical Research Society Inc. LA, 1973.

The Portable Nietzsche.

The works of Pindar, Plato, Lucretius, Catullus, Seneca, Virgil, Juvenal, Persius, Petronius, Apuleius, et al (various editions).

The Holy Bible.

The Dome Books.

John Muir's Alternative Volkswagen Manual (title page missing; somewhat foxed & begreased)

Great Circles, Glover, Taylor Publications, Wellington, 1972.

Grass Roots magazines aplenty.

The Last Whole Earth Cattledog.

Dogrock
David Foster

'D'Arcy D'Oliveres is one of the great comic characters of
twentieth century literature'
E. Annie Proulx, author of *The Shipping News*

'Vividly imagined ... skilfully sustained ... a master
storyteller ... in the moments when he doesn't have you
laughing, Foster manages to get you wondering whodunit'
US Newsday

'... the most original and daring of novelists writing in
Australia today'
Geoffrey Dutton

'... our most original and important living novelist'
The Independent Monthly

Moonlite
David Foster

'A singularly brilliant work ... a great book. Among the black
humour David Foster brings strange places to life with
extraordinary precision'
Judge's report, National Book Council Awards 1981

'... fast-paced and uproariously funny'
Tim Thorne, *Books and Writing*

'*Moonlite* contains the scenes which move the mind round to
considering major questions, not just about the organisation
of society, but about human nature'
Manning Clark

'... our most original and important novelist'
The Independent Monthly